# QUANTITATIVE METHODS

CFA® Program Curriculum
2024 • LEVEL PREREQUISITE READINGS • VOLUME 1

©2023 by CFA Institute. All rights reserved. This copyright covers material written expressly for this volume by the editor/s as well as the compilation itself. It does not cover the individual selections herein that first appeared elsewhere. Permission to reprint these has been obtained by CFA Institute for this edition only. Further reproductions by any means, electronic or mechanical, including photocopying and recording, or by any information storage or retrieval systems, must be arranged with the individual copyright holders noted.

CFA®, Chartered Financial Analyst®, AIMR-PPS®, and GIPS® are just a few of the trademarks owned by CFA Institute. To view a list of CFA Institute trademarks and the Guide for Use of CFA Institute Marks, please visit our website at www.cfainstitute.org.

This publication is designed to provide accurate and authoritative information in regard to the subject matter covered. It is sold with the understanding that the publisher is not engaged in rendering legal, accounting, or other professional service. If legal advice or other expert assistance is required, the services of a competent professional should be sought.

All trademarks, service marks, registered trademarks, and registered service marks are the property of their respective owners and are used herein for identification purposes only.

ISBN: 978-1-953337-81-8

# CONTENTS

**How to Use the CFA Program Curriculum**      vii
    Errata      vii

## Quantitative Methods

**Learning Module 1**      **Interest Rates, Present Value, and Future Value**      3
Introduction      3
Interest Rates      4
Future Value of a Single Cash Flow      6
Non-Annual Compounding (Future Value)      10
Continuous Compounding      12
    Stated and Effective Rates      14
Future Value of a Series of Cash Flows      15
    Equal Cash Flows—Ordinary Annuity      15
    Unequal Cash Flows      17
Present Value of a Single Cash Flow      18
Non-Annual Compounding (Present Value)      20
Present Value of a Series of Equal and Unequal Cash Flows      21
    The Present Value of a Series of Equal Cash Flows      21
    The Present Value of a Series of Unequal Cash Flows      25
Present Value of a Perpetuity      26
    Present Values Indexed at Times Other than $t = 0$      27
Solving for Interest Rates, Growth Rates, and Number of Periods      29
    Solving for Interest Rates and Growth Rates      29
    Solving for the Number of Periods      32
Solving for Size of Annuity Payments      32
Present and Future Value Equivalence and the Additivity Principle      36
    The Cash Flow Additivity Principle      38
*Summary*      39
*Practice Problems*      40
*Solutions*      45

**Learning Module 2**      **Organizing, Visualizing, and Describing Data**      59
Introduction      59
Data Types      60
    Numerical versus Categorical Data      60
    Cross-Sectional versus Time-Series versus Panel Data      63
    Structured versus Unstructured Data      64
    Data Summarization      68
Organizing Data for Quantitative Analysis      68
Summarizing Data Using Frequency Distributions      71
Summarizing Data Using a Contingency Table      77
Data Visualization      80
    Histogram and Frequency Polygon      80
    Bar Chart      82

|  |  |
|---|---|
| Tree-Map | 85 |
| Word Cloud | 86 |
| Line Chart | 88 |
| Scatter Plot | 90 |
| Heat Map | 94 |
| Guide to Selecting among Visualization Types | 96 |
| Measures of Central Tendency | 98 |
| The Arithmetic Mean | 99 |
| The Median | 103 |
| The Mode | 105 |
| Other Concepts of Mean | 106 |
| Quantiles | 115 |
| Quartiles, Quintiles, Deciles, and Percentiles | 115 |
| Quantiles in Investment Practice | 121 |
| Measures of Dispersion | 122 |
| The Range | 122 |
| The Mean Absolute Deviation | 122 |
| Sample Variance and Sample Standard Deviation | 124 |
| Downside Deviation and Coefficient of Variation | 127 |
| Coefficient of Variation | 130 |
| *Summary* | *132* |
| *Practice Problems* | *136* |
| *Solutions* | *147* |

**Learning Module 3**    **Probability Concepts**    **155**

|  |  |
|---|---|
| Probability Concepts and Odds Ratios | 156 |
| Probability and Odds | 156 |
| Conditional and Joint Probability | 161 |
| Principles of Counting | 173 |
| *Summary* | *179* |
| *References* | *182* |
| *Practice Problems* | *183* |
| *Solutions* | *186* |

**Learning Module 4**    **Common Probability Distributions**    **189**

|  |  |
|---|---|
| Discrete Random Variables | 190 |
| Discrete Random Variables | 191 |
| Discrete and Continuous Uniform Distribution | 195 |
| Continuous Uniform Distribution | 197 |
| Binomial Distribution | 200 |
| Normal Distribution | 208 |
| The Normal Distribution | 208 |
| Probabilities Using the Normal Distribution | 212 |
| Standardizing a Random Variable | 214 |
| Probabilities Using the Standard Normal Distribution | 214 |
| Student's *t*-, Chi-Square, and *F*-Distributions | 216 |
| Student's *t*-Distribution | 216 |
| Chi-Square and *F*-Distribution | 218 |
| *Summary* | *223* |

# Contents

| | | |
|---|---|---|
| | *References* | *226* |
| | *Practice Problems* | *227* |
| | *Solutions* | *232* |
| **Learning Module 5** | **Sampling and Estimation** | **237** |
| | Introduction | 237 |
| | Point Estimates of the Population Mean | 238 |
| |     Point Estimators | 238 |
| | Confidence Intervals for the Population Mean and Sample Size Selection | 242 |
| |     Selection of Sample Size | 248 |
| | Sampling-Related Biases | 250 |
| |     Data Snooping Bias | 251 |
| |     Sample Selection Bias | 252 |
| |     Look-Ahead Bias | 254 |
| |     Time-Period Bias | 255 |
| | *Summary* | *256* |
| | *References* | *259* |
| | *Practice Problems* | *260* |
| | *Solutions* | *263* |
| **Learning Module 6** | **Basics of Hypothesis Testing** | **267** |
| | Introduction | 268 |
| |     Why Hypothesis Testing? | 268 |
| |     Implications from a Sampling Distribution | 268 |
| | The Process of Hypothesis Testing | 270 |
| |     Stating the Hypotheses | 271 |
| |     Two-Sided vs. One-Sided Hypotheses | 271 |
| |     Selecting the Appropriate Hypotheses | 272 |
| | Identify the Appropriate Test Statistic | 273 |
| |     Test Statistics | 273 |
| |     Identifying the Distribution of the Test Statistic | 273 |
| | Specify the Level of Significance | 274 |
| | State the Decision Rule | 276 |
| |     Determining Critical Values | 276 |
| |     Decision Rules and Confidence Intervals | 278 |
| |     Collect the Data and Calculate the Test Statistic | 278 |
| | Make a Decision | 279 |
| |     Make a Statistical Decision | 279 |
| |     Make an Economic Decision | 279 |
| |     Statistically Significant but Not Economically Significant? | 279 |
| | The Role of *p*-Values | 280 |
| | Multiple Tests and Significance Interpretation | 283 |
| | Tests Concerning a Single Mean | 286 |
| | Test Concerning Differences between Means with Independent Samples | 290 |
| | Test Concerning Differences between Means with Dependent Samples | 292 |
| | Testing Concerning Tests of Variances | 296 |
| |     Tests of a Single Variance | 296 |
| |     Test Concerning the Equality of Two Variances (*F*-Test) | 299 |
| | *Summary* | *304* |

| | | |
|---|---|---|
| | *References* | *307* |
| | *Practice Problems* | *308* |
| | *Solutions* | *317* |
| **Learning Module 7** | **Appendices** | **323** |
| | Appendices | 323 |
| | **Glossary** | **G-1** |

# How to Use the CFA Program Curriculum

The CFA® Program exams measure your mastery of the core knowledge, skills, and abilities required to succeed as an investment professional. These core competencies are the basis for the Candidate Body of Knowledge (CBOK™). The CBOK consists of four components:

- A broad outline that lists the major CFA Program topic areas (www.cfainstitute.org/programs/cfa/curriculum/cbok)
- Topic area weights that indicate the relative exam weightings of the top-level topic areas (www.cfainstitute.org/programs/cfa/curriculum)
- Learning outcome statements (LOS) that advise candidates about the specific knowledge, skills, and abilities they should acquire from curriculum content covering a topic area: LOS are provided in candidate study sessions and at the beginning of each block of related content and the specific lesson that covers them. We encourage you to review the information about the LOS on our website (www.cfainstitute.org/programs/cfa/curriculum/study-sessions), including the descriptions of LOS "command words" on the candidate resources page at www.cfainstitute.org.
- The CFA Program curriculum that candidates receive upon exam registration

Therefore, the key to your success on the CFA exams is studying and understanding the CBOK. You can learn more about the CBOK on our website: www.cfainstitute.org/programs/cfa/curriculum/cbok.

*The entire curriculum, including the practice questions, is the basis for all exam questions and is selected or developed specifically to teach the knowledge, skills, and abilities reflected in the CBOK.*

## ERRATA

The curriculum development process is rigorous and includes multiple rounds of reviews by content experts. Despite our efforts to produce a curriculum that is free of errors, there are instances where we must make corrections. Curriculum errata are periodically updated and posted by exam level and test date online on the Curriculum Errata webpage (www.cfainstitute.org/en/programs/submit-errata). If you believe you have found an error in the curriculum, you can submit your concerns through our curriculum errata reporting process found at the bottom of the Curriculum Errata webpage.

## DESIGNING YOUR PERSONAL STUDY PROGRAM

An orderly, systematic approach to exam preparation is critical. You should dedicate a consistent block of time every week to reading and studying. Review the LOS both before and after you study curriculum content to ensure that you have mastered the applicable content and can demonstrate the knowledge, skills, and abilities described by the LOS and the assigned reading. Use the LOS self-check to track your progress and highlight areas of weakness for later review.

Successful candidates report an average of more than 300 hours preparing for each exam. Your preparation time will vary based on your prior education and experience, and you will likely spend more time on some study sessions than on others.

## CFA INSTITUTE LEARNING ECOSYSTEM (LES)

Your exam registration fee includes access to the CFA Program Learning Ecosystem (LES). This digital learning platform provides access, even offline, to all of the curriculum content and practice questions and is organized as a series of short online lessons with associated practice questions. This tool is your one-stop location for all study materials, including practice questions and mock exams, and the primary method by which CFA Institute delivers your curriculum experience. The LES offers candidates additional practice questions to test their knowledge, and some questions in the LES provide a unique interactive experience.

## FEEDBACK

Please send any comments or feedback to info@cfainstitute.org, and we will review your suggestions carefully.

# Quantitative Methods

# LEARNING MODULE 1

# Interest Rates, Present Value, and Future Value

by Richard A. DeFusco, PhD, CFA, Dennis W. McLeavey, DBA, CFA, Jerald E. Pinto, PhD, CFA, and David E. Runkle, PhD, CFA.

*Richard A. DeFusco, PhD, CFA, is at the University of Nebraska-Lincoln (USA). Dennis W. McLeavey, DBA, CFA, is at the University of Rhode Island (USA). Jerald E. Pinto, PhD, CFA, is at CFA Institute (USA). David E. Runkle, PhD, CFA, is at Jacobs Levy Equity Management (USA).*

## LEARNING OUTCOMES

| Mastery | The candidate should be able to: |
|---|---|
| ☐ | interpret interest rates as required rates of return, discount rates, or opportunity costs |
| ☐ | explain an interest rate as the sum of a real risk-free rate and premiums that compensate investors for bearing distinct types of risk |
| ☐ | calculate and interpret the future value (FV) and present value (PV) of a single sum of money, an ordinary annuity, an annuity due, a perpetuity (PV only), and a series of unequal cash flows |
| ☐ | demonstrate the use of a time line in modeling and solving time value of money problems |
| ☐ | calculate the solution for time value of money problems with different frequencies of compounding |
| ☐ | calculate and interpret the effective annual rate, given the stated annual interest rate and the frequency of compounding |

## INTRODUCTION

As investment analysts, much of our work also involves evaluating transactions with present and future cash flows. When we place a value on any security, for example, we are attempting to determine the worth of a stream of future cash flows. To carry out all the above tasks accurately, we must understand the mathematics of time value of money problems. Money has time value in that individuals value a given amount of money more highly the earlier it is received. Therefore, a smaller amount of money now may be equivalent in value to a larger amount received at a future date. The

**time value of money** as a topic in investment mathematics deals with equivalence relationships between cash flows with different dates. Mastery of time value of money concepts and techniques is essential for investment analysts.[1]

## 2. INTEREST RATES

☐ interpret interest rates as required rates of return, discount rates, or opportunity costs

☐ explain an interest rate as the sum of a real risk-free rate and premiums that compensate investors for bearing distinct types of risk

In this reading, we will continually refer to interest rates. In some cases, we assume a particular value for the interest rate; in other cases, the interest rate will be the unknown quantity we seek to determine. Before turning to the mechanics of time value of money problems, we must illustrate the underlying economic concepts. In this section, we briefly explain the meaning and interpretation of interest rates.

Time value of money concerns equivalence relationships between cash flows occurring on different dates. The idea of equivalence relationships is relatively simple. Consider the following exchange: You pay $10,000 today and in return receive $9,500 today. Would you accept this arrangement? Not likely. But what if you received the $9,500 today and paid the $10,000 one year from now? Can these amounts be considered equivalent? Possibly, because a payment of $10,000 a year from now would probably be worth less to you than a payment of $10,000 today. It would be fair, therefore, to **discount** the $10,000 received in one year—that is, to cut its value based on how much time passes before the money is paid. An **interest rate**, denoted $r$, is a rate of return that reflects the relationship between differently dated cash flows. If $9,500 today and $10,000 in one year are equivalent in value, then $10,000 − $9,500 = $500 is the required compensation for receiving $10,000 in one year rather than now. The interest rate—the required compensation stated as a rate of return—is $500/$9,500 = 0.0526 or 5.26 percent.

Interest rates can be thought of in three ways. First, they can be considered required rates of return—that is, the minimum rate of return an investor must receive in order to accept the investment. Second, interest rates can be considered discount rates. In the example above, 5.26 percent is that rate at which we discounted the $10,000 future amount to find its value today. Thus, we use the terms "interest rate" and "discount rate" almost interchangeably. Third, interest rates can be considered opportunity costs. An **opportunity cost** is the value that investors forgo by choosing a particular course of action. In the example, if the party who supplied $9,500 had instead decided to spend it today, he would have forgone earning 5.26 percent on the money. So we can view 5.26 percent as the opportunity cost of current consumption.

Economics tells us that interest rates are set in the marketplace by the forces of supply and demand, where investors are suppliers of funds and borrowers are demanders of funds. Taking the perspective of investors in analyzing market-determined interest

---

[1] Examples in this reading and other readings in quantitative methods were updated in 2018 by Professor Sanjiv Sabherwal of the University of Texas, Arlington.

rates, we can view an interest rate $r$ as being composed of a real risk-free interest rate plus a set of four premiums that are required returns or compensation for bearing distinct types of risk:

$r$ = Real risk-free interest rate + Inflation premium + Default risk premium + Liquidity premium + Maturity premium

- The **real risk-free interest rate** is the single-period interest rate for a completely risk-free security if no inflation were expected. In economic theory, the real risk-free rate reflects the time preferences of individuals for current versus future real consumption.
- The **inflation premium** compensates investors for expected inflation and reflects the average inflation rate expected over the maturity of the debt. Inflation reduces the purchasing power of a unit of currency—the amount of goods and services one can buy with it. The sum of the real risk-free interest rate and the inflation premium is the **nominal risk-free interest rate**.[2] Many countries have governmental short-term debt whose interest rate can be considered to represent the nominal risk-free interest rate in that country. The interest rate on a 90-day US Treasury bill (T-bill), for example, represents the nominal risk-free interest rate over that time horizon.[3] US T-bills can be bought and sold in large quantities with minimal transaction costs and are backed by the full faith and credit of the US government.
- The **default risk premium** compensates investors for the possibility that the borrower will fail to make a promised payment at the contracted time and in the contracted amount.
- The **liquidity premium** compensates investors for the risk of loss relative to an investment's fair value if the investment needs to be converted to cash quickly. US T-bills, for example, do not bear a liquidity premium because large amounts can be bought and sold without affecting their market price. Many bonds of small issuers, by contrast, trade infrequently after they are issued; the interest rate on such bonds includes a liquidity premium reflecting the relatively high costs (including the impact on price) of selling a position.
- The **maturity premium** compensates investors for the increased sensitivity of the market value of debt to a change in market interest rates as maturity is extended, in general (holding all else equal). The difference between the interest rate on longer-maturity, liquid Treasury debt and that on short-term Treasury debt reflects a positive maturity premium for the longer-term debt (and possibly different inflation premiums as well).

Using this insight into the economic meaning of interest rates, we now turn to a discussion of solving time value of money problems, starting with the future value of a single cash flow.

---

2 Technically, 1 plus the nominal rate equals the product of 1 plus the real rate and 1 plus the inflation rate. As a quick approximation, however, the nominal rate is equal to the real rate plus an inflation premium. In this discussion we focus on approximate additive relationships to highlight the underlying concepts.

3 Other developed countries issue securities similar to US Treasury bills. The French government issues BTFs or negotiable fixed-rate discount Treasury bills (*Bons du Trésor àtaux fixe et à intérêts précomptés*) with maturities of up to one year. The Japanese government issues a short-term Treasury bill with maturities of 6 and 12 months. The German government issues at discount both Treasury financing paper (*Finanzierungsschätze des Bundes* or, for short, *Schätze*) and Treasury discount paper (*Bubills*) with maturities up to 24 months. In the United Kingdom, the British government issues gilt-edged Treasury bills with maturities ranging from 1 to 364 days. The Canadian government bond market is closely related to the US market; Canadian Treasury bills have maturities of 3, 6, and 12 months.

## 3. FUTURE VALUE OF A SINGLE CASH FLOW

- [ ] calculate and interpret the future value (FV) and present value (PV) of a single sum of money, an ordinary annuity, an annuity due, a perpetuity (PV only), and a series of unequal cash flows
- [ ] demonstrate the use of a time line in modeling and solving time value of money problems

In this section, we introduce time value associated with a single cash flow or lump-sum investment. We describe the relationship between an initial investment or **present value (PV)**, which earns a rate of return (the interest rate per period) denoted as $r$, and its **future value (FV)**, which will be received $N$ years or periods from today.

The following example illustrates this concept. Suppose you invest $100 (PV = $100) in an interest-bearing bank account paying 5 percent annually. At the end of the first year, you will have the $100 plus the interest earned, $0.05 \times \$100 = \$5$, for a total of $105. To formalize this one-period example, we define the following terms:

$PV$ = present value of the investment

$FV_N$ = future value of the investment $N$ periods from today

$r$ = rate of interest per period

For $N = 1$, the expression for the future value of amount PV is

$$FV_1 = PV(1 + r) \tag{1}$$

For this example, we calculate the future value one year from today as $FV_1 = \$100(1.05) = \$105$.

Now suppose you decide to invest the initial $100 for two years with interest earned and credited to your account annually. At the end of the first year (the beginning of the second year), your account will have $105, which you will leave in the bank for another year. Thus, with a beginning amount of $105 (PV = $105), the amount at the end of the second year will be $105(1.05) = $110.25. Note that the $5.25 interest earned during the second year is 5 percent of the amount invested at the beginning of Year 2.

Another way to understand this example is to note that the amount invested at the beginning of Year 2 is composed of the original $100 that you invested plus the $5 interest earned during the first year. During the second year, the original principal again earns interest, as does the interest that was earned during Year 1. You can see how the original investment grows:

| | |
|---|---:|
| Original investment | $100.00 |
| Interest for the first year ($100 × 0.05) | 5.00 |
| Interest for the second year based on original investment ($100 × 0.05) | 5.00 |
| Interest for the second year based on interest earned in the first year (0.05 × $5.00 interest on interest) | 0.25 |
| Total | $110.25 |

The $5 interest that you earned each period on the $100 original investment is known as **simple interest** (the interest rate times the principal). **Principal** is the amount of funds originally invested. During the two-year period, you earn $10 of simple interest. The extra $0.25 that you have at the end of Year 2 is the interest you earned on the Year 1 interest of $5 that you reinvested.

# Future Value of a Single Cash Flow

The interest earned on interest provides the first glimpse of the phenomenon known as **compounding**. Although the interest earned on the initial investment is important, for a given interest rate it is fixed in size from period to period. The compounded interest earned on reinvested interest is a far more powerful force because, for a given interest rate, it grows in size each period. The importance of compounding increases with the magnitude of the interest rate. For example, $100 invested today would be worth about $13,150 after 100 years if compounded annually at 5 percent, but worth more than $20 million if compounded annually over the same time period at a rate of 13 percent.

To verify the $20 million figure, we need a general formula to handle compounding for any number of periods. The following general formula relates the present value of an initial investment to its future value after $N$ periods:

$$FV_N = PV(1 + r)^N \qquad (2)$$

where $r$ is the stated interest rate per period and $N$ is the number of compounding periods. In the bank example, $FV_2 = \$100(1 + 0.05)^2 = \$110.25$. In the 13 percent investment example, $FV_{100} = \$100(1.13)^{100} = \$20{,}316{,}287.42$.

The most important point to remember about using the future value equation is that the stated interest rate, $r$, and the number of compounding periods, $N$, must be compatible. Both variables must be defined in the same time units. For example, if $N$ is stated in months, then $r$ should be the one-month interest rate, unannualized.

A time line helps us to keep track of the compatibility of time units and the interest rate per time period. In the time line, we use the time index $t$ to represent a point in time a stated number of periods from today. Thus the present value is the amount available for investment today, indexed as $t = 0$. We can now refer to a time $N$ periods from today as $t = N$. The time line in Exhibit 1 shows this relationship.

**Exhibit 1: The Relationship between an Initial Investment, PV, and Its Future Value, FV**

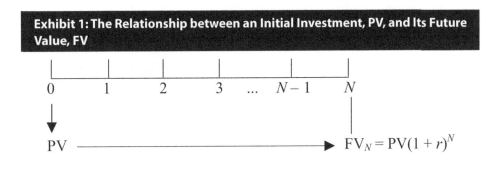

In Exhibit 1, we have positioned the initial investment, PV, at $t = 0$. Using Equation 2, we move the present value, PV, forward to $t = N$ by the factor $(1 + r)^N$. This factor is called a future value factor. We denote the future value on the time line as FV and position it at $t = N$. Suppose the future value is to be received exactly 10 periods from today's date ($N = 10$). The present value, PV, and the future value, FV, are separated in time through the factor $(1 + r)^{10}$.

The fact that the present value and the future value are separated in time has important consequences:

- We can add amounts of money only if they are indexed at the same point in time.
- For a given interest rate, the future value increases with the number of periods.

- For a given number of periods, the future value increases with the interest rate.

To better understand these concepts, consider three examples that illustrate how to apply the future value formula.

### EXAMPLE 1

### The Future Value of a Lump Sum with Interim Cash Reinvested at the Same Rate

1. You are the lucky winner of your state's lottery of $5 million after taxes. You invest your winnings in a five-year certificate of deposit (CD) at a local financial institution. The CD promises to pay 7 percent per year compounded annually. This institution also lets you reinvest the interest at that rate for the duration of the CD. How much will you have at the end of five years if your money remains invested at 7 percent for five years with no withdrawals?

### Solution:

To solve this problem, compute the future value of the $5 million investment using the following values in Equation 2:

$PV = \$5,000,000$
$r = 7\% = 0.07$
$N = 5$
$FV_N = PV(1 + r)^N$
$= \$5,000,000(1.07)^5$
$= \$5,000,000(1.402552)$
$= \$7,012,758.65$

At the end of five years, you will have $7,012,758.65 if your money remains invested at 7 percent with no withdrawals.

*In this and most examples in this reading, note that the factors are reported at six decimal places but the calculations may actually reflect greater precision.* For example, the reported 1.402552 has been rounded up from 1.40255173 (the calculation is actually carried out with more than eight decimal places of precision by the calculator or spreadsheet). Our final result reflects the higher number of decimal places carried by the calculator or spreadsheet.[4]

---

[4] We could also solve time value of money problems using tables of interest rate factors. Solutions using tabled values of interest rate factors are generally less accurate than solutions obtained using calculators or spreadsheets, so practitioners prefer calculators or spreadsheets.

# Future Value of a Single Cash Flow

## EXAMPLE 2

### The Future Value of a Lump Sum with No Interim Cash

1. An institution offers you the following terms for a contract: For an investment of JPY2,500,000, the institution promises to pay you a lump sum six years from now at an 8 percent annual interest rate. What future amount can you expect?

### Solution:

Use the following data in Equation 2 to find the future value:

$PV = ¥2,500,000$
$r = 8\% = 0.08$
$N = 6$
$FV_N = PV(1 + r)^N$
$= ¥2,500,000(1.08)^6$
$= ¥2,500,000(1.586874)$
$= ¥3,967,186$

You can expect to receive JPY3,967,186 six years from now.

Our third example is a more complicated future value problem that illustrates the importance of keeping track of actual calendar time.

## EXAMPLE 3

### The Future Value of a Lump Sum

1. A pension fund manager estimates that his corporate sponsor will make a $10 million contribution five years from now. The rate of return on plan assets has been estimated at 9 percent per year. The pension fund manager wants to calculate the future value of this contribution 15 years from now, which is the date at which the funds will be distributed to retirees. What is that future value?

### Solution:

By positioning the initial investment, PV, at $t = 5$, we can calculate the future value of the contribution using the following data in Equation 2:

$PV = \$10$ million
$r = 9\% = 0.09$
$N = 10$
$FV_N = PV(1 + r)^N$
$= \$10,000,000(1.09)^{10}$
$= \$10,000,000(2.367364)$
$= \$23,673,636.75$

This problem looks much like the previous two, but it differs in one important respect: its timing. From the standpoint of today ($t = 0$), the future amount of $23,673,636.75 is 15 years into the future. Although the future value is 10 years from its present value, the present value of $10 million will not be received for another five years.

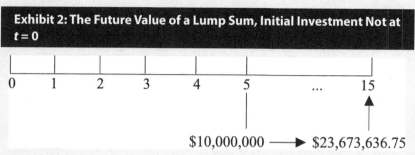

Exhibit 2: The Future Value of a Lump Sum, Initial Investment Not at $t = 0$

$10,000,000 ⟶ $23,673,636.75

As Exhibit 2 shows, we have followed the convention of indexing today as $t = 0$ and indexing subsequent times by adding 1 for each period. The additional contribution of $10 million is to be received in five years, so it is indexed as $t = 5$ and appears as such in the figure. The future value of the investment in 10 years is then indexed at $t = 15$—that is, 10 years following the receipt of the $10 million contribution at $t = 5$. Time lines like this one can be extremely useful when dealing with more-complicated problems, especially those involving more than one cash flow.

In a later section of this reading, we will discuss how to calculate the value today of the $10 million to be received five years from now. For the moment, we can use Equation 2. Suppose the pension fund manager in Example 3 above were to receive $6,499,313.86 today from the corporate sponsor. How much will that sum be worth at the end of five years? How much will it be worth at the end of 15 years?

PV = $6,499,313.86
$r = 9\% = 0.09$
$N = 5$
$FV_N = PV(1 + r)^N$
$= \$6,499,313.86(1.09)^5$
$= \$6,499,313.86(1.538624)$
$= \$10,000,000$ at the five-year mark

and

PV = $6,499,313.86
$r = 9\% = 0.09$
$N = 15$
$FV_N = PV(1 + r)^N$
$= \$6,499,313.86(1.09)^{15}$
$= \$6,499,313.86(3.642482)$
$= \$23,673,636.74$ at the 15-year mark

These results show that today's present value of about $6.5 million becomes $10 million after five years and $23.67 million after 15 years.

# 4

## NON-ANNUAL COMPOUNDING (FUTURE VALUE)

- [ ] calculate the solution for time value of money problems with different frequencies of compounding

# Non-Annual Compounding (Future Value)

In this section, we examine investments paying interest more than once a year. For instance, many banks offer a monthly interest rate that compounds 12 times a year. In such an arrangement, they pay interest on interest every month. Rather than quote the periodic monthly interest rate, financial institutions often quote an annual interest rate that we refer to as the **stated annual interest rate** or **quoted interest rate**. We denote the stated annual interest rate by $r_s$. For instance, your bank might state that a particular CD pays 8 percent compounded monthly. The stated annual interest rate equals the monthly interest rate multiplied by 12. In this example, the monthly interest rate is $0.08/12 = 0.0067$ or 0.67 percent.[5] This rate is strictly a quoting convention because $(1 + 0.0067)^{12} = 1.083$, not 1.08; the term $(1 + r_s)$ is not meant to be a future value factor when compounding is more frequent than annual.

With more than one compounding period per year, the future value formula can be expressed as

$$FV_N = PV\left(1 + \frac{r_s}{m}\right)^{mN} \qquad (3)$$

where $r_s$ is the stated annual interest rate, $m$ is the number of compounding periods per year, and $N$ now stands for the number of years. Note the compatibility here between the interest rate used, $r_s/m$, and the number of compounding periods, $mN$. The periodic rate, $r_s/m$, is the stated annual interest rate divided by the number of compounding periods per year. The number of compounding periods, $mN$, is the number of compounding periods in one year multiplied by the number of years. The periodic rate, $r_s/m$, and the number of compounding periods, $mN$, must be compatible.

### EXAMPLE 4

### The Future Value of a Lump Sum with Quarterly Compounding

1. Continuing with the CD example, suppose your bank offers you a CD with a two-year maturity, a stated annual interest rate of 8 percent compounded quarterly, and a feature allowing reinvestment of the interest at the same interest rate. You decide to invest $10,000. What will the CD be worth at maturity?

### Solution:

Compute the future value with Equation 3 as follows:

PV = $10,000
$r_s$ = 8% = 0.08
m = 4
$r_s/m$ = 0.08/4 = 0.02
N = 2
mN = 4(2) = 8 interest periods

$$FV_N = PV\left(1 + \frac{r_s}{m}\right)^{mN}$$
$= \$10,000(1.02)^8$
$= \$10,000(1.171659)$
$= \$11,716.59$

At maturity, the CD will be worth $11,716.59.

---

[5] To avoid rounding errors when using a financial calculator, divide 8 by 12 and then press the %i key, rather than simply entering 0.67 for %i, so we have $(1 + 0.08/12)^{12} = 1.083000$.

The future value formula in Equation 3 does not differ from the one in Equation 2. Simply keep in mind that the interest rate to use is the rate per period and the exponent is the number of interest, or compounding, periods.

> **EXAMPLE 5**
>
> ### The Future Value of a Lump Sum with Monthly Compounding
>
> 1. An Australian bank offers to pay you 6 percent compounded monthly. You decide to invest AUD 1 million for one year. What is the future value of your investment if interest payments are reinvested at 6 percent?
>
> **Solution:**
>
> Use Equation 3 to find the future value of the one-year investment as follows:
>
> PV = A$1,000,000
> $r_s$ = 6% = 0.06
> $m$ = 12
> $r_s/m$ = 0.06/12 = 0.0050
> $N$ = 1
> $mN$ = 12(1) = 12 interest periods
>
> $$FV_N = PV\left(1 + \frac{r_s}{m}\right)^{mN}$$
>
> = A$1,000,000(1.005)$^{12}$
> = A$1,000,000(1.061678)
> = A$1,061,677.81
>
> If you had been paid 6 percent with annual compounding, the future amount would be only AUD 1,000,000(1.06) = AUD 1,060,000 instead of AUD 1,061,677.81 with monthly compounding.

## 5. CONTINUOUS COMPOUNDING

- [ ] calculate and interpret the effective annual rate, given the stated annual interest rate and the frequency of compounding
- [ ] calculate the solution for time value of money problems with different frequencies of compounding

The preceding discussion on compounding periods illustrates discrete compounding, which credits interest after a discrete amount of time has elapsed. If the number of compounding periods per year becomes infinite, then interest is said to compound continuously. If we want to use the future value formula with continuous compounding, we need to find the limiting value of the future value factor for $m \to \infty$ (infinitely many compounding periods per year) in Equation 3. The expression for the future value of a sum in $N$ years with continuous compounding is

$$FV_N = PV e^{r_s N} \tag{4}$$

# Continuous Compounding

The term $e^{r_s N}$ is the transcendental number $e \approx 2.7182818$ raised to the power $r_s N$. Most financial calculators have the function $e^x$.

### EXAMPLE 6

### The Future Value of a Lump Sum with Continuous Compounding

Suppose a $10,000 investment will earn 8 percent compounded continuously for two years. We can compute the future value with Equation 4 as follows:

PV = $10,000
$r_s$ = 8% = 0.08
N = 2
$FV_N = PV e^{r_s N}$
= $10,000 e^{0.08(2)}$
= $10,000 (1.173511)$
= $11,735.11

With the same interest rate but using continuous compounding, the $10,000 investment will grow to $11,735.11 in two years, compared with $11,716.59 using quarterly compounding as shown in Example 4.

Exhibit 3 shows how a stated annual interest rate of 8 percent generates different ending dollar amounts with annual, semiannual, quarterly, monthly, daily, and continuous compounding for an initial investment of $1 (carried out to six decimal places).

As Exhibit 3 shows, all six cases have the same stated annual interest rate of 8 percent; they have different ending dollar amounts, however, because of differences in the frequency of compounding. With annual compounding, the ending amount is $1.08. More frequent compounding results in larger ending amounts. The ending dollar amount with continuous compounding is the maximum amount that can be earned with a stated annual rate of 8 percent.

### Exhibit 3: The Effect of Compounding Frequency on Future Value

| Frequency | $r_s/m$ | mN | Future Value of $1 | | |
|---|---|---|---|---|---|
| Annual | 8%/1 = 8% | 1 × 1 = 1 | $1.00(1.08) | = | $1.08 |
| Semiannual | 8%/2 = 4% | 2 × 1 = 2 | $1.00(1.04)^2$ | = | $1.081600 |
| Quarterly | 8%/4 = 2% | 4 × 1 = 4 | $1.00(1.02)^4$ | = | $1.082432 |
| Monthly | 8%/12 = 0.6667% | 12 × 1 = 12 | $1.00(1.006667)^{12}$ | = | $1.083000 |
| Daily | 8%/365 = 0.0219% | 365 × 1 = 365 | $1.00(1.000219)^{365}$ | = | $1.083278 |
| Continuous | | | $1.00 e^{0.08(1)}$ | = | $1.083287 |

Exhibit 3 also shows that a $1 investment earning 8.16 percent compounded annually grows to the same future value at the end of one year as a $1 investment earning 8 percent compounded semiannually. This result leads us to a distinction between the stated annual interest rate and the **effective annual rate** (EAR).[6] For an 8 percent stated annual interest rate with semiannual compounding, the EAR is 8.16 percent.

## Stated and Effective Rates

The stated annual interest rate does not give a future value directly, so we need a formula for the EAR. With an annual interest rate of 8 percent compounded semiannually, we receive a periodic rate of 4 percent. During the course of a year, an investment of $1 would grow to $1(1.04)^2 = $1.0816, as illustrated in Exhibit 3. The interest earned on the $1 investment is $0.0816 and represents an effective annual rate of interest of 8.16 percent. The effective annual rate is calculated as follows:

$$\text{EAR} = (1 + \text{Periodic interest rate})^m - 1 \tag{5}$$

The periodic interest rate is the stated annual interest rate divided by $m$, where $m$ is the number of compounding periods in one year. Using our previous example, we can solve for EAR as follows: $(1.04)^2 - 1 = 8.16$ percent.

The concept of EAR extends to continuous compounding. Suppose we have a rate of 8 percent compounded continuously. We can find the EAR in the same way as above by finding the appropriate future value factor. In this case, a $1 investment would grow to $1e^{0.08(1.0)} = $1.0833. The interest earned for one year represents an effective annual rate of 8.33 percent and is larger than the 8.16 percent EAR with semiannual compounding because interest is compounded more frequently. With continuous compounding, we can solve for the effective annual rate as follows:

$$\text{EAR} = e^{r_s} - 1 \tag{6}$$

We can reverse the formulas for EAR with discrete and continuous compounding to find a periodic rate that corresponds to a particular effective annual rate. Suppose we want to find the appropriate periodic rate for a given effective annual rate of 8.16 percent with semiannual compounding. We can use Equation 5 to find the periodic rate:

$0.0816 = (1 + \text{Periodic rate})^2 - 1$
$1.0816 = (1 + \text{Periodic rate})^2$
$(1.0816)^{1/2} - 1 = \text{Periodic rate}$
$(1.04) - 1 = \text{Periodic rate}$
$4\% = \text{Periodic rate}$

To calculate the continuously compounded rate (the stated annual interest rate with continuous compounding) corresponding to an effective annual rate of 8.33 percent, we find the interest rate that satisfies Equation 6:

$0.0833 = e^{r_s} - 1$
$1.0833 = e^{r_s}$

---

[6] Among the terms used for the effective annual return on interest-bearing bank deposits are annual percentage yield (APY) in the United States and equivalent annual rate (EAR) in the United Kingdom. By contrast, the **annual percentage rate** (APR) measures the cost of borrowing expressed as a yearly rate. In the United States, the APR is calculated as a periodic rate times the number of payment periods per year and, as a result, some writers use APR as a general synonym for the stated annual interest rate. Nevertheless, APR is a term with legal connotations; its calculation follows regulatory standards that vary internationally. Therefore, "stated annual interest rate" is the preferred general term for an annual interest rate that does not account for compounding within the year.

To solve this equation, we take the natural logarithm of both sides. (Recall that the natural log of $e^{r_s}$ is $\ln e^{r_s} = r_s$.) Therefore, $\ln 1.0833 = r_s$, resulting in $r_s = 8$ percent. We see that a stated annual rate of 8 percent with continuous compounding is equivalent to an EAR of 8.33 percent.

## FUTURE VALUE OF A SERIES OF CASH FLOWS

6

- ☐ calculate and interpret the future value (FV) and present value (PV) of a single sum of money, an ordinary annuity, an annuity due, a perpetuity (PV only), and a series of unequal cash flows
- ☐ demonstrate the use of a time line in modeling and solving time value of money problems

In this section, we consider series of cash flows, both even and uneven. We begin with a list of terms commonly used when valuing cash flows that are distributed over many time periods.

- An **annuity** is a finite set of level, or identical, and sequential cash flows.
- An **ordinary annuity** has a first cash flow that occurs one period from now (indexed at $t = 1$).
- An **annuity due** has a first cash flow that occurs immediately (indexed at $t = 0$).
- A **perpetuity** is a perpetual annuity, or a set of level, or identical, never-ending sequential cash flows, with the first cash flow occurring one period from now.

### Equal Cash Flows—Ordinary Annuity

Consider an ordinary annuity paying 5 percent annually. Suppose we have five separate deposits of $1,000 occurring at equally spaced intervals of one year, with the first payment occurring at $t = 1$. Our goal is to find the future value of this ordinary annuity after the last deposit at $t = 5$. The increment in the time counter is one year, so the last payment occurs five years from now. As the time line in Exhibit 4 shows, we find the future value of each $1,000 deposit as of $t = 5$ with Equation 2, $FV_N = PV(1 + r)^N$. The arrows in Exhibit 4 extend from the payment date to $t = 5$. For instance, the first $1,000 deposit made at $t = 1$ will compound over four periods. Using Equation 2, we find that the future value of the first deposit at $t = 5$ is $1,000(1.05)^4 = $1,215.51$. We calculate the future value of all other payments in a similar fashion. (Note that we are finding the future value at $t = 5$, so the last payment does not earn any interest.) With all values now at $t = 5$, we can add the future values to arrive at the future value of the annuity. This amount is $5,525.63.

### Exhibit 4: The Future Value of a Five-Year Ordinary Annuity

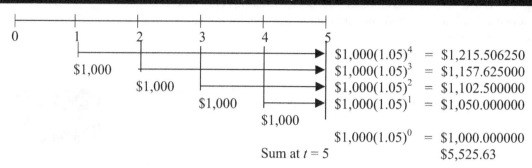

We can arrive at a general annuity formula if we define the annuity amount as $A$, the number of time periods as $N$, and the interest rate per period as $r$. We can then define the future value as

$$FV_N = A\left[(1+r)^{N-1} + (1+r)^{N-2} + (1+r)^{N-3} + \ldots + (1+r)^1 + (1+r)^0\right]$$

which simplifies to

$$FV_N = A\left[\frac{(1+r)^N - 1}{r}\right] \qquad (7)$$

The term in brackets is the future value annuity factor. This factor gives the future value of an ordinary annuity of $1 per period. Multiplying the future value annuity factor by the annuity amount gives the future value of an ordinary annuity. For the ordinary annuity in Exhibit 4, we find the future value annuity factor from Equation 7 as

$$\left[\frac{(1.05)^5 - 1}{0.05}\right] = 5.525631$$

With an annuity amount $A$ = $1,000, the future value of the annuity is $1,000(5.525631) = $5,525.63, an amount that agrees with our earlier work.

The next example illustrates how to find the future value of an ordinary annuity using the formula in Equation 7.

### EXAMPLE 7

### The Future Value of an Annuity

1. Suppose your company's defined contribution retirement plan allows you to invest up to EUR20,000 per year. You plan to invest €20,000 per year in a stock index fund for the next 30 years. Historically, this fund has earned 9 percent per year on average. Assuming that you actually earn 9 percent a

# Future Value of a Series of Cash Flows

year, how much money will you have available for retirement after making the last payment?

## Solution:

Use Equation 7 to find the future amount:

$A = €20,000$

$r = 9\% = 0.09$

$N = 30$

FV annuity factor $= \frac{(1+r)^N - 1}{r} = \frac{(1.09)^{30} - 1}{0.09} = 136.307539$

$FV_N = €20,000(136.307539)$

$= €2,726,150.77$

Assuming the fund continues to earn an average of 9 percent per year, you will have €2,726,150.77 available at retirement.

## Unequal Cash Flows

In many cases, cash flow streams are unequal, precluding the simple use of the future value annuity factor. For instance, an individual investor might have a savings plan that involves unequal cash payments depending on the month of the year or lower savings during a planned vacation. One can always find the future value of a series of unequal cash flows by compounding the cash flows one at a time. Suppose you have the five cash flows described in Exhibit 5, indexed relative to the present ($t = 0$).

**Exhibit 5: A Series of Unequal Cash Flows and Their Future Values at 5 Percent**

| Time | Cash Flow ($) | Future Value at Year 5 | | |
|---|---|---|---|---|
| $t = 1$ | 1,000 | $\$1,000(1.05)^4$ | = | \$1,215.51 |
| $t = 2$ | 2,000 | $\$2,000(1.05)^3$ | = | \$2,315.25 |
| $t = 3$ | 4,000 | $\$4,000(1.05)^2$ | = | \$4,410.00 |
| $t = 4$ | 5,000 | $\$5,000(1.05)^1$ | = | \$5,250.00 |
| $t = 5$ | 6,000 | $\$6,000(1.05)^0$ | = | \$6,000.00 |
| | | Sum | = | \$19,190.76 |

All of the payments shown in Exhibit 5 are different. Therefore, the most direct approach to finding the future value at $t = 5$ is to compute the future value of each payment as of $t = 5$ and then sum the individual future values. The total future value at Year 5 equals \$19,190.76, as shown in the third column. Later in this reading, you will learn shortcuts to take when the cash flows are close to even; these shortcuts will allow you to combine annuity and single-period calculations.

# 7  PRESENT VALUE OF A SINGLE CASH FLOW

☐ calculate and interpret the future value (FV) and present value (PV) of a single sum of money, an ordinary annuity, an annuity due, a perpetuity (PV only), and a series of unequal cash flows

☐ demonstrate the use of a time line in modeling and solving time value of money problems

Just as the future value factor links today's present value with tomorrow's future value, the present value factor allows us to discount future value to present value. For example, with a 5 percent interest rate generating a future payoff of $105 in one year, what current amount invested at 5 percent for one year will grow to $105? The answer is $100; therefore, $100 is the present value of $105 to be received in one year at a discount rate of 5 percent.

Given a future cash flow that is to be received in $N$ periods and an interest rate per period of $r$, we can use the formula for future value to solve directly for the present value as follows:

$$FV_N = PV(1 + r)^N$$
$$PV = FV_N \left[\frac{1}{(1 + r)^N}\right] \tag{8}$$
$$PV = FV_N(1 + r)^{-N}$$

We see from Equation 8 that the present value factor, $(1 + r)^{-N}$, is the reciprocal of the future value factor, $(1 + r)^N$.

### EXAMPLE 8

### The Present Value of a Lump Sum

1. An insurance company has issued a Guaranteed Investment Contract (GIC) that promises to pay $100,000 in six years with an 8 percent return rate. What amount of money must the insurer invest today at 8 percent for six years to make the promised payment?

### Solution:

We can use Equation 8 to find the present value using the following data:

$FV_N = \$100,000$
$r = 8\% = 0.08$
$N = 6$
$PV = FV_N(1 + r)^{-N}$
$= \$100,000 \left[\frac{1}{(1.08)^6}\right]$
$= \$100,000 (0.6301696)$
$= \$63,016.96$

We can say that $63,016.96 today, with an interest rate of 8 percent, is equivalent to $100,000 to be received in six years. Discounting the $100,000 makes a future $100,000 equivalent to $63,016.96 when allowance is made for the time value of money. As the time line in Exhibit 6 shows, the $100,000 has been discounted six full periods.

## Present Value of a Single Cash Flow

### Exhibit 6: The Present Value of a Lump Sum to Be Received at Time $t = 6$

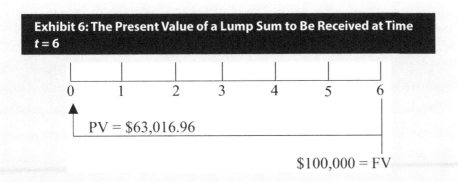

### EXAMPLE 9

## The Projected Present Value of a More Distant Future Lump Sum

1. Suppose you own a liquid financial asset that will pay you $100,000 in 10 years from today. Your daughter plans to attend college four years from today, and you want to know what the asset's present value will be at that time. Given an 8 percent discount rate, what will the asset be worth four years from today?

### Solution:

The value of the asset is the present value of the asset's promised payment. At $t = 4$, the cash payment will be received six years later. With this information, you can solve for the value four years from today using Equation 8:

$FV_N = \$100,000$
$r = 8\% = 0.08$
$N = 6$
$PV = FV_N(1 + r)^{-N}$
$= \$100,000 \dfrac{1}{(1.08)^6}$
$= \$100,000 (0.6301696)$
$= \$63,016.96$

### Exhibit 7: The Relationship between Present Value and Future Value

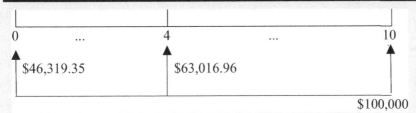

The time line in Exhibit 7 shows the future payment of $100,000 that is to be received at $t = 10$. The time line also shows the values at $t = 4$ and at $t = 0$. Relative to the payment at $t = 10$, the amount at $t = 4$ is a projected present value, while the amount at $t = 0$ is the present value (as of today).

Present value problems require an evaluation of the present value factor, $(1 + r)^{-N}$. Present values relate to the discount rate and the number of periods in the following ways:

- For a given discount rate, the farther in the future the amount to be received, the smaller that amount's present value.
- Holding time constant, the larger the discount rate, the smaller the present value of a future amount.

## 8. NON-ANNUAL COMPOUNDING (PRESENT VALUE)

☐ calculate the solution for time value of money problems with different frequencies of compounding

Recall that interest may be paid semiannually, quarterly, monthly, or even daily. To handle interest payments made more than once a year, we can modify the present value formula (Equation 8) as follows. Recall that $r_s$ is the quoted interest rate and equals the periodic interest rate multiplied by the number of compounding periods in each year. In general, with more than one compounding period in a year, we can express the formula for present value as

$$PV = FV_N \left(1 + \frac{r_s}{m}\right)^{-mN} \tag{9}$$

where

$m$ = number of compounding periods per year

$r_s$ = quoted annual interest rate

$N$ = number of years

The formula in Equation 9 is quite similar to that in Equation 8. As we have already noted, present value and future value factors are reciprocals. Changing the frequency of compounding does not alter this result. The only difference is the use of the periodic interest rate and the corresponding number of compounding periods.

The following example illustrates Equation 9.

### EXAMPLE 10

### The Present Value of a Lump Sum with Monthly Compounding

1. The manager of a Canadian pension fund knows that the fund must make a lump-sum payment of C$5 million 10 years from now. She wants to invest an amount today in a GIC so that it will grow to the required amount. The current interest rate on GICs is 6 percent a year, compounded monthly. How much should she invest today in the GIC?

### Solution:

Use Equation 9 to find the required present value:

$FV_N = C\$5{,}000{,}000$
$r_s = 6\% = 0.06$
$m = 12$
$r_s/m = 0.06/12 = 0.005$
$N = 10$
$mN = 12(10) = 120$
$PV = FV_N\left(1 + \frac{r_s}{m}\right)^{-mN}$
$= C\$5{,}000{,}000\,(1.005)^{-120}$
$= C\$5{,}000{,}000\,(0.549633)$
$= C\$2{,}748{,}163.67$

In applying Equation 9, we use the periodic rate (in this case, the monthly rate) and the appropriate number of periods with monthly compounding (in this case, 10 years of monthly compounding, or 120 periods).

# PRESENT VALUE OF A SERIES OF EQUAL AND UNEQUAL CASH FLOWS

☐ calculate and interpret the future value (FV) and present value (PV) of a single sum of money, an ordinary annuity, an annuity due, a perpetuity (PV only), and a series of unequal cash flows

☐ demonstrate the use of a time line in modeling and solving time value of money problems

Many applications in investment management involve assets that offer a series of cash flows over time. The cash flows may be highly uneven, relatively even, or equal. They may occur over relatively short periods of time or longer periods of time or even stretch on indefinitely. In this section, we discuss how to find the present value of a series of cash flows.

## The Present Value of a Series of Equal Cash Flows

We begin with an ordinary annuity. Recall that an ordinary annuity has equal annuity payments, with the first payment starting one period into the future. In total, the annuity makes $N$ payments, with the first payment at $t = 1$ and the last at $t = N$. We can express the present value of an ordinary annuity as the sum of the present values of each individual annuity payment, as follows:

$$PV = \frac{A}{(1+r)} + \frac{A}{(1+r)^2} + \frac{A}{(1+r)^3} + \ldots + \frac{A}{(1+r)^{N-1}} + \frac{A}{(1+r)^N} \qquad (10)$$

where

$A$ = the annuity amount

$r$ = the interest rate per period corresponding to the frequency of annuity payments (for example, annual, quarterly, or monthly)

$N$ = the number of annuity payments

Because the annuity payment (A) is a constant in this equation, it can be factored out as a common term. Thus the sum of the interest factors has a shortcut expression:

$$PV = A \left[ \frac{1 - \frac{1}{(1+r)^N}}{r} \right] \qquad (11)$$

In much the same way that we computed the future value of an ordinary annuity, we find the present value by multiplying the annuity amount by a present value annuity factor (the term in brackets in Equation 11).

### EXAMPLE 11

## The Present Value of an Ordinary Annuity

1. Suppose you are considering purchasing a financial asset that promises to pay €1,000 per year for five years, with the first payment one year from now. The required rate of return is 12 percent per year. How much should you pay for this asset?

### Solution:

To find the value of the financial asset, use the formula for the present value of an ordinary annuity given in Equation 11 with the following data:

$A = €1,000$

$r = 12\% = 0.12$

$N = 5$

$$PV = A \left[ \frac{1 - \frac{1}{(1+r)^N}}{r} \right]$$

$$= €1,000 \left[ \frac{1 - \frac{1}{(1.12)^5}}{0.12} \right]$$

$= €1,000(3.604776)$

$= €3,604.78$

The series of cash flows of €1,000 per year for five years is currently worth €3,604.78 when discounted at 12 percent.

Keeping track of the actual calendar time brings us to a specific type of annuity with identical payments: the annuity due. An annuity due has its first payment occurring today ($t = 0$). In total, the annuity due will make $N$ payments. Exhibit 8 presents the time line for an annuity due that makes four payments of $100.

**Exhibit 8: An Annuity Due of $100 per Period**

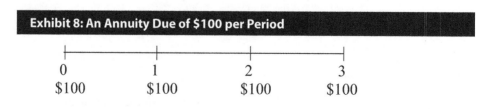

## Present Value of a Series of Equal and Unequal Cash Flows

As Exhibit 8 shows, we can view the four-period annuity due as the sum of two parts: a $100 lump sum today and an ordinary annuity of $100 per period for three periods. At a 12 percent discount rate, the four $100 cash flows in this annuity due example will be worth $340.18.[7]

Expressing the value of the future series of cash flows in today's dollars gives us a convenient way of comparing annuities. The next example illustrates this approach.

### EXAMPLE 12

### An Annuity Due as the Present Value of an Immediate Cash Flow Plus an Ordinary Annuity

1. You are retiring today and must choose to take your retirement benefits either as a lump sum or as an annuity. Your company's benefits officer presents you with two alternatives: an immediate lump sum of $2 million or an annuity with 20 payments of $200,000 a year with the first payment starting today. The interest rate at your bank is 7 percent per year compounded annually. Which option has the greater present value? (Ignore any tax differences between the two options.)

### Solution:

To compare the two options, find the present value of each at time $t = 0$ and choose the one with the larger value. The first option's present value is $2 million, already expressed in today's dollars. The second option is an annuity due. Because the first payment occurs at $t = 0$, you can separate the annuity benefits into two pieces: an immediate $200,000 to be paid today ($t = 0$) and an ordinary annuity of $200,000 per year for 19 years. To value this option, you need to find the present value of the ordinary annuity using Equation 11 and then add $200,000 to it.

$A = \$200,000$
$N = 19$
$r = 7\% = 0.07$

$$PV = A \left[ \frac{1 - \frac{1}{(1+r)^N}}{r} \right]$$

$$= \$200,000 \left[ \frac{1 - \frac{1}{(1.07)^{19}}}{0.07} \right]$$

$= \$200,000 (10.335595)$

$= \$2,067,119.05$

The 19 payments of $200,000 have a present value of $2,067,119.05. Adding the initial payment of $200,000 to $2,067,119.05, we find that the total value of the annuity option is $2,267,119.05. The present value of the annuity is greater than the lump sum alternative of $2 million.

We now look at another example reiterating the equivalence of present and future values.

---

[7] There is an alternative way to calculate the present value of an annuity due. Compared to an ordinary annuity, the payments in an annuity due are each discounted one less period. Therefore, we can modify Equation 11 to handle annuities due by multiplying the right-hand side of the equation by $(1 + r)$:

$$PV(\text{Annuity due}) = A \left\{ [1 - (1 + r)^{-N}] / r \right\} (1 + r)$$

# EXAMPLE 13

## The Projected Present Value of an Ordinary Annuity

1. A German pension fund manager anticipates that benefits of €1 million per year must be paid to retirees. Retirements will not occur until 10 years from now at time $t = 10$. Once benefits begin to be paid, they will extend until $t = 39$ for a total of 30 payments. What is the present value of the pension liability if the appropriate annual discount rate for plan liabilities is 5 percent compounded annually?

### Solution:

This problem involves an annuity with the first payment at $t = 10$. From the perspective of $t = 9$, we have an ordinary annuity with 30 payments. We can compute the present value of this annuity with Equation 11 and then look at it on a time line.

$A = €1,000,000$

$r = 5\% = 0.05$

$N = 30$

$$PV = A \left[ \frac{1 - \frac{1}{(1+r)^N}}{r} \right]$$

$$= €1,000,000 \left[ \frac{1 - \frac{1}{(1.05)^{30}}}{0.05} \right]$$

$= €1,000,000(15.372451)$

$= €15,372,451.03$

### Exhibit 9: The Present Value of an Ordinary Annuity with First Payment at Time $t = 10$ (in Millions)

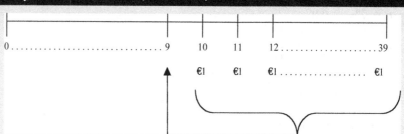

On the time line, we have shown the pension payments of €1 million extending from $t = 10$ to $t = 39$. The bracket and arrow indicate the process of finding the present value of the annuity, discounted back to $t = 9$. The present value of the pension benefits as of $t = 9$ is €15,372,451.03. The problem is to find the present value today (at $t = 0$).

Now we can rely on the equivalence of present value and future value. As Exhibit 9 shows, we can view the amount at $t = 9$ as a future value from the

# Present Value of a Series of Equal and Unequal Cash Flows

> vantage point of $t = 0$. We compute the present value of the amount at $t = 9$ as follows:
>
> $FV_N = €15{,}372{,}451.03$ (the present value at $t = 9$)
>
> $N = 9$
>
> $r = 5\% = 0.05$
>
> $PV = FV_N(1 + r)^{-N}$
>
> $= €15{,}372{,}451.03(1.05)^{-9}$
>
> $= €15{,}372{,}451.03(0.644609)$
>
> $= €9{,}909{,}219.00$
>
> The present value of the pension liability is €9,909,219.00.

Example 13 illustrates three procedures emphasized in this reading:

- finding the present or future value of any cash flow series;
- recognizing the equivalence of present value and appropriately discounted future value; and
- keeping track of the actual calendar time in a problem involving the time value of money.

## The Present Value of a Series of Unequal Cash Flows

When we have unequal cash flows, we must first find the present value of each individual cash flow and then sum the respective present values. For a series with many cash flows, we usually use a spreadsheet. Exhibit 10 lists a series of cash flows with the time periods in the first column, cash flows in the second column, and each cash flow's present value in the third column. The last row of Exhibit 10 shows the sum of the five present values.

**Exhibit 10: A Series of Unequal Cash Flows and Their Present Values at 5 Percent**

| Time Period | Cash Flow ($) | Present Value at Year 0 | | |
|---|---|---|---|---|
| 1 | 1,000 | $1{,}000(1.05)^{-1}$ | = | $952.38 |
| 2 | 2,000 | $2{,}000(1.05)^{-2}$ | = | $1,814.06 |
| 3 | 4,000 | $4{,}000(1.05)^{-3}$ | = | $3,455.35 |
| 4 | 5,000 | $5{,}000(1.05)^{-4}$ | = | $4,113.51 |
| 5 | 6,000 | $6{,}000(1.05)^{-5}$ | = | $4,701.16 |
| | | Sum | = | $15,036.46 |

We could calculate the future value of these cash flows by computing them one at a time using the single-payment future value formula. We already know the present value of this series, however, so we can easily apply time-value equivalence. The future value of the series of cash flows from Exhibit 5, $19,190.76, is equal to the single $15,036.46 amount compounded forward to $t = 5$:

PV = $15,036.46
N = 5
r = 5% = 0.05
$FV_N = PV(1 + r)^N$
= $15,036.46(1.05)^5$
= $15,036.46(1.276282)$
= $19,190.76

## 10. PRESENT VALUE OF A PERPETUITY

☐ calculate and interpret the future value (FV) and present value (PV) of a single sum of money, an ordinary annuity, an annuity due, a perpetuity (PV only), and a series of unequal cash flows

Consider the case of an ordinary annuity that extends indefinitely. Such an ordinary annuity is called a perpetuity (a perpetual annuity). To derive a formula for the present value of a perpetuity, we can modify Equation 10 to account for an infinite series of cash flows:

$$PV = A \sum_{t=1}^{\infty} \left[ \frac{1}{(1+r)^t} \right] \qquad (12)$$

As long as interest rates are positive, the sum of present value factors converges and

$$PV = \frac{A}{r} \qquad (13)$$

To see this, look back at Equation 11, the expression for the present value of an ordinary annuity. As $N$ (the number of periods in the annuity) goes to infinity, the term $1/(1 + r)^N$ approaches 0 and Equation 11 simplifies to Equation 13. This equation will reappear when we value dividends from stocks because stocks have no predefined life span. (A stock paying constant dividends is similar to a perpetuity.) With the first payment a year from now, a perpetuity of $10 per year with a 20 percent required rate of return has a present value of $10/0.2 = $50.

Equation 13 is valid only for a perpetuity with identical payments. In our development above, the first payment occurred at $t = 1$; therefore, we compute the present value as of $t = 0$.

Other assets also come close to satisfying the assumptions of a perpetuity. Certain government bonds and preferred stocks are typical examples of financial assets that make level payments for an indefinite period of time.

### EXAMPLE 14

### The Present Value of a Perpetuity

1. The British government once issued a type of security called a consol bond, which promised to pay an identical cash flow indefinitely. If a consol bond paid GBP100 per year in perpetuity, what would it be worth today if the required rate of return were 5 percent?

### Solution:

To answer this question, we can use Equation 13 with the following data:

# Present Value of a Perpetuity

$A = £100$
$r = 5\% = 0.05$
$PV = A/r$
$= £100/0.05$
$= £2,000$

The bond would be worth GBP2,000.

## Present Values Indexed at Times Other than $t = 0$

In practice with investments, analysts frequently need to find present values indexed at times other than $t = 0$. Subscripting the present value and evaluating a perpetuity beginning with $100 payments in Year 2, we find $PV_1 = \$100/0.05 = \$2,000$ at a 5 percent discount rate. Further, we can calculate today's PV as $PV_0 = \$2,000/1.05 = \$1,904.76$.

Consider a similar situation in which cash flows of $6 per year begin at the end of the 4th year and continue at the end of each year thereafter, with the last cash flow at the end of the 10th year. From the perspective of the end of the third year, we are facing a typical seven-year ordinary annuity. We can find the present value of the annuity from the perspective of the end of the third year and then discount that present value back to the present. At an interest rate of 5 percent, the cash flows of $6 per year starting at the end of the fourth year will be worth $34.72 at the end of the third year ($t = 3$) and $29.99 today ($t = 0$).

The next example illustrates the important concept that an annuity or perpetuity beginning sometime in the future can be expressed in present value terms one period prior to the first payment. That present value can then be discounted back to today's present value.

### EXAMPLE 15

### The Present Value of a Projected Perpetuity

1. Consider a level perpetuity of GBP100 per year with its first payment beginning at $t = 5$. What is its present value today (at $t = 0$), given a 5 percent discount rate?

### Solution:

First, we find the present value of the perpetuity at $t = 4$ and then discount that amount back to $t = 0$. (Recall that a perpetuity or an ordinary annuity has its first payment one period away, explaining the $t = 4$ index for our present value calculation.)

i. Find the present value of the perpetuity at $t = 4$:

$A = £100$
$r = 5\% = 0.05$
$PV = A/r$
$= £100/0.05$
$= £2,000$

ii. Find the present value of the future amount at $t = 4$. From the perspective of $t = 0$, the present value of £2,000 can be considered a future value. Now we need to find the present value of a lump sum:

$FV_N = £2,000$ (the present value at $t = 4$)
$r = 5\% = 0.05$
$N = 4$
$PV = FV_N(1 + r)^{-N}$
$= £2,000 (1.05)^{-4}$
$= £2,000 (0.822702)$
$= £1,645.40$

Today's present value of the perpetuity is £1,645.40.

As discussed earlier, an annuity is a series of payments of a fixed amount for a specified number of periods. Suppose we own a perpetuity. At the same time, we issue a perpetuity obligating us to make payments; these payments are the same size as those of the perpetuity we own. However, the first payment of the perpetuity we issue is at $t = 5$; payments then continue on forever. The payments on this second perpetuity exactly offset the payments received from the perpetuity we own at $t = 5$ and all subsequent dates. We are left with level nonzero net cash flows at $t = 1, 2, 3,$ and 4. This outcome exactly fits the definition of an annuity with four payments. Thus we can construct an annuity as the difference between two perpetuities with equal, level payments but differing starting dates. The next example illustrates this result.

### EXAMPLE 16

### The Present Value of an Ordinary Annuity as the Present Value of a Current Minus Projected Perpetuity

1. Given a 5 percent discount rate, find the present value of a four-year ordinary annuity of £100 per year starting in Year 1 as the difference between the following two level perpetuities:

   Perpetuity 1    £100 per year starting in Year 1 (first payment at $t = 1$)
   Perpetuity 2    £100 per year starting in Year 5 (first payment at $t = 5$)

### Solution:

If we subtract Perpetuity 2 from Perpetuity 1, we are left with an ordinary annuity of £100 per period for four years (payments at $t = 1, 2, 3, 4$). Subtracting the present value of Perpetuity 2 from that of Perpetuity 1, we arrive at the present value of the four-year ordinary annuity:

$PV_0(\text{Perpetuity 1}) = £100/0.05 = £2,000$
$PV_4(\text{Perpetuity 2}) = £100/0.05 = £2,000$
$PV_0(\text{Perpetuity 2}) = £2,000/(1.05)^4 = £1,645.40$
$PV_0(\text{Annuity}) = PV_0(\text{Perpetuity 1}) - PV_0(\text{Perpetuity 2})$
$= £2,000 - £1,645.40$
$= £354.60$

The four-year ordinary annuity's present value is equal to £2,000 − £1,645.40 = £354.60.

# 11 SOLVING FOR INTEREST RATES, GROWTH RATES, AND NUMBER OF PERIODS

☐ calculate and interpret the future value (FV) and present value (PV) of a single sum of money, an ordinary annuity, an annuity due, a perpetuity (PV only), and a series of unequal cash flows

In the previous examples, certain pieces of information have been made available. For instance, all problems have given the rate of interest, $r$, the number of time periods, $N$, the annuity amount, $A$, and either the present value, PV, or future value, FV. In real-world applications, however, although the present and future values may be given, you may have to solve for either the interest rate, the number of periods, or the annuity amount. In the subsections that follow, we show these types of problems.

## Solving for Interest Rates and Growth Rates

Suppose a bank deposit of €100 is known to generate a payoff of €111 in one year. With this information, we can infer the interest rate that separates the present value of €100 from the future value of €111 by using Equation 2, $FV_N = PV(1 + r)^N$, with $N = 1$. With PV, FV, and $N$ known, we can solve for $r$ directly:

$1 + r = FV/PV$

$1 + r = €111/€100 = 1.11$

$r = 0.11$, or 11%

The interest rate that equates €100 at $t = 0$ to €111 at $t = 1$ is 11 percent. Thus we can state that €100 grows to €111 with a growth rate of 11 percent.

As this example shows, an interest rate can also be considered a growth rate. The particular application will usually dictate whether we use the term "interest rate" or "growth rate." Solving Equation 2 for $r$ and replacing the interest rate $r$ with the growth rate $g$ produces the following expression for determining growth rates:

$$g = (FV_N/PV)^{1/N} - 1 \qquad (14)$$

Below are two examples that use the concept of a growth rate.

### EXAMPLE 17

#### Calculating a Growth Rate (1)

Hyundai Steel, the first South Korean steelmaker, was established in 1953. Hyundai Steel's sales increased from ₩14,146.4 billion in 2012 to ₩19,166.0 billion in 2017. However, its net profit declined from ₩796.4 billion in 2012 to ₩727.5 billion in 2017. Calculate the following growth rates for Hyundai Steel for the five-year period from the end of 2012 to the end of 2017:

1. Sales growth rate.

#### Solution to 1:

To solve this problem, we can use Equation 14, $g = (FV_N/PV)^{1/N} - 1$. We denote sales in 2012 as PV and sales in 2017 as $FV_5$. We can then solve for the growth rate as follows:

$$g = \sqrt[5]{₩19{,}166.0/₩14{,}146.4} - 1$$
$$= \sqrt[5]{1.354832} - 1$$
$$= 1.062618 - 1$$
$$= 0.062618 \text{ or about } 6.3\%$$

The calculated growth rate of about 6.3 percent a year shows that Hyundai Steel's sales grew during the 2012–2017 period.

2. Net profit growth rate.

## Solution to 2:

In this case, we can speak of a positive compound rate of decrease or a negative compound growth rate. Using Equation 14, we find

$$g = \sqrt[5]{₩727.5/₩796.4} - 1$$
$$= \sqrt[5]{0.913486} - 1$$
$$= 0.982065 - 1$$
$$= -0.017935 \text{ or about } -1.8\%$$

In contrast to the positive sales growth, the rate of growth in net profit was approximately −1.8 percent during the 2012–2017 period.

### EXAMPLE 18

## Calculating a Growth Rate (2)

1. Toyota Motor Corporation, one of the largest automakers in the world, had consolidated vehicle sales of 8.96 million units in 2018 (fiscal year ending 31 March 2018). This is substantially more than consolidated vehicle sales of 7.35 million units six years earlier in 2012. What was the growth rate in number of vehicles sold by Toyota from 2012 to 2018?

## Solution:

Using Equation 14, we find

$$g = \sqrt[6]{8.96/7.35} - 1$$
$$= \sqrt[6]{1.219048} - 1$$
$$= 1.033563 - 1$$
$$= 0.033563 \text{ or about } 3.4\%$$

The rate of growth in vehicles sold was approximately 3.4 percent during the 2012–2018 period. Note that we can also refer to 3.4 percent as the compound annual growth rate because it is the single number that compounds the number of vehicles sold in 2012 forward to the number of vehicles sold in 2018. Exhibit 11 lists the number of vehicles sold by Toyota from 2012 to 2018.

# Solving for Interest Rates, Growth Rates, and Number of Periods

**Exhibit 11: Number of Vehicles Sold, 2012–2018**

| Year | Number of Vehicles Sold (Millions) | $(1 + g)_t$ | t |
|---|---|---|---|
| 2012 | 7.35 | | 0 |
| 2013 | 8.87 | 8.87/7.35 = 1.206803 | 1 |
| 2014 | 9.12 | 9.12/8.87 = 1.028185 | 2 |
| 2015 | 8.97 | 8.97/9.12 = 0.983553 | 3 |
| 2016 | 8.68 | 8.68/8.97 = 0.967670 | 4 |
| 2017 | 8.97 | 8.97/8.68 = 1.033410 | 5 |
| 2018 | 8.96 | 8.96/8.97 = 0.998885 | 6 |

*Source:* www.toyota.com.

Exhibit 11 also shows 1 plus the one-year growth rate in number of vehicles sold. We can compute the 1 plus six-year cumulative growth in number of vehicles sold from 2012 to 2018 as the product of quantities (1 + one-year growth rate). We arrive at the same result as when we divide the ending number of vehicles sold, 8.96 million, by the beginning number of vehicles sold, 7.35 million:

$$\frac{8.96}{7.35} = \left(\frac{8.87}{7.35}\right)\left(\frac{9.12}{8.87}\right)\left(\frac{8.97}{9.12}\right)\left(\frac{8.68}{8.97}\right)\left(\frac{8.97}{8.68}\right)\left(\frac{8.96}{8.97}\right)$$
$$= (1+g_1)(1+g_2)(1+g_3)(1+g_4)(1+g_5)(1+g_6)$$
$$1.219048 = (1.206803)(1.028185)(0.983553)(0.967670)(1.033410)(0.998885)$$

The right-hand side of the equation is the product of 1 plus the one-year growth rate in number of vehicles sold for each year. Recall that, using Equation 14, we took the sixth root of 8.96/7.35 = 1.219048. In effect, we were solving for the single value of $g$ which, when compounded over six periods, gives the correct product of 1 plus the one-year growth rates.[8]

In conclusion, we do not need to compute intermediate growth rates as in Exhibit 11 to solve for a compound growth rate $g$. Sometimes, however, the intermediate growth rates are interesting or informative. For example, most of the 21.9 percent increase in vehicles sold by Toyota from 2012 to 2018 occurred in 2013 as sales increased by 20.7 percent from 2012 to 2013. Elsewhere in Toyota's disclosures, the company noted that all regions except Europe showed a substantial increase in sales in 2013. We can also analyze the variability in growth rates when we conduct an analysis as in Exhibit 11. Sales continued to increase in 2014 but then declined in 2015 and 2016. Sales then increased but the sales in 2017 and 2018 are about the same as in 2015.

The compound growth rate is an excellent summary measure of growth over multiple time periods. In our Toyota example, the compound growth rate of 3.4 percent is the single growth rate that, when added to 1, compounded over six years, and multiplied by the 2012 number of vehicles sold, yields the 2018 number of vehicles sold.

---

[8] The compound growth rate that we calculate here is an example of a geometric mean, specifically the geometric mean of the growth rates. We define the geometric mean in the reading on statistical concepts.

## Solving for the Number of Periods

In this section, we demonstrate how to solve for the number of periods given present value, future value, and interest or growth rates.

### EXAMPLE 19

### The Number of Annual Compounding Periods Needed for an Investment to Reach a Specific Value

1. You are interested in determining how long it will take an investment of €10,000,000 to double in value. The current interest rate is 7 percent compounded annually. How many years will it take €10,000,000 to double to €20,000,000?

**Solution:**

Use Equation 2, $FV_N = PV(1 + r)^N$, to solve for the number of periods, $N$, as follows:

$$(1 + r)^N = FV_N/PV = 2$$
$$N \ln(1 + r) = \ln(2)$$
$$N = \ln(2)/\ln(1 + r)$$
$$= \ln(2)/\ln(1.07) = 10.24$$

With an interest rate of 7 percent, it will take approximately 10 years for the initial €10,000,000 investment to grow to €20,000,000. Solving for $N$ in the expression $(1.07)^N = 2.0$ requires taking the natural logarithm of both sides and using the rule that $\ln(x^N) = N\ln(x)$. Generally, we find that $N = [\ln(FV/PV)]/\ln(1 + r)$. Here, $N = \ln(€20,000,000/€10,000,000)/\ln(1.07) = \ln(2)/\ln(1.07) = 10.24$.[9]

## 12 SOLVING FOR SIZE OF ANNUITY PAYMENTS

- [ ] calculate and interpret the future value (FV) and present value (PV) of a single sum of money, an ordinary annuity, an annuity due, a perpetuity (PV only), and a series of unequal cash flows
- [ ] demonstrate the use of a time line in modeling and solving time value of money problems

In this section, we discuss how to solve for annuity payments. Mortgages, auto loans, and retirement savings plans are classic examples of applications of annuity formulas.

---

9 To quickly approximate the number of periods, practitioners sometimes use an ad hoc rule called the **Rule of 72**: Divide 72 by the stated interest rate to get the approximate number of years it would take to double an investment at the interest rate. Here, the approximation gives 72/7 = 10.3 years. The Rule of 72 is loosely based on the observation that it takes 12 years to double an amount at a 6 percent interest rate, giving 6 × 12 = 72. At a 3 percent rate, one would guess it would take twice as many years, 3 × 24 = 72.

# Solving for Size of Annuity Payments

## EXAMPLE 20

### Calculating the Size of Payments on a Fixed-Rate Mortgage

1. You are planning to purchase a $120,000 house by making a down payment of $20,000 and borrowing the remainder with a 30-year fixed-rate mortgage with monthly payments. The first payment is due at $t = 1$. Current mortgage interest rates are quoted at 8 percent with monthly compounding. What will your monthly mortgage payments be?

### Solution:

The bank will determine the mortgage payments such that at the stated periodic interest rate, the present value of the payments will be equal to the amount borrowed (in this case, $100,000). With this fact in mind, we can use Equation 11,

$$PV = A \left[ \frac{1 - \frac{1}{(1+r)^N}}{r} \right]$$

to solve for the annuity amount, $A$, as the present value divided by the present value annuity factor:

$PV = \$100,000$
$r_s = 8\% = 0.08$
$m = 12$
$r_s/m = 0.08/12 = 0.006667$
$N = 30$
$mN = 12 \times 30 = 360$

$$\text{Present value annuity factor} = \frac{1 - \frac{1}{[1+(r_s/m)]^{mN}}}{r_s/m} = \frac{1 - \frac{1}{(1.006667)^{360}}}{0.006667}$$

$= 136.283494$
$A = PV/\text{Present value annuity factor}$
$= \$100,000/136.283494$
$= \$733.76$

The amount borrowed, $100,000, is equivalent to 360 monthly payments of $733.76 with a stated interest rate of 8 percent. The mortgage problem is a relatively straightforward application of finding a level annuity payment.

Next, we turn to a retirement-planning problem. This problem illustrates the complexity of the situation in which an individual wants to retire with a specified retirement income. Over the course of a life cycle, the individual may be able to save only a small amount during the early years but then may have the financial resources to save more during later years. Savings plans often involve uneven cash flows, a topic we will examine in the last part of this reading. When dealing with uneven cash flows, we take maximum advantage of the principle that dollar amounts indexed at the same point in time are additive—the **cash flow additivity principle**.

# EXAMPLE 21

## The Projected Annuity Amount Needed to Fund a Future-Annuity Inflow

1. Jill Grant is 22 years old (at $t = 0$) and is planning for her retirement at age 63 (at $t = 41$). She plans to save $2,000 per year for the next 15 years ($t = 1$ to $t = 15$). She wants to have retirement income of $100,000 per year for 20 years, with the first retirement payment starting at $t = 41$. How much must Grant save each year from $t = 16$ to $t = 40$ in order to achieve her retirement goal? Assume she plans to invest in a diversified stock-and-bond mutual fund that will earn 8 percent per year on average.

### Solution:

To help solve this problem, we set up the information on a time line. As Exhibit 12 shows, Grant will save $2,000 (an outflow) each year for Years 1 to 15. Starting in Year 41, Grant will start to draw retirement income of $100,000 per year for 20 years. In the time line, the annual savings is recorded in parentheses ($2) to show that it is an outflow. The problem is to find the savings, recorded as $X$, from Year 16 to Year 40.

**Exhibit 12: Solving for Missing Annuity Payments (in Thousands)**

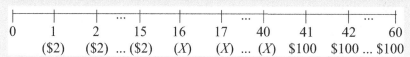

Solving this problem involves satisfying the following relationship: the present value of savings (outflows) equals the present value of retirement income (inflows). We could bring all the dollar amounts to $t = 40$ or to $t = 15$ and solve for $X$.

Let us evaluate all dollar amounts at $t = 15$ (we encourage the reader to repeat the problem by bringing all cash flows to $t = 40$). As of $t = 15$, the first payment of $X$ will be one period away (at $t = 16$). Thus we can value the stream of $X$s using the formula for the present value of an ordinary annuity. This problem involves three series of level cash flows. The basic idea is that the present value of the retirement income must equal the present value of Grant's savings. Our strategy requires the following steps:

1. Find the future value of the savings of $2,000 per year and index it at $t = 15$. This value tells us how much Grant will have saved.

2. Find the present value of the retirement income at $t = 15$. This value tells us how much Grant needs to meet her retirement goals (as of $t = 15$). Two substeps are necessary. First, calculate the present value of the annuity of $100,000 per year at $t = 40$. Use the formula for the present value of an annuity. (Note that the present value is indexed at $t = 40$ because the first payment is at $t = 41$.) Next, discount the present value back to $t = 15$ (a total of 25 periods).

## Solving for Size of Annuity Payments

3. Now compute the difference between the amount Grant has saved (Step 1) and the amount she needs to meet her retirement goals (Step 2). Her savings from $t = 16$ to $t = 40$ must have a present value equal to the difference between the future value of her savings and the present value of her retirement income.

Our goal is to determine the amount Grant should save in each of the 25 years from $t = 16$ to $t = 40$. We start by bringing the $2,000 savings to $t = 15$, as follows:

$A = \$2,000$
$r = 8\% = 0.08$
$N = 15$
$$FV = A\left[\frac{(1+r)^N - 1}{r}\right]$$
$$= \$2,000\left[\frac{(1.08)^{15} - 1}{0.08}\right]$$
$= \$2,000(27.152114)$
$= \$54,304.23$

At $t = 15$, Grant's initial savings will have grown to $54,304.23.

Now we need to know the value of Grant's retirement income at $t = 15$. As stated earlier, computing the retirement present value requires two substeps. First, find the present value at $t = 40$ with the formula in Equation 11; second, discount this present value back to $t = 15$. Now we can find the retirement income present value at $t = 40$:

$A = \$100,000$
$r = 8\% = 0.08$
$N = 20$
$$PV = A\left[\frac{1 - \frac{1}{(1+r)^N}}{r}\right]$$
$$= \$100,000\left[\frac{1 - \frac{1}{(1.08)^{20}}}{0.08}\right]$$
$= \$100,000(9.818147)$
$= \$981,814.74$

The present value amount is as of $t = 40$, so we must now discount it back as a lump sum to $t = 15$:

$FV_N = \$981,814.74$
$N = 25$
$r = 8\% = 0.08$
$PV = FV_N(1+r)^{-N}$
$= \$981,814.74(1.08)^{-25}$
$= \$981,814.74(0.146018)$
$= \$143,362.53$

Now recall that Grant will have saved $54,304.23 by $t = 15$. Therefore, in present value terms, the annuity from $t = 16$ to $t = 40$ must equal the difference between the amount already saved ($54,304.23) and the amount required for retirement ($143,362.53). This amount is equal to $143,362.53 − $54,304.23 = $89,058.30. Therefore, we must now find the annuity payment, $A$, from $t = 16$ to $t = 40$ that has a present value of $89,058.30. We find the annuity payment as follows:

$PV = \$89{,}058.30$
$r = 8\% = 0.08$
$N = 25$

$$\text{Present value annuity factor} = \left[\frac{1 - \frac{1}{(1+r)^N}}{r}\right]$$

$$= \left[\frac{1 - \frac{1}{(1.08)^{25}}}{0.08}\right]$$

$= 10.674776$
$A = PV/\text{Present value annuity factor}$
$= \$89{,}058.30/10.674776$
$= \$8{,}342.87$

Grant will need to increase her savings to $8,342.87 per year from $t = 16$ to $t = 40$ to meet her retirement goal of having a fund equal to $981,814.74 after making her last payment at $t = 40$.

# 13 PRESENT AND FUTURE VALUE EQUIVALENCE AND THE ADDITIVITY PRINCIPLE

☐ calculate and interpret the future value (FV) and present value (PV) of a single sum of money, an ordinary annuity, an annuity due, a perpetuity (PV only), and a series of unequal cash flows

☐ demonstrate the use of a time line in modeling and solving time value of money problems

As we have demonstrated, finding present and future values involves moving amounts of money to different points on a time line. These operations are possible because present value and future value are equivalent measures separated in time. Exhibit 13 illustrates this equivalence; it lists the timing of five cash flows, their present values at $t = 0$, and their future values at $t = 5$.

To interpret Exhibit 13, start with the third column, which shows the present values. Note that each $1,000 cash payment is discounted back the appropriate number of periods to find the present value at $t = 0$. The present value of $4,329.48 is exactly equivalent to the series of cash flows. This information illustrates an important point: A lump sum can actually generate an annuity. If we place a lump sum in an account that earns the stated interest rate for all periods, we can generate an annuity that is equivalent to the lump sum. Amortized loans, such as mortgages and car loans, are examples of this principle.

### Exhibit 13: The Equivalence of Present and Future Values

| Time | Cash Flow ($) | Present Value at $t = 0$ | | | Future Value at $t = 5$ | | |
|---|---|---|---|---|---|---|---|
| 1 | 1,000 | $\$1{,}000(1.05)^{-1}$ | = | $952.38 | $\$1{,}000(1.05)^{4}$ | = | $1,215.51 |
| 2 | 1,000 | $\$1{,}000(1.05)^{-2}$ | = | $907.03 | $\$1{,}000(1.05)^{3}$ | = | $1,157.63 |
| 3 | 1,000 | $\$1{,}000(1.05)^{-3}$ | = | $863.84 | $\$1{,}000(1.05)^{2}$ | = | $1,102.50 |

# Present and Future Value Equivalence and the Additivity Principle

| Time | Cash Flow ($) | Present Value at $t = 0$ | | | Future Value at $t = 5$ | | |
|---|---|---|---|---|---|---|---|
| 4 | 1,000 | $1,000(1.05)^{-4}$ | = | $822.70 | $1,000(1.05)^{1}$ | = | $1,050.00 |
| 5 | 1,000 | $1,000(1.05)^{-5}$ | = | $783.53 | $1,000(1.05)^{0}$ | = | $1,000.00 |
| | | Sum: | | $4,329.48 | Sum: | | $5,525.64 |

To see how a lump sum can fund an annuity, assume that we place $4,329.48 in the bank today at 5 percent interest. We can calculate the size of the annuity payments by using Equation 11. Solving for $A$, we find

$$A = \frac{PV}{\frac{1 - [1/(1+r)^N]}{r}}$$

$$= \frac{\$4,329.48}{\frac{1 - [1/(1.05)^5]}{0.05}}$$

$$= \$1,000$$

Exhibit 14 shows how the initial investment of $4,329.48 can actually generate five $1,000 withdrawals over the next five years.

To interpret Exhibit 14, start with an initial present value of $4,329.48 at $t = 0$. From $t = 0$ to $t = 1$, the initial investment earns 5 percent interest, generating a future value of $4,329.48(1.05) = $4,545.95. We then withdraw $1,000 from our account, leaving $4,545.95 − $1,000 = $3,545.95 (the figure reported in the last column for time period 1). In the next period, we earn one year's worth of interest and then make a $1,000 withdrawal. After the fourth withdrawal, we have $952.38, which earns 5 percent. This amount then grows to $1,000 during the year, just enough for us to make the last withdrawal. Thus the initial present value, when invested at 5 percent for five years, generates the $1,000 five-year ordinary annuity. The present value of the initial investment is exactly equivalent to the annuity.

Now we can look at how future value relates to annuities. In Exhibit 13, we reported that the future value of the annuity was $5,525.64. We arrived at this figure by compounding the first $1,000 payment forward four periods, the second $1,000 forward three periods, and so on. We then added the five future amounts at $t = 5$. The annuity is equivalent to $5,525.64 at $t = 5$ and $4,329.48 at $t = 0$. These two dollar measures are thus equivalent. We can verify the equivalence by finding the present value of $5,525.64, which is $5,525.64 × $(1.05)^{-5}$ = $4,329.48. We found this result above when we showed that a lump sum can generate an annuity.

### Exhibit 14: How an Initial Present Value Funds an Annuity

| Time Period | Amount Available at the Beginning of the Time Period ($) | Ending Amount before Withdrawal | | | Withdrawal ($) | Amount Available after Withdrawal ($) |
|---|---|---|---|---|---|---|
| 1 | 4,329.48 | $4,329.48(1.05) | = | $4,545.95 | 1,000 | 3,545.95 |
| 2 | 3,545.95 | $3,545.95(1.05) | = | $3,723.25 | 1,000 | 2,723.25 |
| 3 | 2,723.25 | $2,723.25(1.05) | = | $2,859.41 | 1,000 | 1,859.41 |
| 4 | 1,859.41 | $1,859.41(1.05) | = | $1,952.38 | 1,000 | 952.38 |
| 5 | 952.38 | $952.38(1.05) | = | $1,000 | 1,000 | 0 |

To summarize what we have learned so far: A lump sum can be seen as equivalent to an annuity, and an annuity can be seen as equivalent to its future value. Thus present values, future values, and a series of cash flows can all be considered equivalent as long as they are indexed at the same point in time.

## The Cash Flow Additivity Principle

The cash flow additivity principle—the idea that amounts of money indexed at the same point in time are additive—is one of the most important concepts in time value of money mathematics. We have already mentioned and used this principle; this section provides a reference example for it.

Consider the two series of cash flows shown on the time line in Exhibit 15. The series are denoted A and B. If we assume that the annual interest rate is 2 percent, we can find the future value of each series of cash flows as follows. Series A's future value is $100(1.02) + $100 = $202. Series B's future value is $200(1.02) + $200 = $404. The future value of (A + B) is $202 + $404 = $606 by the method we have used up to this point. The alternative way to find the future value is to add the cash flows of each series, A and B (call it A + B), and then find the future value of the combined cash flow, as shown in Exhibit 15.

The third time line in Exhibit 15 shows the combined series of cash flows. Series A has a cash flow of $100 at $t = 1$, and Series B has a cash flow of $200 at $t = 1$. The combined series thus has a cash flow of $300 at $t = 1$. We can similarly calculate the cash flow of the combined series at $t = 2$. The future value of the combined series (A + B) is $300(1.02) + $300 = $606—the same result we found when we added the future values of each series.

The additivity and equivalence principles also appear in another common situation. Suppose cash flows are $4 at the end of the first year and $24 (actually separate payments of $4 and $20) at the end of the second year. Rather than finding present values of the first year's $4 and the second year's $24, we can treat this situation as a $4 annuity for two years and a second-year $20 lump sum. If the discount rate were 6 percent, the $4 annuity would have a present value of $7.33 and the $20 lump sum a present value of $17.80, for a total of $25.13.

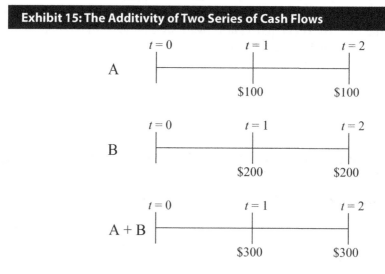

**Exhibit 15: The Additivity of Two Series of Cash Flows**

# SUMMARY

In this reading, we have explored a foundation topic in investment mathematics, the time value of money. We have developed and reviewed the following concepts for use in financial applications:

- The interest rate, $r$, is the required rate of return; $r$ is also called the discount rate or opportunity cost.
- An interest rate can be viewed as the sum of the real risk-free interest rate and a set of premiums that compensate lenders for risk: an inflation premium, a default risk premium, a liquidity premium, and a maturity premium.
- The future value, FV, is the present value, PV, times the future value factor, $(1 + r)^N$.
- The interest rate, $r$, makes current and future currency amounts equivalent based on their time value.
- The stated annual interest rate is a quoted interest rate that does not account for compounding within the year.
- The periodic rate is the quoted interest rate per period; it equals the stated annual interest rate divided by the number of compounding periods per year.
- The effective annual rate is the amount by which a unit of currency will grow in a year with interest on interest included.
- An annuity is a finite set of identical sequential cash flows.
- There are two types of annuities, the annuity due and the ordinary annuity. The annuity due has a first cash flow that occurs immediately; the ordinary annuity has a first cash flow that occurs one period from the present (indexed at $t = 1$).
- On a time line, we can index the present as 0 and then display equally spaced hash marks to represent a number of periods into the future. This representation allows us to index how many periods away each cash flow will be paid.
- Annuities may be handled in a similar approach as single payments if we use annuity factors rather than single-payment factors.
- The present value, PV, is the future value, FV, times the present value factor, $(1 + r)^{-N}$.
- The present value of a perpetuity is $A/r$, where $A$ is the periodic payment to be received forever.
- It is possible to calculate an unknown variable, given the other relevant variables in time value of money problems.
- The cash flow additivity principle can be used to solve problems with uneven cash flows by combining single payments and annuities.

# PRACTICE PROBLEMS

1. The table below gives current information on the interest rates for two two-year and two eight-year maturity investments. The table also gives the maturity, liquidity, and default risk characteristics of a new investment possibility (Investment 3). All investments promise only a single payment (a payment at maturity). Assume that premiums relating to inflation, liquidity, and default risk are constant across all time horizons.

| Investment | Maturity (in Years) | Liquidity | Default Risk | Interest Rate (%) |
|---|---|---|---|---|
| 1 | 2 | High | Low | 2.0 |
| 2 | 2 | Low | Low | 2.5 |
| 3 | 7 | Low | Low | $r_3$ |
| 4 | 8 | High | Low | 4.0 |
| 5 | 8 | Low | High | 6.5 |

Based on the information in the above table, address the following:

A. Explain the difference between the interest rates on Investment 1 and Investment 2.

B. Estimate the default risk premium.

C. Calculate upper and lower limits for the interest rate on Investment 3, $r_3$.

2. The nominal risk-free rate is *best* described as the sum of the real risk-free rate and a premium for:

A. maturity.

B. liquidity.

C. expected inflation.

3. Which of the following risk premiums is most relevant in explaining the difference in yields between 30-year bonds issued by the US Treasury and 30-year bonds issued by a small private issuer?

A. Inflation

B. Maturity

C. Liquidity

4. The value in six years of $75,000 invested today at a stated annual interest rate of 7% compounded quarterly is *closest* to:

A. $112,555.

B. $113,330.

C. $113,733.

5. A bank quotes a stated annual interest rate of 4.00%. If that rate is equal to an effective annual rate of 4.08%, then the bank is compounding interest:

A. daily.

# Practice Problems

   **B.** quarterly.

   **C.** semiannually.

6. Given a €1,000,000 investment for four years with a stated annual rate of 3% compounded continuously, the difference in its interest earnings compared with the same investment compounded daily is *closest* to:

   **A.** €1.

   **B.** €6.

   **C.** €455.

7. A couple plans to set aside $20,000 per year in a conservative portfolio projected to earn 7 percent a year. If they make their first savings contribution one year from now, how much will they have at the end of 20 years?

8. Two years from now, a client will receive the first of three annual payments of $20,000 from a small business project. If she can earn 9 percent annually on her investments and plans to retire in six years, how much will the three business project payments be worth at the time of her retirement?

9. A saver deposits the following amounts in an account paying a stated annual rate of 4%, compounded semiannually:

   | Year | End of Year Deposits ($) |
   |---|---|
   | 1 | 4,000 |
   | 2 | 8,000 |
   | 3 | 7,000 |
   | 4 | 10,000 |

   At the end of Year 4, the value of the account is *closest* to:

   **A.** $30,432

   **B.** $30,447

   **C.** $31,677

10. To cover the first year's total college tuition payments for his two children, a father will make a $75,000 payment five years from now. How much will he need to invest today to meet his first tuition goal if the investment earns 6 percent annually?

11. Given the following time line and a discount rate of 4% a year compounded annually, the present value (PV), as of the end of Year 5 ($PV_5$), of the cash flow received at the end of Year 20 is *closest* to:

    **A.** $22,819.

    **B.** $27,763.

    **C.** $28,873.

12. A client requires £100,000 one year from now. If the stated annual rate is 2.50% compounded weekly, the deposit needed today is *closest* to:

    A. £97,500.

    B. £97,532.

    C. £97,561.

13. A client can choose between receiving 10 annual $100,000 retirement payments, starting one year from today, or receiving a lump sum today. Knowing that he can invest at a rate of 5 percent annually, he has decided to take the lump sum. What lump sum today will be equivalent to the future annual payments?

14. You are considering investing in two different instruments. The first instrument will pay nothing for three years, but then it will pay $20,000 per year for four years. The second instrument will pay $20,000 for three years and $30,000 in the fourth year. All payments are made at year-end. If your required rate of return on these investments is 8 percent annually, what should you be willing to pay for:

    A. The first instrument?

    B. The second instrument (use the formula for a four-year annuity)?

15. Suppose you plan to send your daughter to college in three years. You expect her to earn two-thirds of her tuition payment in scholarship money, so you estimate that your payments will be $10,000 a year for four years. To estimate whether you have set aside enough money, you ignore possible inflation in tuition payments and assume that you can earn 8 percent annually on your investments. How much should you set aside now to cover these payments?

16. An investment pays €300 annually for five years, with the first payment occurring today. The present value (PV) of the investment discounted at a 4% annual rate is *closest* to:

    A. €1,336.

    B. €1,389.

    C. €1,625.

17. At a 5% interest rate per year compounded annually, the present value (PV) of a 10-year ordinary annuity with annual payments of $2,000 is $15,443.47. The PV of a 10-year annuity due with the same interest rate and payments is *closest* to:

    A. $14,708.

    B. $16,216.

    C. $17,443.

18. Grandparents are funding a newborn's future university tuition costs, estimated at $50,000/year for four years, with the first payment due as a lump sum in 18 years. Assuming a 6% effective annual rate, the required deposit today is *closest* to:

    A. $60,699.

    B. $64,341.

**Practice Problems**

C. $68,201.

19. The present value (PV) of an investment with the following year-end cash flows (CF) and a 12% required annual rate of return is *closest* to:

| Year | Cash Flow (€) |
|---|---|
| 1 | 100,000 |
| 2 | 150,000 |
| 5 | −10,000 |

A. €201,747.

B. €203,191.

C. €227,573.

20. A perpetual preferred stock makes its first quarterly dividend payment of $2.00 in five quarters. If the required annual rate of return is 6% compounded quarterly, the stock's present value is *closest* to:

A. $31.

B. $126.

C. $133.

21. A sweepstakes winner may select either a perpetuity of £2,000 a month beginning with the first payment in one month or an immediate lump sum payment of £350,000. If the annual discount rate is 6% compounded monthly, the present value of the perpetuity is:

A. less than the lump sum.

B. equal to the lump sum.

C. greater than the lump sum.

22. For a lump sum investment of ¥250,000 invested at a stated annual rate of 3% compounded daily, the number of months needed to grow the sum to ¥1,000,000 is *closest* to:

A. 555.

B. 563.

C. 576.

23. An investment of €500,000 today that grows to €800,000 after six years has a stated annual interest rate *closest* to:

A. 7.5% compounded continuously.

B. 7.7% compounded daily.

C. 8.0% compounded semiannually.

24. A client plans to send a child to college for four years starting 18 years from now. Having set aside money for tuition, she decides to plan for room and board also.

She estimates these costs at $20,000 per year, payable at the beginning of each year, by the time her child goes to college. If she starts next year and makes 17 payments into a savings account paying 5 percent annually, what annual payments must she make?

25. A couple plans to pay their child's college tuition for 4 years starting 18 years from now. The current annual cost of college is C$7,000, and they expect this cost to rise at an annual rate of 5 percent. In their planning, they assume that they can earn 6 percent annually. How much must they put aside each year, starting next year, if they plan to make 17 equal payments?

26. A sports car, purchased for £200,000, is financed for five years at an annual rate of 6% compounded monthly. If the first payment is due in one month, the monthly payment is *closest* to:

    A. £3,847.

    B. £3,867.

    C. £3,957.

27. Given a stated annual interest rate of 6% compounded quarterly, the level amount that, deposited quarterly, will grow to £25,000 at the end of 10 years is *closest* to:

    A. £461.

    B. £474.

    C. £836.

28. A client invests €20,000 in a four-year certificate of deposit (CD) that annually pays interest of 3.5%. The annual CD interest payments are automatically reinvested in a separate savings account at a stated annual interest rate of 2% compounded monthly. At maturity, the value of the combined asset is *closest* to:

    A. €21,670.

    B. €22,890.

    C. €22,950.

## SOLUTIONS

1.
   **A.** Investment 2 is identical to Investment 1 except that Investment 2 has low liquidity. The difference between the interest rate on Investment 2 and Investment 1 is 0.5 percentage point. This amount represents the liquidity premium, which represents compensation for the risk of loss relative to an investment's fair value if the investment needs to be converted to cash quickly.

   **B.** To estimate the default risk premium, find the two investments that have the same maturity but different levels of default risk. Both Investments 4 and 5 have a maturity of eight years. Investment 5, however, has low liquidity and thus bears a liquidity premium. The difference between the interest rates of Investments 5 and 4 is 2.5 percentage points. The liquidity premium is 0.5 percentage point (from Part A). This leaves 2.5 − 0.5 = 2.0 percentage points that must represent a default risk premium reflecting Investment 5's high default risk.

   **C.** Investment 3 has liquidity risk and default risk comparable to Investment 2, but with its longer time to maturity, Investment 3 should have a higher maturity premium. The interest rate on Investment 3, $r_3$, should thus be above 2.5 percent (the interest rate on Investment 2). If the liquidity of Investment 3 were high, Investment 3 would match Investment 4 except for Investment 3's shorter maturity. We would then conclude that Investment 3's interest rate should be less than the interest rate on Investment 4, which is 4 percent. In contrast to Investment 4, however, Investment 3 has low liquidity. It is possible that the interest rate on Investment 3 exceeds that of Investment 4 despite 3's shorter maturity, depending on the relative size of the liquidity and maturity premiums. However, we expect $r_3$ to be less than 4.5 percent, the expected interest rate on Investment 4 if it had low liquidity. Thus 2.5 percent < $r_3$ < 4.5 percent.

2. C is correct. The sum of the real risk-free interest rate and the inflation premium is the nominal risk-free rate.

3. C is correct. US Treasury bonds are highly liquid, whereas the bonds of small issuers trade infrequently and the interest rate includes a liquidity premium. This liquidity premium reflects the relatively high costs (including the impact on price) of selling a position.

4. C is correct, as shown in the following (where FV is future value and PV is present value):

   $$FV = PV\left(1 + \frac{r_s}{m}\right)^{mN}$$

   $$FV_6 = \$75{,}000\left(1 + \frac{0.07}{4}\right)^{(4\times 6)}$$

   $FV_6 = \$113{,}733.21$.

5. A is correct. The effective annual rate (EAR) when compounded daily is 4.08%.

   EAR = (1 + Periodic interest rate)$^m$ − 1

$$EAR = (1 + 0.04/365)^{365} - 1$$

$$EAR = (1.0408) - 1 = 0.04081 \approx 4.08\%.$$

6. B is correct. The difference between continuous compounding and daily compounding is

   €127,496.85 − €127,491.29

   = €5.56, or ≈ €6, as shown in the following calculations.

   With continuous compounding, the investment earns (where PV is present value)

   $$PV\, e^{r_s N} - PV = €1{,}000{,}000 e^{0.03(4)} - €1{,}000{,}000$$

   $$= €1{,}127{,}496.85 - €1{,}000{,}000$$

   $$= €127{,}496.85$$

   With daily compounding, the investment earns:

   €1,000,000(1 + 0.03/365)$^{365(4)}$ − €1,000,000 = €1,127,491.29 − €1,000,000

   = €127,491.29.

7. 
   i. Draw a time line.

   ii. Identify the problem as the future value of an annuity.
   iii. Use the formula for the future value of an annuity.

   $$FV_N = A \left[ \frac{(1+r)^N - 1}{r} \right]$$
   $$= \$20{,}000 \left[ \frac{(1 + 0.07)^{20} - 1}{0.07} \right]$$
   $$= \$819{,}909.85$$

   iv. Alternatively, use a financial calculator.

   | Notation Used on Most Calculators | Numerical Value for This Problem |
   | --- | --- |
   | N | 20 |
   | %i | 7 |
   | PV | n/a (= 0) |
   | FV **compute** | X |
   | PMT | $20,000 |

# Solutions

Enter 20 for $N$, the number of periods. Enter 7 for the interest rate and 20,000 for the payment size. The present value is not needed, so enter 0. Calculate the future value. Verify that you get $819,909.85 to make sure you have mastered your calculator's keystrokes.

In summary, if the couple sets aside $20,000 each year (starting next year), they will have $819,909.85 in 20 years if they earn 7 percent annually.

8.

i. Draw a time line.

ii. Recognize the problem as the future value of a delayed annuity. Delaying the payments requires two calculations.

iii. Use the formula for the future value of an annuity (Equation 7), $FV_N = A \left[ \frac{(1+r)^N - 1}{r} \right]$ to bring the three $20,000 payments to an equivalent lump sum of $65,562.00 four years from today.

| Notation Used on Most Calculators | Numerical Value for This Problem |
| --- | --- |
| $N$ | 3 |
| $\%i$ | 9 |
| PV | n/a (= 0) |
| FV **compute** | $X$ |
| PMT | $20,000 |

iv. Use the formula for the future value of a lump sum (Equation 2), $FV_N = PV(1 + r)^N$, to bring the single lump sum of $65,562.00 to an equivalent lump sum of $77,894.21 six years from today.

| Notation Used on Most Calculators | Numerical Value for This Problem |
| --- | --- |
| $N$ | 2 |
| $\%i$ | 9 |
| PV | $65,562.00 |
| FV **compute** | $X$ |
| PMT | n/a (= 0) |

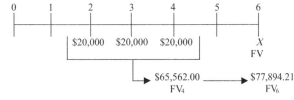

In summary, your client will have $77,894.21 in six years if she receives three yearly payments of $20,000 starting in Year 2 and can earn 9 percent annually on her investments.

9. B is correct. To solve for the future value of unequal cash flows, compute the future value of each payment as of Year 4 at the semiannual rate of 2%, and then sum the individual future values, as follows:

| Year | End of Year Deposits ($) | Factor | Future Value ($) |
|---|---|---|---|
| 1 | 4,000 | $(1.02)^6$ | 4,504.65 |
| 2 | 8,000 | $(1.02)^4$ | 8,659.46 |
| 3 | 7,000 | $(1.02)^2$ | 7,282.80 |
| 4 | 10,000 | $(1.02)^0$ | 10,000.00 |
|   |   | Sum = | 30,446.91 |

10.
   
   i. Draw a time line.

   ii. Identify the problem as the present value of a lump sum.
   
   iii. Use the formula for the present value of a lump sum.

$$PV = FV_N(1 + r)^{-N}$$
$$= \$75,000(1 + 0.06)^{-5}$$
$$= \$56,044.36$$

In summary, the father will need to invest $56,044.36 today in order to have $75,000 in five years if his investments earn 6 percent annually.

11. B is correct. The PV in Year 5 of a $50,000 lump sum paid in Year 20 is $27,763.23 (where FV is future value):

$$PV = FV_N(1 + r)^{-N}$$

$$PV = \$50,000(1 + 0.04)^{-15}$$

$$PV = \$27,763.23$$

12. B is correct because £97,531 represents the present value (PV) of £100,000 received one year from today when today's deposit earns a stated annual rate of 2.50% and interest compounds weekly, as shown in the following equation (where FV is future value):

$$PV = FV_N\left(1 + \frac{r_s}{m}\right)^{-mN}$$

$$PV = £100,000\left(1 + \frac{0.025}{52}\right)^{-52}$$

$$PV = £97,531.58.$$

# Solutions

13.

  i. Draw a time line for the 10 annual payments.

  ii. Identify the problem as the present value of an annuity.

  iii. Use the formula for the present value of an annuity.

  $$PV = A \left[ \frac{1 - \frac{1}{(1+r)^N}}{r} \right]$$

  $$= \$100,000 \left[ \frac{1 - \frac{1}{(1+0.05)^{10}}}{0.05} \right]$$

  $$= \$772,173.49$$

  iv. Alternatively, use a financial calculator.

  | Notation Used on Most Calculators | Numerical Value for This Problem |
  | --- | --- |
  | N | 10 |
  | %i | 5 |
  | PV **compute** | X |
  | FV | n/a (= 0) |
  | PMT | $100,000 |

  In summary, the present value of 10 payments of $100,000 is $772,173.49 if the first payment is received in one year and the rate is 5 percent compounded annually. Your client should accept no less than this amount for his lump sum payment.

14.

  **A.** To evaluate the first instrument, take the following steps:

  i. Draw a time line.

  ii.

$$PV_3 = A\left[\frac{1-\frac{1}{(1+r)^N}}{r}\right]$$

$$= \$20,000\left[\frac{1-\frac{1}{(1+0.08)^4}}{0.08}\right]$$

$$= \$66,242.54$$

iii.

$$PV_0 = \frac{PV_3}{(1+r)^N} = \frac{\$66,242.54}{1.08^3} = \$52,585.46$$

iv. You should be willing to pay $52,585.46 for this instrument.

B. To evaluate the second instrument, take the following steps:

i. Draw a time line.

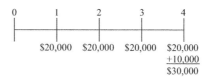

The time line shows that this instrument can be analyzed as an ordinary annuity of $20,000 with four payments (valued in Step ii below) and a $10,000 payment to be received at $t = 4$ (valued in Step iii below).

ii.

$$PV = A\left[\frac{1-\frac{1}{(1+r)^N}}{r}\right]$$

$$= \$20,000\left[\frac{1-\frac{1}{(1+0.08)^4}}{0.08}\right]$$

$$= \$66,242.54$$

iii.

$$PV = \frac{FV_4}{(1+r)^N} = \frac{\$10,000}{(1+0.08)^4} = \$7,350.30$$

iv. Total = $66,242.54 + $7,350.30 = $73,592.84

You should be willing to pay $73,592.84 for this instrument.

15.

i. Draw a time line.

ii. Recognize the problem as a delayed annuity. Delaying the payments requires two calculations.

iii. Use the formula for the present value of an annuity (Equation 11),

# Solutions

$$PV = A\left[\dfrac{1-\dfrac{1}{(1+r)^N}}{r}\right]$$

iv. to bring the four payments of $10,000 back to a single equivalent lump sum of $33,121.27 at $t = 2$. Note that we use $t = 2$ because the first annuity payment is then one period away, giving an ordinary annuity.

| Notation Used on Most Calculators | Numerical Value for This Problem |
|---|---|
| N | 4 |
| %i | 8 |
| PV **compute** | X |
| PMT | $10,000 |

v. Then use the formula for the present value of a lump sum (Equation 8), $PV = FV_N(1 + r)^{-N}$, to bring back the single payment of $33,121.27 (at $t = 2$) to an equivalent single payment of $28,396.15 (at $t = 0$).

| Notation Used on Most Calculators | Numerical Value for This Problem |
|---|---|
| N | 2 |
| %i | 8 |
| PV **compute** | X |
| FV | $33,121.27 |
| PMT | n/a (= 0) |

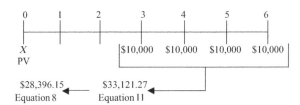

In summary, you should set aside $28,396.15 today to cover four payments of $10,000 starting in three years if your investments earn a rate of 8 percent annually.

16. B is correct, as shown in the following calculation for an annuity (A) due:

$$PV = A\left[\dfrac{1-\dfrac{1}{(1+r)^N}}{r}\right](1+r),$$

where A = €300, $r = 0.04$, and $N = 5$.

$$PV = €300\left[\dfrac{1-\dfrac{1}{(1+.04)^5}}{.04}\right](1.04)$$

PV = €1,388.97, or ≈ €1,389.

17. B is correct.

The present value of a 10-year annuity (A) due with payments of $2,000 at a 5% discount rate is calculated as follows:

$$PV = A \left[ \frac{1 - \frac{1}{(1+r)^N}}{r} \right] + \$2,000$$

$$PV = \$2,000 \left[ \frac{1 - \frac{1}{(1+0.05)^9}}{0.05} \right] + \$2,000$$

PV = $16,215.64.

Alternatively, the PV of a 10-year annuity due is simply the PV of the ordinary annuity multiplied by 1.05:

PV = $15,443.47 × 1.05

PV = $16,215.64.

18. B is correct. First, find the present value (PV) of an ordinary annuity in Year 17 that represents the tuition costs:

$$\$50,000 \left[ \frac{1 - \frac{1}{(1+0.06)^4}}{0.06} \right]$$

= $50,000 × 3.4651

= $173,255.28.

Then, find the PV of the annuity in today's dollars (where FV is future value):

$$PV_0 = \frac{FV}{(1+0.06)^{17}}$$

$$PV_0 = \frac{\$173,255.28}{(1+0.06)^{17}}$$

$PV_0$ = $64,340.85 ≈ $64,341.

19. B is correct, as shown in the following table.

| Year | Cash Flow (€) | Formula CF × (1 + r)$^t$ | PV at Year 0 |
| --- | --- | --- | --- |
| 1 | 100,000 | 100,000(1.12)$^{-1}$ = | 89,285.71 |
| 2 | 150,000 | 150,000(1.12)$^{-2}$ = | 119,579.08 |
| 5 | −10,000 | −10,000(1.12)$^{-5}$ = | −5,674.27 |
| | | | 203,190.52 |

20. B is correct. The value of the perpetuity one year from now is calculated as:

PV = A/r, where PV is present value, A is annuity, and r is expressed as a quarterly required rate of return because the payments are quarterly.

PV = $2.00/(0.06/4)

PV = $133.33.

The value today is (where FV is future value)

$PV = FV_N(1 + r)^{-N}$

$PV = \$133.33(1 + 0.015)^{-4}$

$PV = \$125.62 \approx \$126$.

21. C is correct. As shown below, the present value (PV) of a £2,000 per month perpetuity is worth approximately £400,000 at a 6% annual rate compounded monthly. Thus, the present value of the annuity (A) is worth more than the lump sum offers.

    $A = £2,000$

    $r = (6\%/12) = 0.005$

    $PV = (A/r)$

    $PV = (£2,000/0.005)$

    $PV = £400,000$

22. A is correct. The effective annual rate (EAR) is calculated as follows:

    $EAR = (1 + \text{Periodic interest rate})^m - 1$

    $EAR = (1 + 0.03/365)^{365} - 1$

    $EAR = (1.03045) - 1 = 0.030453 \approx 3.0453\%$.

    Solving for $N$ on a financial calculator results in (where FV is future value and PV is present value):

    $(1 + 0.030453)^N = FV_N/PV = ¥1{,}000{,}000/¥250{,}000$

    = 46.21 years, which multiplied by 12 to convert to months results in 554.5, or ≈ 555 months.

23. C is correct, as shown in the following (where FV is future value and PV is present value):
    If:

    $FV_N = PV\left(1 + \dfrac{r_s}{m}\right)^{mN}$,

    Then:

    $\left(\dfrac{FV_N}{PV}\right)^{\frac{1}{mN}} - 1 = \dfrac{r_s}{m}$

    $\left(\dfrac{800{,}000}{500{,}000}\right)^{\frac{1}{2\times6}} - 1 = \dfrac{r_s}{2}$

    $r_s = 0.07988$ (rounded to 8.0%).

24.
    i.  Draw a time line.

ii. Recognize that you need to equate the values of two annuities.

iii. Equate the value of the four $20,000 payments to a single payment in Period 17 using the formula for the present value of an annuity (Equation 11), with $r = 0.05$. The present value of the college costs as of $t = 17$ is $70,919.

$$PV = \$20,000 \left[ \frac{1 - \frac{1}{(1.05)^4}}{0.05} \right] = \$70,919$$

| Notation Used on Most Calculators | Numerical Value for This Problem |
|---|---|
| N | 4 |
| %i | 5 |
| PV compute | X |
| FV | n/a (= 0) |
| PMT | $20,000 |

iv. Equate the value of the 17 investments of $X$ to the amount calculated in Step iii, college costs as of $t = 17$, using the formula for the future value of an annuity (Equation 7). Then solve for $X$.

$$\$70,919 = \left[ \frac{(1.05)^{17} - 1}{0.05} \right] = 25.840366X$$

$X = \$2,744.50$

| Notation Used on Most Calculators | Numerical Value for This Problem |
|---|---|
| N | 17 |
| %i | 5 |
| PV | n/a (= 0) |
| FV | $70,919 |
| PMT compute | X |

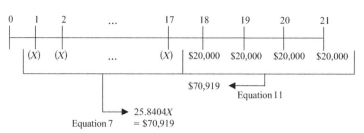

In summary, your client will have to save $2,744.50 each year if she starts next year and makes 17 payments into a savings account paying 5 percent annually.

25.

i. Draw a time line.

# Solutions

ii. Recognize that the payments in Years 18, 19, 20, and 21 are the future values of a lump sum of C$7,000 in Year 0.

iii. With $r = 5\%$, use the formula for the future value of a lump sum (Equation 2), $FV_N = PV (1 + r)^N$, four times to find the payments. These future values are shown on the time line below.

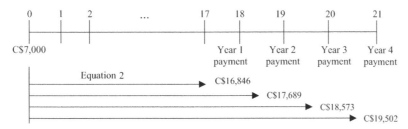

iv. Using the formula for the present value of a lump sum ($r = 6\%$), equate the four college payments to single payments as of $t = 17$ and add them together. C$16,846$(1.06)^{-1}$ + C$17,689$(1.06)^{-2}$ + C$18,573$(1.06)^{-3}$ + C$19,502$(1.06)^{-4}$ = C$62,677

v. Equate the sum of C$62,677 at $t = 17$ to the 17 payments of $X$, using the formula for the future value of an annuity (Equation 7). Then solve for $X$.

$$C\$62,677 = X\left[\frac{(1.06)^{17} - 1}{0.06}\right] = 28.21288X$$

$X = C\$2,221.58$

| Notation Used on Most Calculators | Numerical Value for This Problem |
|---|---|
| N | 17 |
| %i | 6 |
| PV | n/a (= 0) |
| FV | C$62,677 |
| PMT **compute** | X |

```
0    1    2         17   18   19   20   21
|----|----|---...---|----|----|----|----|
    (X)  (X)  ...  (X)
     |_____|
            Equation 7    → 28.21288X
                          = C$62,677
```

In summary, the couple will need to put aside C$2,221.58 each year if they start next year and make 17 equal payments.

26. B is correct, calculated as follows (where A is annuity and PV is present value):

$$A = (\text{PV of annuity}) / \left[ \frac{1 - \frac{1}{(1 + r_s/m)^{mN}}}{r_s/m} \right]$$

$$= (£200,000) / \left[ \frac{1 - \frac{1}{(1 + r_s/m)^{mN}}}{r_s/m} \right]$$

$$(£200,000) / \left[ \frac{1 - \frac{1}{(1 + 0.06/12)^{12(5)}}}{0.06/12} \right]$$

$$= (£200,000) / 51.72556$$
$$= £3,866.56$$

27. A is correct. To solve for an annuity (A) payment, when the future value (FV), interest rate, and number of periods is known, use the following equation:

$$FV = A \left[ \frac{\left(1 + \frac{r_s}{m}\right)^{mN} - 1}{\frac{r}{m}} \right]$$

$$£25,000 = A \left[ \frac{\left(1 + \frac{0.06}{4}\right)^{4 \times 10} - 1}{\frac{0.06}{4}} \right]$$

$$A = £460.68$$

28. B is correct, as the following cash flows show:

annual interest payments (which earn 2.0%/year)
+
€20,000 (return of principal)

The four annual interest payments are based on the CD's 3.5% annual rate.

The first payment grows at 2.0% compounded monthly for three years (where FV is future value):

$$FV_N = €700 \left(1 + \frac{0.02}{12}\right)^{3 \times 12}$$

$$FV_N = 743.25$$

The second payment grows at 2.0% compounded monthly for two years:

$$FV_N = €700 \left(1 + \frac{0.02}{12}\right)^{2 \times 12}$$

$$FV_N = 728.54$$

The third payment grows at 2.0% compounded monthly for one year:

$$FV_N = €700 \left(1 + \frac{0.02}{12}\right)^{1 \times 12}$$

$$FV_N = 714.13$$

The fourth payment is paid at the end of Year 4. Its future value is €700.
The sum of all future value payments is as follows:

# Solutions

| | |
|---|---|
| €20,000.00 | CD |
| €743.25 | First payment's *FV* |
| €728.54 | Second payment's *FV* |
| €714.13 | Third payment's *FV* |
| €700.00 | Fourth payment's *FV* |
| €22,885.92 | Total *FV* |

# LEARNING MODULE 2

## Organizing, Visualizing, and Describing Data

by Pamela Peterson Drake, PhD, CFA, and Jian Wu, PhD.

*Pamela Peterson Drake, PhD, CFA, is at James Madison University (USA). Jian Wu, PhD, is at State Street (USA).*

| LEARNING OUTCOMES | |
|---|---|
| Mastery | The candidate should be able to: |
| ☐ | identify and compare data types |
| ☐ | describe how data are organized for quantitative analysis |
| ☐ | interpret frequency and related distributions |
| ☐ | interpret a contingency table |
| ☐ | describe ways that data may be visualized and evaluate uses of specific visualizations |
| ☐ | describe how to select among visualization types |
| ☐ | calculate and interpret measures of central tendency |
| ☐ | evaluate alternative definitions of mean to address an investment problem |
| ☐ | calculate quantiles and interpret related visualizations |
| ☐ | calculate and interpret measures of dispersion |
| ☐ | calculate and interpret target downside deviation |

## INTRODUCTION

Data have always been a key input for securities analysis and investment management, but the acceleration in the availability and the quantity of data has also been driving the rapid evolution of the investment industry. With the rise of big data and machine learning techniques, investment practitioners are embracing an era featuring large volume, high velocity, and a wide variety of data—allowing them to explore and exploit this abundance of information for their investment strategies.

While this data-rich environment offers potentially tremendous opportunities for investors, turning data into useful information is not so straightforward. Organizing, cleaning, and analyzing data are crucial to the development of successful investment strategies; otherwise, we end up with "garbage in and garbage out" and failed investments. It is often said that 80% of an analyst's time is spent on finding, organizing, cleaning, and analyzing data, while just 20% of her/his time is taken up by model development. So, the importance of having a properly organized, cleansed, and well-analyzed dataset cannot be over-emphasized. With this essential requirement met, an appropriately executed data analysis can detect important relationships within data, uncover underlying structures, identify outliers, and extract potentially valuable insights. Utilizing both visual tools and quantitative methods, like the ones covered in this reading, is the first step in summarizing and understanding data that will be crucial inputs to an investment strategy.

This reading provides a foundation for understanding important concepts that are an indispensable part of the analytical tool kit needed by investment practitioners, from junior analysts to senior portfolio managers. These basic concepts pave the way for more sophisticated tools that will be developed as the quantitative methods topic unfolds and that are integral to gaining competencies in the investment management techniques and asset classes that are presented later in the CFA Program curriculum.

# 2

## DATA TYPES

- ☐ identify and compare data types
- ☐ describe how data are organized for quantitative analysis

**Data** can be defined as a collection of numberpanel data, characters, words, and text—as well as images, audio, and video—in a raw or organized format to represent facts or information. To choose the appropriate statistical methods for summarizing and analyzing data and to select suitable charts for visualizing data, we need to distinguish among different data types. We will discuss data types under three different perspectives of classifications: numerical versus categorical data; cross-sectional vs. time-series versus panel data; and structured versus unstructured data.

### Numerical versus Categorical Data

From a statistical perspective, data can be classified into two basic groups: numerical data and categorical data.

#### Numerical Data

**Numerical data** are values that represent measured or counted quantities as a number and are also called **quantitative data**. Numerical (quantitative) data can be split into two types: continuous data and discrete data.

**Continuous data** are data that can be measured and can take on any numerical value in a specified range of values. For example, the future value of a lump-sum investment measures the amount of money to be received after a certain period of time bearing an interest rate. The future value could take on a range of values depending on the time period and interest rate. Another common example of continuous data is the price returns of a stock that measure price change over a given period in percentage terms.

**Discrete data** are numerical values that result from a counting process. So, practically speaking, the data are limited to a finite number of values. For example, the frequency of discrete compounding, $m$, counts the number of times that interest is accrued and paid out in a given year. The frequency could be monthly ($m = 12$), quarterly ($m = 4$), semi-yearly ($m = 2$), or yearly ($m = 1$).

*Categorical Data*

**Categorical data** (also called **qualitative data**) are values that describe a quality or characteristic of a group of observations and therefore can be used as labels to divide a dataset into groups to summarize and visualize. Usually they can take only a limited number of values that are mutually exclusive. Examples of categorical data for classifying companies include bankrupt vs. not bankrupt and dividends increased vs. no dividend action.

**Nominal data** are categorical values that are not amenable to being organized in a logical order. An example of nominal data is the classification of publicly listed stocks into 11 sectors, as shown in Exhibit 1, that are defined by the Global Industry Classification Standard (GICS). GICS, developed by Morgan Stanley Capital International (MSCI) and Standard & Poor's (S&P), is a four-tiered, hierarchical industry classification system consisting of 11 sectors, 24 industry groups, 69 industries, and 158 sub-industries. Each sector is defined by a unique text label, as shown in the column named "Sector."

**Exhibit 1: Equity Sector Classification by GICS**

| Sector (Text Label) | Code (Numerical Label) |
|---|---|
| Energy | 10 |
| Materials | 15 |
| Industrials | 20 |
| Consumer Discretionary | 25 |
| Consumer Staples | 30 |
| Health Care | 35 |
| Financials | 40 |
| Information Technology | 45 |
| Communication Services | 50 |
| Utilities | 55 |
| Real Estate | 60 |

*Source:* S&P Global Market Intelligence.

Text labels are a common format to represent nominal data, but nominal data can also be coded with numerical labels. As shown below, the column named "Code" contains a corresponding GICS code of each sector as a numerical value. However, the nominal data in numerical format do not indicate ranking, and any arithmetic operations on nominal data are not meaningful. In this example, the energy sector with the code 10 does not represent a lower or higher rank than the real estate sector with the code 60. Often, financial models, such as regression models, require input data to be numerical; so, nominal data in the input dataset must be coded numerically before applying an algorithm (that is, a process for problem solving) for performing the analysis. This would be mainly to identify the category (here, sector) in the model.

**Ordinal data** are categorical values that can be logically ordered or ranked. For example, the Morningstar and Standard & Poor's star ratings for investment funds are ordinal data in which one star represents a group of funds judged to have had relatively the worst performance, with two, three, four, and five stars representing groups with increasingly better performance or quality as evaluated by those firms.

Ordinal data may also involve numbers to identify categories. For example, in ranking growth-oriented investment funds based on their five-year cumulative returns, we might assign the number 1 to the top performing 10% of funds, the number 2 to next best performing 10% of funds, and so on; the number 10 represents the bottom performing 10% of funds. Despite the fact that categories represented by ordinal data can be ranked higher or lower compared to each other, they do not necessarily establish a numerical difference between each category. Importantly, such investment fund ranking tells us nothing about the difference in performance between funds ranked 1 and 2 compared with the difference in performance between funds ranked 3 and 4 or 9 and 10.

Having discussed different data types from a statistical perspective, it is important to note that at first glance, identifying data types may seem straightforward. In some situations, where categorical data are coded in numerical format, they should be distinguished from numerical data. A sound rule of thumb: Meaningful arithmetic operations can be performed on numerical data but not on categorical data.

> **EXAMPLE 1**
>
> ### Identifying Data Types (I)
>
> Identify the data type for each of the following kinds of investment-related information:
>
> 1. *Number of coupon payments for a corporate bond.* As background, a corporate bond is a contractual obligation between an issuing corporation (i.e., borrower) and bondholders (i.e., lenders) in which the issuer agrees to pay interest—in the form of fixed coupon payments—on specified dates, typically semi-annually, over the life of the bond (i.e., to its maturity date) and to repay principal (i.e., the amount borrowed) at maturity.
>
> ### Solution to 1
>
> Number of coupon payments is discrete data. For example, a newly-issued 5-year corporate bond paying interest semi-annually (quarterly) will make 10 (20) coupon payments during its life. In this case, coupon payments are limited to a finite number of values; so, they are discrete.
>
> 2. *Cash dividends per share paid by a public company.* Note that cash dividends are a distribution paid to shareholders based on the number of shares owned.
>
> ### Solution to 2
>
> Cash dividends per share are continuous data since they can take on any non-negative values.
>
> 3. *Credit ratings for corporate bond issues.* As background, credit ratings gauge the bond issuer's ability to meet the promised payments on the bond. Bond rating agencies typically assign bond issues to discrete categories that are

in descending order of credit quality (i.e., increasing probability of non-payment or default).

### Solution to 3

Credit ratings are ordinal data. A rating places a bond issue in a category, and the categories are ordered with respect to the expected probability of default. But arithmetic operations cannot be done on credit ratings, and the difference in the expected probability of default between categories of highly rated bonds, for example, is not necessarily equal to that between categories of lowly rated bonds.

4. *Hedge fund classification types.* Note that hedge funds are investment vehicles that are relatively unconstrained in their use of debt, derivatives, and long and short investment strategies. Hedge fund classification types group hedge funds by the kind of investment strategy they pursue.

### Solution to 4

Hedge fund classification types are nominal data. Each type groups together hedge funds with similar investment strategies. In contrast to credit ratings for bonds, however, hedge fund classification schemes do not involve a ranking. Thus, such classification schemes are not ordinal data.

## Cross-Sectional versus Time-Series versus Panel Data

Another data classification standard is based on how data are collected, and it categorizes data into three types: cross-sectional, time series, and panel.

Prior to the description of the data types, we need to explain two data-related terminologies: variable and observation. A **variable** is a characteristic or quantity that can be measured, counted, or categorized and is subject to change. A variable can also be called a field, an attribute, or a feature. For example, stock price, market capitalization, dividend and dividend yield, earnings per share (EPS), and price-to-earnings ratio (P/E) are basic data variables for the financial analysis of a public company. An **observation** is the value of a specific variable collected at a point in time or over a specified period of time. For example, last year DEF, Inc. recorded EPS of $7.50. This value represented a 15% annual increase.

**Cross-sectional data** are a list of the observations of a specific variable from multiple observational units at a given point in time. The observational units can be individuals, groups, companies, trading markets, regions, etc. For example, January inflation rates (i.e., the variable) for each of the euro-area countries (i.e., the observational units) in the European Union for a given year constitute cross-sectional data.

**Time-series data** are a sequence of observations for a single observational unit of a specific variable collected over time and at discrete and typically equally spaced intervals of time, such as daily, weekly, monthly, annually, or quarterly. For example, the daily closing prices (i.e., the variable) of a particular stock recorded for a given month constitute time-series data.

**Panel data** are a mix of time-series and cross-sectional data that are frequently used in financial analysis and modeling. Panel data consist of observations through time on one or more variables for multiple observational units. The observations in panel data are usually organized in a matrix format called a data table. Exhibit 2 is an example of panel data showing quarterly earnings per share (i.e., the variable) for three companies (i.e., the observational units) in a given year by quarter. Each column is a time series of data that represents the quarterly EPS observations from Q1 to Q4 of a specific company, and each row is cross-sectional data that represent the EPS of all three companies of a particular quarter.

**Exhibit 2: Earnings per Share in Euros of Three Eurozone Companies in a Given Year**

| Time Period | Company A | Company B | Company C |
|---|---|---|---|
| Q1 | 13.53 | 0.84 | −0.34 |
| Q2 | 4.36 | 0.96 | 0.08 |
| Q3 | 13.16 | 0.79 | −2.72 |
| Q4 | 12.95 | 0.19 | 0.09 |

## Structured versus Unstructured Data

Categorizing data into structured and unstructured types is based on whether or not the data are in a highly organized form.

**Structured data** are highly organized in a pre-defined manner, usually with repeating patterns. The typical forms of structured data are one-dimensional arrays, such as a time series of a single variable, or two-dimensional data tables, where each column represents a variable or an observation unit and each row contains a set of values for the same columns. Structured data are relatively easy to enter, store, query, and analyze without much manual processing. Typical examples of structured company financial data are:

- Market data: data issued by stock exchanges, such as intra-day and daily closing stock prices and trading volumes.
- Fundamental data: data contained in financial statements, such as earnings per share, price to earnings ratio, dividend yield, and return on equity.
- Analytical data: data derived from analytics, such as cash flow projections or forecasted earnings growth.

**Unstructured data**, in contrast, are data that do not follow any conventionally organized forms. Some common types of unstructured data are text—such as financial news, posts in social media, and company filings with regulators—and also audio/video, such as managements' earnings calls and presentations to analysts.

Unstructured data are a relatively new classification driven by the rise of alternative data (i.e., data generated from unconventional sources, like electronic devices, social media, sensor networks, and satellites, but also by companies in the normal course of business) and their growing adoption in the financial industry. Unstructured data are typically alternative data as they are usually collected from unconventional sources. By indicating the source from which the data are generated, such data can be classified into three groups:

- Produced by individuals (i.e., via social media posts, web searches, etc.);
- Generated by business processes (i.e., via credit card transactions, corporate regulatory filings, etc.); and
- Generated by sensors (i.e., via satellite imagery, foot traffic by mobile devices, etc.).

## Data Types

Unstructured data may offer new market insights not normally contained in data from traditional sources and may provide potential sources of returns for investment processes. Unlike structured data, however, utilizing unstructured data in investment analysis is challenging. Typically, financial models are able to take only structured data as inputs; therefore, unstructured data must first be transformed into structured data that models can process.

Exhibit 3 shows an excerpt from Form 10-Q (Quarterly Report) filed by Company XYZ with the US Securities and Exchange Commission (SEC) for the fiscal quarter ended 31 March 20XX. The form is an unstructured mix of text and tables, so it cannot be directly used by computers as input to financial models. The SEC has utilized eXtensible Business Reporting Language (XBRL) to structure such data. The data extracted from the XBRL submission can be organized into five tab-delimited TXT format files that contain information about the submission, including taxonomy tags (i.e., financial statement items), dates, units of measure (uom), values (i.e., for the tag items), and more—making it readable by computer. Exhibit 4 shows an excerpt from one of the now structured data tables downloaded from the SEC's EDGAR (Electronic Data Gathering, Analysis, and Retrieval) database.

### Exhibit 3: Excerpt from 10-Q of Company XYZ for Fiscal Quarter Ended 31 March 20XX

Company XYZ
Form 10-Q
Fiscal Quarter Ended 31 March 20XX
Table of Contents

**Part I**

|  |  | Page |
|---|---|---|
| Item 1 | Financial Statements | 1 |
| Item 2 | Management's Discussion and Analysis of Financial Condition and Results of Operations | 21 |
| Item 3 | Quantitative and Qualitative Disclosures About Market Risk | 32 |
| Item 4 | Controls and Procedures | 32 |

**Part II**

| Item 1 | Legal Proceedings | 33 |
|---|---|---|
| Item 1A | Risk Factors | 33 |
| Item 2 | Unregistered Sales of Equity Securities and Use of Proceeds | 43 |
| Item 3 | Defaults Upon Senior Securities | 43 |
| Item 4 | Mine Safety Disclosures | 43 |
| Item 5 | Other Information | 43 |
| Item 6 | Exhibits | 44 |

Condensed Consolidated Statements of Operations (Unaudited)
(in millions, except number of shares, which are reflected in thousands and per share amounts)

|  | 31 March 20XX |
|---|---|
| Net sales: |  |
| Products | $46,565 |
| Services | 11,450 |
| Total net sales | 58,015 |

| | | |
|---|---|---:|
| Cost of sales: | | |
|   Products | | 32,047 |
|   Services | | 4,147 |
|     Total cost of sales | | 36,194 |
|     Gross margin | | 21,821 |
| Operating expenses: | | |
|   Research and development | | 3,948 |
|   Selling, general and administrative | | 4,458 |
|     Total operating expenses | | 8,406 |
| Operating income | | 13,415 |
| Other income/(expense), net | | 378 |
| Income before provision for income taxes | | 13,793 |
| Provision for income taxes | | 2,232 |
| Net income | | $11,561 |

*Source:* EDGAR.

**Exhibit 4: Structured Data Extracted from Form 10-Q of Company XYZ for Fiscal Quarter Ended 31 March 20XX**

| adsh | tag | ddate | uom | value |
|---|---|---|---|---:|
| 0000320193-19-000066 | RevenueFromContractWithCustomerExcludingAssessedTax | 20XX0331 | USD | $58,015,000,000 |
| 0000320193-19-000066 | GrossProfit | 20XX0331 | USD | $21,821,000,000 |
| 0000320193-19-000066 | OperatingExpenses | 20XX0331 | USD | $8,406,000,000 |
| 0000320193-19-000066 | OperatingIncomeLoss | 20XX0331 | USD | $13,415,000,000 |
| 0000320193-19-000066 | NetIncomeLoss | 20XX0331 | USD | $11,561,000,000 |

*Source:* EDGAR.

### EXAMPLE 2

### Identifying Data Types (II)

1. Which of the following is *most likely* to be structured data?

    **A.** Social media posts where consumers are commenting on what they think of a company's new product.

    **B.** Daily closing prices during the past month for all companies listed on Japan's Nikkei 225 stock index.

    **C.** Audio and video of a CFO explaining her company's latest earnings announcement to securities analysts.

## Solution to 1

B is correct as daily closing prices constitute structured data. A is incorrect as social media posts are unstructured data. C is incorrect as audio and video are unstructured data.

2. Which of the following statements describing panel data is *most accurate*?

   A. It is a sequence of observations for a single observational unit of a specific variable collected over time at discrete and equally spaced intervals.
   B. It is a list of observations of a specific variable from multiple observational units at a given point in time.
   C. It is a mix of time-series and cross-sectional data that are frequently used in financial analysis and modeling.

## Solution to 2

C is correct as it most accurately describes panel data. A is incorrect as it describes time-series data. B is incorrect as it describes cross-sectional data.

3. Which of the following data series is *least likely* to be sortable by values?

   A. Daily trading volumes for stocks listed on the Shanghai Stock Exchange.
   B. EPS for a given year for technology companies included in the S&P 500 Index.
   C. Dates of first default on bond payments for a group of bankrupt European manufacturing companies.

## Solution to 3

C is correct as dates are ordinal data that can be sorted by chronological order but not by value. A and B are incorrect as both daily trading volumes and earnings per share (EPS) are numerical data, so they can be sorted by values.

4. Which of the following best describes a time series?

   A. Daily stock prices of the XYZ stock over a 60-month period.
   B. Returns on four-star rated Morningstar investment funds at the end of the most recent month.
   C. Stock prices for all stocks in the FTSE100 on 31 December of the most recent calendar year.

## Solution to 4

A is correct since a time series is a sequence of observations of a specific variable (XYZ stock price) collected over time (60 months) and at discrete intervals of time (daily). B and C are both incorrect as they are cross-sectional data.

## Data Summarization

Given the wide variety of possible formats of **raw data**, which are data available in their original form as collected, such data typically cannot be used by humans or computers to directly extract information and insights. Organizing data into a one-dimensional array or a two-dimensional array is typically the first step in data analytics and modeling. In this section, we will illustrate the construction of these typical data organization formats. We will also introduce two useful tools that can efficiently summarize one-variable and two-variable data: frequency distributions and contingency tables, respectively. Both of them can give us a quick snapshot of the data and allow us to find patterns in the data and associations between variables.

# 3. ORGANIZING DATA FOR QUANTITATIVE ANALYSIS

☐ describe how data are organized for quantitative analysis

Quantitative analysis and modeling typically require input data to be in a clean and formatted form, so raw data are usually not suitable for use directly by analysts. Depending upon the number of variables, raw data can be organized into two typical formats for quantitative analysis: one-dimensional arrays and two-dimensional rectangular arrays.

A **one-dimensional array** is the simplest format for representing a collection of data of the same data type, so it is suitable for representing a single variable. Exhibit 5 is an example of a one-dimensional array that shows the closing price for the first 10 trading days for ABC Inc. stock after the company went public. Closing prices are time-series data collected at daily intervals, so it is natural to organize them into a time-ordered sequence. The time-series format also facilitates future data updates to the existing dataset. In this case, closing prices for future trading sessions can be easily added to the end of the array with no alteration of previously formatted data.

More importantly, in contrast to compiling the data randomly in an unorganized manner, organizing such data by its time-series nature preserves valuable information beyond the basic **descriptive statistics** that summarize central tendency and spread variation in the data's distribution. For example, by simply plotting the data against time, we can learn whether the data demonstrate any increasing or decreasing trends over time or whether the time series repeats certain patterns in a systematic way over time.

### Exhibit 5: One-Dimensional Array: Daily Closing Price of ABC Inc. Stock

| Observation by Day | Stock Price ($) |
|---|---|
| 1 | 57.21 |
| 2 | 58.26 |
| 3 | 58.64 |
| 4 | 56.19 |
| 5 | 54.78 |
| 6 | 54.26 |
| 7 | 56.88 |

# Organizing Data for Quantitative Analysis

| Observation by Day | Stock Price ($) |
|---|---|
| 8 | 54.74 |
| 9 | 52.42 |
| 10 | 50.14 |

A **two-dimensional rectangular array** (also called a **data table**) is one of the most popular forms for organizing data for processing by computers or for presenting data visually for consumption by humans. Similar to the structure in an Excel spreadsheet, a data table is comprised of columns and rows to hold multiple variables and multiple observations, respectively. When a data table is used to organize the data of one single observational unit (i.e., a single company), each column represents a different variable (feature or attribute) of that observational unit, and each row holds an observation for the different variables; successive rows represent the observations for successive time periods. In other words, observations of each variable are a time-series sequence that is sorted in either ascending or descending time order. Consequently, observations of different variables must be sorted and aligned to the same time scale. Example 3 shows how to organize a raw dataset for a company collected online into a machine-readable data table.

## EXAMPLE 3

### Organizing a Company's Raw Data into a Data Table

1. Suppose you are conducting a valuation analysis of ABC Inc., which has been listed on the stock exchange for two years. The metrics to be used in your valuation include revenue, earnings per share (EPS), and dividends paid per share (DPS). You have retrieved the last two years of ABC's quarterly data from the exchange's website, which is shown in Exhibit 6. The data available online are pre-organized into a tabular format, where each column represents a fiscal year and each row represents a particular quarter with values of the three measures clustered together.

#### Exhibit 6: Metrics of ABC Inc. Retrieved Online

| Fiscal Quarter | Year 1 (Fiscal Year) | Year 2 (Fiscal Year) |
|---|---|---|
| March | | |
| Revenue | $3,784(M) | $4,097(M) |
| EPS | 1.37 | −0.34 |
| DPS | N/A | N/A |
| June | | |
| Revenue | $4,236(M) | $5,905(M) |
| EPS | 1.78 | 3.89 |
| DPS | N/A | 0.25 |
| September | | |
| Revenue | $4,187(M) | $4,997(M) |
| EPS | −3.38 | −2.88 |
| DPS | N/A | 0.25 |
| December | | |

| Fiscal Quarter | Year 1 (Fiscal Year) | Year 2 (Fiscal Year) |
|---|---|---|
| Revenue | $3,889(M) | $4,389(M) |
| EPS | −8.66 | −3.98 |
| DPS | N/A | 0.25 |

Use the data to construct a two-dimensional rectangular array (i.e., data table) with the columns representing the metrics for valuation and the observations arranged in a time-series sequence.

## Solution:

To construct a two-dimensional rectangular array, we first need to determine the data table structure. The columns have been specified to represent the three valuation metrics (i.e., variables): revenue, EPS and DPS. The rows should be the observations for each variable in a time ordered sequence. In this example, the data for the valuation measures will be organized in the same quarterly intervals as the raw data retrieved online, starting from Q1 Year 1 to Q4 Year 2. Then, the observations from the original table can be placed accordingly into the data table by variable name and by filing quarter. Exhibit 7 shows the raw data reorganized in the two-dimensional rectangular array (by date and associated valuation metric), which can now be used in financial analysis and is readable by a computer.

It is worth pointing out that in case of missing values while organizing data, how to handle them depends largely on why the data are missing. In this example, dividends (DPS) in the first five quarters are missing because ABC Inc. did not authorize (and pay) any dividends. So, filling the dividend column with zeros is appropriate. If revenue, EPS, and DPS of a given quarter are missing due to particular data source issues, however, these missing values cannot be simply replaced with zeros; this action would result in incorrect interpretation. Instead, the missing values might be replaced with the latest available data or with interpolated values, depending on how the data will be consumed or modeled.

### Exhibit 7: Data Table for ABC Inc.

| | Revenue ($ Million) | EPS ($) | DPS ($) |
|---|---|---|---|
| Q1 Year 1 | 3,784 | 1.37 | 0 |
| Q2 Year 1 | 4,236 | 1.78 | 0 |
| Q3 Year 1 | 4,187 | −3.38 | 0 |
| Q4 Year 1 | 3,889 | −8.66 | 0 |
| Q1 Year 2 | 4,097 | −0.34 | 0 |
| Q2 Year 2 | 5,905 | 3.89 | 0.25 |
| Q3 Year 2 | 4,997 | −2.88 | 0.25 |
| Q4 Year 2 | 4,389 | −3.98 | 0.25 |

# SUMMARIZING DATA USING FREQUENCY DISTRIBUTIONS

☐ interpret frequency and related distributions

We now discuss various tabular formats for describing data based on the count of observations. These tables are a necessary step toward building a true visualization of a dataset. Later, we shall see how bar charts, tree-maps, and heat maps, among other graphic tools, are used to visualize important properties of a dataset.

A **frequency distribution** (also called a one-way table) is a tabular display of data constructed either by counting the observations of a variable by distinct values or groups or by tallying the values of a numerical variable into a set of numerically ordered bins. It is an important tool for initially summarizing data by groups or bins for easier interpretation.

Constructing a frequency distribution of a categorical variable is relatively straightforward and can be stated in the following two basic steps:

1. Count the number of observations for each unique value of the variable.

2. Construct a table listing each unique value and the corresponding counts, and then sort the records by number of counts in descending or ascending order to facilitate the display.

Exhibit 8 shows a frequency distribution of a portfolio's stock holdings by sectors (the variables), which are defined by GICS. The portfolio contains a total of 479 stocks that have been individually classified into 11 GICS sectors (first column). The stocks are counted by sector and are summarized in the second column, absolute frequency. The **absolute frequency**, or simply the raw frequency, is the actual number of observations counted for each unique value of the variable (i.e., each sector). Often it is desirable to express the frequencies in terms of percentages, so we also show the **relative frequency** (in the third column), which is calculated as the absolute frequency of each unique value of the variable divided by the total number of observations. The relative frequency provides a normalized measure of the distribution of the data, allowing comparisons between datasets with different numbers of total observations.

### Exhibit 8: Frequency Distribution for a Portfolio by Sector

| Sector (Variable) | Absolute Frequency | Relative Frequency |
|---|---|---|
| Industrials | 73 | 15.2% |
| Information Technology | 69 | 14.4% |
| Financials | 67 | 14.0% |
| Consumer Discretionary | 62 | 12.9% |
| Health Care | 54 | 11.3% |
| Consumer Staples | 33 | 6.9% |
| Real Estate | 30 | 6.3% |
| Energy | 29 | 6.1% |
| Utilities | 26 | 5.4% |
| Materials | 26 | 5.4% |

| Sector (Variable) | Absolute Frequency | Relative Frequency |
|---|---|---|
| Communication Services | 10 | 2.1% |
| Total | 479 | 100.0% |

A frequency distribution table provides a snapshot of the data, and it facilitates finding patterns. Examining the distribution of absolute frequency in Exhibit 8, we see that the largest number of stocks (73), accounting for 15.2% of the stocks in the portfolio, are held in companies in the industrials sector. The sector with the least number of stocks (10) is communication services, which represents just 2.1% of the stocks in the portfolio.

It is also easy to see that the top four sectors (i.e., industrials, information technology, financials, and consumer discretionary) have very similar relative frequencies, between 15.2% and 12.9%. Similar relative frequencies, between 6.9% and 5.4%, are also seen among several other sectors. Note that the absolute frequencies add up to the total number of stocks in the portfolio (479), and the sum of the relative frequencies should be equal to 100%.

Frequency distributions also help in the analysis of large amounts of numerical data. The procedure for summarizing numerical data is a bit more involved than that for summarizing categorical data because it requires creating non-overlapping bins (also called **intervals** or buckets) and then counting the observations falling into each bin. One procedure for constructing a frequency distribution for numerical data can be stated as follows:

1. Sort the data in ascending order.
2. Calculate the range of the data, defined as Range = Maximum value − Minimum value.
3. Decide on the number of bins ($k$) in the frequency distribution.
4. Determine bin width as Range/$k$.
5. Determine the first bin by adding the bin width to the minimum value. Then, determine the remaining bins by successively adding the bin width to the prior bin's end point and stopping after reaching a bin that includes the maximum value.
6. Determine the number of observations falling into each bin by counting the number of observations whose values are equal to or exceed the bin minimum value yet are less than the bin's maximum value. The exception is in the last bin, where the maximum value is equal to the last bin's maximum, and therefore, the observation with the maximum value is included in this bin's count.
7. Construct a table of the bins listed from smallest to largest that shows the number of observations falling into each bin.

In Step 4, when rounding the bin width, round up (rather than down) to ensure that the final bin includes the maximum value of the data.

These seven steps are basic guidelines for constructing frequency distributions. In practice, however, we may want to refine the above basic procedure. For example, we may want the bins to begin and end with whole numbers for ease of interpretation. Another practical refinement that promotes interpretation is to start the first bin at the nearest whole number below the minimum value.

# Summarizing Data Using Frequency Distributions

As this procedure implies, a frequency distribution groups data into a set of bins, where each bin is defined by a unique set of values (i.e., beginning and ending points). Each observation falls into only one bin, and the total number of bins covers all the values represented in the data. The frequency distribution is the list of the bins together with the corresponding measures of frequency.

To illustrate the basic five-step procedure, suppose we have 12 observations sorted in ascending order (*Step 1*): −4.57, −4.04, −1.64, 0.28, 1.34, 2.35, 2.38, 4.28, 4.42, 4.68, 7.16, and 11.43.

The minimum observation is −4.57, and the maximum observation is +11.43. So, the range is +11.43 − (−4.57) = 16 (*Step 2*).

If we set $k$ = 4 (*Step 3*), then the bin width is 16/4 = 4 (*Step 4*).

Exhibit 9 shows the repeated addition of the bin width of 4 to determine the endpoint for each of the bins (*Step 5*).

### Exhibit 9: Determining Endpoints of the Bins

| | | | | |
|---|---|---|---|---|
| −4.57 | + | 4.0 | = | −0.57 |
| −0.57 | + | 4.0 | = | 3.43 |
| 3.43 | + | 4.0 | = | 7.43 |
| 7.43 | + | 4.0 | = | 11.43 |

Thus, the bins are [−4.57 to −0.57), [−0.57 to 3.43), [3.43 to 7.43), and [7.43 to 11.43], where the notation [−4.57 to −0.57) indicates −4.57 ≤ observation < −0.57. The parentheses indicate that the endpoints are not included in the bins, and the square brackets indicate that the beginning points and the last endpoint are included in the bin. Exhibit 10 summarizes Steps 5 through 7.

### Exhibit 10: Frequency Distribution

| Bin | | | | | Absolute Frequency |
|---|---|---|---|---|---|
| A | −4.57 | ≤ observation < | −0.57 | | 3 |
| B | −0.57 | ≤ observation < | 3.43 | | 4 |
| C | 3.43 | ≤ observation < | 7.43 | | 4 |
| D | 7.43 | ≤ observation ≤ | 11.43 | | 1 |

Note that the bins do not overlap, so each observation can be placed uniquely into one bin, and the last bin includes the maximum value.

We can apply these steps to the construction of frequency distributions for daily returns of the fictitious Euro-Asia-Africa (EAA) Equity Index. The dataset of daily returns of the EAA Equity Index spans a five-year period and consists of 1,258 observations with a minimum value of −4.1% and a maximum value of 5.0%. Thus, the range of the data is 5% − (−4.1%) = 9.1%, approximately. [The mean daily return—mean as a measure of central tendency will be discussed shortly—is 0.04%.]

The decision on the number of bins ($k$) into which we should group the observations often involves inspecting the data and exercising judgment. How much detail should we include? If we use too few bins, we will summarize too much and may lose pertinent characteristics. Conversely, if we use too many bins, we may not summarize enough and may introduce unnecessary noise.

We can establish an appropriate value for k by evaluating the usefulness of the resulting bin width. A large number of empty bins may indicate that we are attempting to over-organize the data to present too much detail. Starting with a relatively small bin width, we can see whether or not the bins are mostly empty and whether or not the value of k associated with that bin width is too large. If the bins are mostly empty, implying that k is too large, we can consider increasingly larger bins (i.e., smaller values of k) until we have a frequency distribution that effectively summarizes the distribution.

Suppose that for ease of interpretation we want to use a bin width stated in whole rather than fractional percentages. In the case of the daily EAA Equity Index returns, a 1% bin width would be associated with 9.1/1 = 9.1 bins, which can be rounded up to k = 10 bins. That number of bins will cover a range of 1% × 10 = 10%. By constructing the frequency distribution in this manner, we will also have bins that end and begin at a value of 0%, thereby allowing us to count the negative and positive returns in the data. Without too much work, we have found an effective way to summarize the data.

Exhibit 11 shows the frequency distribution for the daily returns of the EAA Equity Index using return bins of 1%, where the first bin includes returns from −5.0% to −4.0% (exclusive, meaning < −4%) and the last bin includes daily returns from 4.0% to 5.0% (inclusive, meaning ≤ 5%). Note that to facilitate interpretation, the first bin starts at the nearest whole number below the minimum value (so, at −5.0%).

Exhibit 11 includes two other useful ways to present the data (which can be computed in a straightforward manner once we have established the absolute and relative frequency distributions): the cumulative absolute frequency and the cumulative relative frequency. The **cumulative absolute frequency** cumulates (meaning, adds up) the absolute frequencies as we move from the first bin to the last bin. Similarly, the **cumulative relative frequency** is a sequence of partial sums of the relative frequencies. For the last bin, the cumulative absolute frequency will equal the number observations in the dataset (1,258), and the cumulative relative frequency will equal 100%.

### Exhibit 11: Frequency Distribution for Daily Returns of EAA Equity Index

| Return Bin (%) | Absolute Frequency | Relative Frequency (%) | Cumulative Absolute Frequency | Cumulative Relative Frequency (%) |
|---|---|---|---|---|
| −5.0 to −4.0 | 1 | 0.08 | 1 | 0.08 |
| −4.0 to −3.0 | 7 | 0.56 | 8 | 0.64 |
| −3.0 to −2.0 | 23 | 1.83 | 31 | 2.46 |
| −2.0 to −1.0 | 77 | 6.12 | 108 | 8.59 |
| −1.0 to 0.0 | 470 | 37.36 | 578 | 45.95 |
| 0.0 to 1.0 | 555 | 44.12 | 1,133 | 90.06 |
| 1.0 to 2.0 | 110 | 8.74 | 1,243 | 98.81 |
| 2.0 to 3.0 | 13 | 1.03 | 1,256 | 99.84 |
| 3.0 to 4.0 | 1 | 0.08 | 1,257 | 99.92 |
| 4.0 to 5.0 | 1 | 0.08 | 1,258 | 100.00 |

As Exhibit 11 shows, the absolute frequencies vary widely, ranging from 1 to 555. The bin encompassing returns between 0% and 1% has the most observations (555), and the corresponding relative frequency tells us these observations account for 44.12% of the total number of observations. The frequency distribution gives us a sense of not only where most of the observations lie but also whether the distribution is evenly spread. It is easy to see that the vast majority of observations (37.36% + 44.12% = 81.48%) lie in the middle two bins spanning −1% to 1%. We can also see that not many observations are greater than 3% or less than −4%. Moreover, as there are bins with 0% as ending or beginning points, we are able to count positive and negative returns in the data. Looking at the cumulative relative frequency in the last column, we see that the bin of −1% to 0% shows a cumulative relative frequency of 45.95%. This indicates that 45.95% of the observations lie below the daily return of 0% and that 54.05% of the observations are positive daily returns.

It is worth noting that other than being summarized in tables, frequency distributions also can be effectively represented in visuals, which will be discussed shortly in the section on data visualization.

### EXAMPLE 4

### Constructing a Frequency Distribution of Country Index Returns

1. Suppose we have the annual equity index returns of a given year for 18 different countries, as shown in Exhibit 12, and we are asked to summarize the data.

**Exhibit 12: Annual Equity Index Returns for 18 Countries**

| Market | Index Return (%) |
|---|---|
| Country A | 7.7 |
| Country B | 8.5 |
| Country C | 9.1 |
| Country D | 5.5 |
| Country E | 7.1 |
| Country F | 9.9 |
| Country G | 6.2 |
| Country H | 6.8 |
| Country I | 7.5 |
| Country J | 8.9 |
| Country K | 7.4 |
| Country L | 8.6 |
| Country M | 9.6 |
| Country N | 7.7 |
| Country O | 6.8 |
| Country P | 6.1 |
| Country Q | 8.8 |
| Country R | 7.9 |

Construct a frequency distribution table from these data and state some key findings from the summarized data.

### Solution:

The first step in constructing a frequency distribution table is to sort the return data in ascending order:

| Market | Index Return (%) |
|---|---|
| Country D | 5.5 |
| Country P | 6.1 |
| Country G | 6.2 |
| Country H | 6.8 |
| Country O | 6.8 |
| Country E | 7.1 |
| Country K | 7.4 |
| Country I | 7.5 |
| Country A | 7.7 |
| Country N | 7.7 |
| Country R | 7.9 |
| Country B | 8.5 |
| Country L | 8.6 |
| Country Q | 8.8 |
| Country J | 8.9 |
| Country C | 9.1 |
| Country M | 9.6 |
| Country F | 9.9 |

The second step is to calculate the range of the data, which is 9.9% − 5.5% = 4.4%.

The third step is to decide on the number of bins. Here, we will use $k = 5$.

The fourth step is to determine the bin width. Here, it is 4.4%/5 = 0.88%, which we will round up to 1.0%.

The fifth step is to determine the bins, which are as follows:

5.0% + 1.0% = 6.0%
6.0% + 1.0% = 7.0%
7.0% + 1.0% = 8.0%
8.0% + 1.0% = 9.0%
9.0% + 1.0% = 10.0%

For ease of interpretation, the first bin is set to begin with the nearest whole number (5.0%) below the minimum value (5.5%) of the data series.

The sixth step requires counting the return observations falling into each bin, and the seventh (last) step is to use these results to construct the final frequency distribution table.

Exhibit 13 presents the frequency distribution table, which summarizes the data in Exhibit 12 into five bins spanning 5% to 10%. Note that with 18 countries, the relative frequency for one observation is calculated as 1/18 = 5.56%.

### Exhibit 13: Frequency Distribution of Equity Index Returns

| Return Bin (%) | Absolute Frequency | Relative Frequency (%) | Cumulative Absolute Frequency | Cumulative Relative Frequency (%) |
|---|---|---|---|---|
| 5.0 to 6.0 | 1 | 5.56 | 1 | 5.56 |
| 6.0 to 7.0 | 4 | 22.22 | 5 | 27.78 |
| 7.0 to 8.0 | 6 | 33.33 | 11 | 61.11 |

| Return Bin (%) | Absolute Frequency | Relative Frequency (%) | Cumulative Absolute Frequency | Cumulative Relative Frequency (%) |
|---|---|---|---|---|
| 8.0 to 9.0 | 4 | 22.22 | 15 | 83.33 |
| 9.0 to 10.0 | 3 | 16.67 | 18 | 100.00 |

As Exhibit 13 shows, there is substantial variation in these equity index returns. One-third of the observations fall in the 7.0 to 8.0% bin, making it the bin with the most observations. Both the 6.0 to 7.0% bin and the 8.0 to 9.0% bin hold four observations each, accounting for 22.22% of the total number of the observations, respectively. The two remaining bins have fewer observations, one or three observations, respectively.

# SUMMARIZING DATA USING A CONTINGENCY TABLE

☐ interpret a contingency table

We have shown that the frequency distribution table is a powerful tool to summarize data for one variable. How can we summarize data for two variables simultaneously? A contingency table provides a solution to this question.

A **contingency table** is a tabular format that displays the frequency distributions of two or more categorical variables simultaneously and is used for finding patterns between the variables. A contingency table for two categorical variables is also known as a two-way table. Contingency tables are constructed by listing all the levels (i.e., categories) of one variable as rows and all the levels of the other variable as columns in the table. A contingency table having $R$ levels of one variable in rows and $C$ levels of the other variable in columns is referred to as an $R \times C$ table. Note that each variable in a contingency table must have a finite number of levels, which can be either ordered (ordinal data) or unordered (nominal data). Importantly, the data displayed in the cells of the contingency table can be either a frequency (count) or a relative frequency (percentage) based on either overall total, row totals, or column totals.

Exhibit 14 presents a $5 \times 3$ contingency table that summarizes the number of stocks (i.e., frequency) in a particular portfolio of 1,000 stocks by two variables, sector and company market capitalization. Sector has five levels, with each one being a GICS-defined sector. Market capitalization (commonly referred to as "market cap") is defined for a company as the number of shares outstanding times the price per share. The stocks in this portfolio are categorized by three levels of market capitalization: large cap, more than $10 billion; mid cap, $10 billion to $2 billion; and small cap, less than $2 billion.

### Exhibit 14: Portfolio Frequencies by Sector and Market Capitalization

| Sector Variable (5 Levels) | Market Capitalization Variable (3 Levels) | | | |
|---|---|---|---|---|
| | Small | Mid | Large | Total |
| Communication Services | 55 | 35 | 20 | 110 |
| Consumer Staples | 50 | 30 | 30 | 110 |
| Energy | 175 | 95 | 20 | 290 |
| Health Care | 275 | 105 | 55 | 435 |
| Utilities | 20 | 25 | 10 | 55 |
| Total | 575 | 290 | 135 | 1,000 |

The entries in the cells of the contingency table show the number of stocks of each sector with a given level of market cap. For example, there are 275 small-cap health care stocks, making it the portfolio's largest subgroup in terms of frequency. These data are also called **joint frequencies** because you are joining one variable from the row (i.e., sector) and the other variable from the column (i.e., market cap) to count observations. The joint frequencies are then added across rows and across columns, and these corresponding sums are called **marginal frequencies**. For example, the marginal frequency of health care stocks in the portfolio is the sum of the joint frequencies across all three levels of market cap, so 435 (= 275 + 105 + 55). Similarly, adding the joint frequencies of small-cap stocks across all five sectors gives the marginal frequency of small-cap stocks of 575 (= 55 + 50 + 175 + 275 + 20).

Clearly, health care stocks and small-cap stocks have the largest marginal frequencies among sector and market cap, respectively, in this portfolio. Note the marginal frequencies represent the frequency distribution for each variable. Finally, the marginal frequencies for each variable must sum to the total number of stocks (overall total) in the portfolio—here, 1,000 (shown in the lower right cell).

Similar to the one-way frequency distribution table, we can express frequency in percentage terms as relative frequency by using one of three options. We can divide the joint frequencies by: a) the total count; b) the marginal frequency on a row; or c) the marginal frequency on a column.

Exhibit 15 shows the contingency table using relative frequencies based on total count. It is readily apparent that small-cap health care and energy stocks comprise the largest portions of the total portfolio, at 27.5% (= 275/1,000) and 17.5% (= 175/1,000), respectively, followed by mid-cap health care and energy stocks, at 10.5% and 9.5%, respectively. Together, these two sectors make up nearly three-quarters of the portfolio (43.5% + 29.0% = 72.5%).

### Exhibit 15: Relative Frequencies as Percentage of Total

| Sector Variable (5 Levels) | Market Capitalization Variable (3 Levels) | | | |
|---|---|---|---|---|
| | Small | Mid | Large | Total |
| Communication Services | 5.5% | 3.5% | 2.0% | 11.0% |
| Consumer Staples | 5.0% | 3.0% | 3.0% | 11.0% |
| Energy | 17.5% | 9.5% | 2.0% | 29.0% |
| Health Care | 27.5% | 10.5% | 5.5% | 43.5% |

|  | Market Capitalization Variable (3 Levels) | | | |
|---|---|---|---|---|
| Sector Variable (5 Levels) | Small | Mid | Large | Total |
| Utilities | 2.0% | 2.5% | 1.0% | 5.5% |
| Total | 57.5% | 29.0% | 13.5% | 100% |

Exhibit 16 shows relative frequencies based on marginal frequencies of market cap (i.e., columns). From this perspective, it is clear that the health care and energy sectors dominate the other sectors at each level of market capitalization: 78.3% (= 275/575 + 175/575), 69.0% (= 105/290 + 95/290), and 55.6% (= 55/135 + 20/135), for small, mid, and large caps, respectively. Note that there may be a small rounding error difference between these results and the numbers shown in Exhibit 15.

### Exhibit 16: Relative Frequencies: Sector as Percentage of Market Cap

|  | Market Capitalization Variable (3 Levels) | | | |
|---|---|---|---|---|
| Sector Variable (5 Levels) | Small | Mid | Large | Total |
| Communication Services | 9.6% | 12.1% | 14.8% | 11.0% |
| Consumer Staples | 8.7% | 10.3% | 22.2% | 11.0% |
| Energy | 30.4% | 32.8% | 14.8% | 29.0% |
| Health Care | 47.8% | 36.2% | 40.7% | 43.5% |
| Utilities | 3.5% | 8.6% | 7.4% | 5.5% |
| Total | 100.0% | 100.0% | 100.0% | 100.0% |

In conclusion, the findings from these contingency tables using frequencies and relative frequencies indicate that in terms of the number of stocks, the portfolio can be generally described as a small- to mid-cap-oriented health care and energy sector portfolio that also includes stocks of several other defensive sectors.

As an analytical tool, contingency tables can be used in different applications. One application is for evaluating the performance of a classification model (in this case, the contingency table is called a **confusion matrix**). Suppose we have a model for classifying companies into two groups: those that default on their bond payments and those that do not default. The confusion matrix for displaying the model's results will be a 2 × 2 table showing the frequency of actual defaults versus the model's predicted frequency of defaults. Exhibit 17 shows such a confusion matrix for a sample of 2,000 non-investment-grade bonds. Using company characteristics and other inputs, the model correctly predicts 300 cases of bond defaults and 1,650 cases of no defaults.

### Exhibit 17: Confusion Matrix for Bond Default Prediction Model

| Predicted | Actual Default | | |
|---|---|---|---|
| Default | Yes | No | Total |
| Yes | 300 | 40 | 340 |
| No | 10 | 1,650 | 1,660 |
| Total | 310 | 1,690 | 2,000 |

We can also observe that this classification model incorrectly predicts default in 40 cases where no default actually occurred and also incorrectly predicts no default in 10 cases where default actually did occur. Later in the CFA Program curriculum you will learn how to construct a confusion matrix, how to calculate related model performance metrics, and how to use them to evaluate and tune a classification model.

Another application of contingency tables is to investigate potential association between two categorical variables. For example, revisiting Exhibit 14, one may ask whether the distribution of stocks by sectors is independent of the levels of market capitalization. Given the dominance of small-cap and mid-cap health care and energy stocks, the answer is likely, no.

## 6. DATA VISUALIZATION

> ☐ describe ways that data may be visualized and evaluate uses of specific visualizations
> ☐ describe how to select among visualization types

**Visualization** is the presentation of data in a pictorial or graphical format for the purpose of increasing understanding and for gaining insights into the data. As has been said, "a picture is worth a thousand words." In this section, we discuss a variety of charts that are useful for understanding distributions, making comparisons, and exploring potential relationships among data. Specifically, we will cover visualizing frequency distributions of numerical and categorical data by using plots that represent multi-dimensional data for discovering relationships and by interpreting visuals that display unstructured data.

### Histogram and Frequency Polygon

A **histogram** is a chart that presents the distribution of numerical data by using the height of a bar or column to represent the absolute frequency of each bin or interval in the distribution.

To construct a histogram from a continuous variable, we first need to split the data into bins and summarize the data into a frequency distribution table, such as the one we constructed in Exhibit 11. In a histogram, the $y$-axis generally represents the absolute frequency or the relative frequency in percentage terms, while the $x$-axis usually represents the bins of the variable. Using the frequency distribution table in Exhibit 11, we plot the histogram of daily returns of the EAA Equity Index, as shown in Exhibit 18. The bars are of equal width, representing the bin width of 1% for each return interval. The bars are usually drawn with no spaces in between, but small gaps can also be added between adjacent bars to increase readability, as in this exhibit. In this case, the height of each bar represents the absolute frequency for each return bin. A quick glance can tell us that the return bin 0% to 1% (exclusive) has the highest frequency, with more than 500 observations (555, to be exact), and it is represented by the tallest bar in the histogram.

An advantage of the histogram is that it can effectively present a large amount of numerical data that has been grouped into a frequency distribution and can allow a quick inspection of the shape, center, and spread of the distribution to better understand it. For example, in Exhibit 18, despite the histogram of daily EAA Equity Index returns appearing bell-shaped and roughly symmetrical, most bars to the right side of the origin (i.e., zero) are taller than those on the left side, indicating that more observations lie in the bins in positive territory. Remember that in the earlier discussion of this return distribution, it was noted that 54.1% of the observations are positive daily returns.

As mentioned, histograms can also be created with relative frequencies—the choice of using absolute versus relative frequency depends on the question being answered. An absolute frequency histogram best answers the question of how many items are in each bin, while a relative frequency histogram gives the proportion or percentage of the total observations in each bin.

**Exhibit 18: Histogram Overlaid with Frequency Polygon for Daily Returns of EAA Equity Index**

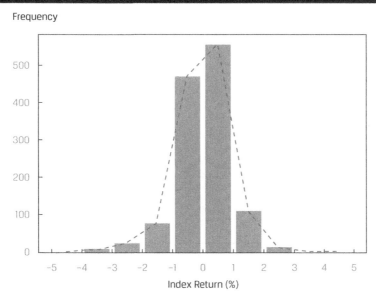

Another graphical tool for displaying frequency distributions is the frequency polygon. To construct a **frequency polygon**, we plot the midpoint of each return bin on the $x$-axis and the absolute frequency for that bin on the $y$-axis. We then connect neighboring points with a straight line. Exhibit 18 shows the frequency polygon that overlays the histogram. In the graph, for example, the return interval 1% to 2% (exclusive) has a frequency of 110, so we plot the return-interval midpoint of 0.5% (which is 1.50% on the $x$-axis) and a frequency of 110 (on the $y$-axis). Importantly, the frequency polygon can quickly convey a visual understanding of the distribution since it displays frequency as an area under the curve.

Another form for visualizing frequency distributions is the **cumulative frequency distribution chart**. Such a chart can plot either the cumulative absolute frequency or the cumulative relative frequency on the $y$-axis against the upper limit of the interval. The cumulative frequency distribution chart allows us to see the number or the percentage of the observations that lie below a certain value. To construct the cumulative frequency distribution, we graph the returns in the fourth (i.e., Cumulative Absolute Frequency) or fifth (i.e., Cumulative Relative Frequency) column of Exhibit 11 against the upper limit of each return interval.

Exhibit 19 presents the graph of the cumulative absolute frequency distribution for the daily returns on the EAA Equity Index. Notice that the cumulative distribution tends to flatten out when returns are extremely negative or extremely positive because the frequencies in these bins are quite small. The steep slope in the middle of Exhibit 19 reflects the fact that most of the observations—[(470 + 555)/1,258], or 81.5%—lie in the neighborhood of −1.0% to 1.0%.

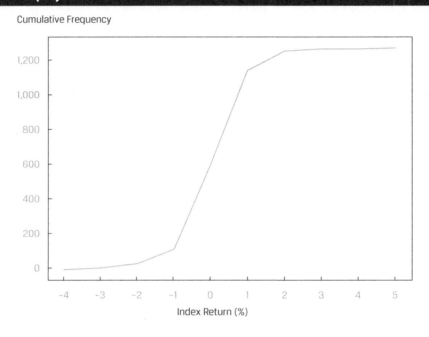

Exhibit 19: Cumulative Absolute Frequency Distribution of Daily Returns of EAA Equity Index

## Bar Chart

As we have demonstrated, the histogram is an efficient graphical tool to present the frequency distribution of numerical data. The frequency distribution of categorical data can be plotted in a similar type of graph called a **bar chart**. In a bar chart, each bar represents a distinct category, with the bar's height proportional to the frequency of the corresponding category.

Similar to plotting a histogram, the construction of a bar chart with one categorical variable first requires a frequency distribution table summarized from the variable. Note that the bars can be plotted vertically or horizontally. In a vertical bar chart, the *y*-axis still represents the absolute frequency or the relative frequency. Different from the histogram, however, is that the *x*-axis in a bar chart represents the mutually exclusive categories to be *compared* rather than bins that group numerical data.

For example, using the marginal frequencies for the five GICS sectors shown in the last column in Exhibit 14, we plot a horizontal bar chart in Exhibit 20 to show the frequency of stocks by sector in the portfolio. The bars are of equal width to represent each sector, and sufficient space should be between adjacent bars to separate them from each other. Because this is a horizontal bar chart—in this case, the *x*-axis shows the absolute frequency and the *y*-axis represents the sectors—the length of each bar represents the absolute frequency of each sector. Since sectors are nominal data with no logical ordering, the bars representing sectors may be arranged in any order. However, in the particular case where the categories in a bar chart are ordered

# Data Visualization

by frequency in descending order and the chart includes a line displaying cumulative relative frequency, it is called a Pareto Chart. The chart is often used to highlight dominant categories or the most important groups.

Bar charts provide a snapshot to show the comparison between categories of data. As shown in Exhibit 20, the sector in which the portfolio holds most stocks is the health care sector, with 435 stocks, followed by the energy sector, with 290 stocks. The sector in which the portfolio has the least number of stocks is utilities, with 55 stocks. To compare categories more accurately, in some cases we may add the frequency count to the right end of each bar (or the top end of each bar in the case of a vertical bar chart).

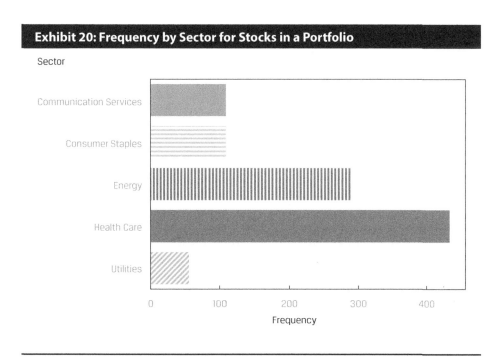

Exhibit 20: Frequency by Sector for Stocks in a Portfolio

The bar chart shown in Exhibit 20 can present the frequency distribution of only one categorical variable. In the case of two categorical variables, we need an enhanced version of the bar chart, called a **grouped bar chart** (also known as a **clustered bar chart**), to show joint frequencies. Using the joint frequencies by sector and by level of market capitalization given in Exhibit 14, for example, we show how a grouped bar chart is constructed in Exhibit 21. While the $y$-axis still represents the same categorical variable (the distinct GICS sectors as in Exhibit 20), in Exhibit 21 three bars are clustered side-by-side within the same sector to represent the three respective levels of market capitalization. The bars within each cluster should be colored differently to distinguish between them, but the color schemes for the sub-groups must be identical across the sector clusters, as shown by the legend at the bottom of Exhibit 21. Additionally, the bars in each sector cluster must always be placed in the same order throughout the chart. It is easy to see that the small-cap health care stocks are the sub-group with the highest frequency (275), and we can also see that small-cap stocks are the largest sub-group within each sector—except for utilities, where mid cap is the largest.

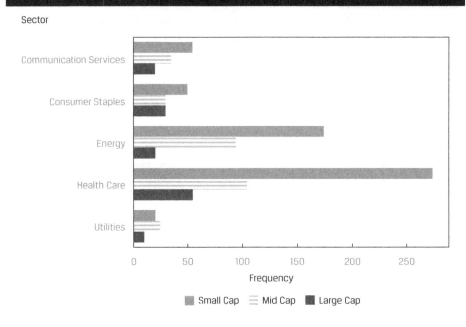

An alternative form for presenting the joint frequency distribution of two categorical variables is a **stacked bar chart**. In the vertical version of a stacked bar chart, the bars representing the sub-groups are placed on top of each other to form a single bar. Each subsection of the bar is shown in a different color to represent the contribution of each sub-group, and the overall height of the stacked bar represents the marginal frequency for the category. Exhibit 21 can be replotted in a stacked bar chart, as shown in Exhibit 22.

## Data Visualization

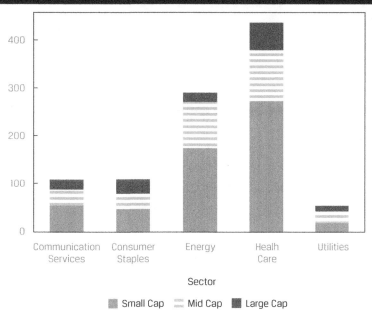

**Exhibit 22: Frequency by Sector and Level of Market Capitalization in a Stacked Bar Chart**

We have shown that the frequency distribution of categorical data can be clearly and efficiently presented by using a bar chart. However, it is worth noting that applications of bar charts may be extended to more general cases when categorical data are associated with numerical data. For example, suppose we want to show a company's quarterly profits over the past one year. In this case, we can plot a vertical bar chart where each bar represents one of the four quarters in a time order and its height indicates the value of profits for that quarter.

## Tree-Map

In addition to bar charts and grouped bar charts, another graphical tool for displaying categorical data is a **tree-map**. It consists of a set of colored rectangles to represent distinct groups, and the area of each rectangle is proportional to the value of the corresponding group. For example, referring back to the marginal frequencies by GICS sector in Exhibit 14, we plot a tree-map in Exhibit 23 to represent the frequency distribution by sector for stocks in the portfolio. The tree-map clearly shows that health care is the sector with the largest number of stocks in the portfolio, which is represented by the rectangle with the largest area.

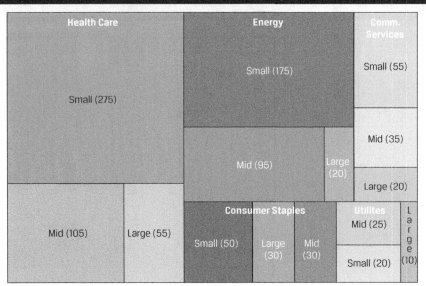

Note that this example also depicts one more categorical variable (i.e., level of market capitalization). The tree-map can represent data with additional dimensions by displaying a set of nested rectangles. To show the joint frequencies of sub-groups by sector and level of market capitalization, as given in Exhibit 14, we can split each existing rectangle for sector into three sub-rectangles to represent small-cap, mid-cap, and large-cap stocks, respectively. In this case, the area of each nested rectangle would be proportional to the number of stocks in each market capitalization sub-group. The exhibit clearly shows that small-cap health care is the sub-group with the largest number of stocks. It is worth noting a caveat for using tree-maps: Tree-maps become difficult to read if the hierarchy involves more than three levels.

## Word Cloud

So far, we have shown how to visualize the frequency distribution of numerical data or categorical data. However, can we find a chart to depict the frequency of unstructured data—particularly, textual data? A **word cloud** (also known as **tag cloud**) is a visual device for representing textual data. A word cloud consists of words extracted from a source of textual data, with the size of each distinct word being proportional to the frequency with which it appears in the given text. Note that common words (e.g., "a," "it," "the") are generally stripped out to focus on key words that convey the most meaningful information. This format allows us to quickly perceive the most frequent terms among the given text to provide information about the nature of the text, including topic and whether or not the text conveys positive or negative news. Moreover, words conveying different sentiment may be displayed in different colors. For example, "profit" typically indicates positive sentiment so might be displayed in green, while "loss" typically indicates negative sentiment and may be shown in red.

Exhibit 24 is an excerpt from the Management's Discussion and Analysis (MDA) section of the 10-Q filing for QXR Inc. for the quarter ended 31 March 20XX. Taking this text, we can create a word cloud, as shown in Exhibit 25. A quick glance at the word cloud tells us that the following words stand out (i.e., they were used most frequently in the MDA text): "billion," "revenue," "year," "income," "growth," and "financial." Note that specific words, such as "income" and "growth," typically convey positive sentiment, as contrasted with such words as "loss" and "decline," which typically convey negative sentiment. In conclusion, word clouds are a useful tool for visualizing textual data that can facilitate understanding the topic of the text as well as the sentiment it may convey.

> **Exhibit 24: Excerpt of MDA Section in Form 10-Q of QXR Inc. for Quarter Ended 31 March 20XX**

## MANAGEMENT'S DISCUSSION AND ANALYSIS OF FINANCIAL CONDITION AND RESULTS OF OPERATIONS

Please read the following discussion and analysis of our financial condition and results of operations together with our consolidated financial statements and related notes included under Part I, Item 1 of this Quarterly Report on Form 10-Q.

### Executive Overview of Results

Below are our key financial results for the three months ended March 31, 20XX (consolidated unless otherwise noted):

- Revenues of $36.3 billion and revenue growth of 17% year over year, constant currency revenue growth of 19% year over year.
- Major segment revenues of $36.2 billion with revenue growth of 17% year over year and other segments' revenues of $170 million with revenue growth of 13% year over year.
- Revenues from the United States, EMEA, APAC, and Other Americas were $16.5 billion, $11.8 billion, $6.1 billion, and $1.9 billion, respectively.
- Cost of revenues was $16.0 billion, consisting of TAC of $6.9 billion and other cost of revenues of $9.2 billion. Our TAC as a percentage of advertising revenues were 22%.
- Operating expenses (excluding cost of revenues) were $13.7 billion, including the EC AFS fine of $1.7 billion.
- Income from operations was $6.6 billion.
- Other income (expense), net, was $1.5 billion.
- Effective tax rate was 18%.
- Net income was $6.7 billion with diluted net income per share of $9.50.
- Operating cash flow was $12.0 billion.
- Capital expenditures were $4.6 billion.

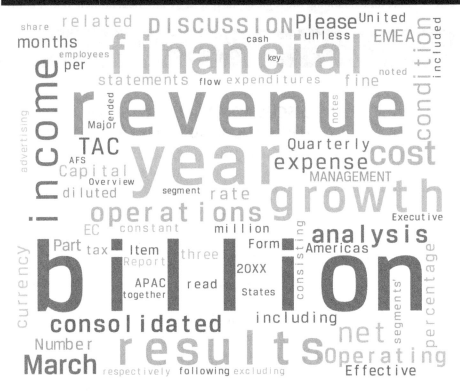

Exhibit 25: Word Cloud Visualizing Excerpted Text in MDA Section in Form 10-Q of QXR Inc.

## Line Chart

A **line chart** is a type of graph used to visualize ordered observations. Often a line chart is used to display the change of data series over time. Note that the frequency polygon in Exhibit 18 and the cumulative frequency distribution chart in Exhibit 19 are also line charts but are used particularly in those instances for representing data frequency distributions.

Constructing a line chart is relatively straightforward: We first plot all the data points against horizontal and vertical axes and then connect the points by straight line segments. For example, to show the 10-day daily closing prices of ABC Inc. stock presented in Exhibit 5, we first construct a chart with the $x$-axis representing time (in days) and the $y$-axis representing stock price (in dollars). Next, plot each closing price as points against both axes, and then use straight line segments to join the points together, as shown in Exhibit 26.

An important benefit of a line chart is that it facilitates showing changes in the data and underlying trends in a clear and concise way. This helps to understand the current data and also helps with forecasting the data series. In Exhibit 26, for example, it is easy to spot the price changes over the first 10 trading days since ABC's initial public offering (IPO). We see that the stock price peaked on Day 3 and then traded lower. Following a partial recovery on Day 7, it declined steeply to around $50 on Day 10. In contrast, although the one-dimensional data array table in Exhibit 5 displays the same values as the line chart, the data table by itself does not provide a quick snapshot of changes in the data or facilitate understanding underlying trends. This is why line charts are helpful for visualization, particularly in cases of large amounts of data (i.e., hundreds, or even thousands, of data points).

**Exhibit 26: Daily Closing Prices of ABC Inc.'s Stock and Its Sector Index**

A line chart is also capable of accommodating more than one set of data points, which is especially helpful for making comparisons. We can add a line to represent each group of data (e.g., a competitor's stock price or a sector index), and each line would have a distinct color or line pattern identified in a legend. For example, Exhibit 26 also includes a plot of ABC's sector index (i.e., the sector index for which ABC stock is a member, like health care or energy) over the same period. The sector index is displayed with its own distinct color to facilitate comparison. Note also that because the sector index has a different range (approximately 6,230 to 6,390) than ABCs' stock ($50 to $59 per share), we need a secondary $y$-axis to correctly display the sector index, which is on the right-hand side of the exhibit.

This comparison can help us understand whether ABC's stock price movement over the period is due to potential mispricing of its share issuance or instead due to industry-specific factors that also affect its competitors' stock prices. The comparison shows that over the period, the sector index moved in a nearly opposite trend versus ABC's stock price movement. This indicates that the steep decline in ABC's stock price is less likely attributable to sector-specific factors and more likely due to potential over-pricing of its IPO or to other company-specific factors.

When an observational unit (here, ABC Inc.) has more than two features (or variables) of interest, it would be useful to show the multi-dimensional data all in one chart to gain insights from a more holistic view. How can we add an additional dimension to a two-dimensional line chart? We can replace the data points with varying-sized bubbles to represent a third dimension of the data. Moreover, these bubbles may even be color-coded to present additional information. This version of a line chart is called a **bubble line chart**.

Exhibit 7, for example, presented three types of quarterly data for ABC Inc. for use in a valuation analysis. We would like to plot two of them, revenue and earnings per share (EPS), over the two-year period. As shown in Exhibit 27, with the $x$-axis representing time (i.e., quarters) and the $y$-axis representing revenue in millions of dollars, we can plot the revenue data points against both axes to form a typical line chart. Next, each marker representing a revenue data point is replaced by a circular bubble with its size proportional to the magnitude of the EPS in the corresponding quarter. Moreover, the bubbles are colored in a binary scheme with green representing profits and red representing losses. In this way, the bubble line chart reflects the changes for both revenue and EPS simultaneously, and it also shows whether the EPS represents a profit or a loss.

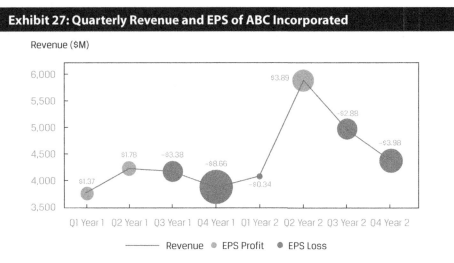

**Exhibit 27: Quarterly Revenue and EPS of ABC Incorporated**

As depicted, ABC's earnings were quite volatile during its initial two years as a public company. Earnings started off as a profit of $1.37/share but finished the first year with a big loss of −$8.66/share, during which time revenue experienced only small fluctuations. Furthermore, while revenues and earnings both subsequently recovered sharply—peaking in Q2 of Year 2—revenues then declined, and the company returned to significant losses (−3.98/share) by the end of Year 2.

## Scatter Plot

A **scatter plot** is a type of graph for visualizing the joint variation in two numerical variables. It is a useful tool for displaying and understanding potential relationships between the variables.

A scatter plot is constructed with the $x$-axis representing one variable and the $y$-axis representing the other variable. It uses dots to indicate the values of the two variables for a particular point in time, which are plotted against the corresponding axes. Suppose an analyst is investigating potential relationships between sector index returns and returns for the broad market, such as the S&P 500 Index. Specifically, he or she is interested in the relative performance of two sectors, information technology (IT) and utilities, compared to the market index over a specific five-year period. The analyst has obtained the sector and market index returns for each month over the five years under investigation and plotted the data points in the scatter plots, shown in Exhibit 28 for IT versus the S&P 500 returns and in Exhibit 29 for utilities versus the S&P 500 returns.

Despite their relatively straightforward construction, scatter plots convey lots of valuable information. First, it is important to inspect for any potential association between the two variables. The pattern of the scatter plot may indicate no apparent relationship, a linear association, or a non-linear relationship. A scatter plot with randomly distributed data points would indicate no clear association between the two variables. However, if the data points seem to align along a straight line, then there may exist a significant relationship among the variables. A positive (negative) slope for the line of data points indicates a positive (negative) association, *meaning the variables move in the same (opposite) direction.* Furthermore, the strength of the association can be determined by how closely the data points are clustered around the line. Tight (loose) clustering signals a potentially stronger (weaker) relationship.

**Exhibit 28: Scatter Plot of Information Technology Sector Index Return vs. S&P 500 Index Return**

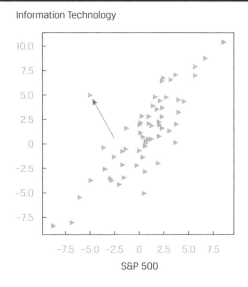

**Exhibit 29: Scatter Plot of Utilities Sector Index Return vs. S&P 500 Index Return**

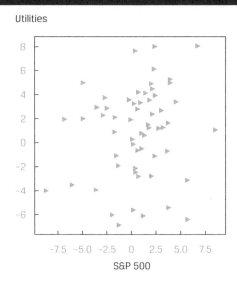

Examining Exhibit 28, we can see the returns of the IT sector are highly positively associated with S&P 500 Index returns because the data points are tightly clustered along a positively sloped line. Exhibit 29 tells a different story for relative performance of the utilities sector and S&P 500 index returns: The data points appear to be distributed in no discernable pattern, indicating no clear relationship among these variables. Second, observing the data points located toward the ends of each axis, which represent the maximum or minimum values, provides a quick sense of the data range. Third, assuming that a relationship among the variables is apparent, inspecting the scatter plot can help to spot extreme values (i.e., outliers). For example, an outlier data point is readily detected in Exhibit 28, as indicated by the arrow. As you will learn later in the CFA Program curriculum, finding these extreme values and handling them with appropriate measures is an important part of the financial modeling process.

Scatter plots are a powerful tool for finding patterns between two variables, for assessing data range, and for spotting extreme values. In practice, however, there are situations where we need to inspect for pairwise associations among many variables—for example, when conducting feature selection from dozens of variables to build a predictive model.

A **scatter plot matrix** is a useful tool for organizing scatter plots between pairs of variables, making it easy to inspect all pairwise relationships in one combined visual. For example, suppose the analyst would like to extend his or her investigation by adding another sector index. He or she can use a scatter plot matrix, as shown in Exhibit 30, which now incorporates four variables, including index returns for the S&P 500 and for three sectors: IT, utilities, and financials.

# Data Visualization

## Exhibit 30: Pairwise Scatter Plot Matrix

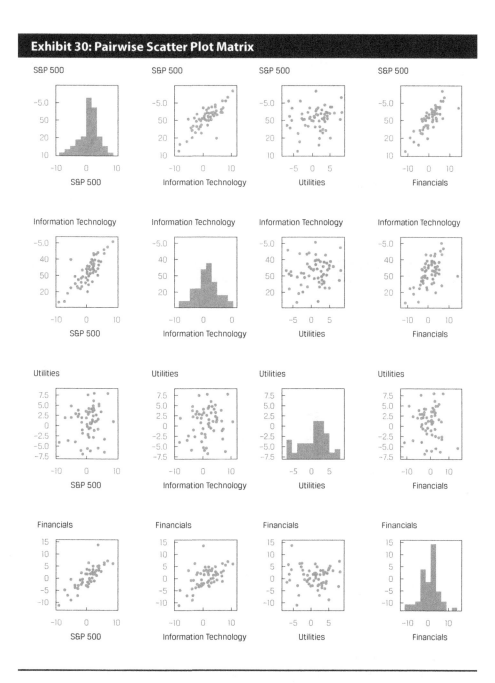

The scatter plot matrix contains each combination of bivariate scatter plot (i.e., S&P 500 vs. each sector, IT vs. utilities, IT vs. financials, and financials vs. utilities) as well as univariate frequency distribution histograms for each variable plotted along the diagonal. In this way, the scatter plot matrix provides a concise visual summary of each variable and of potential relationships among them. Importantly, the construction of the scatter plot matrix is typically a built-in function in most major statistical software packages, so it is relatively easy to implement. It is worth pointing out that the upper triangle of the matrix is the mirror image of the lower triangle, so the compact form of the scatter plot matrix that uses only the lower triangle is also appropriate.

With the addition of the financial sector, the bottom panel of Exhibit 30 reveals the following additional information, which can support sector allocation in the portfolio construction process:

- Strong positive relationship between returns of financials and the S&P 500;
- Positive relationship between returns of financials and IT; and

- No clear relationship between returns of financials and utilities.

It is important to note that despite their usefulness, scatter plots and scatter plot matrixes should not be considered as a substitute for robust statistical tests; rather, they should be used alongside such tests for best results.

## Heat Map

A **heat map** is a type of graphic that organizes and summarizes data in a tabular format and represents them using a color spectrum. For example, given a portfolio, we can create a contingency table that summarizes the joint frequencies of the stock holdings by sector and by level of market capitalization, as in Exhibit 31.

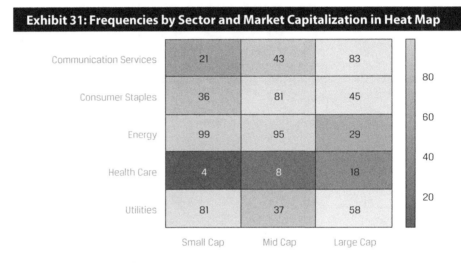

Cells in the chart are color-coded to differentiate high values from low values by using the color scheme defined in the color spectrum on the right side of the chart. As shown by the heat map, this portfolio has the largest exposure (in terms of number of stocks) to small- and mid-cap energy stocks. It has substantial exposures to large-cap communications services, mid-cap consumer staples, and small-cap utilities; however, exposure to the health care sector is limited. In sum, the heat map reveals this portfolio to be relatively well-diversified among sectors and market-cap levels. Besides their use in displaying frequency distributions, heat maps are commonly used for visualizing the degree of correlation among different variables. **Correlation** is a measure of the linear relationship between two random variables. This concept will be discussed in detail in the CFA Program curriculum.

### EXAMPLE 5

### Evaluating Data Visuals

1. You have a cumulative absolute frequency distribution graph (similar to the one in Exhibit 19) of daily returns over a five-year period for an index of Asian equity markets.

   Interpret the meaning of the slope of such a graph.

## Solution 1

The slope of the graph of a cumulative absolute frequency distribution reflects the change in the number of observations between two adjacent return bins. A steep (flat) slope indicates a large (small) change in the frequency of observations between adjacent return bins.

2. You are creating a word cloud for a visual representation of text on a company's quarterly earnings announcements over the past three years. The word cloud uses font size to indicate word frequency. This particular company has experienced both quarterly profits and losses during the period under investigation.

   Describe how the word cloud might be used to convey information besides word frequency.

## Solution 2

Color can add an additional dimension to the information conveyed in the word cloud. For example, red can be used for "losses" and other words conveying negative sentiment, and green can be used for "profit" and other words indicative of positive sentiment.

3. You are examining a scatter plot of monthly stock returns, similar to the one in Exhibit 28, for two technology companies: one is a hardware manufacturer, and the other is a software developer. The scatter plot shows a strong positive association among their returns.

   Describe what other information the scatter plot can provide.

## Solution 3

Besides the sign and degree of association of the stocks' returns, the scatter plot can provide a visual representation of whether the association is linear or non-linear, the maximum and minimum values for the return observations, and an indication of which observations may have extreme values (i.e., are potential outliers).

4. You are reading a vertical bar chart displaying the sales of a company over the past five years. The sales of the first four years seem nearly flat as the corresponding bars are nearly the same height, but the bar representing the sales of the most recent year is approximately three times as high as the other bars.

   Explain whether we can conclude that the sales of the fifth year tripled compared to sales in the earlier years.

## Solution 4

Typically, the heights of bars in a vertical bar chart are proportional to the values that they represent. However, if the graph is using a truncated $y$-axis (i.e., one that does not start at zero), then values are not accurately represented by the height of bars. Therefore, we need to examine the $y$-axis of the bar chart before concluding that sales in the fifth year were triple the sales of the prior years.

## Guide to Selecting among Visualization Types

We have introduced and discussed a variety of different visualization types that are regularly used in investment practice. When it comes to selecting a chart for visualizing data, the intended purpose is the key consideration: Is it for exploring and/or presenting distributions or relationships, or is it for making comparisons? Given your intended purpose, the best selection is typically the simplest visual that conveys the message or achieves the specific goal. Exhibit 32 presents a flow chart for facilitating selection among the visualization types we have discussed. Finally, note that some visualization types, such as bar chart and heat map, may be suitable for several different purposes.

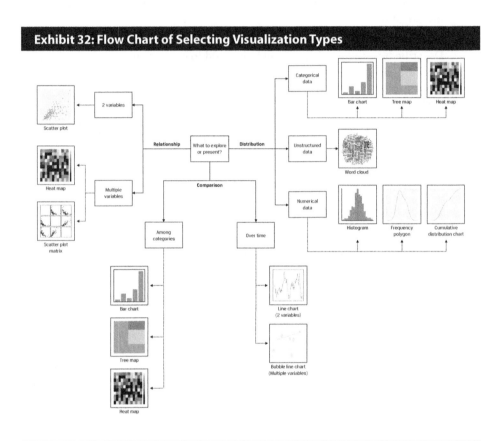

Exhibit 32: Flow Chart of Selecting Visualization Types

Data visualization is a powerful tool to show data and gain insights into data. However, we need to be cautious that a graph could be misleading if data are mispresented or the graph is poorly constructed. There are numerous different ways that may lead to a misleading graph. We list four typical pitfalls here that analysts should avoid.

First, an improper chart type is selected to present data, which would hinder the accurate interpretation of data. For example, to investigate the correlation between two data series, we can construct a scatter plot to visualize the joint variation between two variables. In contrast, plotting the two data series separately in a line chart would make it rather difficult to examine the relationship.

Second, data are selectively plotted in favor of the conclusion an analyst intends to draw. For example, data presented for an overly short time period may appear to show a trend that is actually noise—that is, variation within the data's normal range if examining the data over a longer time period. So, presenting data for too short a time window may mistakenly point to a non-existing trend.

Third, data are improperly plotted in a truncated graph that has a $y$-axis that does not start at zero. In some situations, the truncated graph can create the false impression of significant differences when there is actually only a small difference. For example, suppose a vertical bar chart is used to compare annual revenues of two companies, one with $9 billion and the other with $10 billion. If the $y$-axis starts at $8 billion, then the bar heights would inaccurately imply that the latter company's revenue is twice the former company's revenue.

Last, but not least, is the improper scaling of axes. For example, given a line chart, setting a higher than necessary maximum on the $y$-axis tends to compress the graph into an area close to the $x$-axis. This causes the graph to appear to be less steep and less volatile than if it was properly plotted. In sum, analysts need to avoid these misuses of visualization when charting data and must ensure the ethical use of data visuals.

**EXAMPLE 6**

## Selecting Visualization Types

1. A portfolio manager plans to buy several stocks traded on a small emerging market exchange but is concerned whether the market can provide sufficient liquidity to support her purchase order size. As the first step, she wants to analyze the daily trading volumes of one of these stocks over the past five years.

   Explain which type of chart can best provide a quick view of trading volume for the given period.

### Solution to 1

The five-year history of daily trading volumes contains a large amount of numerical data. Therefore, a histogram is the best chart for grouping these data into frequency distribution bins and for showing a quick snapshot of the shape, center, and spread of the data's distribution.

2. An analyst is building a model to predict stock market downturns. According to the academic literature and his practitioner knowledge and expertise, he has selected 10 variables as potential predictors. Before continuing to construct the model, the analyst would like to get a sense of how closely these variables are associated with the broad stock market index and whether any pair of variables are associated with each other.

   Describe the most appropriate visual to select for this purpose.

### Solution to 2

To inspect for a potential relationship between two variables, a scatter plot is a good choice. But with 10 variables, plotting individual scatter plots is not an efficient approach. Instead, utilizing a scatter plot matrix would give the analyst a good overview in one comprehensive visual of all the pairwise associations between the variables.

3. Central Bank members meet regularly to assess the economy and decide on any interest rate changes. Minutes of their meetings are published on the

Central Bank's website. A quantitative researcher wants to analyze the meeting minutes for use in building a model to predict future economic growth.

Explain which type of chart is most appropriate for creating an overview of the meeting minutes.

## Solution to 3

Since the meeting minutes consist of textual data, a word cloud would be the most suitable tool to visualize the textual data and facilitate the researcher's understanding of the topic of the text as well as the sentiment, positive or negative, it may convey.

4. A private investor wants to add a stock to her portfolio, so she asks her financial adviser to compare the three-year financial performances (by quarter) of two companies. One company experienced consistent revenue and earnings growth, while the other experienced volatile revenue and earnings growth, including quarterly losses.

   Describe the chart the adviser should use to best show these performance differences.

## Solution to 4

The best chart for making this comparison would be a bubble line chart using two different color lines to represent the quarterly revenues for each company. The bubble sizes would then indicate the magnitude of each company's quarterly earnings, with green bubbles signifying profits and red bubbles indicating losses.

# 7. MEASURES OF CENTRAL TENDENCY

- [ ] calculate and interpret measures of central tendency
- [ ] evaluate alternative definitions of mean to address an investment problem

So far, we have discussed methods we can use to organize and present data so that they are more understandable. The frequency distribution of an asset return series, for example, reveals much about the nature of the risks that investors may encounter in a particular asset. Although frequency distributions, histograms, and contingency tables provide a convenient way to summarize a series of observations, these methods are just a first step toward describing the data. In this section, we discuss the use of quantitative measures that explain characteristics of data. Our focus is on measures of central tendency and other measures of location. A **measure of central tendency** specifies where the data are centered. Measures of central tendency are probably more widely used than any other statistical measure because they can be computed and applied relatively easily. **Measures of location** include not only measures of central tendency but other measures that illustrate the location or distribution of data.

# Measures of Central Tendency

In the following subsections, we explain the common measures of central tendency—the arithmetic mean, the median, the mode, the weighted mean, the geometric mean, and the harmonic mean. We also explain other useful measures of location, including quartiles, quintiles, deciles, and percentiles.

A **statistic** is a summary measure of a set of observations, and descriptive statistics summarize the central tendency and spread variation in the distribution of data. If the statistic summarizes the set of all possible observations of a **population**, we refer to the statistic as a parameter. If the statistic summarizes a set of observations that is a subset of the population, we refer to the statistic as a **sample statistic**, often leaving off the word "sample" and simply referring to it as a statistic. While measures of central tendency and location can be calculated for populations and **samples**, our focus is on sample measures (i.e., sample statistics) as it is rare that an investment manager would be dealing with an entire population of data.

## The Arithmetic Mean

Analysts and portfolio managers often want one number that describes a representative possible outcome of an investment decision. The arithmetic mean is one of the most frequently used measures of the center of data.

> **Definition of Arithmetic Mean.** The **arithmetic mean** is the sum of the values of the observations divided by the number of observations.

### The Sample Mean

The sample mean is the arithmetic mean or arithmetic average computed for a sample. As you will see, we use the terms "mean" and "average" interchangeably. Often, we cannot observe every member of a population; instead, we observe a subset or sample of the population.

> **Sample Mean Formula.** The **sample mean** or average, $\bar{X}$ (read "X-bar"), is the arithmetic mean value of a sample:

$$\bar{X} = \frac{\sum_{i=1}^{n} X_i}{n}, \qquad (1)$$

> where $n$ is the number of observations in the sample.

Equation 1 tells us to sum the values of the observations ($X_i$) and divide the sum by the number of observations. For example, if a sample of market capitalizations for six publicly traded Australian companies contains the values (in AUD billions) 35, 30, 22, 18, 15, and 12, the sample mean market cap is 132/6 = A$22 billion. As previously noted, the sample mean is a statistic (that is, a descriptive measure of a sample).

Means can be computed for individual units or over time. For instance, the sample might be the return on equity (ROE) in a given year for a sample of 25 companies in the FTSE Eurotop 100, an index of Europe's 100 largest companies. In this case, we calculate the mean ROE in that year as an average across 25 individual units. When we examine the characteristics of some units at a specific point in time (such as ROE for the FTSE Eurotop 100), we are examining cross-sectional data; the mean of these observations is the cross-sectional mean. If the sample consists of the historical monthly returns on the FTSE Eurotop 100 for the past five years, however, then we have time-series data; the mean of these observations is the time-series mean. We will examine specialized statistical methods related to the behavior of time series in the reading on time-series analysis.

Except in cases of large datasets with many observations, we should not expect any of the actual observations to equal the mean; sample means provide only a summary of the data being analyzed. Also, although in some cases the number of values below the mean is quite close to the number of values above the mean, this need not be the case. As an analyst, you will often need to find a few numbers that describe the characteristics of the distribution, and we will consider more later. The mean is generally the statistic that you use as a measure of the typical outcome for a distribution. You can then use the mean to compare the performance of two different markets. For example, you might be interested in comparing the stock market performance of investments in Asia Pacific with investments in Europe. You can use the mean returns in these markets to compare investment results.

### EXAMPLE 7

### Calculating a Cross-Sectional Mean

1. Suppose we want to examine the performance of a sample of selected stock indexes from 11 different countries. The 52-week percentage change is reported in Exhibit 33 for Year 1, Year 2, and Year 3 for the sample of indexes.

**Exhibit 33: Annual Returns for Years 1 to 3 for Selected Countries' Stock Indexes**

| | 52-Week Return (%) | | |
|---|---|---|---|
| Index | Year 1 | Year 2 | Year 3 |
| Country A | −15.6 | −5.4 | 6.1 |
| Country B | 7.8 | 6.3 | −1.5 |
| Country C | 5.3 | 1.2 | 3.5 |
| Country D | −2.4 | −3.1 | 6.2 |
| Country E | −4.0 | −3.0 | 3.0 |
| Country F | 5.4 | 5.2 | −1.0 |
| Country G | 12.7 | 6.7 | −1.2 |
| Country H | 3.5 | 4.3 | 3.4 |
| Country I | 6.2 | 7.8 | 3.2 |
| Country J | 8.1 | 4.1 | −0.9 |
| Country K | 11.5 | 3.4 | 1.2 |

# Measures of Central Tendency

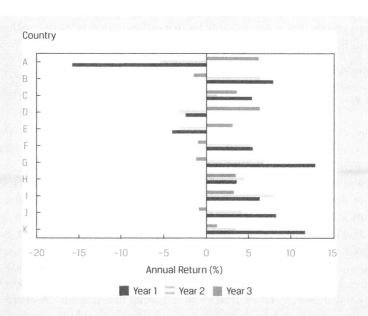

Using the data provided, calculate the sample mean return for the 11 indexes for each year.

## Solution:

For Year 3, the calculation applies Equation 1 to the returns for Year 3: (6.1 − 1.5 + 3.5 + 6.2 + 3.0 − 1.0 − 1.2 + 3.4 + 3.2 − 0.9 + 1.2)/11 = 22.0/11 = 2.0%. Using a similar calculation, the sample mean is 3.5% for Year 1 and 2.5% for Year 2.

### Properties of the Arithmetic Mean

The arithmetic mean can be likened to the center of gravity of an object. Exhibit 34 expresses this analogy graphically by plotting nine hypothetical observations on a bar. The nine observations are 2, 4, 4, 6, 10, 10, 12, 12, and 12; the arithmetic mean is 72/9 = 8. The observations are plotted on the bar with various heights based on their frequency (that is, 2 is one unit high, 4 is two units high, and so on). When the bar is placed on a fulcrum, it balances only when the fulcrum is located at the point on the scale that corresponds to the arithmetic mean.

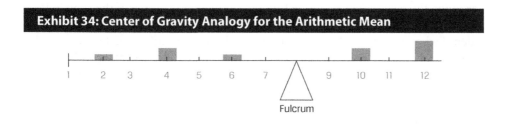

**Exhibit 34: Center of Gravity Analogy for the Arithmetic Mean**

As analysts, we often use the mean return as a measure of the typical outcome for an asset. As in Example 7, however, some outcomes are above the mean and some are below it. We can calculate the distance between the mean and each outcome, which is the deviation. Mathematically, it is always true that the sum of the deviations around the mean equals 0. We can see this by using the definition of the arithmetic mean shown in Equation 1, multiplying both sides of the equation by $n$: $n\bar{X} = \sum_{i=1}^{n} X_i$. The sum of the deviations from the mean is calculated as follows:

$$\sum_{i=1}^{n}(X_i - \bar{X}) = \sum_{i=1}^{n} X_i - \sum_{i=1}^{n} \bar{X} = \sum_{i=1}^{n} X_i - n\bar{X} = 0.$$

Deviations from the arithmetic mean are important information because they indicate risk. The concept of deviations around the mean forms the foundation for the more complex concepts of variance, skewness, and kurtosis.

Skewness measures the lack of symmetry in a distribution. A symmetric distribution of data has identical shape to the left and right of its mean point. A normal distribution is a symmetric distribution, is not skewed, and has a skewness of zero. Other distributions that may not be symmetric have different shapes around their mean point and have skewness different from zero. Negative skewness indicates that the data in the distribution is skewed left and positive skewness indicates that the distribution is skewed right. Kurtosis measures whether the distribution of the data is heavy-tailed or light-tailed relative to a normal distribution. A distribution with high kurtosis tends to have long tails, or outliers. A distribution with low kurtosis tends to have short tails, or a lack of outliers. We will address these concepts in depth in the curriculum.

A property and potential drawback of the arithmetic mean is its sensitivity to extreme values, or outliers. Because all observations are used to compute the mean and are given equal weight (i.e., importance), the arithmetic mean can be pulled sharply upward or downward by extremely large or small observations, respectively. For example, suppose we compute the arithmetic mean of the following seven numbers: 1, 2, 3, 4, 5, 6, and 1,000. The mean is 1,021/7 = 145.86, or approximately 146. Because the magnitude of the mean, 146, is so much larger than most of the observations (the first six), we might question how well it represents the location of the data. Perhaps the most common approach in such cases is to report the median, or middle value, in place of or in addition to the mean.

### Outliers

In practice, although an extreme value or outlier in a financial dataset may just represent a rare value in the population, it may also reflect an error in recording the value of an observation or an observation generated from a different population from that producing the other observations in the sample. In the latter two cases, in particular, the arithmetic mean could be misleading. So, what do we do? The first step is to examine the data, either by inspecting the sample observations if the sample is not too large or by using visualization approaches. Once we are comfortable that we have identified and eliminated errors (that is, we have "cleaned" the data), we can then address what to do with extreme values in the sample. When dealing with a sample that has extreme values, there may be a possibility of transforming the variable (e.g., a log transformation) or of selecting another variable that achieves the same purpose. However, if alternative model specifications or variable transformations are not possible, then here are three options for dealing with extreme values:

| | |
|---|---|
| Option 1 | Do nothing; use the data without any adjustment. |
| Option 2 | Delete all the outliers. |
| Option 3 | Replace the outliers with another value. |

The first option is appropriate if the values are legitimate, correct observations, and it is important to reflect the whole of the sample distribution. Outliers may contain meaningful information, so excluding or altering these values may reduce valuable information. Further, because identifying a data point as extreme leaves it up to the judgment of the analyst, leaving in all observations eliminates that need to judge a value as extreme.

The second option excludes the extreme observations. One measure of central tendency in this case is the **trimmed mean**, which is computed by excluding a stated small percentage of the lowest and highest values and then computing an arithmetic mean of the remaining values. For example, a 5% trimmed mean discards the lowest 2.5% and the highest 2.5% of values and computes the mean of the remaining 95% of values. A trimmed mean is used in sports competitions when judges' lowest and highest scores are discarded in computing a contestant's score.

The third option involves substituting values for the extreme values. A measure of central tendency in this case is the **winsorized mean**. It is calculated by assigning a stated percentage of the lowest values equal to one specified low value and a stated percentage of the highest values equal to one specified high value and then computing a mean from the restated data. For example, a 95% winsorized mean sets the bottom 2.5% of values equal to the value at or below which 2.5% of all the values lie (as will be seen shortly, this is called the "2.5th percentile" value) and the top 2.5% of values equal to the value at or below which 97.5% of all the values lie (the "97.5th percentile" value).

In Exhibit 35, we show the differences among these options for handling outliers using daily returns for the fictitious Euro-Asia-Africa (EAA) Equity Index in Exhibit 11.

### Exhibit 35: Handling Outliers: Daily Returns to an Index

Consider the fictitious EAA Equity Index. Using daily returns on the EAA Equity Index for the period of five years, consisting of 1,258 trading days, we can see the effect of trimming and winsorizing the data:

|  | Arithmetic Mean (%) | Trimmed Mean [Trimmed 5%] (%) | Winsorized Mean [95%] (%) |
|---|---|---|---|
| Mean | 0.035 | 0.048 | 0.038 |
| Number of Observations | 1,258 | 1,194 | 1,258 |

The trimmed mean eliminates the lowest 2.5% of returns, which in this sample is any daily return less than −1.934%, and it eliminates the highest 2.5%, which in this sample is any daily return greater than 1.671%. The result of this trimming is that the mean is calculated using 1,194 observations instead of the original sample's 1,258 observations.

The winsorized mean substitutes −1.934% for any return below −1.934 and substitutes 1.671% for any return above 1.671. The result in this case is that the trimmed and winsorized means are above the arithmetic mean.

## The Median

A second important measure of central tendency is the median.

> **Definition of Median.** The **median** is the value of the middle item of a set of items that has been sorted into ascending or descending order. In an odd-numbered sample of $n$ items, the median is the value of the item that

occupies the $(n + 1)/2$ position. In an even-numbered sample, we define the median as the mean of the values of items occupying the $n/2$ and $(n + 2)/2$ positions (the two middle items).

Suppose we have a return on assets (in %) for each of three companies: 0.0, 2.0, and 2.1. With an odd number of observations ($n = 3$), the median occupies the $(n + 1)/2 = 4/2 =$ 2nd position. The median is 2.0%. The value of 2.0% is the "middlemost" observation: One lies above it, and one lies below it. Whether we use the calculation for an even- or odd-numbered sample, an equal number of observations lie above and below the median. A distribution has only one median.

A potential advantage of the median is that, unlike the mean, extreme values do not affect it. For example, if a sample consists of the observations of 1, 2, 3, 4, 5, 6 and 1,000, the median is 4. The median is not influenced by the extremely large outcome of 1,000. In other words, the median is affected less by outliers than the mean and therefore is useful in describing data that follow a distribution that is not symmetric, such as revenues.

The median, however, does not use all the information about the size of the observations; it focuses only on the relative position of the ranked observations. Calculating the median may also be more complex. To do so, we need to order the observations from smallest to largest, determine whether the sample size is even or odd, and then on that basis, apply one of two calculations. Mathematicians express this disadvantage by saying that the median is less mathematically tractable than the mean.

We use the data from Exhibit 33 to demonstrate finding the median, reproduced in Exhibit 36 in ascending order of the return for Year 3, with the ranked position from 1 (lowest) to 11 (highest) indicated. Because this sample has 11 observations, the median is the value in the sorted array that occupies the $(11 + 1)/2 =$ 6th position. Country E's index occupies the sixth position and is the median. The arithmetic mean for Year 3 for this sample of indexes is 2.0%, whereas the median is 3.0%.

**Exhibit 36: Returns on Selected Country Stock Indexes for Year 3 in Ascending Order**

| Index | Year 3 Return (%) | Position |
|---|---|---|
| Country B | −1.5 | 1 |
| Country G | −1.2 | 2 |
| Country F | −1.0 | 3 |
| Country J | −0.9 | 4 |
| Country K | 1.2 | 5 |
| Country E | 3.0 ← | 6 |
| Country I | 3.2 | 7 |
| Country H | 3.4 | 8 |
| Country C | 3.5 | 9 |
| Country A | 6.1 | 10 |
| Country D | 6.2 | 11 |

# Measures of Central Tendency

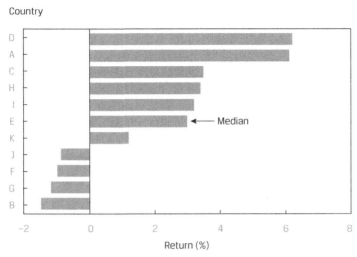

If a sample has an even number of observations, the median is the mean of the two values in the middle. For example, if our sample in Exhibit 36 had 12 indexes instead of 11, the median would be the mean of the values in the sorted array that occupy the sixth and the seventh positions.

## The Mode

The third important measure of central tendency is the mode.

> **Definition of Mode.** The **mode** is the most frequently occurring value in a distribution.

A distribution can have more than one mode, or even no mode. When a distribution has a single value that is most frequently occurring, the distribution is said to be **unimodal**. If a distribution has two most frequently occurring values, then it has two modes and is called **bimodal**. If the distribution has three most frequently occurring values, then it is **trimodal**. When all the values in a dataset are different, the distribution has no mode because no value occurs more frequently than any other value.

Stock return data and other data from continuous distributions may not have a modal outcome. When such data are grouped into bins, however, we often find an interval (possibly more than one) with the highest frequency: the **modal interval** (or intervals). Consider the frequency distribution of the daily returns for the EAA Equity Index over five years that we looked at in Exhibit 11. A histogram for the frequency distribution of these daily returns is shown in Exhibit 37. The modal interval always has the highest bar in the histogram; in this case, the modal interval is 0.0 to 0.9%, and this interval has 493 observations out of a total of 1,258 observations.

Notice that this histogram in Exhibit 37 looks slightly different from the one in Exhibit 11, since this one has 11 bins and follows the seven-step procedure exactly. Thus, the bin width is 0.828 [= (5.00 − −4.11)/11], and the first bin begins at the minimum value of −4.11%. It was noted previously that for ease of interpretation, in practice bin width is often rounded up to the nearest whole number; the first bin can start at the nearest whole number below the minimum value. These refinements and the use of 10 bins were incorporated into the histogram in Exhibit 11, which has a modal interval of 0.0% to 1.0%.

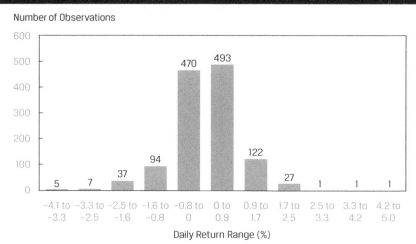

The mode is the only measure of central tendency that can be used with nominal data. For example, when we categorize investment funds into different styles and assign a number to each style, the mode of these categorized data is the most frequent investment fund style.

## Other Concepts of Mean

Earlier we explained the arithmetic mean, which is a fundamental concept for describing the central tendency of data. An advantage of the arithmetic mean over two other measures of central tendency, the median and mode, is that the mean uses all the information about the size of the observations. The mean is also relatively easy to work with mathematically.

However, other concepts of mean are very important in investments. In the following sections, we discuss such concepts.

### The Weighted Mean

The concept of weighted mean arises repeatedly in portfolio analysis. In the arithmetic mean, all sample observations are equally weighted by the factor $1/n$. In working with portfolios, we often need the more general concept of weighted mean to allow for different (i.e., unequal) weights on different observations.

To illustrate the weighted mean concept, an investment manager with $100 million to invest might allocate $70 million to equities and $30 million to bonds. The portfolio, therefore, has a weight of 0.70 on stocks and 0.30 on bonds. How do we calculate the return on this portfolio? The portfolio's return clearly involves an averaging of the returns on the stock and bond investments. The mean that we compute, however, must reflect the fact that stocks have a 70% weight in the portfolio and bonds have a 30% weight. The way to reflect this weighting is to multiply the return on the stock investment by 0.70 and the return on the bond investment by 0.30, then sum the two results. This sum is an example of a weighted mean. It would be incorrect to take an arithmetic mean of the return on the stock and bond investments, equally weighting the returns on the two asset classes.

**Weighted Mean Formula.** The **weighted mean** $\overline{X}_w$ (read "X-bar sub-w"), for a set of observations $X_1, X_2, \ldots, X_n$ with corresponding weights of $w_1, w_2, \ldots, w_n$, is computed as:

# Measures of Central Tendency

$$\overline{X}_w = \sum_{i=1}^{n} w_i X_i, \quad (2)$$

where the sum of the weights equals 1; that is, $\sum w_i = 1$.

In the context of portfolios, a positive weight represents an asset held long and a negative weight represents an asset held short.

The formula for the weighted mean can be compared to the formula for the arithmetic mean. For a set of observations $X_1, X_2, ..., X_n$, let the weights $w_1, w_2, ..., w_n$ all equal $1/n$. Under this assumption, the formula for the weighted mean is $(1/n) \sum_{i=1}^{n} X_i$. This is the formula for the arithmetic mean. Therefore, the arithmetic mean is a special case of the weighted mean in which all the weights are equal.

## EXAMPLE 8

### Calculating a Weighted Mean

1. Using the country index data shown in Exhibit 33, consider a portfolio that consists of three funds that track three countries' indexes: Country C, Country G, and Country K. The portfolio weights and index returns are as follows:

| Index Tracked by Fund | Allocation (%) | Annual Return (%) | | |
|---|---|---|---|---|
| | | Year 1 | Year 2 | Year 3 |
| Country C | 25% | 5.3 | 1.2 | 3.5 |
| Country G | 45% | 12.7 | 6.7 | −1.2 |
| Country K | 30% | 11.5 | 3.4 | 1.2 |

Using the information provided, calculate the returns on the portfolio for each year.

### Solution

Converting the percentage asset allocation to decimal form, we find the mean return as the weighted average of the funds' returns. We have:

Mean portfolio return for Year 1 = 0.25 (5.3) + 0.45 (12.7) + 0.30(11.5)
= 10.50%

Mean portfolio return for Year 2 = 0.25 (1.2) + 0.45 (6.7) + 0.30 (3.4)
= 4.34%

Mean portfolio return for Year 3 = 0.25 (3.5) + 0.45 (−1.2) + 0.30 (1.2)
= 0.70%

This example illustrates the general principle that a portfolio return is a weighted sum. Specifically, a portfolio's return is the weighted average of the returns on the assets in the portfolio; the weight applied to each asset's return is the fraction of the portfolio invested in that asset.

Market indexes are computed as weighted averages. For market-capitalization weighted indexes, such as the CAC-40 in France, the TOPIX in Japan, or the S&P 500 in the United States, each included stock receives a weight corresponding to its market value divided by the total market value of all stocks in the index.

Our illustrations of weighted mean use past data, but they might just as well use forward-looking data. When we take a weighted average of forward-looking data, the weighted mean is the expected value, which will be discussed in the CFA Program curriculum later. In all cases, the weights to be used are the probabilities, which must sum to 1, satisfying the condition on the weights in the expression for weighted mean, Equation 3.

### The Geometric Mean

The geometric mean is most frequently used to average rates of change over time or to compute the growth rate of a variable. In investments, we frequently use the geometric mean to either average a time series of rates of return on an asset or a portfolio or to compute the growth rate of a financial variable, such as earnings or sales. The geometric mean is defined by the following formula.

**Geometric Mean Formula.** The **geometric mean**, $\overline{X}_G$, of a set of observations $X_1, X_2, ..., X_n$ is:

$$\overline{X}_G = \sqrt[n]{X_1 X_2 X_3 ... X_n} \text{ with } X_i \geq 0 \text{ for } i = 1, 2, ..., n. \tag{3}$$

Equation 3 has a solution, and the geometric mean exists only if the product under the square root sign is non-negative. Therefore, we must impose the restriction that all the observations $X_i$ are greater than or equal to zero. We can solve for the geometric mean directly with any calculator that has an exponentiation key (on most calculators, $y^x$). We can also solve for the geometric mean using natural logarithms. Equation 3 can also be stated as

$$ln \overline{X}_G = \tfrac{1}{n} ln\left(X_1 X_2 X_3 ... X_n\right),$$

or, because the logarithm of a product of terms is equal to the sum of the logarithms of each of the terms, as

$$ln \overline{X}_G = \frac{\sum_{i=1}^{n} ln X_i}{n}.$$

When we have computed $ln \overline{X}_G$, then $\overline{X}_G = e^{ln \overline{X}_G}$ (on most calculators, the key for this step is $e^x$).

Risky assets can have negative returns up to –100% (if their price falls to zero), so we must take some care in defining the relevant variables to average in computing a geometric mean. We cannot just use the product of the returns for the sample and then take the $n$th root because the returns for any period could be negative. We must recast the returns to make them positive. We do this by adding 1.0 to the returns expressed as decimals, where $R_t$ represents the return in period $t$. The term $(1 + R_t)$ represents the year-ending value relative to an initial unit of investment at the beginning of the year. As long as we use $(1 + R_t)$, the observations will never be negative because the biggest negative return is –100%. The result is the geometric mean of $1 + R_t$; by then subtracting 1.0 from this result, we obtain the geometric mean of the individual returns $R_t$.

An equation that summarizes the calculation of the geometric mean return, $R_G$, is a slightly modified version of Equation 3 in which $X_i$ represents "1 + return in decimal form." Because geometric mean returns use time series, we use a subscript $t$ indexing time as well. We calculate one plus the geometric mean return as:

$$1 + R_G = \sqrt[T]{\left(1 + R_1\right)\left(1 + R_2\right) ... \left(1 + R_T\right)}.$$

We can represent this more compactly as:

$$1 + R_G = \left[\prod_{t=1}^{T}(1 + R_t)\right]^{\frac{1}{T}},$$

# Measures of Central Tendency

where the capital Greek letter 'pi,' Π, denotes the arithmetical operation of multiplication of the $T$ terms. Once we subtract one, this becomes the formula for the geometric mean return.

For example, the returns on Country B's index are given in Exhibit 33 as 7.8, 6.3, and −1.5%. Putting the returns into decimal form and adding 1.0 produces 1.078, 1.063, and 0.985. Using Equation 4, we have $\sqrt[3]{(1.078)(1.063)(0.985)} = \sqrt[3]{1.128725} = 1.041189$. This number is 1 plus the geometric mean rate of return. Subtracting 1.0 from this result, we have 1.041189 − 1.0 = 0.041189, or approximately 4.12%. This is lower than the arithmetic mean for County B's index of 4.2%.

> **Geometric Mean Return Formula.** Given a time series of holding period returns $R_t$, $t = 1, 2, ..., T$, the geometric mean return over the time period spanned by the returns $R_1$ through $R_T$ is:

$$R_G = \left[\prod_{t=1}^{T}(1+R_t)\right]^{\frac{1}{T}} - 1. \tag{4}$$

We can use Equation 5 to solve for the geometric mean return for any return data series. Geometric mean returns are also referred to as compound returns. If the returns being averaged in Equation 5 have a monthly frequency, for example, we may call the geometric mean monthly return the compound monthly return. The next example illustrates the computation of the geometric mean while contrasting the geometric and arithmetic means.

### EXAMPLE 9

### Geometric and Arithmetic Mean Returns

1. Using the data in Exhibit 33, calculate the arithmetic mean and the geometric mean returns over the three years for each of the three stock indexes: those of Country D, Country E, and Country F.

### Solution

The arithmetic mean returns calculations are:

|  | Annual Return (%) | | | Sum $\sum_{i=1}^{3} R_i$ | Arithmetic Mean |
|---|---|---|---|---|---|
|  | Year 1 | Year 2 | Year 3 |  |  |
| Country D | −2.4 | −3.1 | 6.2 | 0.7 | 0.233 |
| Country E | −4.0 | −3.0 | 3.0 | −4.0 | −1.333 |
| Country F | 5.4 | 5.2 | −1.0 | 9.6 | 3.200 |

Geometric mean returns calculations are:

|  | 1 + Return in Decimal Form $(1 + R_t)$ | | | $\prod_{t}^{T}(1+R_t)$ | 3rd root $\left[\prod_{t}^{3}(1+R_t)\right]^{\frac{1}{3}}$ | Geometric mean return (%) |
|---|---|---|---|---|---|---|
|  | Year 1 | Year 2 | Year 3 | | | |
| Country D | 0.976 | 0.969 | 1.062 | 1.00438 | 1.00146 | 0.146 |
| Country E | 0.960 | 0.970 | 1.030 | 0.95914 | 0.98619 | −1.381 |
| Country F | 1.054 | 1.052 | 0.990 | 1.09772 | 1.03157 | 3.157 |

In Example 9, the geometric mean return is less than the arithmetic mean return for each country's index returns. In fact, the geometric mean is always less than or equal to the arithmetic mean. The only time that the two means will be equal is when there is no variability in the observations—that is, when all the observations in the series are the same.

In general, the difference between the arithmetic and geometric means increases with the variability within the sample; the more disperse the observations, the greater the difference between the arithmetic and geometric means. Casual inspection of the returns in Exhibit 33 and the associated graph of means suggests a greater variability for Country A's index relative to the other indexes, and this is confirmed with the greater deviation of the geometric mean return (−5.38%) from the arithmetic mean return (−4.97%), as we show in Exhibit 38. How should the analyst interpret these results?

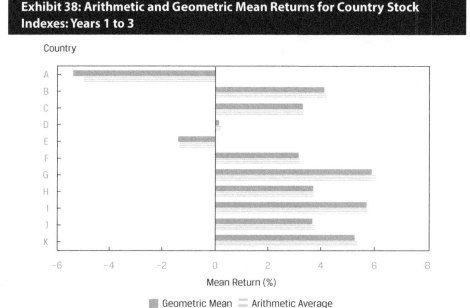

**Exhibit 38: Arithmetic and Geometric Mean Returns for Country Stock Indexes: Years 1 to 3**

The geometric mean return represents the growth rate or compound rate of return on an investment. One unit of currency invested in a fund tracking the Country B index at the beginning of Year 1 would have grown to $(1.078)(1.063)(0.985) = 1.128725$ units of currency, which is equal to 1 plus the geometric mean return compounded over three periods: $[1 + 0.041189]^3 = 1.128725$, confirming that the geometric mean is the compound rate of return. With its focus on the profitability of an investment over a multi-period horizon, the geometric mean is of key interest to investors. The arithmetic mean return, focusing on average single-period performance, is also of interest. Both arithmetic and geometric means have a role to play in investment management, and both are often reported for return series.

For reporting historical returns, the geometric mean has considerable appeal because it is the rate of growth or return we would have to earn each year to match the actual, cumulative investment performance. Suppose we purchased a stock for €100 and two years later it was worth €100, with an intervening year at €200. The geometric mean of 0% is clearly the compound rate of growth during the two years, which we can confirm by compounding the returns: $[(1 + 1.00)(1 - 0.50)]^{1/2} - 1 = 0\%$. Specifically, the ending amount is the beginning amount times $(1 + R_G)^2$. The geometric mean is an excellent measure of past performance.

The arithmetic mean, which is $[100\% + -50\%]/2 = 25\%$ in the above example, can distort our assessment of historical performance. As we noted previously, the arithmetic mean is always greater than or equal to the geometric mean. If we want to estimate the average return over a one-period horizon, we should use the arithmetic mean because the arithmetic mean is the average of one-period returns. If we want to estimate the average returns over more than one period, however, we should use the geometric mean of returns because the geometric mean captures how the total returns are linked over time.

Dispersion in cash flows or returns causes the arithmetic mean to be larger than the geometric mean. The more dispersion in the sample of returns, the more divergence exists between the arithmetic and geometric means. If there is zero variance in a sample of observations, the geometric and arithmetic returns are equal.

### *The Harmonic Mean*

The arithmetic mean, the weighted mean, and the geometric mean are the most frequently used concepts of mean in investments. A fourth concept, the **harmonic mean**, $\bar{X}_H$, is another measure of central tendency. The harmonic mean is appropriate in cases in which the variable is a rate or a ratio. The terminology "harmonic" arises from its use of a type of series involving reciprocals known as a harmonic series.

**Harmonic Mean Formula.** The harmonic mean of a set of observations $X_1$, $X_2$, ..., $X_n$ is:

$$\bar{X}_H = \frac{n}{\sum_{i=1}^{n}(1/X_i)} \text{ with } X_i > 0 \text{ for } i = 1, 2, ..., n. \tag{5}$$

The harmonic mean is the value obtained by summing the reciprocals of the observations—terms of the form $1/X_i$—then averaging that sum by dividing it by the number of observations $n$, and, finally, taking the reciprocal of the average.

The harmonic mean may be viewed as a special type of weighted mean in which an observation's weight is inversely proportional to its magnitude. For example, if there is a sample of observations of 1, 2, 3, 4, 5, 6, and 1,000, the harmonic mean is 2.8560. Compared to the arithmetic mean of 145.8571, we see the influence of the outlier (the 1,000) to be much less than in the case of the arithmetic mean. So, the harmonic mean is quite useful as a measure of central tendency in the presence of outliers.

The harmonic mean is used most often when the data consist of rates and ratios, such as P/Es. Suppose three peer companies have P/Es of 45, 15, and 15. The arithmetic mean is 25, but the harmonic mean, which gives less weight to the P/E of 45, is 19.3.

# EXAMPLE 10

## Harmonic Mean Returns and the Returns on Selected Country Stock Indexes

Using data in Exhibit 33, calculate the harmonic mean return over the 2016–2018 period for three stock indexes: Country D, Country E, and Country F.

| | Calculating the Harmonic Mean for the Indexes | | | | | |
|---|---|---|---|---|---|---|
| | Inverse of 1+ Return, or $(1 + X_i)$ where $X_i$ is the return in decimal form | | | | | |
| Index | Year 1 | Year 2 | Year 3 | $\sum_{i}^{n} 1/X_i$ | $\dfrac{n}{\sum_{i}^{n} 1/X_i}$ | Harmonic Mean (%) |
| Country D | 1.02459 | 1.03199 | 0.94162 | 2.99820 | 1.00060 | 0.05999 |
| Country E | 1.04167 | 1.03093 | 0.97087 | 3.04347 | 0.98572 | −1.42825 |
| Country F | 0.94877 | 0.95057 | 1.01010 | 2.90944 | 1.03113 | 3.11270 |

Comparing the three types of means, we see the arithmetic mean is higher than the geometric mean return, and the geometric mean return is higher than the harmonic mean return. We can see the differences in these means in the following graph:

## Harmonic, Geometric, and Arithmetic Means of Selected Country Indexes

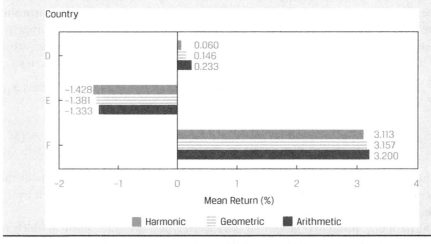

The harmonic mean is a relatively specialized concept of the mean that is appropriate for averaging ratios ("amount per unit") when the ratios are repeatedly applied to a fixed quantity to yield a variable number of units. The concept is best explained through an illustration. A well-known application arises in the investment strategy known as **cost averaging**, which involves the periodic investment of a fixed amount of money. In this application, the ratios we are averaging are prices per share at different purchase dates, and we are applying those prices to a constant amount of money to yield a variable number of shares. An illustration of the harmonic mean to cost averaging is provided in Example 11.

# Measures of Central Tendency

> **EXAMPLE 11**
>
> ## Cost Averaging and the Harmonic Mean
>
> 1. Suppose an investor purchases €1,000 of a security each month for $n = 2$ months. The share prices are €10 and €15 at the two purchase dates. What is the average price paid for the security?
>
> ### Solution:
>
> Purchase in the first month = €1,000/€10 = 100 shares
>
> Purchase in the second month = €1,000/€15 = 66.67 shares
>
> The purchases are 166.67 shares in total, and the price paid per share is €2,000/166.67 = €12.
>
> The average price paid is in fact the harmonic mean of the asset's prices at the purchase dates. Using Equation 6, the harmonic mean price is 2/[(1/10) + (1/15)] = €12. The value €12 is less than the arithmetic mean purchase price (€10 + €15)/2 = €12.5.
>
> However, we could find the correct value of €12 using the weighted mean formula, where the weights on the purchase prices equal the shares purchased at a given price as a proportion of the total shares purchased. In our example, the calculation would be (100/166.67)€10.00 + (66.67/166.67)€15.00 = €12. If we had invested varying amounts of money at each date, we could not use the harmonic mean formula. We could, however, still use the weighted mean formula.

Since they use the same data but involve different progressions in their respective calculations (that is, arithmetic, geometric, and harmonic progressions), the arithmetic, geometric, and harmonic means are mathematically related to one another. While we will not go into the proof of this relationship, the basic result follows:

Arithmetic mean × Harmonic mean = Geometric mean$^2$.

However, the key question is: Which mean to use in what circumstances?

> **EXAMPLE 12**
>
> ## Calculating the Arithmetic, Geometric, and Harmonic Means for P/Es
>
> Each year in December, a securities analyst selects her 10 favorite stocks for the next year. Exhibit 39 gives the P/E, the ratio of share price to projected earnings per share (EPS), for her top-10 stock picks for the next year.
>
> **Exhibit 39: Analyst's 10 Favorite Stocks for Next Year**
>
> | Stock | P/E |
> |---|---|
> | Stock 1 | 22.29 |
> | Stock 2 | 15.54 |
> | Stock 3 | 9.38 |
> | Stock 4 | 15.12 |
> | Stock 5 | 10.72 |

| Stock | P/E |
|---|---|
| Stock 6 | 14.57 |
| Stock 7 | 7.20 |
| Stock 8 | 7.97 |
| Stock 9 | 10.34 |
| Stock 10 | 8.35 |

For these 10 stocks,

1. Calculate the arithmetic mean P/E.

## Solution to 1:

The arithmetic mean is 121.48/10 = 12.1480.

2. Calculate the geometric mean P/E.

## Solution to 2:

The geometric mean is $e^{24.3613/10}$ = 11.4287.

3. Calculate the harmonic mean P/E.

## Solution to 3:

The harmonic mean is 10/0.9247 = 10.8142.

A mathematical fact concerning the harmonic, geometric, and arithmetic means is that unless all the observations in a dataset have the same value, the harmonic mean is less than the geometric mean, which, in turn, is less than the arithmetic mean. The choice of which mean to use depends on many factors, as we describe in Exhibit 40:

- Are there outliers that we want to include?
- Is the distribution symmetric?
- Is there compounding?
- Are there extreme outliers?

**Exhibit 40: Deciding Which Central Tendency Measure to Use**

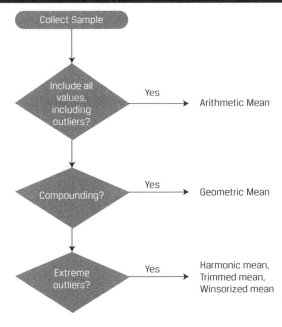

# QUANTILES

☐ calculate quantiles and interpret related visualizations

Having discussed measures of central tendency, we now examine an approach to describing the location of data that involves identifying values at or below which specified proportions of the data lie. For example, establishing that 25, 50, and 75% of the annual returns on a portfolio are at or below the values −0.05, 0.16, and 0.25, respectively, provides concise information about the distribution of portfolio returns. Statisticians use the word **quantile** (or **fractile**) as the most general term for a value at or below which a stated fraction of the data lies. In the following section, we describe the most commonly used quantiles—quartiles, quintiles, deciles, and percentiles—and their application in investments.

## Quartiles, Quintiles, Deciles, and Percentiles

We know that the median divides a distribution of data in half. We can define other dividing lines that split the distribution into smaller sizes. **Quartiles** divide the distribution into quarters, **quintiles** into fifths, **deciles** into tenths, and **percentiles** into hundredths. Given a set of observations, the $y$th percentile is the value at or below which $y$% of observations lie. Percentiles are used frequently, and the other measures can be defined with respect to them. For example, the first quartile ($Q_1$) divides a distribution such that 25% of the observations lie at or below it; therefore, the first quartile is also the 25th percentile. The second quartile ($Q_2$) represents the

50th percentile, and the third quartile ($Q_3$) represents the 75th percentile (i.e., 75% of the observations lie at or below it). The **interquartile range** (IQR) is the difference between the third quartile and the first quartile, or IQR = $Q_3 - Q_1$.

When dealing with actual data, we often find that we need to approximate the value of a percentile. For example, if we are interested in the value of the 75th percentile, we may find that no observation divides the sample such that exactly 75% of the observations lie at or below that value. The following procedure, however, can help us determine or estimate a percentile. The procedure involves first locating the position of the percentile within the set of observations and then determining (or estimating) the value associated with that position.

Let $P_y$ be the value at or below which $y\%$ of the distribution lies, or the $y$th percentile. (For example, $P_{18}$ is the point at or below which 18% of the observations lie; this implies that $100 - 18 = 82\%$ of the observations are greater than $P_{18}$.) The formula for the position (or location) of a percentile in an array with $n$ entries sorted in ascending order is:

$$L_y = (n+1)\frac{y}{100}, \qquad (6)$$

where $y$ is the percentage point at which we are dividing the distribution, and $L_y$ is the location ($L$) of the percentile ($P_y$) in the array sorted in ascending order. The value of $L_y$ may or may not be a whole number. In general, as the sample size increases, the percentile location calculation becomes more accurate; in small samples it may be quite approximate.

To summarize:

- When the location, $L_y$, is a whole number, the location corresponds to an actual observation. For example, if we are determining the third quartile ($Q_3$) in a sample of size $n = 11$, then $L_y$ would be $L_{75} = (11 + 1)(75/100) = 9$, and the third quartile would be $P_{75} = X_9$, where $X_i$ is defined as the value of the observation in the $i$th ($i = L_{75}$, so 9th), position of the data sorted in ascending order.

- When $L_y$ is not a whole number or integer, $L_y$ lies between the two closest integer numbers (one above and one below), and we use **linear interpolation** between those two places to determine $P_y$. Interpolation means estimating an unknown value on the basis of two known values that surround it (i.e., lie above and below it); the term "linear" refers to a straight-line estimate.

Example 13 illustrates the calculation of various quantiles for the daily return on the EAA Equity Index.

### EXAMPLE 13

### Percentiles, Quintiles, and Quartiles for the EAA Equity Index

Using the daily returns on the fictitious EAA Equity Index over five years and ranking them by return, from lowest to highest daily return, we show the return bins from 1 (the lowest 5%) to 20 (the highest 5%) as follows:

## Exhibit 41: EAA Equity Index Daily Returns Grouped by Size of Return

| Bin | Cumulative Percentage of Sample Trading Days (%) | Daily Return (%) Between* | | Number of Observations |
|---|---|---|---|---|
| | | Lower Bound | Upper Bound | |
| 1 | 5 | −4.108 | −1.416 | 63 |
| 2 | 10 | −1.416 | −0.876 | 63 |
| 3 | 15 | −0.876 | −0.629 | 63 |
| 4 | 20 | −0.629 | −0.432 | 63 |
| 5 | 25 | −0.432 | −0.293 | 63 |
| 6 | 30 | −0.293 | −0.193 | 63 |
| 7 | 35 | −0.193 | −0.124 | 62 |
| 8 | 40 | −0.124 | −0.070 | 63 |
| 9 | 45 | −0.070 | −0.007 | 63 |
| 10 | 50 | −0.007 | 0.044 | 63 |
| 11 | 55 | 0.044 | 0.108 | 63 |
| 12 | 60 | 0.108 | 0.173 | 63 |
| 13 | 65 | 0.173 | 0.247 | 63 |
| 14 | 70 | 0.247 | 0.343 | 62 |
| 15 | 75 | 0.343 | 0.460 | 63 |
| 16 | 80 | 0.460 | 0.575 | 63 |
| 17 | 85 | 0.575 | 0.738 | 63 |
| 18 | 90 | 0.738 | 0.991 | 63 |
| 19 | 95 | 0.991 | 1.304 | 63 |
| 20 | 100 | 1.304 | 5.001 | 63 |

Note that because of the continuous nature of returns, it is not likely for a return to fall on the boundary for any bin other than the minimum (Bin = 1) and maximum (Bin = 20).

1. Identify the 10th and 90th percentiles.

## Solution to 1

The 10th and 90th percentiles correspond to the bins or ranked returns that include 10% and 90% of the daily returns, respectively. The 10th percentile corresponds to the return of −0.876% (and includes returns of that much and lower), and the 90th percentile corresponds to the return of 0.991% (and lower).

2. Identify the first, second, and third quintiles.

## Solution to 2

The first quintile corresponds to the lowest 20% of the ranked data, or −0.432% (and lower).

The second quintile corresponds to the lowest 40% of the ranked data, or −0.070% (and lower).

The third quintile corresponds to the lowest 60% of the ranked data, or 0.173% (and lower).

3. Identify the first and third quartiles.

## Solution to 3

The first quartile corresponds to the lowest 25% of the ranked data, or −0.293% (and lower).

The third quartile corresponds to the lowest 75% of the ranked data, or 0.460% (and lower).

4. Identify the median.

## Solution to 4

The median is the return for which 50% of the data lies on either side, which is 0.044%, the highest daily return in the 10th bin out of 20.

5. Calculate the interquartile range.

## Solution to 5

The interquartile range is the difference between the third and first quartiles, 0.460% and −0.293%, or 0.753%.

One way to visualize the dispersion of data across quartiles is to use a diagram, such as a box and whisker chart. A **box and whisker plot** consists of a "box" with "whiskers" connected to the box, as shown in Exhibit 42. The "box" represents the lower bound of the second quartile and the upper bound of the third quartile, with the median or arithmetic average noted as a measure of central tendency of the entire distribution. The whiskers are the lines that run from the box and are bounded by the "fences," which represent the lowest and highest values of the distribution.

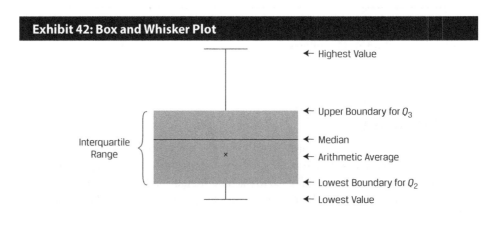

**Exhibit 42: Box and Whisker Plot**

There are several variations for box and whisker displays. For example, for ease in detecting potential outliers, the fences of the whiskers may be a function of the interquartile range instead of the highest and lowest values like that in Exhibit 42.

In Exhibit 42, visually, the interquartile range is the height of the box and the fences are set at extremes. But another form of box and whisker plot typically uses 1.5 times the interquartile range for the fences. Thus, the upper fence is 1.5 times the

# Quantiles

interquartile range added to the upper bound of $Q_3$, and the lower fence is 1.5 times the interquartile range subtracted from the lower bound of $Q_2$. Observations beyond the fences (i.e., outliers) may also be displayed.

We can see the role of outliers in such a box and whisker plot using the EAA Equity Index daily returns, as shown in Exhibit 43. Referring back to Exhibit 41 (Example 13), we know:

- The maximum and minimum values of the distribution are 5.001 and −4.108, respectively, while the median (50th percentile) value is 0.044.
- The interquartile range is 0.753 [= 0.460 − (−0.293)], and when multiplied by 1.5 and added to the $Q_3$ upper bound of 0.460 gives an upper fence of 1.589 [= (1.5 × 0.753) + 0.460].
- The lower fence is determined in a similar manner, using the $Q_2$ lower bound, to be −1.422 [= −(1.5 × 0.753) + (−0.293)].

As noted, any observation above (below) the upper (lower) fence is deemed to be an outlier.

**Exhibit 43: Box and Whisker Chart for EAA Equity Index Daily Returns**

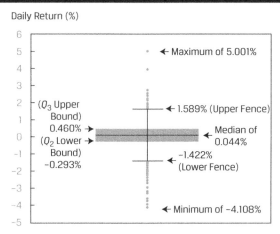

## EXAMPLE 14

### Quantiles

Consider the results of an analysis focusing on the market capitalizations of a sample of 100 firms:

| Bin | Cumulative Percentage of Sample (%) | Market Capitalization (in billions of €) | | Number of Observations |
|---|---|---|---|---|
| | | Lower Bound | Upper Bound | |
| 1 | 5 | 0.28 | 15.45 | 5 |
| 2 | 10 | 15.45 | 21.22 | 5 |
| 3 | 15 | 21.22 | 29.37 | 5 |
| 4 | 20 | 29.37 | 32.57 | 5 |
| 5 | 25 | 32.57 | 34.72 | 5 |

| Bin | Cumulative Percentage of Sample (%) | Market Capitalization (in billions of €) | | Number of Observations |
|---|---|---|---|---|
| | | Lower Bound | Upper Bound | |
| 6 | 30 | 34.72 | 37.58 | 5 |
| 7 | 35 | 37.58 | 39.90 | 5 |
| 8 | 40 | 39.90 | 41.57 | 5 |
| 9 | 45 | 41.57 | 44.86 | 5 |
| 10 | 50 | 44.86 | 46.88 | 5 |
| 11 | 55 | 46.88 | 49.40 | 5 |
| 12 | 60 | 49.40 | 51.27 | 5 |
| 13 | 65 | 51.27 | 53.58 | 5 |
| 14 | 70 | 53.58 | 56.66 | 5 |
| 15 | 75 | 56.66 | 58.34 | 5 |
| 16 | 80 | 58.34 | 63.10 | 5 |
| 17 | 85 | 63.10 | 67.06 | 5 |
| 18 | 90 | 67.06 | 73.00 | 5 |
| 19 | 95 | 73.00 | 81.62 | 5 |
| 20 | 100 | 81.62 | 96.85 | 5 |

Using this information, answer the following five questions.

1. The tenth percentile corresponds to observations in bin(s):

    A. 2.

    B. 1 and 2.

    C. 19 and 20.

## Solution to 1

B is correct because the tenth percentile corresponds to the lowest 10% of the observations in the sample, which are in bins 1 and 2.

2. The second quintile corresponds to observations in bin(s):

    A. 8

    B. 5, 6, 7, and 8.

    C. 6, 7, 8, 9, and 10.

## Solution to 2

B is correct because the second quintile corresponds to the second 20% of observations. The first 20% consists of bins 1 through 4. The second 20% of observations consists of bins 5 through 8.

3. The fourth quartile corresponds to observations in bin(s):

    A. 17.

    B. 17, 18, 19, and 20.

    C. 16, 17, 18, 19, and 20.

### Solution to 3

C is correct because a quartile consists of 25% of the data, and the last 25% of the 20 bins are 16 through 20.

4. The median is *closest* to:

    A. 44.86.
    B. 46.88.
    C. 49.40.

### Solution to 4

B is correct because this is the center of the 20 bins. The market capitalization of 46.88 is the highest value of the 10th bin and the lowest value of the 11th bin.

5. The interquartile range is *closest* to:

    A. 20.76.
    B. 23.62.
    C. 25.52.

### Solution to 5

B is correct because the interquartile range is the difference between the lowest value in the second quartile and the highest value in the third quartile. The lowest value of the second quartile is 34.72, and the highest value of the third quartile is 58.34. Therefore, the interquartile range is 58.34 − 34.72 = 23.62.

## Quantiles in Investment Practice

In this section, we briefly discuss the use of quantiles in investments. Quantiles are used in portfolio performance evaluation as well as in investment strategy development and research.

Investment analysts use quantiles every day to rank performance—for example, the performance of portfolios. The performance of investment managers is often characterized in terms of the percentile or quartile in which they fall relative to the performance of their peer group of managers. The Morningstar investment fund star rankings, for example, associate the number of stars with percentiles of performance relative to similar-style investment funds.

Another key use of quantiles is in investment research. For example, analysts often refer to the set of companies with returns falling below the 10th percentile cutoff point as the bottom return decile. Dividing data into quantiles based on some characteristic allows analysts to evaluate the impact of that characteristic on a quantity of interest. For instance, empirical finance studies commonly rank companies based on the market value of their equity and then sort them into deciles. The first decile contains the portfolio of those companies with the smallest market values, and the tenth decile contains those companies with the largest market values. Ranking companies by decile allows analysts to compare the performance of small companies with large ones.

## 9   MEASURES OF DISPERSION

☐ calculate and interpret measures of dispersion

Few would disagree with the importance of expected return or mean return in investments: The mean return tells us where returns, and investment results, are centered. To more completely understand an investment, however, we also need to know how returns are dispersed around the mean. **Dispersion** is the variability around the central tendency. If mean return addresses reward, then dispersion addresses risk.

In this section, we examine the most common measures of dispersion: range, mean absolute deviation, variance, and standard deviation. These are all measures of **absolute dispersion**. Absolute dispersion is the amount of variability present without comparison to any reference point or benchmark.

These measures are used throughout investment practice. The variance or standard deviation of return is often used as a measure of risk pioneered by Nobel laureate Harry Markowitz. Other measures of dispersion, mean absolute deviation and range, are also useful in analyzing data.

### The Range

We encountered range earlier when we discussed the construction of frequency distributions. It is the simplest of all the measures of dispersion.

> **Definition of Range.** The **range** is the difference between the maximum and minimum values in a dataset:

$$\text{Range} = \text{Maximum value} - \text{Minimum value}. \tag{7}$$

As an illustration of range, consider Exhibit 33, our example of annual returns for countries' stock indexes. The range of returns for Year 1 is the difference between the returns of Country G's index and Country A's index, or 12.7 − (−15.6) = 28.3%. The range of returns for Year 3 is the difference between the returns for the Country D index and the Country B index, or 6.2 − (−1.5) = 7.7%.

An alternative definition of range specifically reports the maximum and minimum values. This alternative definition provides more information than does the range as defined in Equation 7. In other words, in the above-mentioned case for Year 1, the range is reported as "from 12.7% to −15.6%."

One advantage of the range is ease of computation. A disadvantage is that the range uses only two pieces of information from the distribution. It cannot tell us how the data are distributed (that is, the shape of the distribution). Because the range is the difference between the maximum and minimum returns, it can reflect extremely large or small outcomes that may not be representative of the distribution.

### The Mean Absolute Deviation

Measures of dispersion can be computed using all the observations in the distribution rather than just the highest and lowest. But how should we measure dispersion? Our previous discussion on properties of the arithmetic mean introduced the notion of distance or deviation from the mean $(X_i - \overline{X})$ as a fundamental piece of information used in statistics. We could compute measures of dispersion as the arithmetic average of the deviations around the mean, but we would encounter a problem: The deviations

# Measures of Dispersion

around the mean always sum to 0. If we computed the mean of the deviations, the result would also equal 0. Therefore, we need to find a way to address the problem of negative deviations canceling out positive deviations.

One solution is to examine the absolute deviations around the mean as in the **mean absolute deviation**. This is also known as the average absolute deviation.

**Mean Absolute Deviation Formula.** The mean absolute deviation (MAD) for a sample is:

$$\text{MAD} = \frac{\sum_{i=1}^{n}|X_i - \bar{X}|}{n}, \tag{8}$$

where $\bar{X}$ is the sample mean, $n$ is the number of observations in the sample, and the $|\ |$ indicate the absolute value of what is contained within these bars.

In calculating MAD, we ignore the signs of the deviations around the mean. For example, if $X_i = -11.0$ and $\bar{X} = 4.5$, the absolute value of the difference is $|-11.0 - 4.5| = |-15.5| = 15.5$. The mean absolute deviation uses all of the observations in the sample and is thus superior to the range as a measure of dispersion. One technical drawback of MAD is that it is difficult to manipulate mathematically compared with the next measure we will introduce, sample variance. Example 15 illustrates the use of the range and the mean absolute deviation in evaluating risk.

## EXAMPLE 15

## Mean Absolute Deviation for Selected Countries' Stock Index Returns

1. Using the country stock index returns in Exhibit 33, calculate the mean absolute deviation of the index returns for each year. Note the sample mean returns ($\bar{X}$) are 3.5%, 2.5%, and 2.0% for Years 1, 2, and 3, respectively.

### Solution

| | Absolute Value of Deviation from the Mean $|X_i - \bar{X}|$ | | |
|---|---|---|---|
| | Year 1 | Year 2 | Year 3 |
| Country A | 19.1 | 7.9 | 4.1 |
| Country B | 4.3 | 3.8 | 3.5 |
| Country C | 1.8 | 1.3 | 1.5 |
| Country D | 5.9 | 5.6 | 4.2 |
| Country E | 7.5 | 5.5 | 1.0 |
| Country F | 1.9 | 2.7 | 3.0 |
| Country G | 9.2 | 4.2 | 3.2 |
| Country H | 0.0 | 1.8 | 1.4 |
| Country I | 2.7 | 5.3 | 1.2 |
| Country J | 4.6 | 1.6 | 2.9 |
| Country K | 8.0 | 0.9 | 0.8 |
| Sum | 65.0 | 40.6 | 26.8 |

|  | Absolute Value of Deviation from the Mean $\|X_i - \bar{X}\|$ | | |
| --- | --- | --- | --- |
|  | Year 1 | Year 2 | Year 3 |
| MAD | 5.91 | 3.69 | 2.44 |

For Year 3, for example, the sum of the absolute deviations from the arithmetic mean ($\bar{X}$ = 2.0) is 26.8. We divide this by 11, with the resulting MAD of 2.44.

## Sample Variance and Sample Standard Deviation

The mean absolute deviation addressed the issue that the sum of deviations from the mean equals zero by taking the absolute value of the deviations. A second approach to the treatment of deviations is to square them. The variance and standard deviation, which are based on squared deviations, are the two most widely used measures of dispersion. **Variance** is defined as the average of the squared deviations around the mean. **Standard deviation** is the positive square root of the variance. The following discussion addresses the calculation and use of variance and standard deviation.

### Sample Variance

In investments, we often do not know the mean of a population of interest, usually because we cannot practically identify or take measurements from each member of the population. We then estimate the population mean using the mean from a sample drawn from the population, and we calculate a sample variance or standard deviation.

**Sample Variance Formula.** The **sample variance**, $s^2$, is:

$$s^2 = \frac{\sum_{i=1}^{n}(X_i - \bar{X})^2}{n-1}, \tag{9}$$

where $\bar{X}$ is the sample mean and $n$ is the number of observations in the sample.

Given knowledge of the sample mean, we can use Equation 10 to calculate the sum of the squared differences from the mean, taking account of all $n$ items in the sample, and then to find the mean squared difference by dividing the sum by $n - 1$. Whether a difference from the mean is positive or negative, squaring that difference results in a positive number. Thus, variance takes care of the problem of negative deviations from the mean canceling out positive deviations by the operation of squaring those deviations.

For the sample variance, by dividing by the sample size minus 1 (or $n - 1$) rather than $n$, we improve the statistical properties of the sample variance. In statistical terms, the sample variance defined in Equation 10 is an unbiased estimator of the population variance (a concept covered later in the curriculum on sampling). The quantity $n - 1$ is also known as the number of degrees of freedom in estimating the population variance. To estimate the population variance with $s^2$, we must first calculate the sample mean, which itself is an estimated parameter. Therefore, once we have computed the sample mean, there are only $n - 1$ independent pieces of information from the sample; that is, if you know the sample mean and $n - 1$ of the observations, you could calculate the missing sample observation.

## Sample Standard Deviation

Because the variance is measured in squared units, we need a way to return to the original units. We can solve this problem by using standard deviation, the square root of the variance. Standard deviation is more easily interpreted than the variance because standard deviation is expressed in the same unit of measurement as the observations. By taking the square root, we return the values to the original unit of measurement. Suppose we have a sample with values in euros. Interpreting the standard deviation in euros is easier than interpreting the variance in squared euros.

**Sample Standard Deviation Formula.** The **sample standard deviation**, $s$, is:

$$s = \sqrt{\frac{\sum_{i=1}^{n}(X_i - \bar{X})^2}{n-1}}, \qquad (10)$$

where $\bar{X}$ is the sample mean and $n$ is the number of observations in the sample.

To calculate the sample standard deviation, we first compute the sample variance. We then take the square root of the sample variance. The steps for computing the sample variance and the standard deviation are provided in Exhibit 44.

### Exhibit 44: Steps to Calculate Sample Standard Deviation and Variance

| Step | Description | Notation |
|---|---|---|
| 1 | Calculate the sample mean | $\bar{X}$ |
| 2 | Calculate the deviations from the sample mean | $(X_i - \bar{X})$ |
| 3 | Calculate each observation's squared deviation from the sample mean | $(X_i - \bar{X})^2$ |
| 4 | Sum the squared deviations from the mean | $\sum_{i=1}^{n}(X_i - \bar{X})^2$ |
| 5 | Divide the sum of squared deviations from the mean by $n - 1$. This is the variance ($s^2$). | $\frac{\sum_{i=1}^{n}(X_i - \bar{X})^2}{n-1}$ |
| 6 | Take the square root of the sum of the squared deviations divided by $n - 1$. This is the standard deviation ($s$). | $\sqrt{\frac{\sum_{i=1}^{n}(X_i - \bar{X})^2}{n-1}}$ |

We illustrate the process of calculating the sample variance and standard deviation in Example 16 using the returns of the selected country stock indexes presented in Exhibit 33.

## EXAMPLE 16

### Calculating Sample Variance and Standard Deviation for Returns on Selected Country Stock Indexes

1. Using the sample information on country stock indexes in Exhibit 33, calculate the sample variance and standard deviation of the sample of index returns for Year 3.

### Solution

| Index | Sample Observation | Deviation from the Sample Mean | Squared Deviation |
|---|---|---|---|
| Country A | 6.1 | 4.1 | 16.810 |
| Country B | −1.5 | −3.5 | 12.250 |
| Country C | 3.5 | 1.5 | 2.250 |
| Country D | 6.2 | 4.2 | 17.640 |
| Country E | 3.0 | 1.0 | 1.000 |
| Country F | −1.0 | −3.0 | 9.000 |
| Country G | −1.2 | −3.2 | 10.240 |
| Country H | 3.4 | 1.4 | 1.960 |
| Country I | 3.2 | 1.2 | 1.440 |
| Country J | −0.9 | −2.9 | 8.410 |
| Country K | 1.2 | −0.8 | 0.640 |
| **Sum** | **22.0** | **0.0** | **81.640** |

Sample variance = 81.640/10 = 8.164
Sample standard deviation = $\sqrt{8.164}$ = 2.857

In addition to looking at the cross-sectional standard deviation as we did in Example 16, we could also calculate the standard deviation of a given country's returns across time (that is, the three years). Consider Country F, which has an arithmetic mean return of 3.2%. The sample standard deviation is calculated as:

$$\sqrt{\frac{(0.054 - 0.032)^2 + (0.052 - 0.032)^2 + (-0.01 - 0.032)^2}{2}}$$
$$= \sqrt{\frac{0.000484 + 0.000400 + 0.001764}{2}}$$
$$= \sqrt{0.001324}$$
$$= 3.6387\%.$$

Because the standard deviation is a measure of dispersion about the arithmetic mean, we usually present the arithmetic mean and standard deviation together when summarizing data. When we are dealing with data that represent a time series of percentage changes, presenting the geometric mean—representing the compound rate of growth—is also very helpful.

### *Dispersion and the Relationship between the Arithmetic and the Geometric Means*

We can use the sample standard deviation to help us understand the gap between the arithmetic mean and the geometric mean. The relation between the arithmetic mean ($\overline{X}$) and geometric mean ($\overline{X}_G$) is:

$$\overline{X}_G \approx \overline{X} - \frac{s^2}{2}.$$

In other words, the larger the variance of the sample, the wider the difference between the geometric mean and the arithmetic mean.

Using the data for Country F from Example 8, the geometric mean return is 3.1566%, the arithmetic mean return is 3.2%, and the factor $s^2/2$ is $0.001324/2 = 0.0662\%$:

$3.1566\% \approx 3.2\% - 0.0662\%$

$3.1566\% \approx 3.1338\%$.

This relation informs us that the more disperse or volatile the returns, the larger the gap between the geometric mean return and the arithmetic mean return.

# DOWNSIDE DEVIATION AND COEFFICIENT OF VARIATION

10

☐ calculate and interpret target downside deviation

An asset's variance or standard deviation of returns is often interpreted as a measure of the asset's risk. Variance and standard deviation of returns take account of returns above and below the mean, or upside and downside risks, respectively. However, investors are typically concerned only with **downside risk**—for example, returns below the mean or below some specified minimum target return. As a result, analysts have developed measures of downside risk.

In practice, we may be concerned with values of return (or another variable) below some level other than the mean. For example, if our return objective is 6.0% annually (our minimum acceptable return), then we may be concerned particularly with returns below 6.0% a year. The 6.0% is the target. The target downside deviation, also referred to as the **target semideviation**, is a measure of dispersion of the observations (here, returns) below the target. To calculate a sample target semideviation, we first specify the target. After identifying observations below the target, we find the sum of the squared negative deviations from the target, divide that sum by the total number of observations in the sample minus 1, and, finally, take the square root.

**Sample Target Semideviation Formula.** The target semideviation, $s_{Target}$, is:

$$s_{Target} = \sqrt{\sum_{\substack{\text{for all} X_i \leq B}}^{n} \frac{(X_i - B)^2}{n-1}}, \tag{11}$$

where $B$ is the target and $n$ is the total number of sample observations. We illustrate this in Example 17.

# EXAMPLE 17

## Calculating Target Downside Deviation

Suppose the monthly returns on a portfolio are as shown:

| Monthly Portfolio Returns | |
|---|---|
| Month | Return (%) |
| January | 5 |
| February | 3 |

| Month | Return (%) |
|---|---|
| March | −1 |
| April | −4 |
| May | 4 |
| June | 2 |
| July | 0 |
| August | 4 |
| September | 3 |
| October | 0 |
| November | 6 |
| December | 5 |

1. Calculate the target downside deviation when the target return is 3%.

## Solution to 1

| Month | Observation | Deviation from the 3% Target | Deviations below the Target | Squared Deviations below the Target |
|---|---|---|---|---|
| January | 5 | 2 | — | — |
| February | 3 | 0 | — | — |
| March | −1 | −4 | −4 | 16 |
| April | −4 | −7 | −7 | 49 |
| May | 4 | 1 | — | — |
| June | 2 | −1 | −1 | 1 |
| July | 0 | −3 | −3 | 9 |
| August | 4 | 1 | — | — |
| September | 3 | 0 | — | — |
| October | 0 | −3 | −3 | 9 |
| November | 6 | 3 | — | — |
| December | 5 | 2 | — | — |
| **Sum** | | | | **84** |

**Target semideviation** = $\sqrt{\frac{84}{11}}$ = 2.7634%

2. If the target return were 4%, would your answer be different from that for question 1? Without using calculations, explain how would it be different?

## Solution to 2

If the target return is higher, then the existing deviations would be larger and there would be several more values in the deviations and squared deviations below the target; so, the target semideviation would be larger.

How does the target downside deviation relate to the sample standard deviation? We illustrate the differences between the target downside deviation and the standard deviation in Example 18, using the data in Example 17.

# EXAMPLE 18

## Comparing the Target Downside Deviation with the Standard Deviation

1. Given the data in Example 17, calculate the sample standard deviation.

### Solution to 1

| Month | Observation | Deviation from the mean | Squared deviation |
|---|---|---|---|
| January | 5 | 2.75 | 7.5625 |
| February | 3 | 0.75 | 0.5625 |
| March | −1 | −3.25 | 10.5625 |
| April | −4 | −6.25 | 39.0625 |
| May | 4 | 1.75 | 3.0625 |
| June | 2 | −0.25 | 0.0625 |
| July | 0 | −2.25 | 5.0625 |
| August | 4 | 1.75 | 3.0625 |
| September | 3 | 0.75 | 0.5625 |
| October | 0 | −2.25 | 5.0625 |
| November | 6 | 3.75 | 14.0625 |
| December | 5 | 2.75 | 7.5625 |
| **Sum** | 27 | | 96.2500 |

The sample standard deviation is $\sqrt{\frac{96.2500}{11}} = 2.958\%$.

2. Given the data in Example 17, calculate the target downside deviation if the target is 2%.

### Solution to 2

| Month | Observation | Deviation from the 2% Target | Deviations below the Target | Squared Deviations below the Target |
|---|---|---|---|---|
| January | 5 | 3 | — | — |
| February | 3 | 1 | — | — |
| March | −1 | −3 | −3 | 9 |
| April | −4 | −6 | −6 | 36 |
| May | 4 | 2 | — | — |
| June | 2 | 0 | — | — |
| July | 0 | −2 | −2 | 4 |
| August | 4 | 2 | — | — |
| September | 3 | 1 | — | — |
| October | 0 | −2 | −2 | 4 |
| November | 6 | 4 | — | — |

| Month | Observation | Deviation from the 2% Target | Deviations below the Target | Squared Deviations below the Target |
|---|---|---|---|---|
| December | 5 | 3 | — | — |
| **Sum** | | | | 53 |

The target semideviation with 2% target = $\sqrt{\frac{53}{11}}$ = 2.195%.

3. Compare the standard deviation, the target downside deviation if the target is 2%, and the target downside deviation if the target is 3%.

### Solution to 3

The standard deviation is based on the deviation from the mean, which is 2.25%. The standard deviation includes all deviations from the mean, not just those below it. This results in a sample standard deviation of 2.958%.

Considering just the four observations below the 2% target, the target semideviation is 2.195%. It is less than the sample standard deviation since target semideviation captures only the downside risk (i.e., deviations below the target). Considering target semideviation with a 3% target, there are now five observations below 3%, so the target semideviation is higher, at 2.763%.

## Coefficient of Variation

We noted earlier that the standard deviation is more easily interpreted than variance because standard deviation uses the same units of measurement as the observations. We may sometimes find it difficult to interpret what standard deviation means in terms of the relative degree of variability of different sets of data, however, either because the datasets have markedly different means or because the datasets have different units of measurement. In this section, we explain a measure of relative dispersion, the coefficient of variation, that can be useful in such situations. **Relative dispersion** is the amount of dispersion relative to a reference value or benchmark.

The coefficient of variation is helpful in such situations as that just described (i.e., datasets with markedly different means or different units of measurement).

> **Coefficient of Variation Formula.** The **coefficient of variation**, CV, is the ratio of the standard deviation of a set of observations to their mean value:
>
> $$\text{CV} = s/\overline{X}, \tag{12}$$
>
> where $s$ is the sample standard deviation and $\overline{X}$ is the sample mean.

When the observations are returns, for example, the coefficient of variation measures the amount of risk (standard deviation) per unit of reward (mean return). An issue that may arise, especially when dealing with returns, is that if $\overline{X}$ is negative, the statistic is meaningless.

The CV may be stated as a multiple (e.g., 2 times) or as a percentage (e.g., 200%). Expressing the magnitude of variation among observations relative to their average size, the coefficient of variation permits direct comparisons of dispersion across different datasets. Reflecting the correction for scale, the coefficient of variation is a scale-free measure (that is, it has no units of measurement).

# Downside Deviation and Coefficient of Variation

We illustrate the usefulness of coefficient of variation for comparing datasets with markedly different standard deviations using two hypothetical samples of companies in Example 19.

## EXAMPLE 19

### Coefficient of Variation of Returns on Assets

Suppose an analyst collects the return on assets (in percentage terms) for ten companies for each of two industries:

| Company | Industry A | Industry B |
|---|---|---|
| 1 | −5 | −10 |
| 2 | −3 | −9 |
| 3 | −1 | −7 |
| 4 | 2 | −3 |
| 5 | 4 | 1 |
| 6 | 6 | 3 |
| 7 | 7 | 5 |
| 8 | 9 | 18 |
| 9 | 10 | 20 |
| 10 | 11 | 22 |

These data can be represented graphically as the following:

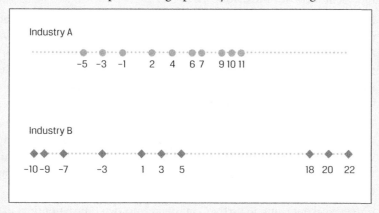

1. Calculate the average return on assets (ROA) for each industry.

### Solution to 1

The arithmetic mean for both industries is the sum divided by 10, or 40/10 = 4%.

2. Calculate the standard deviation of ROA for each industry.

### Solution to 2

The standard deviation using Equation 11 for Industry A is 5.60, and for Industry B the standard deviation is 12.12.

3. Calculate the coefficient of variation of ROA for each industry.

**Solution to 3**

The coefficient of variation for Industry A = 5.60/4 = 1.40.

The coefficient of variation for Industry B = 12.12/4 = 3.03.

Though the two industries have the same arithmetic mean ROA, the dispersion is different—with Industry B's returns on assets being much more disperse than those of Industry A. The coefficients of variation for these two industries reflects this, with Industry B having a larger coefficient of variation. The interpretation is that the risk per unit of mean return is more than two times (2.16 = 3.03/1.40) greater for Industry B compared to Industry A.

# SUMMARY

In this reading, we have presented tools and techniques for organizing, visualizing, and describing data that permit us to convert raw data into useful information for investment analysis.

- Data can be defined as a collection of numbers, characters, words, and text—as well as images, audio, and video—in a raw or organized format to represent facts or information.

- From a statistical perspective, data can be classified as numerical data and categorical data. Numerical data (also called quantitative data) are values that represent measured or counted quantities as a number. Categorical data (also called qualitative data) are values that describe a quality or characteristic of a group of observations and usually take only a limited number of values that are mutually exclusive.

- Numerical data can be further split into two types: continuous data and discrete data. Continuous data can be measured and can take on any numerical value in a specified range of values. Discrete data are numerical values that result from a counting process and therefore are limited to a finite number of values.

- Categorical data can be further classified into two types: nominal data and ordinal data. Nominal data are categorical values that are not amenable to being organized in a logical order, while ordinal data are categorical values that can be logically ordered or ranked.

- Based on how they are collected, data can be categorized into three types: cross-sectional, time series, and panel. Time-series data are a sequence of observations for a single observational unit on a specific variable collected over time and at discrete and typically equally spaced intervals of time. Cross-sectional data are a list of the observations of a specific variable from multiple observational units at a given point in time. Panel data are a mix of time-series and cross-sectional data that consists of observations through time on one or more variables for multiple observational units.

- Based on whether or not data are in a highly organized form, they can be classified into structured and unstructured types. Structured data are highly organized in a pre-defined manner, usually with repeating patterns.

- Unstructured data do not follow any conventionally organized forms; they are typically alternative data as they are usually collected from unconventional sources.
- Raw data are typically organized into either a one-dimensional array or a two-dimensional rectangular array (also called a data table) for quantitative analysis.
- A frequency distribution is a tabular display of data constructed either by counting the observations of a variable by distinct values or groups or by tallying the values of a numerical variable into a set of numerically ordered bins. Frequency distributions permit us to evaluate how data are distributed.
- The relative frequency of observations in a bin (interval or bucket) is the number of observations in the bin divided by the total number of observations. The cumulative relative frequency cumulates (adds up) the relative frequencies as we move from the first bin to the last, thus giving the fraction of the observations that are less than the upper limit of each bin.
- A contingency table is a tabular format that displays the frequency distributions of two or more categorical variables simultaneously. One application of contingency tables is for evaluating the performance of a classification model (using a confusion matrix).
- Visualization is the presentation of data in a pictorial or graphical format for the purpose of increasing understanding and for gaining insights into the data.
- A histogram is a bar chart of data that have been grouped into a frequency distribution. A frequency polygon is a graph of frequency distributions obtained by drawing straight lines joining successive midpoints of bars representing the class frequencies.
- A bar chart is used to plot the frequency distribution of categorical data, with each bar representing a distinct category and the bar's height (or length) proportional to the frequency of the corresponding category. Grouped bar charts or stacked bar charts can present the frequency distribution of multiple categorical variables simultaneously.
- A tree-map is a graphical tool to display categorical data. It consists of a set of colored rectangles to represent distinct groups, and the area of each rectangle is proportional to the value of the corresponding group. Additional dimensions of categorical data can be displayed by nested rectangles.
- A word cloud is a visual device for representing textual data, with the size of each distinct word being proportional to the frequency with which it appears in the given text.
- A line chart is a type of graph used to visualize ordered observations and often to display the change of data series over time. A bubble line chart is a special type of line chart that uses varying-sized bubbles as data points to represent an additional dimension of data.
- A scatter plot is a type of graph for visualizing the joint variation in two numerical variables. It is constructed by drawing dots to indicate the values of the two variables plotted against the corresponding axes. A scatter plot matrix organizes scatter plots between pairs of variables into a matrix format to inspect all pairwise relationships between more than two variables in one combined visual.

- A heat map is a type of graphic that organizes and summarizes data in a tabular format and represents it using a color spectrum. It is often used in displaying frequency distributions or visualizing the degree of correlation among different variables.
- The key consideration when selecting among chart types is the intended purpose of visualizing data (i.e., whether it is for exploring/presenting distributions or relationships or for making comparisons).
- A population is defined as all members of a specified group. A sample is a subset of a population.
- A parameter is any descriptive measure of a population. A sample statistic (statistic, for short) is a quantity computed from or used to describe a sample.
- Sample statistics—such as measures of central tendency, measures of dispersion, skewness, and kurtosis—help with investment analysis, particularly in making probabilistic statements about returns.
- Measures of central tendency specify where data are centered and include the mean, median, and mode (i.e., the most frequently occurring value).
- The arithmetic mean is the sum of the observations divided by the number of observations. It is the most frequently used measure of central tendency.
- The median is the value of the middle item (or the mean of the values of the two middle items) when the items in a set are sorted into ascending or descending order. The median is not influenced by extreme values and is most useful in the case of skewed distributions.
- The mode is the most frequently observed value and is the only measure of central tendency that can be used with nominal data. A distribution may be unimodal (one mode), bimodal (two modes), or trimodal (three modes) or have even more modes.
- A portfolio's return is a weighted mean return computed from the returns on the individual assets, where the weight applied to each asset's return is the fraction of the portfolio invested in that asset.
- The geometric mean, $\bar{X}_G$, of a set of observations $X_1, X_2, ..., X_n$, is $\bar{X}_G = \sqrt[n]{X_1 X_2 X_3 ... X_n}$, with $X_i \geq 0$ for $i = 1, 2, ..., n$. The geometric mean is especially important in reporting compound growth rates for time-series data. The geometric mean will always be less than an arithmetic mean whenever there is variance in the observations.
- The harmonic mean, $\bar{X}_H$, is a type of weighted mean in which an observation's weight is inversely proportional to its magnitude.
- Quantiles—such as the median, quartiles, quintiles, deciles, and percentiles—are location parameters that divide a distribution into halves, quarters, fifths, tenths, and hundredths, respectively.
- A box and whiskers plot illustrates the interquartile range (the "box") as well as a range outside of the box that is based on the interquartile range, indicated by the "whiskers."
- Dispersion measures—such as the range, mean absolute deviation (MAD), variance, standard deviation, target downside deviation, and coefficient of variation—describe the variability of outcomes around the arithmetic mean.
- The range is the difference between the maximum value and the minimum value of the dataset. The range has only a limited usefulness because it uses information from only two observations.

- The MAD for a sample is the average of the absolute deviations of observations from the mean, $\dfrac{\sum_{i=1}^{n} |X_i - \bar{X}|}{n}$, where $\bar{X}$ is the sample mean and $n$ is the number of observations in the sample.
- The variance is the average of the squared deviations around the mean, and the standard deviation is the positive square root of variance. In computing sample variance ($s^2$) and sample standard deviation ($s$), the average squared deviation is computed using a divisor equal to the sample size minus 1.
- The target downside deviation, or target semideviation, is a measure of the risk of being below a given target. It is calculated as the square root of the average squared deviations from the target, but it includes only those observations below the target ($B$), or $\sqrt{\sum_{\text{for all } X_i \leq B}^{n} \dfrac{(X_i - B)^2}{n-1}}$.
- The coefficient of variation, CV, is the ratio of the standard deviation of a set of observations to their mean value. By expressing the magnitude of variation among observations relative to their average size, the CV permits direct comparisons of dispersion across different datasets. Reflecting the correction for scale, the CV is a scale-free measure (i.e., it has no units of measurement).

# PRACTICE PROBLEMS

1. Published ratings on stocks ranging from 1 (strong sell) to 5 (strong buy) are examples of which measurement scale?
   
   **A.** Ordinal
   
   **B.** Continuous
   
   **C.** Nominal

2. Data values that are categorical and not amenable to being organized in a logical order are *most likely* to be characterized as:
   
   **A.** ordinal data.
   
   **B.** discrete data.
   
   **C.** nominal data.

3. Which of the following data types would be classified as being categorical?
   
   **A.** Discrete
   
   **B.** Nominal
   
   **C.** Continuous

4. A fixed-income analyst uses a proprietary model to estimate bankruptcy probabilities for a group of firms. The model generates probabilities that can take any value between 0 and 1. The resulting set of estimated probabilities would *most likely* be characterized as:
   
   **A.** ordinal data.
   
   **B.** discrete data.
   
   **C.** continuous data.

5. An analyst uses a software program to analyze unstructured data—specifically, management's earnings call transcript for one of the companies in her research coverage. The program scans the words in each sentence of the transcript and then classifies the sentences as having negative, neutral, or positive sentiment. The resulting set of sentiment data would *most likely* be characterized as:
   
   **A.** ordinal data.
   
   **B.** discrete data.
   
   **C.** nominal data.

## The following information relates to questions 6-7

An equity analyst gathers total returns for three country equity indexes over the past four years. The data are presented below.

## Practice Problems

| Time Period | Index A | Index B | Index C |
|---|---|---|---|
| Year $t-3$ | 15.56% | 11.84% | −4.34% |
| Year t−2 | −4.12% | −6.96% | 9.32% |
| Year $t-1$ | 11.19% | 10.29% | −12.72% |
| Year $t$ | 8.98% | 6.32% | 21.44% |

6. Each individual column of data in the table can be *best* characterized as:

    A. panel data.

    B. time-series data.

    C. cross-sectional data.

7. Each individual row of data in the table can be *best* characterized as:

    A. panel data.

    B. time-series data.

    C. cross-sectional data.

8. A two-dimensional rectangular array would be most suitable for organizing a collection of raw:

    A. panel data.

    B. time-series data.

    C. cross-sectional data.

9. In a frequency distribution, the absolute frequency measure:

    A. represents the percentages of each unique value of the variable.

    B. represents the actual number of observations counted for each unique value of the variable.

    C. allows for comparisons between datasets with different numbers of total observations.

10. An investment fund has the return frequency distribution shown in the following exhibit.

    | Return Interval (%) | Absolute Frequency |
    |---|---|
    | −10.0 to −7.0 | 3 |
    | −7.0 to −4.0 | 7 |
    | −4.0 to −1.0 | 10 |
    | −1.0 to +2.0 | 12 |
    | +2.0 to +5.0 | 23 |
    | +5.0 to +8.0 | 5 |

    Which of the following statements is correct?

A. The relative frequency of the bin "−1.0 to +2.0" is 20%.

B. The relative frequency of the bin "+2.0 to +5.0" is 23%.

C. The cumulative relative frequency of the bin "+5.0 to +8.0" is 91.7%.

11. An analyst is using the data in the following exhibit to prepare a statistical report.

| Portfolio's Deviations from Benchmark Return for a 12-Year Period (%) | | | |
|---|---|---|---|
| Year 1 | 2.48 | Year 7 | −9.19 |
| Year 2 | −2.59 | Year 8 | −5.11 |
| Year 3 | 9.47 | Year 9 | 1.33 |
| Year 4 | −0.55 | Year 10 | 6.84 |
| Year 5 | −1.69 | Year 11 | 3.04 |
| Year 6 | −0.89 | Year 12 | 4.72 |

The cumulative relative frequency for the bin −1.71% ≤ $x$ < 2.03% is *closest* to:

A. 0.250.

B. 0.333.

C. 0.583.

# The following information relates to questions 12-13

A fixed-income portfolio manager creates a contingency table of the number of bonds held in her portfolio by sector and bond rating. The contingency table is presented here:

| | Bond Rating | | |
|---|---|---|---|
| Sector | A | AA | AAA |
| Communication Services | 25 | 32 | 27 |
| Consumer Staples | 30 | 25 | 25 |
| Energy | 100 | 85 | 30 |
| Health Care | 200 | 100 | 63 |
| Utilities | 22 | 28 | 14 |

12. The marginal frequency of energy sector bonds is *closest* to:

A. 27.

B. 85.

C. 215.

13. The relative frequency of AA rated energy bonds, based on the total count, is

**Practice Problems**

*closest* to:

**A.** 10.5%.

**B.** 31.5%.

**C.** 39.5%.

---

14. The following is a frequency polygon of monthly exchange rate changes in the US dollar/Japanese yen spot exchange rate for a four-year period. A positive change represents yen appreciation (the yen buys more dollars), and a negative change represents yen depreciation (the yen buys fewer dollars).

**Exhibit 1: Monthly Changes in the US Dollar/Japanese Yen Spot Exchange Rate**

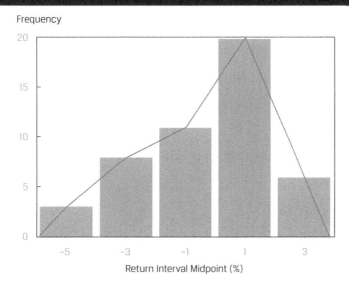

Based on the chart, yen appreciation:

**A.** occurred more than 50% of the time.

**B.** was less frequent than yen depreciation.

**C.** in the 0.0 to 2.0 interval occurred 20% of the time.

15. A bar chart that orders categories by frequency in descending order and includes a line displaying cumulative relative frequency is referred to as a:

**A.** Pareto Chart.

**B.** grouped bar chart.

**C.** frequency polygon.

16. Which visualization tool works *best* to represent unstructured, textual data?

**A.** Tree-Map

**B.** Scatter plot

C. Word cloud

17. A tree-map is best suited to illustrate:
    A. underlying trends over time.
    B. joint variations in two variables.
    C. value differences of categorical groups.

18. A line chart with two variables—for example, revenues and earnings per share—is best suited for visualizing:
    A. the joint variation in the variables.
    B. underlying trends in the variables over time.
    C. the degree of correlation between the variables.

19. A heat map is best suited for visualizing the:
    A. frequency of textual data.
    B. degree of correlation between different variables.
    C. shape, center, and spread of the distribution of numerical data.

20. Which valuation tool is recommended to be used if the goal is to make comparisons of three or more variables over time?
    A. Heat map
    B. Bubble line chart
    C. Scatter plot matrix

# The following information relates to questions 21-22

The following histogram shows a distribution of the S&P 500 Index annual returns for a 50-year period:

**Practice Problems**

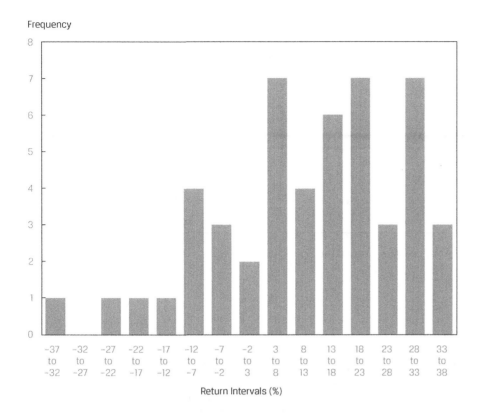

21. The bin containing the median return is:

    A. 3% to 8%.

    B. 8% to 13%.

    C. 13% to 18%.

22. Based on the previous histogram, the distribution is *best* described as being:

    A. unimodal.

    B. bimodal.

    C. trimodal.

23. The annual returns for three portfolios are shown in the following exhibit. Portfolios P and R were created in Year 1, Portfolio Q in Year 2.

| | **Annual Portfolio Returns (%)** | | | | |
|---|---|---|---|---|---|
| | Year 1 | Year 2 | Year 3 | Year 4 | Year 5 |
| Portfolio P | −3.0 | 4.0 | 5.0 | 3.0 | 7.0 |
| Portfolio Q | | −3.0 | 6.0 | 4.0 | 8.0 |
| Portfolio R | 1.0 | −1.0 | 4.0 | 4.0 | 3.0 |

The median annual return from portfolio creation to Year 5 for:

A. Portfolio P is 4.5%.

B. Portfolio Q is 4.0%.

C. Portfolio R is higher than its arithmetic mean annual return.

24. At the beginning of Year X, an investor allocated his retirement savings in the asset classes shown in the following exhibit and earned a return for Year X as also shown.

| Asset Class | Asset Allocation (%) | Asset Class Return for Year X (%) |
| --- | --- | --- |
| Large-cap US equities | 20.0 | 8.0 |
| Small-cap US equities | 40.0 | 12.0 |
| Emerging market equities | 25.0 | −3.0 |
| High-yield bonds | 15.0 | 4.0 |

The portfolio return for Year X is *closest to*:

A. 5.1%.

B. 5.3%.

C. 6.3%.

25. The following exhibit shows the annual returns for Fund Y.

| | Fund Y (%) |
| --- | --- |
| Year 1 | 19.5 |
| Year 2 | −1.9 |
| Year 3 | 19.7 |
| Year 4 | 35.0 |
| Year 5 | 5.7 |

The geometric mean return for Fund Y is *closest* to:

A. 14.9%.

B. 15.6%.

C. 19.5%.

26. A portfolio manager invests €5,000 annually in a security for four years at the prices shown in the following exhibit.

| | Purchase Price of Security (€ per unit) |
| --- | --- |
| Year 1 | 62.00 |
| Year 2 | 76.00 |
| Year 3 | 84.00 |
| Year 4 | 90.00 |

The average price is *best* represented as the:

A. harmonic mean of €76.48.

B. geometric mean of €77.26.

C. arithmetic average of €78.00.

**Practice Problems**

27. When analyzing investment returns, which of the following statements is correct?

    **A.** The geometric mean will exceed the arithmetic mean for a series with non-zero variance.

    **B.** The geometric mean measures an investment's compound rate of growth over multiple periods.

    **C.** The arithmetic mean measures an investment's terminal value over multiple periods.

# The following information relates to questions 28-32

A fund had the following experience over the past 10 years:

| Year | Return |
|---|---|
| 1 | 4.5% |
| 2 | 6.0% |
| 3 | 1.5% |
| 4 | −2.0% |
| 5 | 0.0% |
| 6 | 4.5% |
| 7 | 3.5% |
| 8 | 2.5% |
| 9 | 5.5% |
| 10 | 4.0% |

28. The arithmetic mean return over the 10 years is *closest* to:

    **A.** 2.97%.

    **B.** 3.00%.

    **C.** 3.33%.

29. The geometric mean return over the 10 years is *closest* to:

    **A.** 2.94%.

    **B.** 2.97%.

    **C.** 3.00%.

30. The harmonic mean return over the 10 years is *closest* to:

    **A.** 2.94%.

    **B.** 2.97%.

    **C.** 3.00%.

31. The standard deviation of the 10 years of returns is *closest* to:

   A. 2.40%.

   B. 2.53%.

   C. 7.58%.

32. The target semideviation of the returns over the 10 years if the target is 2% is *closest* to:

   A. 1.42%.

   B. 1.50%.

   C. 2.01%.

# The following information relates to questions 33-34

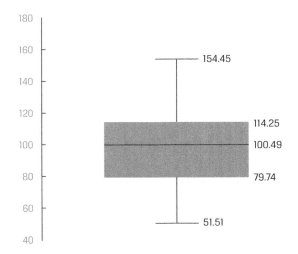

33. The median is *closest* to:

   A. 34.51.

   B. 100.49.

   C. 102.98.

34. The interquartile range is *closest* to:

   A. 13.76.

   B. 25.74.

   C. 34.51.

## Practice Problems

## The following information relates to questions 35-36

The following exhibit shows the annual MSCI World Index total returns for a 10-year period.

| Year 1 | 15.25%  | Year 6  | 30.79% |
|--------|---------|---------|--------|
| Year 2 | 10.02%  | Year 7  | 12.34% |
| Year 3 | 20.65%  | Year 8  | −5.02% |
| Year 4 | 9.57%   | Year 9  | 16.54% |
| Year 5 | −40.33% | Year 10 | 27.37% |

35. The fourth quintile return for the MSCI World Index is *closest* to:

    A. 20.65%.

    B. 26.03%.

    C. 27.37%.

36. For Year 6–Year 10, the mean absolute deviation of the MSCI World Index total returns is *closest* to:

    A. 10.20%.

    B. 12.74%.

    C. 16.40%.

37. Annual returns and summary statistics for three funds are listed in the following exhibit:

    | | Annual Returns (%) | | |
    |---|---|---|---|
    | Year | Fund ABC | Fund XYZ | Fund PQR |
    | Year 1 | −20.0 | −33.0 | −14.0 |
    | Year 2 | 23.0 | −12.0 | −18.0 |
    | Year 3 | −14.0 | −12.0 | 6.0 |
    | Year 4 | 5.0 | −8.0 | −2.0 |
    | Year 5 | −14.0 | 11.0 | 3.0 |
    | | | | |
    | Mean | −4.0 | −10.8 | −5.0 |
    | Standard deviation | 17.8 | 15.6 | 10.5 |

    The fund with the highest absolute dispersion is:

    A. Fund PQR if the measure of dispersion is the range.

    B. Fund XYZ if the measure of dispersion is the variance.

    C. Fund ABC if the measure of dispersion is the mean absolute deviation.

38. The average return for Portfolio A over the past twelve months is 3%, with a standard deviation of 4%. The average return for Portfolio B over this same period is also 3%, but with a standard deviation of 6%. The geometric mean return of Portfolio A is 2.85%. The geometric mean return of Portfolio B is:

   A. less than 2.85%.

   B. equal to 2.85%.

   C. greater than 2.85%.

39. The mean monthly return and the standard deviation for three industry sectors are shown in the following exhibit.

| Sector | Mean Monthly Return (%) | Standard Deviation of Return (%) |
| --- | --- | --- |
| Utilities (UTIL) | 2.10 | 1.23 |
| Materials (MATR) | 1.25 | 1.35 |
| Industrials (INDU) | 3.01 | 1.52 |

   Based on the coefficient of variation, the riskiest sector is:

   A. utilities.

   B. materials.

   C. industrials.

# SOLUTIONS

1. A is correct. Ordinal scales sort data into categories that are ordered with respect to some characteristic and may involve numbers to identify categories but do not assure that the differences between scale values are equal. The buy rating scale indicates that a stock ranked 5 is expected to perform better than a stock ranked 4, but it tells us nothing about the performance difference between stocks ranked 4 and 5 compared with the performance difference between stocks ranked 1 and 2, and so on.

2. C is correct. Nominal data are categorical values that are not amenable to being organized in a logical order. A is incorrect because ordinal data are categorical data that can be logically ordered or ranked. B is incorrect because discrete data are numerical values that result from a counting process; thus, they can be ordered in various ways, such as from highest to lowest value.

3. B is correct. Categorical data (or qualitative data) are values that describe a quality or characteristic of a group of observations and therefore can be used as labels to divide a dataset into groups to summarize and visualize. The two types of categorical data are nominal data and ordinal data. Nominal data are categorical values that are not amenable to being organized in a logical order, while ordinal data are categorical values that can be logically ordered or ranked. A is incorrect because discrete data would be classified as numerical data (not categorical data). C is incorrect because continuous data would be classified as numerical data (not categorical data).

4. C is correct. Continuous data are data that can be measured and can take on any numerical value in a specified range of values. In this case, the analyst is estimating bankruptcy probabilities, which can take on any value between 0 and 1. Therefore, the set of bankruptcy probabilities estimated by the analyst would likely be characterized as continuous data. A is incorrect because ordinal data are categorical values that can be logically ordered or ranked. Therefore, the set of bankruptcy probabilities would not be characterized as ordinal data. B is incorrect because discrete data are numerical values that result from a counting process, and therefore the data are limited to a finite number of values. The proprietary model used can generate probabilities that can take any value between 0 and 1; therefore, the set of bankruptcy probabilities would not be characterized as discrete data.

5. A is correct. Ordinal data are categorical values that can be logically ordered or ranked. In this case, the classification of sentences in the earnings call transcript into three categories (negative, neutral, or positive) describes ordinal data, as the data can be logically ordered from positive to negative. B is incorrect because discrete data are numerical values that result from a counting process. In this case, the analyst is categorizing sentences (i.e., unstructured data) from the earnings call transcript as having negative, neutral, or positive sentiment. Thus, these categorical data do not represent discrete data. C is incorrect because nominal data are categorical values that are not amenable to being organized in a logical order. In this case, the classification of unstructured data (i.e., sentences from the earnings call transcript) into three categories (negative, neutral, or positive) describes ordinal (not nominal) data, as the data can be logically ordered from positive to negative.

6. B is correct. Time-series data are a sequence of observations of a specific variable collected over time and at discrete and typically equally spaced intervals of time,

such as daily, weekly, monthly, annually, and quarterly. In this case, each column is a time series of data that represents annual total return (the specific variable) for a given country index, and it is measured annually (the discrete interval of time). A is incorrect because panel data consist of observations through time on one or more variables for multiple observational units. The entire table of data is an example of panel data showing annual total returns (the variable) for three country indexes (the observational units) by year. C is incorrect because cross-sectional data are a list of the observations of a specific variable from multiple observational units at a given point in time. Each row (not column) of data in the table represents cross-sectional data.

7. C is correct. Cross-sectional data are observations of a specific variable from multiple observational units at a given point in time. Each row of data in the table represents cross-sectional data. The specific variable is annual total return, the multiple observational units are the three countries' indexes, and the given point in time is the time period indicated by the particular row. A is incorrect because panel data consist of observations through time on one or more variables for multiple observational units. The entire table of data is an example of panel data showing annual total returns (the variable) for three country indexes (the observational units) by year. B is incorrect because time-series data are a sequence of observations of a specific variable collected over time and at discrete and typically equally spaced intervals of time, such as daily, weekly, monthly, annually, and quarterly. In this case, each column (not row) is a time series of data that represents annual total return (the specific variable) for a given country index, and it is measured annually (the discrete interval of time).

8. A is correct. Panel data consist of observations through time on one or more variables for multiple observational units. A two-dimensional rectangular array, or data table, would be suitable here as it is comprised of columns to hold the variable(s) for the observational units and rows to hold the observations through time. B is incorrect because a one-dimensional (not a two-dimensional rectangular) array would be most suitable for organizing a collection of data of the same data type, such as the time-series data from a single variable. C is incorrect because a one-dimensional (not a two-dimensional rectangular) array would be most suitable for organizing a collection of data of the same data type, such as the same variable for multiple observational units at a given point in time (cross-sectional data).

9. B is correct. In a frequency distribution, the absolute frequency, or simply the raw frequency, is the actual number of observations counted for each unique value of the variable. A is incorrect because the relative frequency, which is calculated as the absolute frequency of each unique value of the variable divided by the total number of observations, presents the absolute frequencies in terms of percentages. C is incorrect because the relative (not absolute) frequency provides a normalized measure of the distribution of the data, allowing comparisons between datasets with different numbers of total observations.

10. A is correct. The relative frequency is the absolute frequency of each bin divided by the total number of observations. Here, the relative frequency is calculated as: $(12/60) \times 100 = 20\%$. B is incorrect because the relative frequency of this bin is $(23/60) \times 100 = 38.33\%$. C is incorrect because the cumulative relative frequency of the last bin must equal 100%.

11. C is correct. The cumulative relative frequency of a bin identifies the fraction of observations that are less than the upper limit of the given bin. It is determined by summing the relative frequencies from the lowest bin up to and including the given bin. The following exhibit shows the relative frequencies for all the bins of

# Solutions

the data from the previous exhibit:

| Lower Limit (%) | Upper Limit (%) | Absolute Frequency | Relative Frequency | Cumulative Relative Frequency |
|---|---|---|---|---|
| −9.19 ≤ | < −5.45 | 1 | 0.083 | 0.083 |
| −5.45 ≤ | < −1.71 | 2 | 0.167 | 0.250 |
| −1.71 ≤ | < 2.03 | 4 | 0.333 | 0.583 |
| 2.03 ≤ | < 5.77 | 3 | 0.250 | 0.833 |
| 5.77 ≤ | ≤ 9.47 | 2 | 0.167 | 1.000 |

The bin −1.71% ≤ $x$ < 2.03% has a cumulative relative frequency of 0.583.

12. C is correct. The marginal frequency of energy sector bonds in the portfolio is the sum of the joint frequencies across all three levels of bond rating, so 100 + 85 + 30 = 215. A is incorrect because 27 is the relative frequency for energy sector bonds based on the total count of 806 bonds, so 215/806 = 26.7%, not the marginal frequency. B is incorrect because 85 is the joint frequency for AA rated energy sector bonds, not the marginal frequency.

13. A is correct. The relative frequency for any value in the table based on the total count is calculated by dividing that value by the total count. Therefore, the relative frequency for AA rated energy bonds is calculated as 85/806 = 10.5%.

    B is incorrect because 31.5% is the relative frequency for AA rated energy bonds, calculated based on the marginal frequency for all AA rated bonds, so 85/(32 + 25 + 85 + 100 + 28), not based on total bond counts. C is incorrect because 39.5% is the relative frequency for AA rated energy bonds, calculated based on the marginal frequency for all energy bonds, so 85/(100 + 85 + 30), not based on total bond counts.

14. A is correct. Twenty observations lie in the interval "0.0 to 2.0," and six observations lie in the "2.0 to 4.0" interval. Together, they represent 26/48, or 54.17%, of all observations, which is more than 50%.

15. A is correct. A bar chart that orders categories by frequency in descending order and includes a line displaying cumulative relative frequency is called a Pareto Chart. A Pareto Chart is used to highlight dominant categories or the most important groups. B is incorrect because a grouped bar chart or clustered bar chart is used to present the frequency distribution of two categorical variables. C is incorrect because a frequency polygon is used to display frequency distributions.

16. C is correct. A word cloud, or tag cloud, is a visual device for representing unstructured, textual data. It consists of words extracted from text with the size of each word being proportional to the frequency with which it appears in the given text. A is incorrect because a tree-map is a graphical tool for displaying and comparing categorical data, not for visualizing unstructured, textual data. B is incorrect because a scatter plot is used to visualize the joint variation in two numerical variables, not for visualizing unstructured, textual data.

17. C is correct. A tree-map is a graphical tool used to display and compare categorical data. It consists of a set of colored rectangles to represent distinct groups, and the area of each rectangle is proportional to the value of the corresponding group. A is incorrect because a line chart, not a tree-map, is used to display the change in a data series over time. B is incorrect because a scatter plot, not a tree-map, is used to visualize the joint variation in two numerical variables.

18. B is correct. An important benefit of a line chart is that it facilitates showing

changes in the data and underlying trends in a clear and concise way. Often a line chart is used to display the changes in data series over time. A is incorrect because a scatter plot, not a line chart, is used to visualize the joint variation in two numerical variables. C is incorrect because a heat map, not a line chart, is used to visualize the values of joint frequencies among categorical variables.

19. B is correct. A heat map is commonly used for visualizing the degree of correlation between different variables. A is incorrect because a word cloud, or tag cloud, not a heat map, is a visual device for representing textual data with the size of each distinct word being proportional to the frequency with which it appears in the given text. C is incorrect because a histogram, not a heat map, depicts the shape, center, and spread of the distribution of numerical data.

20. B is correct. A bubble line chart is a version of a line chart where data points are replaced with varying-sized bubbles to represent a third dimension of the data. A line chart is very effective at visualizing trends in three or more variables over time. A is incorrect because a heat map differentiates high values from low values and reflects the correlation between variables but does not help in making comparisons of variables over time. C is incorrect because a scatterplot matrix is a useful tool for organizing scatterplots between pairs of variables, making it easy to inspect all pairwise relationships in one combined visual. However, it does not help in making comparisons of these variables over time.

21. C is correct. Because 50 data points are in the histogram, the median return would be the mean of the 50/2 = 25th and (50 + 2)/2 = 26th positions. The sum of the return bin frequencies to the left of the 13% to 18% interval is 24. As a result, the 25th and 26th returns will fall in the 13% to 18% interval.

22. C is correct. The mode of a distribution with data grouped in intervals is the interval with the highest frequency. The three intervals of 3% to 8%, 18% to 23%, and 28% to 33% all have a high frequency of 7.

23. C is correct. The median of Portfolio R is 0.8% higher than the mean for Portfolio R.

24. C is correct. The portfolio return must be calculated as the weighted mean return, where the weights are the allocations in each asset class:

    $(0.20 \times 8\%) + (0.40 \times 12\%) + (0.25 \times -3\%) + (0.15 \times 4\%) = 6.25\%$, or $\approx 6.3\%$.

25. A is correct. The geometric mean return for Fund Y is found as follows:

    Fund Y = $[(1 + 0.195) \times (1 - 0.019) \times (1 + 0.197) \times (1 + 0.350) \times (1 + 0.057)]^{(1/5)} - 1$

    = 14.9%.

26. A is correct. The harmonic mean is appropriate for determining the average price per unit. It is calculated by summing the reciprocals of the prices, then averaging that sum by dividing by the number of prices, then taking the reciprocal of the average:

    $4/[(1/62.00) + (1/76.00) + (1/84.00) + (1/90.00)] = €76.48$.

27. B is correct. The geometric mean compounds the periodic returns of every period, giving the investor a more accurate measure of the terminal value of an investment.

# Solutions

28. B is correct. The sum of the returns is 30.0%, so the arithmetic mean is 30.0%/10 = 3.0%.

29. B is correct.

| Year | Return | 1+ Return |
|---|---|---|
| 1 | 4.5% | 1.045 |
| 2 | 6.0% | 1.060 |
| 3 | 1.5% | 1.015 |
| 4 | −2.0% | 0.980 |
| 5 | 0.0% | 1.000 |
| 6 | 4.5% | 1.045 |
| 7 | 3.5% | 1.035 |
| 8 | 2.5% | 1.025 |
| 9 | 5.5% | 1.055 |
| 10 | 4.0% | 1.040 |

The product of the 1 + Return is 1.3402338.
Therefore, $\bar{X}_G = \sqrt[10]{1.3402338} - 1 = 2.9717\%$.

30. A is correct.

| Year | Return | 1+ Return | 1/(1+Return) |
|---|---|---|---|
| 1 | 4.5% | 1.045 | 0.957 |
| 2 | 6.0% | 1.060 | 0.943 |
| 3 | 1.5% | 1.015 | 0.985 |
| 4 | −2.0% | 0.980 | 1.020 |
| 5 | 0.0% | 1.000 | 1.000 |
| 6 | 4.5% | 1.045 | 0.957 |
| 7 | 3.5% | 1.035 | 0.966 |
| 8 | 2.5% | 1.025 | 0.976 |
| 9 | 5.5% | 1.055 | 0.948 |
| 10 | 4.0% | 1.040 | 0.962 |
| Sum | | | 9.714 |

The harmonic mean return = ($n$/Sum of reciprocals) − 1 = (10 / 9.714) − 1.

The harmonic mean return = 2.9442%.

31. B is correct.

| Year | Return | Deviation | Deviation Squared |
|---|---|---|---|
| 1 | 4.5% | 0.0150 | 0.000225 |
| 2 | 6.0% | 0.0300 | 0.000900 |
| 3 | 1.5% | −0.0150 | 0.000225 |
| 4 | −2.0% | −0.0500 | 0.002500 |
| 5 | 0.0% | −0.0300 | 0.000900 |
| 6 | 4.5% | 0.0150 | 0.000225 |

| Year | Return | Deviation | Deviation Squared |
|---|---|---|---|
| 7 | 3.5% | 0.0050 | 0.000025 |
| 8 | 2.5% | −0.0050 | 0.000025 |
| 9 | 5.5% | 0.0250 | 0.000625 |
| 10 | 4.0% | 0.0100 | 0.000100 |
| Sum | | 0.0000 | **0.005750** |

The standard deviation is the square root of the sum of the squared deviations divided by $n - 1$:

$$s = \sqrt{\frac{0.005750}{9}} = 2.5276\%.$$

32. B is correct.

| Year | Return | Deviation Squared below Target of 2% |
|---|---|---|
| 1 | 4.5% | |
| 2 | 6.0% | |
| 3 | 1.5% | 0.000025 |
| 4 | −2.0% | 0.001600 |
| 5 | 0.0% | 0.000400 |
| 6 | 4.5% | |
| 7 | 3.5% | |
| 8 | 2.5% | |
| 9 | 5.5% | |
| 10 | 4.0% | |
| Sum | | 0.002025 |

The target semi-deviation is the square root of the sum of the squared deviations from the target, divided by $n - 1$:

$$s_{Target} = \sqrt{\frac{0.002025}{9}} = 1.5\%.$$

33. B is correct. The median is indicated within the box, which is the 100.49 in this diagram.

34. C is correct. The interquartile range is the difference between 114.25 and 79.74, which is 34.51.

35. B is correct. Quintiles divide a distribution into fifths, with the fourth quintile occurring at the point at which 80% of the observations lie below it. The fourth quintile is equivalent to the 80th percentile. To find the $y$th percentile ($P_y$), we first must determine its location. The formula for the location ($L_y$) of a $y$th percentile in an array with $n$ entries sorted in ascending order is $L_y = (n + 1) \times (y/100)$. In this case, $n = 10$ and $y = 80\%$, so

$$L_{80} = (10 + 1) \times (80/100) = 11 \times 0.8 = 8.8.$$

With the data arranged in ascending order (−40.33%, −5.02%, 9.57%, 10.02%, 12.34%, 15.25%, 16.54%, 20.65%, 27.37%, and 30.79%), the 8.8th position would be between the 8th and 9th entries, 20.65% and 27.37%, respectively. Using linear

# Solutions

interpolation, $P_{80} = X_8 + (L_y - 8) \times (X_9 - X_8)$,

$P_{80} = 20.65 + (8.8 - 8) \times (27.37 - 20.65)$

$= 20.65 + (0.8 \times 6.72) = 20.65 + 5.38$

$= 26.03\%$.

36. A is correct. The formula for mean absolute deviation (MAD) is

$$\text{MAD} = \frac{\sum_{i=1}^{n}|X_i - \overline{X}|}{n}.$$

**Column 1**: Sum annual returns and divide by $n$ to find the arithmetic mean $(\overline{X})$ of 16.40%.

**Column 2**: Calculate the absolute value of the difference between each year's return and the mean from Column 1. Sum the results and divide by $n$ to find the MAD.

These calculations are shown in the following exhibit:

| Year | Column 1<br>Return | | Column 2<br>$\|X_i - \overline{X}\|$ |
|---|---|---|---|
| Year 6 | 30.79% | | 14.39% |
| Year 7 | 12.34% | | 4.06% |
| Year 8 | −5.02% | | 21.42% |
| Year 9 | 16.54% | | 0.14% |
| Year 10 | 27.37% | | 10.97% |
| Sum: | 82.02% | Sum: | 50.98% |
| $n$: | 5 | $n$: | 5 |
| $\overline{X}$: | 16.40% | MAD: | 10.20% |

37. C is correct. The mean absolute deviation (MAD) of Fund ABC's returns is greater than the MAD of both of the other funds.

$\text{MAD} = \frac{\sum_{i=1}^{n}|X_i - \overline{X}|}{n}$, where $\overline{X}$ is the arithmetic mean of the series.

MAD for Fund ABC =

$\frac{|-20 - (-4)| + |23 - (-4)| + |-14 - (-4)| + |5 - (-4)| + |-14 - (-4)|}{5} = 14.4\%$.

MAD for Fund XYZ =

$\frac{|-33 - (-10.8)| + |-12 - (-10.8)| + |-12 - (-10.8)| + |-8 - (-10.8)| + |11 - (-10.8)|}{5}$

$= 9.8\%$.

MAD for Fund PQR =

$\frac{|-14 - (-5)| + |-18 - (-5)| + |6 - (-5)| + |-2 - (-5)| + |3 - (-5)|}{5} = 8.8\%$.

A and B are incorrect because the range and variance of the three funds are as follows:

|  | Fund ABC | Fund XYZ | Fund PQR |
|---|---|---|---|
| Range | 43% | 44% | 24% |
| Variance | 317 | 243 | 110 |

The numbers shown for variance are understood to be in "percent squared" terms so that when taking the square root, the result is standard deviation in percentage terms. Alternatively, by expressing standard deviation and variance in decimal form, one can avoid the issue of units. In decimal form, the variances for Fund ABC, Fund XYZ, and Fund PQR are 0.0317, 0.0243, and 0.0110, respectively.

38. A is correct. The more disperse a distribution, the greater the difference between the arithmetic mean and the geometric mean.

39. B is correct. The coefficient of variation (CV) is the ratio of the standard deviation to the mean, where a higher CV implies greater risk per unit of return.

$$CV_{UTIL} = \frac{s}{\bar{X}} = \frac{1.23\%}{2.10\%} = 0.59.$$

$$CV_{MATR} = \frac{s}{\bar{X}} = \frac{1.35\%}{1.25\%} = 1.08.$$

$$CV_{INDU} = \frac{s}{\bar{X}} = \frac{1.52\%}{3.01\%} = 0.51.$$

# LEARNING MODULE
# 3

## Probability Concepts

by Richard A. DeFusco, PhD, CFA, Dennis W. McLeavey, DBA, CFA, Jerald E. Pinto, PhD, CFA, and David E. Runkle, PhD, CFA.

*Richard A. DeFusco, PhD, CFA, is at the University of Nebraska-Lincoln (USA). Dennis W. McLeavey, DBA, CFA, is at the University of Rhode Island (USA). Jerald E. Pinto, PhD, CFA, is at CFA Institute (USA). David E. Runkle, PhD, CFA, is at Jacobs Levy Equity Management (USA).*

## LEARNING OUTCOMES

| Mastery | The candidate should be able to: |
|---|---|
| ☐ | define a random variable, an outcome, and an event |
| ☐ | identify the two defining properties of probability, including mutually exclusive and exhaustive events, and compare and contrast empirical, subjective, and a priori probabilities |
| ☐ | describe the probability of an event in terms of odds for and against the event |
| ☐ | calculate and interpret conditional probabilities |
| ☐ | demonstrate the application of the multiplication and addition rules for probability |
| ☐ | compare and contrast dependent and independent events |
| ☐ | calculate and interpret an unconditional probability using the total probability rule |
| ☐ | identify the most appropriate method to solve a particular counting problem and analyze counting problems using factorial, combination, and permutation concepts |

CFA Institute would like to thank John Stowe, PhD, CFA, for his significant contributions in revising this reading.

# 1  PROBABILITY CONCEPTS AND ODDS RATIOS

- [ ] define a random variable, an outcome, and an event
- [ ] identify the two defining properties of probability, including mutually exclusive and exhaustive events, and compare and contrast empirical, subjective, and a priori probabilities
- [ ] describe the probability of an event in terms of odds for and against the event

Investment decisions are made in a risky environment. The tools that allow us to make decisions with consistency and logic in this setting are based on probability concepts. This reading presents the essential probability tools needed to frame and address many real-world problems involving risk. These tools apply to a variety of issues, such as predicting investment manager performance, forecasting financial variables, and pricing bonds so that they fairly compensate bondholders for default risk. Our focus is practical. We explore the concepts of independence of events, conditional, unconditional and joint probabilities, and the principle of counting using factorial, permutation and combination.

## Probability and Odds

The probability concepts and tools necessary for most of an analyst's work are relatively few and straightforward but require thought to apply. This section presents the essentials for working with probability, drawing on examples from equity and fixed income analysis.

An investor's concerns center on returns. The return on a risky asset is an example of a random variable.

- Definition of Random Variable. A **random variable** is a quantity whose future outcomes are uncertain.
- Definition of Outcome. An **outcome** is a possible value of a random variable.

Using Exhibit 1 as an example, a portfolio manager may have a return objective of 10% a year. The portfolio manager's focus at the moment may be on the likelihood of earning a return that is less than 10% over the next year. Ten percent is a particular value or outcome of the random variable "portfolio return." Although we may be concerned about a single outcome, frequently our interest may be in a set of outcomes. The concept of "event" covers both.

- Definition of Event. An **event** is a specified set of outcomes.

## Exhibit 1: Visualizing Probability

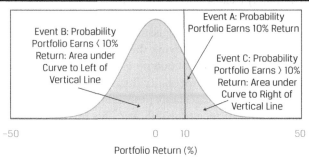

An event can be a single outcome—for example, the portfolio earns a return of (exactly) 10%. We can capture the portfolio manager's concerns by defining another event as the portfolio earns a return below 10%. This second event, referring as it does to all possible returns greater than or equal to −100% (the worst possible return, losing all the money in the portfolio) but less than 10%, contains an infinite number of outcomes. To save words, it is common to use a capital letter in italics to represent a defined event. We could define *A = the portfolio earns a return of 10%* and *B = the portfolio earns a return below 10%*.

To return to the portfolio manager's concern, how likely is it that the portfolio will earn a return below 10%? The answer to this question is a **probability**: a number between 0 and 1 that measures the chance that a stated event will occur. If the probability is 0.65 that the portfolio earns a return below 10%, there is a 65% chance of that event happening. If an event is impossible, it has a probability of 0. If an event is certain to happen, it has a probability of 1. If an event is impossible or a sure thing, it is not random at all. So, 0 and 1 bracket all the possible values of a probability.

To reiterate, a probability can be thought of as the likelihood that something will happen. If it has a probability of 1, it is likely to happen 100% of the time, and if it has a probably of 0, it is likely to never happen. Some people think of probabilities as akin to relative frequencies. If something is expected to happen 30 times out of 100, the probability is 0.30. The probability is the number of ways that an (equally likely) event can happen divided by the total number of possible outcomes.

Probability has two properties, which together constitute its definition.

- Definition of Probability. The two defining properties of a probability are:
    1. The probability of any event $E$ is a number between 0 and 1: $0 \leq P(E) \leq 1$.
    2. The sum of the probabilities of any set of mutually exclusive and exhaustive events equals 1.

$P$ followed by parentheses stands for "the probability of (the event in parentheses)," as in $P(E)$ for "the probability of event $E$." We can also think of $P$ as a rule or function that assigns numerical values to events consistent with Properties 1 and 2.

In the above definition, the term **mutually exclusive** means that only one event can occur at a time; **exhaustive** means that the events cover all possible outcomes. Referring back to Exhibit 1, the events *A = the portfolio earns a return of 10%* and *B = the portfolio earns a return below 10%* are mutually exclusive because *A* and *B* cannot both occur at the same time. For example, a return of 8.1% means that *B* has occurred and *A* has not occurred. Although events *A* and *B* are mutually exclusive, they are not exhaustive because they do not cover outcomes such as a return of 11%.

Suppose we define a third event: C = *the portfolio earns a return above 10%*. Clearly, A, B, and C are mutually exclusive and exhaustive events. Each of P(A), P(B), and P(C) is a number between 0 and 1, and P(A) + P(B) + P(C) = 1.

Earlier, to illustrate a concept, we assumed a probability of 0.65 for a portfolio earning less than 10%, without justifying the particular assumption. We also talked about using assigned probabilities of outcomes to calculate the probability of events, without explaining how such a probability distribution might be estimated. Making actual financial decisions using inaccurate probabilities could have grave consequences. How, in practice, do we estimate probabilities? This topic is a field of study in itself, but there are three broad approaches to estimating probabilities. In investments, we often estimate the probability of an event as a relative frequency of occurrence based on historical data. This method produces an **empirical probability**. For example, suppose you noted that 51 of the 60 stocks in a particular large-cap equity index pay dividends. The empirical probability of the stocks in the index paying a dividend is *P(stock is dividend paying)* = 51 / 60 = 0.85.

Relationships must be stable through time for empirical probabilities to be accurate. We cannot calculate an empirical probability of an event not in the historical record or a reliable empirical probability for a very rare event. In some cases, then, we may adjust an empirical probability to account for perceptions of changing relationships. In other cases, we have no empirical probability to use at all. We may also make a personal assessment of probability without reference to any particular data. Another type of probability is a **subjective probability**, one drawing on personal or subjective judgment. Subjective probabilities are of great importance in investments. Investors, in making buy and sell decisions that determine asset prices, often draw on subjective probabilities.

For many well-defined problems, we can deduce probabilities by reasoning about the problem. The resulting probability is an **a priori probability**, one based on logical analysis rather than on observation or personal judgment. Because a priori and empirical probabilities generally do not vary from person to person, they are often grouped as **objective probabilities**.

For examples of the three types of probabilities, suppose you want to estimate the probability of flipping a coin and getting exactly two heads out of five flips. For the empirical probability, you do the experiment 100 times (five flips each time) and find that you get two heads 33 times. The empirical probability would be 33/100 = 0.33. For a subjective judgement, you think the probability is somewhere between 0.25 and 0.50, so you split the difference and choose 0.375. For the a priori probability, you assume that the binomial probability function (discussed later in the curriculum) applies, and the mathematical probability of two heads out of five flips is 0.3125.

Another way of stating probabilities often encountered in investments is in terms of odds—for instance, "the odds for *E*" or the "odds against *E*." A probability is the fraction of the time you expect an event to occur, and the odds for an event is the probability that an event will occur divided by the probability that the event will not occur. Consider a football team that has a 0.25 probability of winning the World Cup, and a 0.75 probability of losing. The odds for winning are 0.25/0.75 = 0.33 (and the odds for losing are 0.75/0.25 = 3.0). If another team has a 0.80 probability of winning, the odds for winning would be 0.80/0.20 = 4.0. If, for a third team, the probability of winning was 0.50, the odds are even: odds = 0.50/0.50 = 1. If the probability is low, the odds are very close to the probability. For example, if the probability of winning is 0.05, the odds for winning are 0.05/0.95 = 0.0526.

## Probability Concepts and Odds Ratios

> **EXAMPLE 1**
>
> ### Odds of Passing a Quantitative Methods Investment Course
>
> Two of your colleagues are taking a quantitative methods investment course.
>
> 1. If your first colleague has a 0.40 probability of passing, what are his odds for passing?
>
> ### Solution for 1:
>
> The odds are the probability of passing divided by the probability of not passing. The odds are 0.40 / 0.60 = 2/3 ≈ 0.667.
>
> 2. If your second colleague has odds of passing of 4 to 1, what is the probability of her passing?
>
> ### Solution for 2:
>
> The odds = *Probability (passing) / Probability (not passing)*. If $Y$ = Probability of passing, then $4 = Y / (1 - Y)$. Solving for $Y$, we get 0.80 as the probability of passing.

We interpret probabilities stated in terms of odds as follows:

- Probability Stated as Odds. Given a probability $P(E)$,

    1. **Odds for E** = $P(E)/[1 - P(E)]$. The odds for $E$ are the probability of $E$ divided by 1 minus the probability of $E$. Given odds for $E$ of "$a$ to $b$," the implied probability of $E$ is $a/(a + b)$.

    In the example, the statement that your second colleague's odds of passing the exam are 4 to 1 means that the probability of the event is $4/(4 + 1) = 4/5 = 0.80$.

    2. **Odds against E** = $[1 - P(E)]/P(E)$, the reciprocal of odds for $E$. Given odds against $E$ of "$a$ to $b$," the implied probability of $E$ is $b/(a + b)$.

    In the example, if the odds against your second colleague passing the exam are 1 to 4, this means that the probability of the event is $1/(4 + 1) = 1/5 = 0.20$.

To further explain odds for an event, if $P(E) = 1/8$, the odds for $E$ are $(1/8)/(7/8) = (1/8)(8/7) = 1/7$, or "1 to 7." For each occurrence of $E$, we expect seven cases of non-occurrence; out of eight cases in total, therefore, we expect $E$ to happen once, and the probability of $E$ is 1/8. In wagering, it is common to speak in terms of the odds against something, as in Statement 2. For odds of "15 to 1" against $E$ (an implied probability of $E$ of 1/16), a $1 wager on $E$, if successful, returns $15 in profits plus the $1 staked in the wager. We can calculate the bet's anticipated profit as follows:

Win:        Probability = 1/16; Profit = $15
Loss:       Probability = 15/16; Profit = –$1
 Anticipated profit = (1/16)($15) + (15/16)(–$1) = $0

Weighting each of the wager's two outcomes by the respective probability of the outcome, if the odds (probabilities) are accurate, the anticipated profit of the bet is $0.

> **EXAMPLE 2**
>
> ## Profiting from Inconsistent Probabilities
>
> 1. You are examining the common stock of two companies in the same industry in which an important antitrust decision will be announced next week. The first company, SmithCo Corporation, will benefit from a governmental decision that there is no antitrust obstacle related to a merger in which it is involved. You believe that SmithCo's share price reflects a 0.85 probability of such a decision. A second company, Selbert Corporation, will equally benefit from a "go ahead" ruling. Surprisingly, you believe Selbert stock reflects only a 0.50 probability of a favorable decision. Assuming your analysis is correct, what investment strategy would profit from this pricing discrepancy?
>
>    Consider the logical possibilities. One is that the probability of 0.50 reflected in Selbert's share price is accurate. In that case, Selbert is fairly valued, but SmithCo is overvalued, because its current share price overestimates the probability of a "go ahead" decision. The second possibility is that the probability of 0.85 is accurate. In that case, SmithCo shares are fairly valued, but Selbert shares, which build in a lower probability of a favorable decision, are undervalued. You diagram the situation as shown in Exhibit 2.
>
>    **Exhibit 2: Worksheet for Investment Problem**
>
>    |  | True Probability of a "Go Ahead" Decision | |
>    | --- | --- | --- |
>    |  | 0.50 | 0.85 |
>    | SmithCo | Shares Overvalued | Shares Fairly Valued |
>    | Selbert | Shares Fairly Valued | Shares Undervalued |
>    | Strategy | Short-Sell Smith / Buy Selbert | Sell Smith / Buy Selbert |
>
>    The 0.50 probability column shows that Selbert shares are a better value than SmithCo shares. Selbert shares are also a better value if a 0.85 probability is accurate. Thus, SmithCo shares are overvalued relative to Selbert shares.
>
>    Your investment actions depend on your confidence in your analysis and on any investment constraints you face (such as constraints on selling stock short). Selling short or shorting stock means selling borrowed shares in the hope of repurchasing them later at a lower price. A conservative strategy would be to buy Selbert shares and reduce or eliminate any current position in SmithCo. The most aggressive strategy is to short SmithCo stock (relatively overvalued) and simultaneously buy the stock of Selbert (relatively undervalued). The prices of SmithCo and Selbert shares reflect probabilities that are not consistent. According to one of the most important probability results for investments, the **Dutch Book Theorem**, inconsistent probabilities create profit opportunities. In our example, investors' buy and sell decisions exploit the inconsistent probabilities to eliminate the profit opportunity and inconsistency.

# CONDITIONAL AND JOINT PROBABILITY

☐ calculate and interpret conditional probabilities

☐ demonstrate the application of the multiplication and addition rules for probability

☐ compare and contrast dependent and independent events

☐ calculate and interpret an unconditional probability using the total probability rule

To understand the meaning of a probability in investment contexts, we need to distinguish between two types of probability: unconditional and conditional. Both unconditional and conditional probabilities satisfy the definition of probability stated earlier, but they are calculated or estimated differently and have different interpretations. They provide answers to different questions.

A probability of an event not conditioned on another event having occurred or occurring sometime in the future is an unconditional probability, or sometimes called marginal probability. Suppose the question is "What is the probability that *the stock earns a return above the risk-free rate* (event A)?" The answer is an unconditional probability that can be viewed as the ratio of two quantities. The numerator is the sum of the probabilities of stock returns above the risk-free rate. Suppose that sum is 0.70. The denominator is 1, the sum of the probabilities of all possible returns. The answer to the question is $P(A) = 0.70$.

Contrast the question "What is the probability of A?" with the question "What is the probability of A, given that B has occurred?" The probability in answer to this last question is a **conditional probability**, denoted $P(A \mid B)$ (read: "the probability of A given B").

Suppose we want to know the probability that *the stock earns a return above the risk-free rate* (event A), given that *the stock earns a positive return* (event B). With the words "given that," we are restricting returns to those larger than 0%—a new element in contrast to the question that brought forth an unconditional probability. The conditional probability is calculated as the ratio of two quantities. The numerator is the sum of the probabilities of stock returns above the risk-free rate; in this particular case, the numerator is the same as it was in the unconditional case, which we gave as 0.70. The denominator, however, changes from 1 to the sum of the probabilities for all outcomes (returns) above 0%. Suppose that number is 0.80, a larger number than 0.70 because returns between 0 and the risk-free rate have some positive probability of occurring. Then $P(A \mid B) = 0.70/0.80 = 0.875$. If we observe that the stock earns a positive return, the probability of a return above the risk-free rate is greater than the unconditional probability, which is the probability of the event given no other information. To review, an unconditional probability is the probability of an event without any restriction (i.e., a standalone probability). A conditional probability, in contrast, is a probability of an event given that another event has occurred.

To state an exact definition of conditional probability, we first need to introduce the concept of joint probability. Suppose we ask the question "What is the probability of both A and B happening?" The answer to this question is a **joint probability**, denoted $P(AB)$ (read: "the probability of A and B"). If we think of the probability of A and the probability of B as sets built of the outcomes of one or more random variables, the joint probability of A and B is the sum of the probabilities of the outcomes they have in common. For example, consider two events: *the stock earns a return above the risk-free* rate (A) and *the stock earns a positive return* (B). The outcomes of A are contained within (a subset of) the outcomes of B, so P(AB) equals P(A). We can now state a formal definition of conditional probability that provides a formula for calculating it.

- **Definition of Conditional Probability.** The conditional probability of A given that B has occurred is equal to the joint probability of A and B divided by the probability of B (assumed not to equal 0).

$$P(A \mid B) = P(AB)/P(B), P(B) \neq 0 \tag{1}$$

For example, suppose B happens half the time, $P(B) = 0.50$, and A and B both happen 10% of the time, $P(AB) = 0.10$. What is the probability that A happens, given that B happens? That is $P(A \mid B) = P(AB)/P(B) = 0.10 / 0.50 = 0.20$. Sometimes we know the conditional probability $P(A \mid B)$ and we want to know the joint probability $P(AB)$. We can obtain the joint probability from the following multiplication rule for probabilities.

- **Multiplication Rule for Probability**. The joint probability of A and B can be expressed as

$$P(AB) = P(A \mid B)P(B) \tag{2}$$

With the same numbers above, if B happens 50% of the time, and the probability of A given that B happens is 20%, the joint probability of A and B happening is $P(AB) = P(A \mid B)P(B) = 0.20 \times 0.50 = 0.10$.

> **EXAMPLE 3**
>
> ## Conditional Probabilities and Predictability of Mutual Fund Performance (1)
>
> An analyst conducts a study of the returns of 200 mutual funds over a two-year period. For each year, the total returns for the funds were ranked, and the top 50% of funds were labeled winners; the bottom 50% were labeled losers. Exhibit 3 shows the percentage of those funds that were winners in two consecutive years, winners in one year and then losers in the next year, losers then winners, and finally losers in both years. The winner–winner entry, for example, shows that 66% of the first-year winner funds were also winners in the second year. The four entries in the table can be viewed as conditional probabilities.
>
> **Exhibit 3: Persistence of Returns: Conditional Probability for Year 2 Performance Given Year 1 Performance**
>
> |  | Year 2 Winner | Year 2 Loser |
> | --- | --- | --- |
> | Year 1 Winner | 66% | 34% |
> | Year 1 Loser | 34% | 66% |
>
> Based on the data in Exhibit 3, answer the following questions:

1. State the four events needed to define the four conditional probabilities.

## Solution to 1:

The four events needed to define the conditional probabilities are as follows:

*Fund is a Year 1 winner*

*Fund is a Year 1 loser*

*Fund is a Year 2 loser*

*Fund is a Year 2 winner*

---

2. State the four entries of the table as conditional probabilities using the form P(*this event* | *that event*) = number.

### Solution to 2:

From Row 1:

P(*fund is a Year 2 winner* | *fund is a Year 1 winner*) = 0.66
P(*fund is a Year 2 loser* | *fund is a Year 1 winner*) = 0.34

From Row 2:

P(*fund is a Year 2 winner* | *fund is a Year 1 loser*) = 0.34
P(*fund is a Year 2 loser* | *fund is a Year 1 loser*) = 0.66

3. Are the conditional probabilities in Question 2 empirical, a priori, or subjective probabilities?

### Solution to 3:

These probabilities are calculated from data, so they are empirical probabilities.

4. Using information in the table, calculate the probability of the event a *fund is a loser in both Year 1 and Year 2*. (Note that because 50% of funds are categorized as losers in each year, the unconditional probability that a fund is labeled a loser in either year is 0.5.)

### Solution to 4:

The estimated probability is 0.33. Let $A$ represent the event that a *fund is a Year 2 loser*, and let $B$ represent the event that the *fund is a Year 1 loser*. Therefore, the event $AB$ is the event that a *fund is a loser in both Year 1 and Year 2*. From Exhibit 3, $P(A | B) = 0.66$ and $P(B) = 0.50$. Thus, using Equation 2, we find that

$$P(AB) = P(A | B)P(B) = 0.66(0.50) = 0.33$$

or a probability of 0.33. Note that Equation 2 states that the joint probability of $A$ and $B$ equals the probability of $A$ given $B$ times the probability of $B$. Because $P(AB) = P(BA)$, the expression $P(AB) = P(BA) = P(B | A)P(A)$ is equivalent to Equation 2.

---

When we have two events, $A$ and $B$, that we are interested in, we often want to know the probability that either $A$ or $B$ occurs. Here the word "or" is inclusive, meaning that either $A$ or $B$ occurs or that both $A$ and $B$ occur. Put another way, the probability of $A$ or $B$ is the probability that at least one of the two events occurs. Such probabilities are calculated using the **addition rule for probabilities**.

- **Addition Rule for Probabilities.** Given events $A$ and $B$, the probability that $A$ or $B$ occurs, or both occur, is equal to the probability that $A$ occurs, plus the probability that $B$ occurs, minus the probability that both $A$ and $B$ occur.

$$P(A \text{ or } B) = P(A) + P(B) - P(AB) \tag{3}$$

If we think of the individual probabilities of A and B as sets built of outcomes of one or more random variables, the first step in calculating the probability of A or B is to sum the probabilities of the outcomes in A to obtain P(A). If A and B share any outcomes, then if we now added P(B) to P(A), we would count twice the probabilities of those shared outcomes. So we add to P(A) the quantity [P(B) − P(AB)], which is the probability of outcomes in B net of the probability of any outcomes already counted when we computed P(A). Exhibit 4 illustrates this process; we avoid double-counting the outcomes in the intersection of A and B by subtracting P(AB). As an example of the calculation, if P(A) = 0.50, P(B) = 0.40, and P(AB) = 0.20, then P(A or B) = 0.50 + 0.40 − 0.20 = 0.70. Only if the two events A and B were mutually exclusive, so that P(AB) = 0, would it be correct to state that P(A or B) = P(A) + P(B).

**Exhibit 4: Addition Rule for Probabilities**

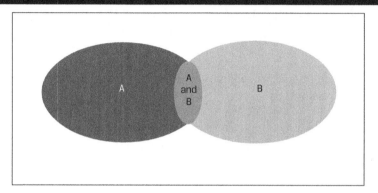

Example 4 illustrates the relation between empirical frequencies and unconditional, conditional, and joint probabilities as well as the multiplication and addition rules for probability.

### EXAMPLE 4

### Frequencies and Probability Concepts

1. Analysts often discuss the frequencies of events as well as their probabilities. In Exhibit 5, there are 150 cells, each representing one trading day. Outcome A, one of the 80 trading days when the stock market index increased, is represented by the dark-shaded rectangle with 80 cells. Outcome B, one of the 30 trading days when interest rates decreased, is represented by the light-bordered rectangle with 30 cells. The overlap between these two rectangles, when both events A and B occurred—the stock market index increased,

# Conditional and Joint Probability

and interest rates decreased—happened 15 times and is represented by the intermediate-shaded rectangle.

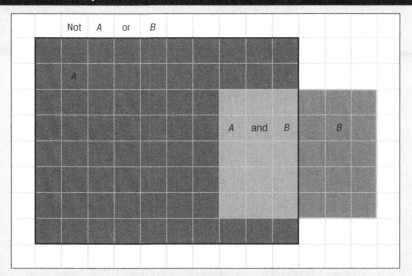

**Exhibit 5: Frequencies for Two Events**

- The frequency of A (stock market index increased) is 80 and has an unconditional probability $P(A) = 80/150 = 0.533$.
- The frequency of B (interest rates decreased) is 30 and has an unconditional probability $P(B) = 30/150 = 0.20$.
- The frequency of A and B (stock market index increased, and interest rates decreased) is 15 and has a joint probability, $P(AB) = 15/150 = 0.10$.

The frequency of A or B (stock market index increased or interest rates decreased) is 95, and $P(A \text{ or } B)$ is $95/150 = 0.633$. Using the addition rule for probabilities, the probability of A or B is $P(A \text{ or } B) = P(A) + P(B) - P(AB) = 80/150 + 30/150 - 15/150 = 95/150 = 0.633$. The probability of not A or B (stock market index did not increase or interest rates did not decrease) $= 1 - 95/150 = 55/150 = 0.367$.

The conditional probability of A given B, $P(A|B)$, stock market index increased given that interest rates decreased, was $15/30 = 0.50$, which is also $P(A|B) = P(AB) / P(B) = (15/150) / (30/150) = 0.10 / 0.20 = 0.50$.

The next example shows how much useful information can be obtained using the probability rules presented to this point.

## EXAMPLE 5

### Probability of a Limit Order Executing

You have two buy limit orders outstanding on the same stock. A limit order to buy stock at a stated price is an order to buy at that price or lower. A number of vendors, including an internet service that you use, supply the estimated probability that a limit order will be filled within a stated time horizon, given the current stock price and the price limit. One buy order (Order 1) was placed at a price limit of $10. The probability that it will execute within one hour is 0.35. The second buy order (Order 2) was placed at a price limit of $9.75; it has a 0.25 probability of executing within the same one-hour time frame.

1. What is the probability that either Order 1 or Order 2 will execute?

## Solution to 1:

The probability is 0.35. The two probabilities that are given are P(Order 1 executes) = 0.35 and P(Order 2 executes) = 0.25. Note that if Order 2 executes, it is certain that Order 1 also executes because the price must pass through $10 to reach $9.75. Thus,

P(Order 1 executes | Order 2 executes) = 1

and using the multiplication rule for probabilities,

P(Order 1 executes and Order 2 executes) = P(Order 1 executes | Order 2 executes)P(Order 2 executes) = 1(0.25)

= 0.25

To answer the question, we use the addition rule for probabilities:

P(Order 1 executes or Order 2 executes) = P(Order 1 executes) + P(Order 2 executes) − P(Order 1 executes and Order 2 executes)
= 0.35 + 0.25 − 0.25

= 0.35

Note that the outcomes for which Order 2 executes are a subset of the outcomes for which Order 1 executes. After you count the probability that Order 1 executes, you have counted the probability of the outcomes for which Order 2 also executes. Therefore, the answer to the question is the probability that Order 1 executes, 0.35.

2. What is the probability that Order 2 executes, given that Order 1 executes?

## Solution to 2:

If the first order executes, the probability that the second order executes is 0.714. In the solution to Part 1, you found that P(Order 1 executes and Order 2 executes) = P(Order 1 executes | Order 2 executes)P(Order 2 executes) = 1(0.25) = 0.25. An equivalent way to state this joint probability is useful here:

P(Order 1 executes and Order 2 executes) = 0.25

= P(Order 2 executes | Order 1 executes)P(Order 1 executes)

Because P(Order 1 executes) = 0.35 was a given, you have one equation with one unknown:

0.25 = P(Order 2 executes | Order 1 executes)(0.35)

You conclude that P(Order 2 executes | Order 1 executes) = 0.25/0.35 = 0.714. You can also use Equation 1 to obtain this answer.

The concepts of independence and dependence are of great interest to investment analysts. These concepts bear on such basic investment questions as which financial variables are useful for investment analysis, whether asset returns can be predicted, and whether superior investment managers can be selected based on their past records.

Two events are independent if the occurrence of one event does not affect the probability of occurrence of the other event.

- Definition of Independent Events. Two events $A$ and $B$ are **independent** if and only if $P(A \mid B) = P(A)$ or, equivalently, $P(B \mid A) = P(B)$.

# Conditional and Joint Probability

The logic of independence is clear: A and B are independent if the conditional probability of A given B, $P(A \mid B)$, is the same as the unconditional probability of A, $P(A)$. Independence means that knowing B tells you nothing about A.

For an example of independent events, suppose that event A is the bankruptcy of Company A, and event B is the bankruptcy of Company B. If the probability of bankruptcy of Company A is $P(A) = 0.20$, and the probability of bankruptcy of Company A given that Company B goes bankrupt is the same, $P(A \mid B) = 0.20$, then event A is independent of event B.

When two events are not independent, they are **dependent**: The probability of occurrence of one is related to the occurrence of the other. If we are trying to forecast one event, information about a dependent event may be useful, but information about an independent event will not be useful. For example, suppose an announcement is released that a biotech company will be acquired at an attractive price by another company. If the prices of pharmaceutical companies increase as a result of this news, the companies' stock prices are not independent of the biotech takeover announcement event. For a different example, if two events are mutually exclusive, then knowledge that one event has occurred gives us information that the other (mutually exclusive) event cannot occur.

When two events are independent, the multiplication rule for probabilities, Equation 2, simplifies because $P(A \mid B)$ in that equation then equals $P(A)$.

- **Multiplication Rule for Independent Events**. When two events are independent, the joint probability of A and B equals the product of the individual probabilities of A and B.

$$P(AB) = P(A)P(B) \tag{4}$$

Therefore, if we are interested in two independent events with probabilities of 0.75 and 0.50, respectively, the probability that both will occur is $0.375 = 0.75(0.50)$. The multiplication rule for independent events generalizes to more than two events; for example, if A, B, and C are independent events, then $P(ABC) = P(A)P(B)P(C)$.

### EXAMPLE 6

#### BankCorp's Earnings per Share (1)

As part of your work as a banking industry analyst, you build models for forecasting earnings per share of the banks you cover. Today you are studying BankCorp. The historical record shows that in 55% of recent quarters, BankCorp's EPS has increased sequentially, and in 45% of quarters, EPS has decreased or remained unchanged sequentially. At this point in your analysis, you are assuming that changes in sequential EPS are independent.

Earnings per share for 2Q:Year 1 (that is, EPS for the second quarter of Year 1) were larger than EPS for 1Q:Year 1.

1. What is the probability that *3Q:Year 1 EPS will be larger than 2Q:Year 1 EPS* (a positive change in sequential EPS)?

#### Solution to 1:

Under the assumption of independence, the probability that *3Q:Year 1 EPS will be larger than 2Q:Year 1 EPS* is the unconditional probability of positive change, 0.55. The fact that 2Q:Year 1 EPS was larger than 1Q:Year 1 EPS is not useful information, because the next change in EPS is independent of the prior change.

2. What is the probability that EPS decreases or remains unchanged in the next two quarters?

**Solution to 2:**

Assuming independence, the probability is 0.2025 = 0.45(0.45).

The following example illustrates how difficult it is to satisfy a set of independent criteria even when each criterion by itself is not necessarily stringent.

### EXAMPLE 7

### Screening Stocks for Investment

You have developed a stock screen—a set of criteria for selecting stocks. Your investment universe (the set of securities from which you make your choices) is 905 large- and medium-cap US equities, specifically all stocks that are members of the S&P 500 and S&P 400 Indexes. Your criteria capture different aspects of the stock selection problem; you believe that the criteria are independent of each other, to a close approximation.

| Criterion | Number of stocks meeting criterion | Fraction of stocks meeting criterion |
|---|---|---|
| First valuation criterion | 556 | 0.614 |
| Second valuation criterion | 489 | 0.540 |
| Analyst coverage criterion | 600 | 0.663 |
| Profitability criterion | 490 | 0.541 |
| Financial strength criterion | 313 | 0.346 |

How many stocks do you expect to pass your screen?

Only 37 stocks out of 905 should pass through your screen. If you define five events—*the stock passes the first valuation criterion, the stock passes the second valuation criterion, the stock passes the analyst coverage criterion, the company passes the profitability criterion, the company passes the financial strength criterion* (say events $A$, $B$, $C$, $D$, and $E$, respectively)—then the probability that a stock will pass all five criteria, under independence, is

$$P(ABCDE) = P(A)P(B)P(C)P(D)P(E) = (0.614)(0.540)(0.663)(0.541)(0.346)$$
$$= 0.0411$$

Although only one of the five criteria is even moderately strict (the strictest lets 34.6% of stocks through), the probability that a stock can pass all five criteria is only 0.0411, or about 4%. If the criteria are independent, the size of the list of candidate investments is expected to be 0.0411(905) = 37 stocks.

An area of intense interest to investment managers and their clients is whether records of past performance are useful in identifying repeat winners and losers. The following example shows how this issue relates to the concept of independence.

# EXAMPLE 8

## Conditional Probabilities and Predictability of Mutual Fund Performance (2)

1. The purpose of the mutual fund study introduced in Example 3 was to address the question of repeat mutual fund winners and losers. If the status of a fund as a winner or a loser in one year is independent of whether it is a winner in the next year, the practical value of performance ranking is questionable. Using the four events defined in Example 3 as building blocks, we can define the following events to address the issue of predictability of mutual fund performance:

   *Fund is a Year 1 winner* and *fund is a Year 2 winner*
   *Fund is a Year 1 winner* and *fund is a Year 2 loser*
   *Fund is a Year 1 loser* and *fund is a Year 2 winner*
   *Fund is a Year 1 loser* and *fund is a Year 2 loser*

   In Part 4 of Example 3, you calculated that

   P(*fund is a Year 2 loser* and *fund is a Year 1 loser*) = 0.33

   If the ranking in one year is independent of the ranking in the next year, what will you expect P(*fund is a Year 2 loser* and *fund is a Year 1 loser*) to be? Interpret the empirical probability 0.33.

   By the multiplication rule for independent events, P(*fund is a Year 2 loser* and *fund is a Year 1 loser*) = P(*fund is a Year 2 loser*)P(*fund is a Year 1 loser*). Because 50% of funds are categorized as losers in each year, the unconditional probability that a fund is labeled a loser in either year is 0.50. Thus P(*fund is a Year 2 loser*)P(*fund is a Year 1 loser*) = 0.50(0.50) = 0.25. If the status of a fund as a loser in one year is independent of whether it is a loser in the prior year, we conclude that P(*fund is a Year 2 loser* and *fund is a Year 1 loser*) = 0.25. This probability is a priori because it is obtained from reasoning about the problem. You could also reason that the four events described above define categories and that if funds are randomly assigned to the four categories, there is a 1/4 probability of *fund is a Year 1 loser* and *fund is a Year 2 loser*. If the classifications in Year 1 and Year 2 were dependent, then the assignment of funds to categories would not be random. The empirical probability of 0.33 is above 0.25. Is this apparent predictability the result of chance? Further analysis would be necessary to determine whether these results would allow you to reject the hypothesis that investment returns are independent between Year 1 and Year 2.

In many practical problems, we logically analyze a problem as follows: We formulate scenarios that we think affect the likelihood of an event that interests us. We then estimate the probability of the event, given the scenario. When the scenarios (conditioning events) are mutually exclusive and exhaustive, no possible outcomes are left out. We can then analyze the event using the **total probability rule**. This rule explains the unconditional probability of the event in terms of probabilities conditional on the scenarios.

The total probability rule is stated below for two cases. Equation 5 gives the simplest case, in which we have two scenarios. One new notation is introduced: If we have an event or scenario S, the event not-S, called the **complement** of S, is written $S^C$. Note that $P(S) + P(S^C) = 1$, as either S or not-S must occur. Equation 6 states the rule for the general case of n mutually exclusive and exhaustive events or scenarios.

- **Total Probability Rule.**

$$P(A) = P(AS) + P(AS^C)$$
$$= P(A|S)P(S) + P(A|S^C)P(S^C) \quad (5)$$

$$P(A) = P(AS_1) + P(AS_2) + \ldots + P(AS_n)$$
$$= P(A|S_1)P(S_1) + P(A|S_2)P(S_2) + \ldots + P(A|S_n)P(S_n) \quad (6)$$

where $S_1, S_2, \ldots, S_n$ are mutually exclusive and exhaustive scenarios or events.

Equation 6 states the following: The probability of any event [$P(A)$] can be expressed as a weighted average of the probabilities of the event, given scenarios [terms such $P(A \mid S_1)$]; the weights applied to these conditional probabilities are the respective probabilities of the scenarios [terms such as $P(S_1)$ multiplying $P(A \mid S_1)$], and the scenarios must be mutually exclusive and exhaustive. Among other applications, this rule is needed to understand Bayes' formula, which we discuss later.

Exhibit 6 is a visual representation of the total probability rule. Panel A illustrates Equation 5 for the total probability rule when there are two scenarios (S and its complement $S^C$). For two scenarios, the probabilities of S and $S^C$ sum to 1, and the probability of A is a weighted average where the probability of A in each scenario is weighted by the probability of each scenario. Panel B of Exhibit 6 illustrates Equation 6 for the total probability rule when there are n scenarios. The scenarios are mutually exclusive and exhaustive, and the sum of the probabilities for the scenarios is 1. Like the two-scenario case, the probability of A given the n-scenarios is a weighted average of the conditional probabilities of A in each scenario, using as weights the probability of each scenario.

# Conditional and Joint Probability

**Exhibit 6: The Total Probability Rule for Two Scenarios and for *n* Scenarios**

### A. Total Probability Rule for Two Scenarios (S and $S^c$)

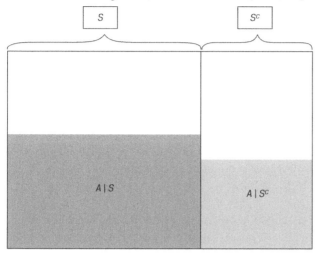

$P(S) + P(S^c) = 1$; $P(A) = P(AS) + P(AS^c) = P(A \mid S) P(S) + P(A \mid S^c) P(S^c)$

### B. Total Probability Rule for n Scenarios

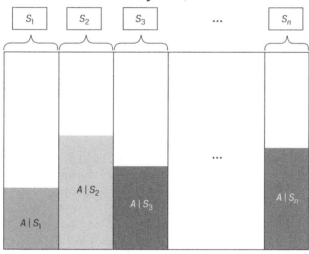

$S_1, S_2, \ldots S_n$, are mutually exclusive and exhaustive scenarios, such that

$$\sum_{i=1}^{n} P(S_i) = 1$$

$P(A) = P(AS_1) + P(AS_2) + \ldots + P(AS_n)$
$= P(A \mid S_1) P(S_1) + P(A \mid S_2) P(S_2) + \ldots + P(A \mid S_n) P(S_n)$

---

In the next example, we use the total probability rule to develop a consistent set of views about BankCorp's earnings per share.

## EXAMPLE 9

### BankCorp's Earnings per Share (2)

You are continuing your investigation into whether you can predict the direction of changes in BankCorp's quarterly EPS. You define four events:

| Event | Probability |
|---|---|
| $A$ = Change in sequential EPS is positive next quarter | 0.55 |
| $A^C$ = Change in sequential EPS is 0 or negative next quarter | 0.45 |
| $S$ = Change in sequential EPS is positive in the prior quarter | 0.55 |
| $S^C$ = Change in sequential EPS is 0 or negative in the prior quarter | 0.45 |

On inspecting the data, you observe some persistence in EPS changes: Increases tend to be followed by increases, and decreases by decreases. The first probability estimate you develop is P(*change in sequential EPS is positive next quarter | change in sequential EPS is 0 or negative in the prior quarter*) = $P(A \mid S^C)$ = 0.40. The most recent quarter's EPS (2Q:Year 1) is announced, and the change is a positive sequential change (the event *S*). You are interested in forecasting EPS for 3Q:Year 1.

1. Write this statement in probability notation: "the probability that the change in sequential EPS is positive next quarter, given that the change in sequential EPS is positive the prior quarter."

## Solution to 1:

In probability notation, this statement is written $P(A \mid S)$.

2. Calculate the probability in Part 1. (Calculate the probability that is consistent with your other probabilities or beliefs.)

## Solution to 2:

The probability is 0.673 that the change in sequential EPS is positive for 3Q:Year 1, given the positive change in sequential EPS for 2Q:Year 1, as shown below.

According to Equation 5, $P(A) = P(A \mid S)P(S) + P(A \mid S^C)P(S^C)$. The values of the probabilities needed to calculate $P(A \mid S)$ are already known: $P(A)$ = 0.55, $P(S)$ = 0.55, $P(S^C)$ = 0.45, and $P(A \mid S^C)$ = 0.40. Substituting into Equation 5,

$0.55 = P(A \mid S)(0.55) + 0.40(0.45)$

Solving for the unknown, $P(A \mid S) = [0.55 - 0.40(0.45)]/0.55 = 0.672727$, or 0.673.

You conclude that P(*change in sequential EPS is positive next quarter | change in sequential EPS is positive the prior quarter*) = 0.673. Any other probability is not consistent with your other estimated probabilities. Reflecting the persistence in EPS changes, this conditional probability of a positive EPS change, 0.673, is greater than the unconditional probability of an EPS increase, 0.55.

## PRINCIPLES OF COUNTING

☐ identify the most appropriate method to solve a particular counting problem and analyze counting problems using factorial, combination, and permutation concepts

The first step in addressing a question often involves determining the different logical possibilities. We may also want to know the number of ways that each of these possibilities can happen. In the back of our mind is often a question about probability. How likely is it that I will observe this particular possibility? Records of success and failure are an example. For instance, the counting methods presented in this section have been used to evaluate a market timer's record. We can also use the methods in this section to calculate what we earlier called a priori probabilities. When we can assume that the possible outcomes of a random variable are equally likely, the probability of an event equals the number of possible outcomes favorable for the event divided by the total number of outcomes.

In counting, enumeration (counting the outcomes one by one) is of course the most basic resource. What we discuss in this section are shortcuts and principles. Without these shortcuts and principles, counting the total number of outcomes can be very difficult and prone to error. The first and basic principle of counting is the multiplication rule.

- **Multiplication Rule for Counting.** If one task can be done in $n_1$ ways, and a second task, given the first, can be done in $n_2$ ways, and a third task, given the first two tasks, can be done in $n_3$ ways, and so on for $k$ tasks, then the number of ways the $k$ tasks can be done is $(n_1)(n_2)(n_3) \ldots (n_k)$.

Exhibit 7 illustrates the multiplication rule where, for example, we have three steps in an investment decision process. In the first step, stocks are classified two ways, as domestic or foreign (represented by dark- and light-shaded circles, respectively). In the second step, stocks are assigned to one of four industries in our investment universe: consumer, energy, financial, or technology (represented by four circles with progressively darker shades, respectively). In the third step, stocks are classified three ways by size: small-cap, mid-cap, and large-cap (represented by light-, medium-, and dark-shaded circles, respectively). Because the first step can be done in two ways, the second in four ways, and the third in three ways, using the multiplication rule, we can carry out the three steps in (2)(4)(3) = 24 different ways.

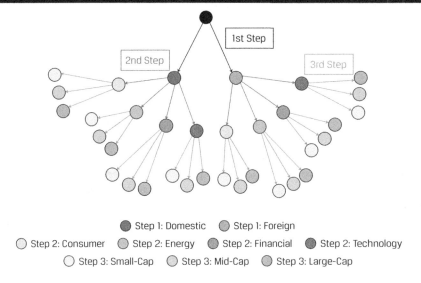

**Exhibit 7: Investment Decision Process Using Multiplication Rule:** $n_1 = 2$, $n_2 = 4$, $n_3 = 3$

- Step 1: Domestic ● Step 1: Foreign
- Step 2: Consumer ● Step 2: Energy ● Step 2: Financial ● Step 2: Technology
- Step 3: Small-Cap ● Step 3: Mid-Cap ● Step 3: Large-Cap

Another illustration is the assignment of members of a group to an equal number of positions. For example, suppose you want to assign three security analysts to cover three different industries. In how many ways can the assignments be made? The first analyst can be assigned in three different ways. Then two industries remain. The second analyst can be assigned in two different ways. Then one industry remains. The third and last analyst can be assigned in only one way. The total number of different assignments equals (3)(2)(1) = 6. The compact notation for the multiplication we have just performed is 3! (read: 3 factorial). If we had $n$ analysts, the number of ways we could assign them to $n$ tasks would be

$$n! = n(n-1)(n-2)(n-3)\ldots 1$$

or ***n* factorial**. (By convention, 0! = 1.) To review, in this application, we repeatedly carry out an operation (here, job assignment) until we use up all members of a group (here, three analysts). With $n$ members in the group, the multiplication formula reduces to $n$ factorial.

The next type of counting problem can be called labeling problems.[1] We want to give each object in a group a label, to place it in a category. The following example illustrates this type of problem.

A mutual fund guide ranked 18 bond mutual funds by total returns for the last year. The guide also assigned each fund one of five risk labels: *high risk* (four funds), *above-average risk* (four funds), *average risk* (three funds), *below-average risk* (four funds), and *low risk* (three funds); as 4 + 4 + 3 + 4 + 3 = 18, all the funds are accounted for. How many different ways can we take 18 mutual funds and label 4 of them *high risk*, 4 *above-average risk*, 3 *average risk*, 4 *below-average risk*, and 3 *low risk*, so that each fund is labeled?

The answer is close to 13 billion. We can label any of 18 funds *high risk* (the first slot), then any of 17 remaining funds, then any of 16 remaining funds, then any of 15 remaining funds (now we have 4 funds in the *high risk* group); then we can label any of 14 remaining funds *above-average risk*, then any of 13 remaining funds, and so forth. There are 18! possible sequences. However, order of assignment within a

---

[1] This discussion follows Kemeny, Schleifer, Snell, and Thompson (1972) in terminology and approach.

**Principles of Counting**

category does not matter. For example, whether a fund occupies the first or third slot of the four funds labeled *high risk*, the fund has the same label (*high risk*). Thus, there are 4! ways to assign a given group of four funds to the four *high risk* slots. Making the same argument for the other categories, in total there are (4!)(4!)(3!)(4!)(3!) equivalent sequences. To eliminate such redundancies from the 18! total, we divide 18! by (4!)(4!)(3!)(4!)(3!). We have 18!/[(4!)(4!)(3!)(4!)(3!)] = 18!/[(24)(24)(6)(24)(6)] = 12,864,852,000. This procedure generalizes as follows.

- **Multinomial Formula (General Formula for Labeling Problems).** The number of ways that $n$ objects can be labeled with $k$ different labels, with $n_1$ of the first type, $n_2$ of the second type, and so on, with $n_1 + n_2 + ... + n_k = n$, is given by

$$\frac{n!}{n_1!\, n_2!...n_k!} \quad (7)$$

The multinomial formula with two different labels ($k = 2$) is especially important. This special case is called the combination formula. A **combination** is a listing in which the order of the listed items does not matter. We state the combination formula in a traditional way, but no new concepts are involved. Using the notation in the formula below, the number of objects with the first label is $r = n_1$ and the number with the second label is $n - r = n_2$ (there are just two categories, so $n_1 + n_2 = n$). Here is the formula:

- **Combination Formula (Binomial Formula).** The number of ways that we can choose $r$ objects from a total of $n$ objects, when the order in which the $r$ objects are listed does not matter, is

$$_nC_r = \binom{n}{r} = \frac{n!}{(n-r)!\,r!} \quad (8)$$

Here $_nC_r$ and $\binom{n}{r}$ are shorthand notations for $n!/(n-r)!r!$ (read: $n$ choose $r$, or $n$ combination $r$).

If we label the $r$ objects as *belongs to the group* and the remaining objects as *does not belong to the group*, whatever the group of interest, the combination formula tells us how many ways we can select a group of size $r$. We can illustrate this formula with the binomial option pricing model. (The binomial pricing model is covered in the next learning module. The only intuition we are concerned with here is that a number of different pricing paths can end up with the same final stock price.) This model describes the movement of the underlying asset as a series of moves, price up (U) or price down (D). For example, two sequences of five moves containing three up moves, such as UUUDD and UDUUD, result in the same final stock price. At least for an option with a payoff dependent on final stock price, the number but not the order of up moves in a sequence matters. How many sequences of five moves *belong to the group with three up moves?* The answer is 10, calculated using the combination formula ("5 choose 3"):

$_5C_3 = 5!/[(5-3)!3!]$

$= [(5)(4)(3)(2)(1)]/[(2)(1)(3)(2)(1)] = 120/12 = 10$ ways

A useful fact can be illustrated as follows: $_5C_3 = 5!/(2!3!)$ equals $_5C_2 = 5!/(3!2!)$, as $3 + 2 = 5$; $_5C_4 = 5!/(1!4!)$ equals $_5C_1 = 5!/(4!1!)$, as $4 + 1 = 5$. This symmetrical relationship can save work when we need to calculate many possible combinations.

Suppose jurors want to select three companies out of a group of five to receive the first-, second-, and third-place awards for the best annual report. In how many ways can the jurors make the three awards? Order does matter if we want to distinguish among the three awards (the rank within the group of three); clearly the question makes order important. On the other hand, if the question were "In how many ways can the jurors choose three winners, without regard to place of finish?" we would use the combination formula.

To address the first question above, we need to count ordered listings such as *first place, New Company; second place, Fir Company; third place, Well Company*. An ordered listing is known as a **permutation**, and the formula that counts the number of permutations is known as the permutation formula. A more formal definition states that a permutation is an ordered subset of $n$ distinct objects.

- **Permutation Formula**. The number of ways that we can choose $r$ objects from a total of $n$ objects, when the order in which the $r$ objects are listed does matter, is

$$_nP_r = \frac{n!}{(n-r)!} \tag{9}$$

So the jurors have $_5P_3 = 5!/(5-3)! = [(5)(4)(3)(2)(1)]/[(2)(1)] = 120/2 = 60$ ways in which they can make their awards. To see why this formula works, note that $[(5)(4)(3)(2)(1)]/[(2)(1)]$ reduces to $(5)(4)(3)$, after cancellation of terms. This calculation counts the number of ways to fill three slots choosing from a group of five companies, according to the multiplication rule of counting. This number is naturally larger than it would be if order did not matter (compare 60 to the value of 10 for "5 choose 3" that we calculated above). For example, *first place, Well Company; second place, Fir Company; third place, New Company* contains the same three companies as *first place, New Company; second place, Fir Company; third place, Well Company*. If we were concerned only with award winners (without regard to place of finish), the two listings would count as one combination. But when we are concerned with the order of finish, the listings count as two permutations.

### EXAMPLE 10

### Permutations and Combinations for Two Out of Four Outcomes

1. There are four balls numbered 1, 2, 3, and 4 in a basket. You are running a contest in which two of the four balls are selected at random from the basket. To win, a player must have correctly chosen the numbers of the two randomly selected balls. Suppose the winning numbers are numbers 1 and 3. If the player must choose the balls in the same order in which they are drawn, she wins if she chose 1 first and 3 second. On the other hand, if order is not important, the player wins if the balls drawn are 1 and then 3 or if the balls drawn are 3 and then 1. The number of possible outcomes for permutations and combinations of choosing 2 out of 4 items is illustrated in Exhibit 8. If order is not important, for choosing 2 out of 4 items, the winner wins twice as often.

# Principles of Counting

> **Exhibit 8: Permutations and Combinations for Choosing 2 out of 4 Items**
>
> | Permutations: Order matters | Combinations: Order does not matter |
> |---|---|
> | List of all possible outcomes:<br>(1 2) (2 1) (3 1) (4 1)<br>(1 3) (2 3) (3 2) (4 2)<br>(1 4) (2 4) (3 4) (4 3) | List of all possible outcomes:<br>(1 2) (2 3) (3 4)<br>(1 3) (2 4)<br>(1 4) |
> | Number of permutations:<br>$_nP_r = \dfrac{n!}{(n-r)!}$<br>$_4P_2 = \dfrac{4!}{(4-2)!} = \dfrac{4 \times 3 \times 2 \times 1}{2 \times 1} = 12$ | Number of combinations:<br>$_nC_r = \dfrac{n!}{(n-r)!r!}$<br>$_4C_2 = \dfrac{4!}{(4-2)!2!} = \dfrac{4 \times 3 \times 2 \times 1}{2 \times 1 \times 2 \times 1} = 6$ |
>
> If order is important, the number of permutations (possible outcomes) is much larger than the number of combinations when order is not important.

## EXAMPLE 11

### Reorganizing the Analyst Team Assignments

1. Gehr-Flint Investors classifies the stocks in its investment universe into 11 industries and is assigning each research analyst one or two industries. Five of the industries have been assigned, and you are asked to cover two industries from the remaining six.

    How many possible pairs of industries remain?

    **A.** 12

    **B.** 15

    **C.** 36

### Solution:

B is correct. The number of combinations of selecting two industries out of six is equal to

$$_nC_r = \begin{bmatrix} n \\ r \end{bmatrix} = \dfrac{n!}{(n-r)!r!} = \dfrac{6!}{4!2!} = 15$$

The number of possible combinations for picking two industries out of six is 15.

## EXAMPLE 12

### Australian Powerball Lottery

To win the Australian Powerball jackpot, you must match the numbers of seven balls pulled from a basket (the balls are numbered 1 through 35) plus the number of the Powerball (numbered 1 through 20). The order in which the seven balls are drawn is not important. The number of combinations of matching 7 out of 35 balls is

$$_nC_r = \begin{bmatrix} n \\ r \end{bmatrix} = \frac{n!}{(n-r)!r!} = \frac{35!}{28!7!} = 6,724,520$$

The number of combinations for picking the Powerball, 1 out of 20, is

$$_nC_r = \begin{bmatrix} n \\ r \end{bmatrix} = \frac{n!}{(n-r)!r!} = \frac{20!}{19!1!} = 20$$

The number of ways to pick the seven balls plus the Powerball is

$$_{35}C_7 \times {}_{20}C_1 = 6,724,520 \times 20 = 134,490,400$$

Your probability of winning the Australian Powerball with one ticket is 1 in 134,490,400.

Exhibit 9 is a flow chart that may help you apply the counting methods we have presented in this section.

# Principles of Counting

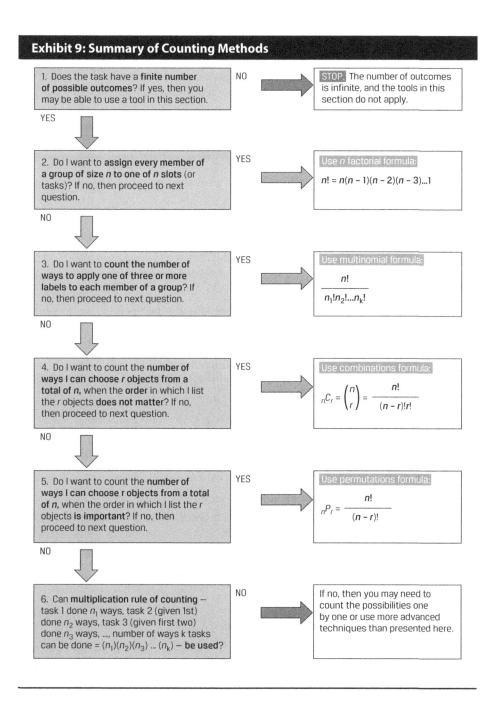

# SUMMARY

In this reading, we have discussed the essential concepts and tools of probability. We have also analyzed counting problems using factorial, combination, and permutation concepts.

- A random variable is a quantity whose outcome is uncertain.
- Probability is a number between 0 and 1 that describes the chance that a stated event will occur.
- An event is a specified set of outcomes of a random variable.

- Mutually exclusive events can occur only one at a time. Exhaustive events cover or contain all possible outcomes.
- The two defining properties of a probability are, first, that $0 \le P(E) \le 1$ (where $P(E)$ denotes the probability of an event $E$) and, second, that the sum of the probabilities of any set of mutually exclusive and exhaustive events equals 1.
- A probability estimated from data as a relative frequency of occurrence is an empirical probability. A probability drawing on personal or subjective judgment is a subjective probability. A probability obtained based on logical analysis is an a priori probability.
- A probability of an event $E$, $P(E)$, can be stated as odds for $E = P(E)/[1 - P(E)]$ or odds against $E = [1 - P(E)]/P(E)$. In other words, given the odds for $E$ of "$a$ to $b$," the implied probability of $E$ is $a/(a + b)$.
- Probabilities that are inconsistent create profit opportunities, according to the Dutch Book Theorem.
- A probability of an event *not* conditioned on another event is an unconditional probability. The unconditional probability of an event $A$ is denoted $P(A)$. Unconditional probabilities are also called marginal probabilities.
- A probability of an event given (conditioned on) another event is a conditional probability. The probability of an event $A$ given an event $B$ is denoted $P(A \mid B)$, and $P(A \mid B) = P(AB)/P(B)$, $P(B) \ne 0$.
- The probability of both $A$ and $B$ occurring is the joint probability of $A$ and $B$, denoted $P(AB)$.
- The multiplication rule for probabilities is $P(AB) = P(A \mid B)P(B)$.
- The probability that $A$ or $B$ occurs, or both occur, is denoted by $P(A \text{ or } B)$.
- The addition rule for probabilities is $P(A \text{ or } B) = P(A) + P(B) - P(AB)$.
- When events are independent, the occurrence of one event does not affect the probability of occurrence of the other event. Otherwise, the events are dependent.
- The multiplication rule for independent events states that if $A$ and $B$ are independent events, $P(AB) = P(A)P(B)$. The rule generalizes in similar fashion to more than two events.
- According to the total probability rule, if $S_1, S_2, ..., S_n$ are mutually exclusive and exhaustive scenarios or events, then $P(A) = P(A \mid S_1)P(S_1) + P(A \mid S_2)P(S_2) + ... + P(A \mid S_n)P(S_n)$.
- The multiplication rule of counting states that, if one task can be done in $n_1$ ways, and a second task, given the first, can be done in $n_2$ ways, and a third task, given the first two tasks, can be done in $n_3$ ways, and so on for k tasks, then the number of ways the k tasks can be done is $(n_1)(n_2)(n_3) ... (n_k)$.
- The number of ways to assign every member of a group of size $n$ to $n$ slots is $n! = n(n-1)(n-2)(n-3) ... 1$. (By convention, $0! = 1$.)
- The number of ways that $n$ objects can be labeled with $k$ different labels, with $n_1$ of the first type, $n_2$ of the second type, and so on, with $n_1 + n_2 + ... + n_k = n$, is given by $n!/(n_1!n_2! ... n_k!)$. This expression is the multinomial formula.
- A special case of the multinomial formula is the combination formula. The number of ways to choose $r$ objects from a total of $n$ objects, when the order in which the $r$ objects are listed does not matter, is

$$_nC_r = \binom{n}{r} = \frac{n!}{(n-r)!r!}$$

# Principles of Counting

- The number of ways to choose $r$ objects from a total of $n$ objects, when the order in which the $r$ objects are listed does matter, is

$$_nP_r = \frac{n!}{(n-r)!}$$

This expression is the permutation formula.

# REFERENCES

Kemeny, John G., Arthur Schleifer, J. Laurie Snell, Gerald L. Thompson. 1972. Finite Mathematics with Business Applications, 2nd edition. Englewood Cliffs: Prentice-Hall.

# PRACTICE PROBLEMS

1. In probability theory, exhaustive events are *best* described as the set of events that:

    A. have a probability of zero.

    B. are mutually exclusive.

    C. include all potential outcomes.

2. Which probability estimate *most likely* varies greatly between people?

    A. An *a priori* probability

    B. An empirical probability

    C. A subjective probability

3. If the probability that Zolaf Company sales exceed last year's sales is 0.167, the odds for exceeding sales are *closest* to:

    A. 1 to 5.

    B. 1 to 6.

    C. 5 to 1.

4. After six months, the growth portfolio that Rayan Khan manages has outperformed its benchmark. Khan states that his odds of beating the benchmark for the year are 3 to 1. If these odds are correct, what is the probability that Khan's portfolio will beat the benchmark for the year?

    A. 0.33

    B. 0.67

    C. 0.75

5. Suppose that 5% of the stocks meeting your stock-selection criteria are in the telecommunications (telecom) industry. Also, dividend-paying telecom stocks are 1% of the total number of stocks meeting your selection criteria. What is the probability that a stock is dividend paying, given that it is a telecom stock that has met your stock selection criteria?

6. You are using the following three criteria to screen potential acquisition targets from a list of 500 companies:

| Criterion | Fraction of the 500 Companies Meeting the Criterion |
| --- | --- |
| Product lines compatible | 0.20 |
| Company will increase combined sales growth rate | 0.45 |
| Balance sheet impact manageable | 0.78 |

    If the criteria are independent, how many companies will pass the screen?

7. Florence Hixon is screening a set of 100 stocks based on two criteria (Criterion

1 and Criterion 2). She set the passing level such that 50% of the stocks passed each screen. For these stocks, the values for Criterion 1 and Criterion 2 are not independent but are positively related. How many stocks should pass Hixon's two screens?

   **A.** Less than 25

   **B.** 25

   **C.** More than 25

8. You apply both valuation criteria and financial strength criteria in choosing stocks. The probability that a randomly selected stock (from your investment universe) meets your valuation criteria is 0.25. Given that a stock meets your valuation criteria, the probability that the stock meets your financial strength criteria is 0.40. What is the probability that a stock meets both your valuation and financial strength criteria?

9. The probability of an event given that another event has occurred is a:

   **A.** joint probability.

   **B.** marginal probability.

   **C.** conditional probability.

10. After estimating the probability that an investment manager will exceed his benchmark return in each of the next two quarters, an analyst wants to forecast the probability that the investment manager will exceed his benchmark return over the two-quarter period in total. Assuming that each quarter's performance is independent of the other, which probability rule should the analyst select?

    **A.** Addition rule

    **B.** Multiplication rule

    **C.** Total probability rule

11. Which of the following is a property of two dependent events?

    **A.** The two events must occur simultaneously.

    **B.** The probability of one event influences the probability of the other event.

    **C.** The probability of the two events occurring is the product of each event's probability.

12. A manager will select 20 bonds out of his universe of 100 bonds to construct a portfolio. Which formula provides the number of possible portfolios?

    **A.** Permutation formula

    **B.** Multinomial formula

    **C.** Combination formula

13. A firm will select two of four vice presidents to be added to the investment committee. How many different groups of two are possible?

    **A.** 6

**Practice Problems**

   B. 12

   C. 24

14. From an approved list of 25 funds, a portfolio manager wants to rank 4 mutual funds from most recommended to least recommended. Which formula is *most* appropriate to calculate the number of possible ways the funds could be ranked?

   A. Permutation formula

   B. Multinomial formula

   C. Combination formula

15. Himari Fukumoto has joined a new firm and is selecting mutual funds in the firm's pension plan. If 10 mutual funds are available, and she plans to select four, how many different sets of mutual funds can she choose?

   A. 210

   B. 720

   C. 5,040

# The following information relates to questions 16-18

Gerd Sturm wants to sponsor a contest with a $1 million prize. The winner must pick the stocks that will be the top five performers next year among the 30 stocks in a well-known large-cap stock index. He asks you to estimate the chances that contestants can win the contest.

16. What are the chances of winning if the contestants must pick the five stocks in the correct order of their total return? If choosing five stocks randomly, a contestant's chance of winning is one out of:

   A. 142,506.

   B. 17,100,720.

   C. 24,300,000.

17. What are the chances of winning if the contestants must pick the top five stocks without regard to order? If choosing five stocks randomly, a contestant's chance of winning is one out of:

   A. 142,506.

   B. 17,100,720.

   C. 24,300,000.

18. Sturm asks, "Can we trust these probabilities of winning?"

# SOLUTIONS

1. C is correct. The term "exhaustive" means that the events cover all possible outcomes.

2. C is correct. A subjective probability draws on personal or subjective judgment that may be without reference to any particular data.

3. A is correct. Given odds for $E$ of $a$ to $b$, the implied probability of $E = a/(a + b)$. Stated in terms of odds $a$ to $b$ with $a = 1$, $b = 5$, the probability of $E = 1/(1 + 5) = 1/6 = 0.167$. This result confirms that a probability of 0.167 for beating sales is odds of 1 to 5.

4. C is correct. The odds for beating the benchmark = $P(beating\ benchmark) / [1 - P(beating\ benchmark)]$. Let $P(A) = P(beating\ benchmark)$. Odds for beating the benchmark = $P(A) / [1 - P(A)]$.

   $3 = P(A) / [1 - P(A)]$

   Solving for $P(A)$, the probability of beating the benchmark is 0.75.

5. Use this equation to find this conditional probability: $P(stock\ is\ dividend\ paying\ |\ telecom\ stock\ that\ meets\ criteria) = P(stock\ is\ dividend\ paying\ and\ telecom\ stock\ that\ meets\ criteria)/P(telecom\ stock\ that\ meets\ criteria) = 0.01/0.05 = 0.20$.

6. According to the multiplication rule for independent events, the probability of a company meeting all three criteria is the product of the three probabilities. Labeling the event that a company passes the first, second, and third criteria, $A$, $B$, and $C$, respectively, $P(ABC) = P(A)P(B)P(C) = (0.20)(0.45)(0.78) = 0.0702$. As a consequence, $(0.0702)(500) = 35.10$, so 35 companies pass the screen.

7. C is correct. Let event $A$ be a stock passing the first screen (Criterion 1) and event $B$ be a stock passing the second screen (Criterion 2). The probability of passing each screen is $P(A) = 0.50$ and $P(B) = 0.50$. If the two criteria are independent, the joint probability of passing both screens is $P(AB) = P(A)P(B) = 0.50 \times 0.50 = 0.25$, so 25 out of 100 stocks would pass both screens. However, the two criteria are positively related, and $P(AB) \neq 0.25$. Using the multiplication rule for probabilities, the joint probability of $A$ and $B$ is $P(AB) = P(A\ |\ B)P(B)$. If the two criteria are not independent, and if $P(B) = 0.50$, then the contingent probability of $P(A\ |\ B)$ is greater than 0.50. So the joint probability of $P(AB) = P(A\ |\ B)P(B)$ is greater than 0.25. More than 25 stocks should pass the two screens.

8. Use the equation for the multiplication rule for probabilities $P(AB) = P(A\ |\ B)P(B)$, defining $A$ as the event that *a stock meets the financial strength criteria* and defining $B$ as the event that *a stock meets the valuation criteria*. Then $P(AB) = P(A\ |\ B)P(B) = 0.40 \times 0.25 = 0.10$. The probability that a stock meets both the financial and valuation criteria is 0.10.

9. C is correct. A conditional probability is the probability of an event given that another event has occurred.

10. B is correct. Because the events are independent, the multiplication rule is most appropriate for forecasting their joint probability. The multiplication rule for independent events states that the joint probability of both $A$ and $B$ occurring is $P(AB) = P(A)P(B)$.

11. B is correct. The probability of the occurrence of one is related to the occurrence

of the other. If we are trying to forecast one event, information about a dependent event may be useful.

12. C is correct. The combination formula provides the number of ways that $r$ objects can be chosen from a total of $n$ objects, when the order in which the $r$ objects are listed does not matter. The order of the bonds within the portfolio does not matter.

13. A is correct. The answer is found using the combination formula

$$_nC_r = \binom{n}{r} = \frac{n!}{(n-r)!r!}$$

Here, $n = 4$ and $r = 2$, so the answer is $4!/[(4-2)!2!] = 24/[(2) \times (2)] = 6$. This result can be verified by assuming there are four vice presidents, VP1–VP4. The six possible additions to the investment committee are VP1 and VP2, VP1 and VP3, VP1 and VP4, VP2 and VP3, VP2 and VP4, and VP3 and VP4.

14. A is correct. The permutation formula is used to choose $r$ objects from a total of $n$ objects when order matters. Because the portfolio manager is trying to rank the four funds from most recommended to least recommended, the order of the funds matters; therefore, the permutation formula is most appropriate.

15. A is correct. The number of combinations is the number of ways to pick four mutual funds out of 10 without regard to order, which is

$$_nC_r = \frac{n!}{(n-r)!r!}$$

$$_{10}C_4 = \frac{10!}{(10-4)!4!} = \frac{10 \times 9 \times 8 \times 7}{4 \times 3 \times 2 \times 1} = 210$$

16. B is correct. The number of permutations is the number of ways to pick five stocks out of 30 in the correct order.

$$_nP_r = \frac{n!}{(n-r)!r!}$$

$$_{30}P_5 = \frac{30!}{(30-5)!} = \frac{30!}{25!} = 30 \times 29 \times 28 \times 27 \times 26 = 17,100,720$$

The contestant's chance of winning is one out of 17,100,720.

17. A is correct. The number of combinations is the number of ways to pick five stocks out of 30 without regard to order.

$$_nC_r = \frac{n!}{(n-r)!r!}$$

$$_{30}C_5 = \frac{30!}{(30-5)!5!} = \frac{30 \times 29 \times 28 \times 27 \times 26}{5 \times 4 \times 3 \times 2 \times 1} = 142,506$$

The contestant's chance of winning is one out of 142,506.

18. This contest does not resemble a usual lottery. Each of the 30 stocks does not have an equal chance of having the highest returns. Furthermore, contestants may have some favored investments, and the 30 stocks will not be chosen with the same frequencies. To guard against more than one person selecting the winners correctly, Sturm may wish to stipulate that if there is more than one winner, the winners will share the $1 million prize.

# LEARNING MODULE 4

## Common Probability Distributions

by Richard A. DeFusco, PhD, CFA, Dennis W. McLeavey, DBA, CFA, Jerald E. Pinto, PhD, CFA, and David E. Runkle, PhD, CFA.

*Richard A. DeFusco, PhD, CFA, is at the University of Nebraska–Lincoln (USA). Dennis W. McLeavey, DBA, CFA, is at the University of Rhode Island (USA). Jerald E. Pinto, PhD, CFA. David E. Runkle, PhD, CFA, is at Jacobs Levy Equity Management (USA).*

*CFA Institute would like to thank Adam Kobor, PhD, CFA, at New York University Investment Office (USA), for this major revision of "Common Probability Distributions," including new visuals, graphics, Microsoft Excel functions, code snippets, and related text content throughout the reading.*

## LEARNING OUTCOMES

| Mastery | The candidate should be able to: |
|---|---|
| ☐ | define a probability distribution and compare and contrast discrete and continuous random variables and their probability functions |
| ☐ | calculate and interpret probabilities for a random variable given its cumulative distribution function |
| ☐ | describe the properties of a discrete uniform random variable, and calculate and interpret probabilities given the discrete uniform distribution function |
| ☐ | describe the properties of the continuous uniform distribution, and calculate and interpret probabilities given a continuous uniform distribution |
| ☐ | describe the properties of a Bernoulli random variable and a binomial random variable, and calculate and interpret probabilities given the binomial distribution function |
| ☐ | explain the key properties of the normal distribution |
| ☐ | contrast a multivariate distribution and a univariate distribution, and explain the role of correlation in the multivariate normal distribution |
| ☐ | calculate the probability that a normally distributed random variable lies inside a given interval |
| ☐ | explain how to standardize a random variable |

# LEARNING OUTCOMES

| Mastery | The candidate should be able to: |
|---|---|
| ☐ | calculate and interpret probabilities using the standard normal distribution |
| ☐ | describe the properties of the Student's $t$-distribution, and calculate and interpret its degrees of freedom |
| ☐ | describe the properties of the chi-square distribution and the $F$-distribution, and calculate and interpret their degrees of freedom |

# 1 DISCRETE RANDOM VARIABLES

| | |
|---|---|
| ☐ | define a probability distribution and compare and contrast discrete and continuous random variables and their probability functions |
| ☐ | calculate and interpret probabilities for a random variable given its cumulative distribution function |

Probabilities play a critical role in investment decisions. Although we cannot predict the future, informed investment decisions are based on some kind of probabilistic thinking. An analyst may put probability estimates behind the success of her high-conviction or low-conviction stock recommendations. Risk managers would typically think in probabilistic terms: What is the probability of not achieving the target return, or what kind of losses are we facing with high likelihood over the relevant time horizon? Probability distributions also underpin validating trade signal–generating models: For example, does earnings revision play a significant role in forecasting stock returns?

In nearly all investment decisions, we work with random variables. The return on a stock and its earnings per share are familiar examples of random variables. To make probability statements about a random variable, we need to understand its probability distribution. A **probability distribution** specifies the probabilities associated with the possible outcomes of a random variable.

In this reading, we present important facts about seven probability distributions and their investment uses. These seven distributions—the uniform, binomial, normal, lognormal, Student's $t$-, chi-square, and $F$-distributions—are used extensively in investment analysis. Normal and binomial distributions are used in such basic valuation models as the Black–Scholes–Merton option pricing model, the binomial option pricing model, and the capital asset pricing model. Student's $t$-, chi-square, and $F$-distributions are applied in validating statistical significance and in hypothesis testing. With the working knowledge of probability distributions provided in this reading, you will be better prepared to study and use other quantitative methods, such as regression analysis, time-series analysis, and hypothesis testing.

We start by defining basic concepts and terms, then illustrate the operation of these concepts through the simplest distribution, the uniform distribution, and then address probability distributions that have more applications in investment work but also greater complexity.

## Discrete Random Variables

A **random variable** is a quantity whose future outcomes are uncertain. The two basic types of random variables are discrete random variables and continuous random variables. A **discrete random variable** can take on at most a countable (possibly infinite) number of possible values. For example, a discrete random variable $X$ can take on a limited number of outcomes $x_1, x_2, \ldots, x_n$ ($n$ possible outcomes), or a discrete random variable $Y$ can take on an unlimited number of outcomes $y_1, y_2, \ldots$ (without end). The number of "yes" votes at a corporate board meeting, for example, is a discrete variable that is countable and finite (from 0 to the voting number of board members). The number of trades at a stock exchange is also countable but is infinite, since there is no limit to the number of trades by the market participants. Note that $X$ refers to the random variable, and $x$ refers to an outcome of $X$. We subscript outcomes, as in $x_1$ and $x_2$, when we need to distinguish among different outcomes in a list of outcomes of a random variable. Since we can count all the possible outcomes of $X$ and $Y$ (even if we go on forever in the case of $Y$), both $X$ and $Y$ satisfy the definition of a discrete random variable.

In contrast, we cannot count the outcomes of a **continuous random variable**. We cannot describe the possible outcomes of a continuous random variable $Z$ with a list $z_1, z_2, \ldots$, because the outcome $(z_1 + z_2)/2$, not in the list, would always be possible. The volume of water in a glass is an example of a continuous random variable since we cannot "count" water on a discrete scale but can only measure its volume. In finance, unless a variable exhibits truly discrete behavior—for example, a positive or negative earnings surprise or the number of central bank board members voting for a rate hike—it is practical to work with a continuous distribution in many cases. The rate of return on an investment is an example of such a continuous random variable.

In working with a random variable, we need to understand its possible outcomes. For example, a majority of the stocks traded on the New Zealand Stock Exchange are quoted in increments of NZ$0.01. Quoted stock price is thus a discrete random variable with possible values NZ$0, NZ$0.01, NZ$0.02, ..., but we can also model stock price as a continuous random variable (as a lognormal random variable, to look ahead). In many applications, we have a choice between using a discrete or a continuous distribution. We are usually guided by which distribution is most efficient for the task we face. This opportunity for choice is not surprising, because many discrete distributions can be approximated with a continuous distribution, and vice versa. In most practical cases, a probability distribution is only a mathematical idealization, or approximate model, of the relative frequencies of a random variable's possible outcomes.

Every random variable is associated with a probability distribution that describes the variable completely. We can view a probability distribution in two ways. The basic view is the **probability function**, which specifies the probability that the random variable takes on a specific value: $P(X = x)$ is the probability that a random variable $X$ takes on the value $x$. For a discrete random variable, the shorthand notation for the probability function (sometimes referred to as the "probability mass function") is $p(x) = P(X = x)$. For continuous random variables, the probability function is denoted $f(x)$ and called the **probability density function** (pdf), or just the density.

A probability function has two key properties (which we state, without loss of generality, using the notation for a discrete random variable):

- $0 \leq p(x) \leq 1$, because probability is a number between 0 and 1.
- The sum of the probabilities $p(x)$ over all values of $X$ equals 1. If we add up the probabilities of all the distinct possible outcomes of a random variable, that sum must equal 1.

We are often interested in finding the probability of a range of outcomes rather than a specific outcome. In these cases, we take the second view of a probability distribution, the cumulative distribution function (cdf). The **cumulative distribution function**, or distribution function for short, gives the probability that a random variable $X$ is less than or equal to a particular value $x$, $P(X \leq x)$. For both discrete and continuous random variables, the shorthand notation is $F(x) = P(X \leq x)$. How does the cumulative distribution function relate to the probability function? The word "cumulative" tells the story. To find $F(x)$, we sum up, or accumulate, values of the probability function for all outcomes less than or equal to $x$. The function of the cdf is parallel to that of cumulative relative frequency.

We illustrate the concepts of probability density functions and cumulative distribution functions with an empirical example using daily returns (i.e., percentage changes) of the fictitious Euro-Asia-Africa (EAA) Equity Index. This dataset spans five years and consists of 1,258 observations, with a minimum value of −4.1%, a maximum value of 5.0%, a range of 9.1%, and a mean daily return of 0.04%.

Exhibit 1 depicts the histograms, representing pdfs, and empirical cdfs (i.e., accumulated values of the bars in the histograms) based on daily returns of the EAA Equity Index. Panels A and B represent the same dataset; the only difference is the histogram bins used in Panel A are wider than those used in Panel B, so naturally Panel B has more bins. Note that in Panel A, we divided the range of observed daily returns (−5% to 5%) into 10 bins, so we chose the bin width to be 1.0%. In Panel B, we wanted a more granular histogram with a narrower range, so we divided the range into 20 bins, resulting in a bin width of 0.5%. Panel A gives a sense of the observed range of daily index returns, whereas Panel B is much more granular, so it more closely resembles continuous pdf and cdf graphs.

# Discrete Random Variables

## Exhibit 1: PDFs and CDFs of Daily Returns for EAA Equity Index

### A. Wide Bin Widths

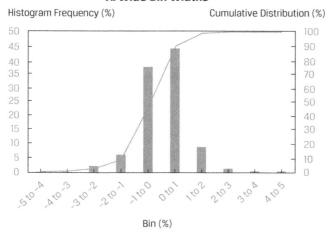

### B. Narrow Bin Widths

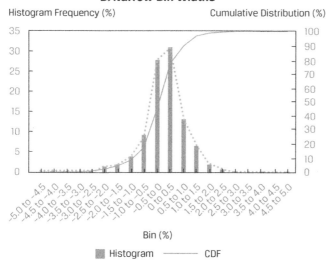

---

### EXAMPLE 1

## Using PDFs and CDFs of Discrete and Continuous Random Variables to Calculate Probabilities

### Discrete Random Variables: Rolling a Die

The example of rolling a six-sided die is an easy and intuitive way to illustrate a discrete random variable's pdf and cdf.

1. What is the probability that you would roll the number 3?

## Solution to 1:

Assuming the die is fair, rolling any number from 1 to 6 has a probability of 1/6 each, so the chance of rolling the number 3 would also equal 1/6. This outcome represents the pdf of this game; the pdf at number 3 takes a value of 1/6. In fact, it takes a value of 1/6 at every number from 1 to 6.

2. What is the probability that you would roll a number less than or equal to 3?

## Solution to 2:

Answering this question involves the cdf of the die game. Three possible events would satisfy our criterion—namely, rolling 1, 2, or 3. The probability of rolling any of these numbers would be 1/6, so by accumulating them from 1 to 3, we get a probability of 3/6, or ½. The cdf of rolling a die takes a value of 1/6 at number 1, 3/6 (or 50%) at number 3, and 6/6 (or 100%) at number 6.

## Continuous Random Variables: EAA Index Return

3. We use the EAA Index to illustrate the pdf and cdf for a continuously distributed random variable. Since daily returns can take on *any* numbers within a reasonable range rather than having discrete outcomes, we represent the pdf in the context of bins (as shown in the following table).

| Bin | PDF | Bin | PDF |
|---|---|---|---|
| –5% to –4% | 0.1% | 0% to 1% | 44.1% |
| –4% to –3% | 0.6% | 1% to 2% | 8.8% |
| –3% to –2% | 1.8% | 2% to 3% | 1.0% |
| –2% to –1% | 6.1% | 3% to 4% | 0.1% |
| –1% to 0% | 37.4% | 4% to 5% | 0.1% |

In our sample, we did not find any daily returns below –5%, and we found only 0.1% of the total observations between –5% and –4%. In the next bin, –4% to –3%, we found 0.6% of the total observations, and so on.

If this empirical pdf is a guide for the future, what is the probability that we will see a daily return less than –2%?

## Solution to 3:

We must calculate the cdf up to –2%. The answer is the sum of the pdfs of the first three bins (see the shaded rectangle in the table provided); 0.1% + 0.6% + 1.8% = 2.5%. So, the probability that we will see a daily return less than –2% is 2.5%.

Next, we illustrate these concepts with examples and show how we use discrete and continuous distributions. We start with the simplest distribution, the discrete uniform distribution.

## DISCRETE AND CONTINUOUS UNIFORM DISTRIBUTION

☐ describe the properties of a discrete uniform random variable, and calculate and interpret probabilities given the discrete uniform distribution function

☐ describe the properties of the continuous uniform distribution, and calculate and interpret probabilities given a continuous uniform distribution

The simplest of all probability distributions is the discrete uniform distribution. Suppose that the possible outcomes are the integers (whole numbers) 1–8, inclusive, and the probability that the random variable takes on any of these possible values is the same for all outcomes (that is, it is uniform). With eight outcomes, $p(x) = 1/8$, or 0.125, for all values of $X$ ($X = 1, 2, 3, 4, 5, 6, 7, 8$); this statement is a complete description of this discrete uniform random variable. The distribution has a finite number of specified outcomes, and each outcome is equally likely. Exhibit 2 summarizes the two views of this random variable, the probability function and the cumulative distribution function, with Panel A in tabular form and Panel B in graphical form.

### Exhibit 2: PDF and CDF for Discrete Uniform Random Variable

**A. Probability Function and Cumulative Distribution Function for a Discrete Uniform Random Variable**

| $X = x$ | Probability Function $p(x) = P(X = x)$ | Cumulative Distribution Function $F(x) = P(X \leq x)$ |
| --- | --- | --- |
| 1 | 0.125 | 0.125 |
| 2 | 0.125 | 0.250 |
| 3 | 0.125 | 0.375 |
| 4 | 0.125 | 0.500 |
| 5 | 0.125 | 0.625 |
| 6 | 0.125 | 0.750 |

**A. Probability Function and Cumulative Distribution Function for a Discrete Uniform Random Variable**

| $X = x$ | Probability Function $p(x) = P(X = x)$ | Cumulative Distribution Function $F(x) = P(X \leq x)$ |
|---|---|---|
| 7 | 0.125 | 0.875 |
| 8 | 0.125 | 1.000 |

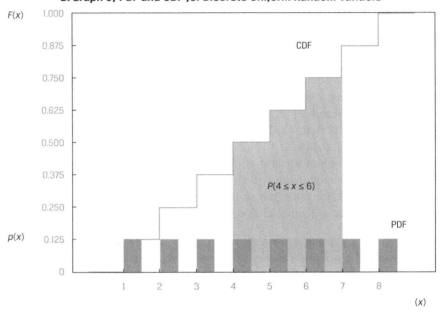

**B. Graph of PDF and CDF for Discrete Uniform Random Variable**

We can use the table in Panel A to find three probabilities: $P(X \leq 7)$, $P(4 \leq X \leq 6)$, and $P(4 < X \leq 6)$. The following examples illustrate how to use the cdf to find the probability that a random variable will fall in any interval (for any random variable, not only the uniform one). The results can also be gleaned visually from the graph in Panel B.

- The probability that $X$ is less than or equal to 7, $P(X \leq 7)$, is the next-to-last entry in the third column: 0.875, or 87.5%.
- To find $P(4 \leq X \leq 6)$, we need to find the sum of three probabilities: $p(4)$, $p(5)$, and $p(6)$. We can find this sum in two ways. We can add $p(4)$, $p(5)$, and $p(6)$ from the second column. Or we can calculate the probability as the difference between two values of the cumulative distribution function:

$$F(6) = P(X \leq 6) = p(6) + p(5) + p(4) + p(3) + p(2) + p(1),$$

and

$$F(3) = P(X \leq 3) = p(3) + p(2) + p(1),$$

so

$$P(4 \leq X \leq 6) = F(6) - F(3) = p(6) + p(5) + p(4) = 3/8.$$

So, we calculate the second probability as $F(6) - F(3) = 3/8$. This can be seen as the shaded area under the step function cdf graph in Panel B.

- The third probability, $P(4 < X \leq 6)$, the probability that $X$ is less than or equal to 6 but greater than 4, is $p(5) + p(6)$. We compute it as follows, using the cdf:

$P(4 < X \leq 6) = P(X \leq 6) - P(X \leq 4) = F(6) - F(4) = p(6) + p(5) = 2/8$.

So we calculate the third probability as $F(6) - F(4) = 2/8$.

Suppose we want to check that the discrete uniform probability function satisfies the general properties of a probability function given earlier. The first property is $0 \leq p(x) \leq 1$. We see that $p(x) = 1/8$ for all $x$ in the first column of in Panel A. [Note that $p(x)$ equals 0 for numbers $x$ that are not in that column, such as −14 or 12.215.] The first property is satisfied. The second property is that the probabilities sum to 1. The entries in the second column of Panel A do sum to 1.

The cdf has two other characteristic properties:

- The cdf lies between 0 and 1 for any $x$: $0 \leq F(x) \leq 1$.
- As $x$ increases, the cdf either increases or remains constant.

Check these statements by looking at the third column in the table in Panel A and at the graph in Panel B.

We now have some experience working with probability functions and cdfs for discrete random variables. As we will see next, the uniform distribution has an important technical use: it is the basis for generating random numbers, which, in turn, produce random observations for all other probability distributions.

## Continuous Uniform Distribution

The continuous uniform distribution is the simplest continuous probability distribution. The uniform distribution has two main uses. As the basis of techniques for generating random numbers, the uniform distribution plays a role in Monte Carlo simulation, which will be covered in the CFA Program curriculum. As the probability distribution that describes equally likely outcomes, the uniform distribution is an appropriate probability model to represent a particular kind of uncertainty in beliefs in which all outcomes appear equally likely.

The pdf for a uniform random variable is

$$f(x) = \begin{cases} \frac{1}{b-a} & \text{for } a \leq x \leq b \\ 0 & \text{otherwise} \end{cases}$$

For example, with $a = 0$ and $b = 8$, $f(x) = 1/8$, or 0.125. We graph this density in Exhibit 3.

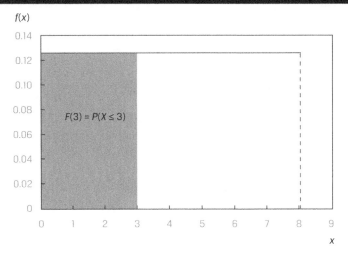

**Exhibit 3: Probability Density Function for a Continuous Uniform Distribution**

The graph of the density function plots as a horizontal line with a value of 0.125.

What is the probability that a uniform random variable with limits $a = 0$ and $b = 8$ is less than or equal to 3, or $F(3) = P(X \leq 3)$? When we were working with the discrete uniform random variable with possible outcomes 1, 2, . . ., 8, we summed individual probabilities: $p(1) + p(2) + p(3) = 0.375$. In contrast, the probability that a continuous uniform random variable or any continuous random variable assumes any given fixed value is 0. To illustrate this point, consider the narrow interval 2.510–2.511. Because that interval holds an infinity of possible values, the sum of the probabilities of values in that interval alone would be infinite if each individual value in it had a positive probability. To find the probability $F(3)$, we find the area under the curve graphing the pdf, between 0 and 3 on the $x$-axis (shaded area in Exhibit 3). In calculus, this operation is called integrating the probability function $f(x)$ from 0 to 3. This area under the curve is a rectangle with base $3 - 0 = 3$ and height 1/8. The area of this rectangle equals base times height: $3(1/8) = 3/8$, or 0.375. So $F(3) = 3/8$, or 0.375.

The interval from 0 to 3 is three-eighths of the total length between the limits of 0 and 8, and $F(3)$ is three-eighths of the total probability of 1. The middle line of the expression for the cdf captures this relationship:

$$F(x) = \begin{cases} 0 \text{ for } x < a \\ \dfrac{x - a}{b - a} \text{ for } a \leq x \leq b. \\ 1 \text{ for } x < b \end{cases}$$

For our problem, $F(x) = 0$ for $x \leq 0$, $F(x) = x/8$ for $0 < x < 8$, and $F(x) = 1$ for $x \geq 8$. Exhibit 4 shows a graph of this cdf.

# Discrete and Continuous Uniform Distribution

**Exhibit 4: Continuous Uniform Cumulative Distribution**

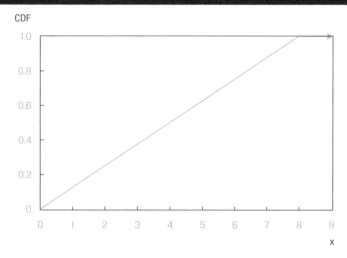

The mathematical operation that corresponds to finding the area under the curve of a pdf $f(x)$ from $a$ to $b$ is the definite integral of $f(x)$ from $a$ to $b$:

$$P(a \leq X \leq b) = \int_a^b f(x)\,dx, \tag{1}$$

where $\int dx$ is the symbol for summing $\int$ over small changes $dx$ and the limits of integration ($a$ and $b$) can be any real numbers or $-\infty$ and $+\infty$. All probabilities of continuous random variables can be computed using Equation 1. For the uniform distribution example considered previously, $F(7)$ is Equation 1 with lower limit $a = 0$ and upper limit $b = 7$. The integral corresponding to the cdf of a uniform distribution reduces to the three-line expression given previously. To evaluate Equation 1 for nearly all other continuous distributions, including the normal and lognormal, we rely on spreadsheet functions, computer programs, or tables of values to calculate probabilities. Those tools use various numerical methods to evaluate the integral in Equation 1.

Recall that the probability of a continuous random variable equaling any fixed point is 0. This fact has an important consequence for working with the cumulative distribution function of a continuous random variable: For any continuous random variable $X$, $P(a \leq X \leq b) = P(a < X \leq b) = P(a \leq X < b) = P(a < X < b)$, because the probabilities at the endpoints $a$ and $b$ are 0. For discrete random variables, these relations of equality are not true, because for them probability accumulates at points.

### EXAMPLE 2

## Probability That a Lending Facility Covenant Is Breached

You are evaluating the bonds of a below-investment-grade borrower at a low point in its business cycle. You have many factors to consider, including the terms of the company's bank lending facilities. The contract creating a bank lending facility such as an unsecured line of credit typically has clauses known as covenants. These covenants place restrictions on what the borrower can do. The company will be in breach of a covenant in the lending facility if the interest coverage ratio, EBITDA/interest, calculated on EBITDA over the four trailing quarters, falls below 2.0. EBITDA is earnings before interest, taxes, depreciation, and amortization. Compliance with the covenants will be checked at the end of the current quarter. If the covenant is breached, the bank can demand immediate repayment of all borrowings on the facility. That action would probably trigger a liquidity crisis for the company. With a high degree of confidence, you forecast interest charges of $25 million. Your estimate of EBITDA runs from $40 million on the low end to $60 million on the high end.

Address two questions (treating projected interest charges as a constant):

1. If the outcomes for EBITDA are equally likely, what is the probability that EBITDA/interest will fall below 2.0, breaching the covenant?

### Solution to 1:

EBITDA/interest is a continuous uniform random variable because all outcomes are equally likely. The ratio can take on values between 1.6 = ($40 million)/($25 million) on the low end and 2.4 = ($60 million/$25 million) on the high end. The range of possible values is 2.4 − 1.6 = 0.8. The fraction of possible values falling below 2.0, the level that triggers default, is the distance between 2.0 and 1.6, or 0.40; the value 0.40 is one-half the total length of 0.8, or 0.4/0.8 = 0.50. So, the probability that the covenant will be breached is 50%.

2. Estimate the mean and standard deviation of EBITDA/interest. For a continuous uniform random variable, the mean is given by $\mu = (a + b)/2$ and the variance is given by $\sigma^2 = (b - a)^2/12$.

### Solution to 2:

In Solution 1, we found that the lower limit of EBITDA/interest is 1.6. This lower limit is $a$. We found that the upper limit is 2.4. This upper limit is $b$. Using the formula given previously,

$\mu = (a + b)/2 = (1.6 + 2.4)/2 = 2.0$.

The variance of the interest coverage ratio is

$\sigma^2 = (b - a)^2/12 = (2.4 - 1.6)^2/12 = 0.053333$.

The standard deviation is the positive square root of the variance, 0.230940 = $(0.053333)^{1/2}$. However, the standard deviation is not particularly useful as a risk measure for a uniform distribution. The probability that lies within various standard deviation bands around the mean is sensitive to different specifications of the upper and lower. Here, a one standard deviation interval around the mean of 2.0 runs from 1.769 to 2.231 and captures 0.462/0.80 = 0.5775, or 57.8%, of the probability. A two standard deviation interval runs from 1.538 to 2.462, which extends past both the lower and upper limits of the random variable.

## 3. BINOMIAL DISTRIBUTION

> describe the properties of a Bernoulli random variable and a binomial random variable, and calculate and interpret probabilities given the binomial distribution function

# Binomial Distribution

In many investment contexts, we view a result as either a success or a failure or as binary (twofold) in some other way. When we make probability statements about a record of successes and failures or about anything with binary outcomes, we often use the binomial distribution. What is a good model for how a stock price moves over time? Different models are appropriate for different uses. Cox, Ross, and Rubinstein (1979) developed an option pricing model based on binary moves—price up or price down—for the asset underlying the option. Their binomial option pricing model was the first of a class of related option pricing models that have played an important role in the development of the derivatives industry. That fact alone would be sufficient reason for studying the binomial distribution, but the binomial distribution has uses in decision making as well.

The building block of the binomial distribution is the **Bernoulli random variable**, named after the Swiss probabilist Jakob Bernoulli (1654–1704). Suppose we have a trial (an event that may repeat) that produces one of two outcomes. Such a trial is a **Bernoulli trial**. If we let $Y$ equal 1 when the outcome is success and $Y$ equal 0 when the outcome is failure, then the probability function of the Bernoulli random variable $Y$ is

$$p(1) = P(Y = 1) = p$$

and

$$p(0) = P(Y = 0) = 1 - p,$$

where $p$ is the probability that the trial is a success.

In $n$ Bernoulli trials, we can have 0 to $n$ successes. If the outcome of an individual trial is random, the total number of successes in $n$ trials is also random. A **binomial random variable** $X$ is defined as the number of successes in $n$ Bernoulli trials. A binomial random variable is the sum of Bernoulli random variables $Y_i$, where $i = 1, 2, \ldots, n$:

$$X = Y_1 + Y_2 + \ldots + Y_n,$$

where $Y_i$ is the outcome on the $i$th trial (1 if a success, 0 if a failure). We know that a Bernoulli random variable is defined by the parameter $p$. The number of trials, $n$, is the second parameter of a binomial random variable. The binomial distribution makes these assumptions:

- The probability, $p$, of success is constant for all trials.
- The trials are independent.

The second assumption has great simplifying force. If individual trials were correlated, calculating the probability of a given number of successes in $n$ trials would be much more complicated.

Under these two assumptions, a binomial random variable is completely described by two parameters, $n$ and $p$. We write

$$X \sim B(n, p),$$

which we read as "$X$ has a binomial distribution with parameters $n$ and $p$." You can see that a Bernoulli random variable is a binomial random variable with $n = 1$: $Y \sim B(1, p)$.

Now we can find the general expression for the probability that a binomial random variable shows $x$ successes in $n$ trials (also known as the probability mass function). We can think in terms of a model of stock price dynamics that can be generalized to allow any possible stock price movements if the periods are made extremely small. Each period is a Bernoulli trial: With probability $p$, the stock price moves up; with probability $1 - p$, the price moves down. A success is an up move, and $x$ is the number of up moves or successes in $n$ periods (trials). With each period's moves independent and $p$ constant, the number of up moves in $n$ periods is a binomial random variable. We now develop an expression for $P(X = x)$, the probability function for a binomial random variable.

Any sequence of $n$ periods that shows exactly $x$ up moves must show $n - x$ down moves. We have many different ways to order the up moves and down moves to get a total of $x$ up moves, but given independent trials, any sequence with $x$ up moves must occur with probability $p^x(1 - p)^{n-x}$. Now we need to multiply this probability by the number of different ways we can get a sequence with $x$ up moves. Using a basic result in counting, there are

$$\frac{n!}{(n - x)!x!}$$

different sequences in $n$ trials that result in $x$ up moves (or successes) and $n - x$ down moves (or failures). Recall that for positive integers $n$, $n$ factorial ($n!$) is defined as $n(n - 1)(n - 2) \ldots 1$ (and $0! = 1$ by convention). For example, $5! = (5)(4)(3)(2)(1) = 120$. The combination formula $n!/[(n - x)!x!]$ is denoted by

$$\binom{n}{x}$$

(read "$n$ combination $x$" or "$n$ choose $x$"). For example, over three periods, exactly three different sequences have two up moves: $uud$, $udu$, and $duu$. We confirm this by

$$\binom{3}{2} = \frac{3!}{(3 - 2)!2!} = \frac{(3)(2)(1)}{(1)(2)(1)} = 3.$$

If, hypothetically, each sequence with two up moves had a probability of 0.15, then the total probability of two up moves in three periods would be $3 \times 0.15 = 0.45$. This example should persuade you that for a binomial random variable X ~ B(n,p), the probability of x successes in n trials is given by

$$p(x) = P(X = x) = \binom{n}{x} p^x (1 - p)^{n-x} = \frac{n!}{(n - x)!x!} p^x (1 - p)^{n-x}. \tag{2}$$

Some distributions are always symmetric, such as the normal, and others are always asymmetric or skewed, such as the lognormal. The binomial distribution is symmetric when the probability of success on a trial is 0.50, but it is asymmetric or skewed otherwise.

We illustrate Equation 2 (the probability function) and the cdf through the symmetrical case by modeling the behavior of stock price movements on four consecutive trading days in a binomial tree framework. Each day is an independent trial. The stock moves up with constant probability $p$ (the **up transition probability**); if it moves up, $u$ is 1 plus the rate of return for an up move. The stock moves down with constant probability $1 - p$ (the **down transition probability**); if it moves down, $d$ is 1 plus the rate of return for a down move. The **binomial tree** is shown in Exhibit 5, where we now associate each of the $n = 4$ stock price moves with time indexed by $t$; the shape of the graph suggests why it is a called a binomial tree. Each boxed value from which successive moves or outcomes branch out in the tree is called a **node**. The initial node, at $t = 0$, shows the beginning stock price, $S$. Each subsequent node represents a potential value for the stock price at the specified future time.

# Binomial Distribution

### Exhibit 5: A Binomial Model of Stock Price Movement

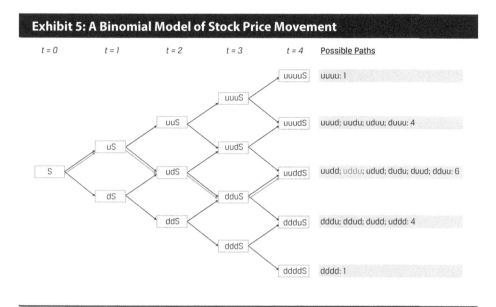

We see from the tree that the stock price at $t = 4$ has five possible values: $uuuuS$, $uuudS$, $uuddS$, $ddduS$, and $ddddS$. The probability that the stock price equals *any* one of these five values is given by the binomial distribution. For example, four sequences of moves result in a final stock price of $uuudS$: These are $uuud$, $uudu$, $uduu$, and $duuu$. These sequences have three up moves out of four moves in total; the combination formula confirms that the number of ways to get three up moves (successes) in four periods (trials) is $4!/(4 − 3)!3! = 4$. Next, note that each of these sequences—$uuud$, $uudu$, $uduu$, and $duuu$—has probability $p^3(1 − p)^1$, which equals 0.0625 (= $0.50^3 \times 0.50^1$). So, $P(S_4 = uuudS) = 4[p^3(1 − p)]$, or 0.25, where $S_4$ indicates the stock's price after four moves. This is shown numerically in Panel A of Exhibit 6, in the line indicating three up moves in $x$, as well as graphically in Panel B, as the height of the bar above $x = 3$. Note that in Exhibit 6, columns 5 and 6 in Panel A show the pdf and cdf, respectively, for this binomial distribution, and in Panel B, the pdf and cdf are represented by the bars and the line graph, respectively.

### Exhibit 6: PDF and CDF of Binomial Probabilities for Stock Price Movements

A. Binomial Probabilities, $n = 4$ and $p = 0.50$

| Col. 1 Number of Up Moves, $x$ | Col. 2 Implied Number of Down Moves, $n − x$ | Col. 3[A] Number of Possible Ways to Reach $x$ Up Moves | Col. 4[B] Probability for Each Way, $p(x)$ | Col. 5[C] Probability for $x\,p(x)$ | Col. 6 $F(x) = P(X \leq x)$ |
|---|---|---|---|---|---|
| 0 | 4 | 1 | 0.0625 | 0.0625 | 0.0625 |
| 1 | 3 | 4 | 0.0625 | 0.2500 | 0.3125 |
| 2 | 2 | 6 | 0.0625 | 0.3750 | 0.6875 |
| 3 | 1 | 4 | 0.0625 | 0.2500 | 0.9375 |
| 4 | 0 | 1 | 0.0625 | 0.0625 | 1.0000 |
| | | | | 1.0000 | |

A: Column 3 = $n! / [(n − x)!\,x!]$

B: Column 4 = $p^x(1 − p)^{n−x}$

C: Column 5 = Column 3 × Column 4

### B. Graphs of Binomial PDF and CDF

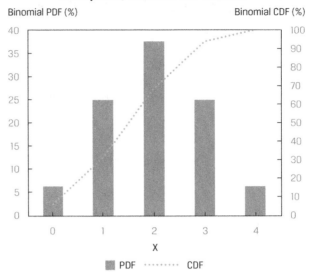

To be clear, the binomial random variable in this application is the number of up moves. Final stock price distribution is a function of the initial stock price, the *number* of up moves, and the *size* of the up moves and down moves. We cannot say that stock price itself is a binomial random variable; rather, it is a function of a binomial random variable, as well as of $u$ and $d$, and initial price, $S$. This richness is actually one key to why this way of modeling stock price is useful: It allows us to choose values of these parameters to approximate various distributions for stock price (using a large number of time periods). One distribution that can be approximated is the lognormal, an important continuous distribution model for stock price that we will discuss later. The flexibility extends further. In the binomial tree shown in Exhibit 5, the transition probabilities are the same at each node: $p$ for an up move and $1 - p$ for a down move. That standard formula describes a process in which stock return volatility is constant over time. Derivatives experts, however, sometimes model changing volatility over time using a binomial tree in which the probabilities for up and down moves differ at different nodes.

> **EXAMPLE 3**
>
> ### A Trading Desk Evaluates Block Brokers
>
> Blocks are orders to sell or buy that are too large for the liquidity ordinarily available in dealer networks or stock exchanges. Your firm has known interests in certain kinds of stock. Block brokers call your trading desk when they want to sell blocks of stocks that they think your firm may be interested in buying. You know that these transactions have definite risks. For example, if the broker's client (the seller) has unfavorable information on the stock or if the total amount he or she is selling through all channels is not truthfully communicated, you may see an immediate loss on the trade. Your firm regularly audits the performance of block brokers by calculating the post-trade, market-risk-adjusted returns on stocks purchased from block brokers. On that basis, you classify each trade as unprofitable or profitable. You have summarized the performance of the brokers in a spreadsheet, excerpted in the following table for November of last year. The broker names are coded BB001 and BB002.

# Binomial Distribution

| Block Trading Gains and Losses | | |
|---|---|---|
| | **Profitable Trades** | **Losing Trades** |
| BB001 | 3 | 9 |
| BB002 | 5 | 3 |

You now want to evaluate the performance of the block brokers, and you begin with two questions:

1. If you are paying a fair price on average in your trades with a broker, what should be the probability of a profitable trade?

### Solution to 1:

If the price you trade at is fair, then 50% of the trades you do with a broker should be profitable.

2. Did each broker meet or miss that expectation on probability?

### Solution to 2:

Your firm has logged 3 + 9 = 12 trades with block broker BB001. Since 3 of the 12 trades were profitable, the portion of profitable trades was 3/12, or 25%. With broker BB002, the portion of profitable trades was 5/8, or 62.5%. The rate of profitable trades with broker BB001 of 25% clearly missed your performance expectation of 50%. Broker BB002, at 62.5% profitable trades, exceeded your expectation.

3. You also realize that the brokers' performance has to be evaluated in light of the sample sizes, and for that you need to use the binomial probability function (Equation 2).

Under the assumption that the prices of trades were fair,

   **A.** calculate the probability of three or fewer profitable trades with broker BB001.
   
   **B.** calculate the probability of five or more profitable trades with broker BB002.

### Solution to 3:

**A.** For broker BB001, the number of trades (the trials) was $n = 12$, and 3 were profitable. You are asked to calculate the probability of three or fewer profitable trades, $F(3) = p(3) + p(2) + p(1) + p(0)$.

Suppose the underlying probability of a profitable trade with BB001 is $p = 0.50$. With $n = 12$ and $p = 0.50$, according to Equation 2 the probability of three profitable trades is

$$p(3) = \binom{n}{x} p^x (1-p)^{n-x} = \binom{12}{3}(0.50^3)(0.50^9)$$
$$= \frac{12!}{(12-3)!\,3!} 0.50^{12} = 220(0.000244) = 0.053711.$$

The probability of exactly 3 profitable trades out of 12 is 5.4% if broker BB001 were giving you fair prices. Now you need to calculate the other probabilities:

$p(2) = [12!/(12 − 2)!2!](0.50^2)(0.50^{10}) = 66(0.000244) = 0.016113.$

$p(1) = [12!/(12 − 1)!1!](0.50^1)(0.50^{11}) = 12(0.000244) = 0.00293.$

$p(0) = [12!/(12 − 0)!0!](0.50^0)(0.50^{12}) = 1(0.000244) = 0.000244.$

Adding all the probabilities, $F(3) = 0.053711 + 0.016113 + 0.00293 + 0.000244 = 0.072998$, or 7.3%. The probability of making 3 or fewer profitable trades out of 12 would be 7.3% if your trading desk were getting fair prices from broker BB001.

B. For broker BB002, you are assessing the probability that the underlying probability of a profitable trade with this broker was 50%, despite the good results. The question was framed as the probability of making five or more profitable trades if the underlying probability is 50%: $1 − F(4) = p(5) + p(6) + p(7) + p(8)$. You could calculate $F(4)$ and subtract it from 1, but you can also calculate $p(5) + p(6) + p(7) + p(8)$ directly.

You begin by calculating the probability that exactly five out of eight trades would be profitable if BB002 were giving you fair prices:

$$p(5) = \binom{8}{5}(0.50^5)(0.50^3)$$
$$= 56(0.003906) = 0.21875.$$

The probability is about 21.9%. The other probabilities are as follows:

$p(6) = 28(0.003906) = 0.109375.$

$p(7) = 8(0.003906) = 0.03125.$

$p(8) = 1(0.003906) = 0.003906.$

So, $p(5) + p(6) + p(7) + p(8) = 0.21875 + 0.109375 + 0.03125 + 0.003906 = 0.363281$, or 36.3%. A 36.3% probability is substantial; the underlying probability of executing a fair trade with BB002 might well have been 0.50 despite your success with BB002 in November of last year. If one of the trades with BB002 had been reclassified from profitable to unprofitable, exactly half the trades would have been profitable. In summary, your trading desk is getting at least fair prices from BB002; you will probably want to accumulate additional evidence before concluding that you are trading at better-than-fair prices.

The magnitude of the profits and losses in these trades is another important consideration. If all profitable trades had small profits but all unprofitable trades had large losses, for example, you might lose money on your trades even if the majority of them were profitable.

Two descriptors of a distribution that are often used in investments are the mean and the variance (or the standard deviation, the positive square root of variance). Exhibit 7 gives the expressions for the mean and variance of binomial random variables.

# Binomial Distribution

### Exhibit 7: Mean and Variance of Binomial Random Variables

|  | Mean | Variance |
|---|---|---|
| Bernoulli, $B(1, p)$ | $p$ | $p(1-p)$ |
| Binomial, $B(n, p)$ | $Np$ | $np(1-p)$ |

Because a single Bernoulli random variable, $Y \sim B(1, p)$, takes on the value 1 with probability $p$ and the value 0 with probability $1 - p$, its mean or weighted-average outcome is $p$. Its variance is $p(1 - p)$. A general binomial random variable, $B(n, p)$, is the sum of $n$ Bernoulli random variables, and so the mean of a $B(n, p)$ random variable is $np$. Given that a $B(1, p)$ variable has variance $p(1 - p)$, the variance of a $B(n, p)$ random variable is $n$ times that value, or $np(1 - p)$, assuming that all the trials (Bernoulli random variables) are independent. We can illustrate the calculation for two binomial random variables with differing probabilities as follows:

| Random Variable | Mean | Variance |
|---|---|---|
| $B(n = 5, p = 0.50)$ | $2.50 = 5(0.50)$ | $1.25 = 5(0.50)(0.50)$ |
| $B(n = 5, p = 0.10)$ | $0.50 = 5(0.10)$ | $0.45 = 5(0.10)(0.90)$ |

For a $B(n = 5, p = 0.50)$ random variable, the expected number of successes is 2.5, with a standard deviation of $1.118 = (1.25)^{1/2}$; for a $B(n = 5, p = 0.10)$ random variable, the expected number of successes is 0.50, with a standard deviation of $0.67 = (0.45)^{1/2}$.

### EXAMPLE 4

## The Expected Number of Defaults in a Bond Portfolio

Suppose as a bond analyst you are asked to estimate the number of bond issues expected to default over the next year in an unmanaged high-yield bond portfolio with 25 US issues from distinct issuers. The credit ratings of the bonds in the portfolio are tightly clustered around Moody's B2/Standard & Poor's B, meaning that the bonds are speculative with respect to the capacity to pay interest and repay principal. The estimated annual default rate for B2/B rated bonds is 10.7%.

1. Over the next year, what is the expected number of defaults in the portfolio, assuming a binomial model for defaults?

### Solution to 1:

For each bond, we can define a Bernoulli random variable equal to 1 if the bond defaults during the year and zero otherwise. With 25 bonds, the expected number of defaults over the year is $np = 25(0.107) = 2.675$, or approximately 3.

2. Estimate the standard deviation of the number of defaults over the coming year.

### Solution to 2:

The variance is $np(1 - p) = 25(0.107)(0.893) = 2.388775$. The standard deviation is $(2.388775)^{1/2} = 1.55$. Thus, a two standard deviation confidence interval ($\pm 3.10$) about the expected number of defaults ($\approx 3$), for example, would run from approximately 0 to approximately 6.

> 3. Critique the use of the binomial probability model in this context.
>
> **Solution to 3:**
>
> > An assumption of the binomial model is that the trials are independent. In this context, a trial relates to whether an individual bond issue will default over the next year. Because the issuing companies probably share exposure to common economic factors, the trials may not be independent. Nevertheless, for a quick estimate of the expected number of defaults, the binomial model may be adequate.

## 4. NORMAL DISTRIBUTION

☐ explain the key properties of the normal distribution

☐ contrast a multivariate distribution and a univariate distribution, and explain the role of correlation in the multivariate normal distribution

☐ calculate the probability that a normally distributed random variable lies inside a given interval

☐ explain how to standardize a random variable

☐ calculate and interpret probabilities using the standard normal distribution

In this section, we focus on the two most important continuous distributions in investment work, the normal and lognormal.

### The Normal Distribution

The normal distribution may be the most extensively used probability distribution in quantitative work. It plays key roles in modern portfolio theory and in several risk management technologies. Because it has so many uses, the normal distribution must be thoroughly understood by investment professionals.

The role of the normal distribution in statistical inference and regression analysis is vastly extended by a crucial result known as the **central limit theorem**. The central limit theorem states that the sum (and mean) of a large number of independent random variables (with finite variance) is approximately normally distributed.

The French mathematician Abraham de Moivre (1667–1754) introduced the normal distribution in 1733 in developing a version of the central limit theorem. As Exhibit 8 shows, the normal distribution is symmetrical and bell-shaped. The range of possible outcomes of the normal distribution is the entire real line: all real numbers lying between $-\infty$ and $+\infty$. The tails of the bell curve extend without limit to the left and to the right.

### Exhibit 8: PDFs of Two Different Normal Distributions

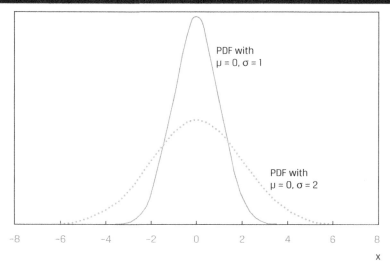

The defining characteristics of a normal distribution are as follows:

- The normal distribution is completely described by two parameters—its mean, μ, and variance, $\sigma^2$. We indicate this as $X \sim N(\mu, \sigma^2)$ (read "$X$ follows a normal distribution with mean μ and variance $\sigma^2$"). We can also define a normal distribution in terms of the mean and the standard deviation, σ (this is often convenient because σ is measured in the same units as $X$ and μ). As a consequence, we can answer any probability question about a normal random variable if we know its mean and variance (or standard deviation).
- The normal distribution has a skewness of 0 (it is symmetric). The normal distribution has a kurtosis of 3; its excess kurtosis (kurtosis − 3.0) equals 0. As a consequence of symmetry, the mean, the median, and the mode are all equal for a normal random variable. More details of these characteristics will be discussed later in the CFA Program curriculum.
- A linear combination of two or more normal random variables is also normally distributed.

The foregoing bullet points and descriptions concern a single variable or univariate normal distribution: the distribution of one normal random variable. A **univariate distribution** describes a single random variable. A **multivariate distribution** specifies the probabilities for a group of related random variables. You will encounter the **multivariate normal distribution** in investment work and readings and should know the following about it.

When we have a group of assets, we can model the distribution of returns on each asset individually or on the assets as a group. "As a group" implies that we take account of all the statistical interrelationships among the return series. One model that has often been used for security returns is the multivariate normal distribution. A multivariate normal distribution for the returns on $n$ stocks is completely defined by three lists of parameters:

- the list of the mean returns on the individual securities ($n$ means in total);
- the list of the securities' variances of return ($n$ variances in total); and
- the list of all the distinct pairwise return correlations: $n(n − 1)/2$ distinct correlations in total.

The need to specify correlations is a distinguishing feature of the multivariate normal distribution in contrast to the univariate normal distribution. We will discuss the concept of correlation in the CFA Program curriculum.

The statement "assume returns are normally distributed" is sometimes used to mean a joint normal distribution. For a portfolio of 30 securities, for example, portfolio return is a weighted average of the returns on the 30 securities. A weighted average is a linear combination. Thus, portfolio return is normally distributed if the individual security returns are (joint) normally distributed. To review, in order to specify the normal distribution for portfolio return, we need the means, the variances, and the distinct pairwise correlations of the component securities.

With these concepts in mind, we can return to the normal distribution for one random variable. The curves graphed in Exhibit 8 are the normal density function:

$$f(x) = \frac{1}{\sigma\sqrt{2\pi}} \exp\left(\frac{-(x-\mu)^2}{2\sigma^2}\right) \text{ for } -\infty < x < +\infty. \tag{3}$$

The two densities graphed in Exhibit 8 correspond to a mean of $\mu = 0$ and standard deviations of $\sigma = 1$ and $\sigma = 2$. The normal density with $\mu = 0$ and $\sigma = 1$ is called the **standard normal distribution** (or **unit normal distribution**). Plotting two normal distributions with the same mean and different standard deviations helps us appreciate why standard deviation is a good measure of dispersion for the normal distribution: Observations are much more concentrated around the mean for the normal distribution with $\sigma = 1$ than for the normal distribution with $\sigma = 2$.

Exhibit 9 illustrates the relationship between the pdf (density function) and cdf (distribution function) of the standard normal distribution (mean = 0, standard deviation = 1). Most of the time, we associate a normal distribution with the "bell curve," which, in fact, is the probability density function of the normal distribution, depicted in Panel A. The cumulative distribution function, depicted in Panel B, in fact plots the size of the shaded areas of the pdfs. Let's take a look at the third row: In Panel A, we have shaded the bell curve up to $x = 0$, the mean of the standard normal distribution. This shaded area corresponds to 50% in the cdf graph, as seen in Panel B, meaning that 50% of the observations of a normally distributed random variable would be equal to or less than the mean.

## Exhibit 9: Density and Distribution Functions of the Standard Normal Distribution

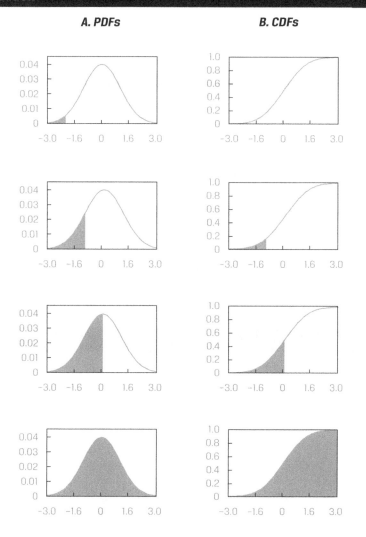

Although not literally accurate, the normal distribution can be considered an approximate model for asset returns. Nearly all the probability of a normal random variable is contained within three standard deviations of the mean. For realistic values of mean return and return standard deviation for many assets, the normal probability of outcomes below −100% is very small.

Whether the approximation is useful in a given application is an empirical question. For example, Fama (1976) and Campbell, Lo, and MacKinlay (1997) showed that the normal distribution is a closer fit for quarterly and yearly holding period returns on a diversified equity portfolio than it is for daily or weekly returns. A persistent departure from normality in most equity return series is kurtosis greater than 3, the fat-tails problem. So when we approximate equity return distributions with the normal distribution, we should be aware that the normal distribution tends to underestimate the probability of extreme returns.

Fat tails can be modeled, among other things, by a mixture of normal random variables or by a Student's $t$-distribution (which we shall cover shortly). In addition, since option returns are skewed, we should be cautious in using the symmetrical normal distribution to model the returns on portfolios containing significant positions in options.

The normal distribution is also less suitable as a model for asset prices than as a model for returns. An asset price can drop only to 0, at which point the asset becomes worthless. As a result, practitioners generally do not use the normal distribution to model the distribution of asset prices but work with the lognormal distribution, which we will discuss later.

## Probabilities Using the Normal Distribution

Having established that the normal distribution is the appropriate model for a variable of interest, we can use it to make the following probability statements:

- Approximately 50% of all observations fall in the interval $\mu \pm (2/3)\sigma$.
- Approximately 68% of all observations fall in the interval $\mu \pm \sigma$.
- Approximately 95% of all observations fall in the interval $\mu \pm 2\sigma$.
- Approximately 99% of all observations fall in the interval $\mu \pm 3\sigma$.

One, two, and three standard deviation intervals are illustrated in Exhibit 10. The intervals indicated are easy to remember but are only approximate for the stated probabilities. More precise intervals are $\mu \pm 1.96\sigma$ for 95% of the observations and $\mu \pm 2.58\sigma$ for 99% of the observations.

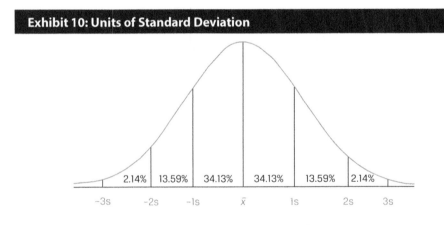

**Exhibit 10: Units of Standard Deviation**

In general, we do not observe the mean or the standard deviation of the distribution of the whole population, so we need to estimate them from an observable sample. We estimate the population mean, $\mu$, using the sample mean, $\bar{X}$ (sometimes denoted as $\hat{\mu}$), and estimate the population standard deviation, $\sigma$, using the sample standard deviation, $s$ (sometimes denoted as $\hat{\sigma}$).

### EXAMPLE 5

### Calculating Probabilities from the Normal Distribution

The chief investment officer of Fund XYZ would like to present some investment return scenarios to the Investment Committee, so she asks your assistance with some indicative numbers. Assuming daily asset returns are normally distributed, she would like to know the following:

# Normal Distribution

## Note on Answering Questions 1–4:

Normal distribution–related functions are part of spreadsheets, R, Python, and all statistical packages. Here, we use Microsoft Excel functions to answer these questions. When we speak in terms of "number of standard deviations above or below the mean," we are referring to the standard normal distribution (i.e., mean of 0 and standard deviation of 1), so it is best to use Excel's "=NORM.S.DIST(Z, 0 or 1)" function. "Z" represents the distance in number of standard deviations away from the mean, and the second parameter of the function is either 0 (Excel returns pdf value) or 1 (Excel returns cdf value).

1. What is the probability that returns would be less than or equal to 1 standard deviation below the mean?

## Solution to 1:

To answer Question 1, we need the normal cdf value (so, set the second parameter equal to 1) that is associated with a $Z$ value of −1 (i.e., one standard deviation below the mean). Thus, "=NORM.S.DIST(-1,1)" returns 0.1587, or 15.9%.

2. What is the probability that returns would be between +1 and −1 standard deviation around the mean?

## Solution to 2:

Here, we need to calculate the area under the normal pdf within the range of the mean ±1 standard deviation. The area under the pdf is the cdf, so we must calculate the difference between the cdf one standard deviation above the mean and the cdf one standard deviation below the mean. Note that "=NORM.S.DIST(1,1)" returns 0.8413, or 84.1%, which means that 84.1% of all observations of a normally distributed random variable would fall below the mean plus one standard deviation. We already calculated 15.9% for the probability that observations for such a variable would fall less than one standard deviation below the mean in the Solution to 1, so the answer here is 84.1% − 15.9% = 68.3%.

3. What is the probability that returns would be less than or equal to −2 standard deviations below the mean?

## Solution to 3:

Similar to Solution 1, use the Excel function "=NORM.S.DIST(-2,1)"— which returns a probability of 0.0228, or 2.3%.

4. How far (in terms of standard deviation) must returns fall below the mean for the probability to equal 95%?

## Solution to 4:

This question is a typical way of phrasing "value at risk." In statistical terms, we want to know the lowest return value below which only 5% of the observations would fall. Thus, we need to find the $Z$ value for which the normal cdf would be 5% probability. To do this, we use the inverse of the cdf function—that is, "=NORM.S.INV(0.05)"—which results in −1.6449, or −1.64. In other words, only 5% of the observations should fall below the mean minus

> 1.64 standard deviations, or equivalently, 95% of the observations should exceed this threshold.

There are as many different normal distributions as there are choices for mean ($\mu$) and variance ($\sigma^2$). We can answer all the previous questions in terms of any normal distribution. Spreadsheets, for example, have functions for the normal cdf for any specification of mean and variance. For the sake of efficiency, however, we would like to refer all probability statements to a single normal distribution. The standard normal distribution (the normal distribution with $\mu = 0$ and $\sigma = 1$) fills that role.

## Standardizing a Random Variable

There are two steps in **standardizing** a normal random variable $X$: Subtract the mean of $X$ from $X$ and then divide that result by the standard deviation of $X$ (this is also known as computing the Z-score). If we have a list of observations on a normal random variable, $X$, we subtract the mean from each observation to get a list of deviations from the mean and then divide each deviation by the standard deviation. The result is the standard normal random variable, $Z$ ($Z$ is the conventional symbol for a standard normal random variable). If we have $X \sim N(\mu, \sigma^2)$ (read "$X$ follows the normal distribution with parameters $\mu$ and $\sigma^2$"), we standardize it using the formula

$$Z = (X - \mu)/\sigma. \tag{4}$$

Suppose we have a normal random variable, $X$, with $\mu = 5$ and $\sigma = 1.5$. We standardize $X$ with $Z = (X - 5)/1.5$. For example, a value $X = 9.5$ corresponds to a standardized value of 3, calculated as $Z = (9.5 - 5)/1.5 = 3$. The probability that we will observe a value as small as or smaller than 9.5 for $X \sim N(5, 1.5)$ is exactly the same as the probability that we will observe a value as small as or smaller than 3 for $Z \sim N(0, 1)$.

## Probabilities Using the Standard Normal Distribution

We can answer all probability questions about $X$ using standardized values. We generally do not know the population mean and standard deviation, so we often use the sample mean $\bar{X}$ for $\mu$ and the sample standard deviation $s$ for $\sigma$. Standard normal probabilities are computed with spreadsheets, statistical and econometric software, and programming languages. Tables of the cumulative distribution function for the standard normal random variable are also readily available.

To find the probability that a standard normal variable is less than or equal to 0.24, for example, calculate NORM.S.DIST(0.24,1)=0.5948; thus, $P(Z \leq 0.24) = 0.5948$, or 59.48%. If we want to find the probability of observing a value 1.65 standard deviations below the mean, calculate NORM.S.DIST(-1.65,1)=0.04947, or roughly 5%.

The following are some of the most frequently referenced values when using the normal distribution, and for these values, =NORM.S.INV(Probability) is a convenient Excel function:

- The 90th percentile point is 1.282, or NORM.S.INV(0.90)=1.28155. Thus, only 10% of values remain in the right tail beyond the mean plus 1.28 standard deviations;
- The 95th percentile point is 1.65, or NORM.S.INV(0.95)=1.64485, which means that $P(Z \leq 1.65) = N(1.65) = 0.95$, or 95%, and 5% of values remain in the right tail. The 5th percentile point, in contrast, is NORM.S.INV(0.05)=-1.64485—that is, the same number as for 95%, but with a negative sign.

# Normal Distribution

- Note the difference between the use of a percentile point when dealing with one tail rather than two tails. We used 1.65 because we are concerned with the 5% of values that lie only on one side, the right tail. If we want to cut off both the left and right 5% tails, then 90% of values would stay within the mean ±1.65 standard deviations range.
- The 99th percentile point is 2.327: $P(Z \leq 2.327) = N(2.327) = 0.99$, or 99%, and 1% of values remain in the right tail.

### EXAMPLE 6

## Probabilities for a Common Stock Portfolio

Assume the portfolio mean return is 12% and the standard deviation of return estimate is 22% per year. Note also that if $X$ is portfolio return, the standardized portfolio return is $Z = (X - \bar{X})/s = (X - 12\%)/22\%$. We use this expression throughout the solutions.

You want to calculate the following probabilities, assuming that a normal distribution describes returns.

1. What is the probability that portfolio return will exceed 20%?

## Solution to 1:

For $X = 20\%$, $Z = (20\% - 12\%)/22\% = 0.363636$. You want to find $P(Z > 0.363636)$. First, note that $P(Z > x) = P(Z \geq x)$ because the normal distribution is a continuous distribution. Also, recall that $P(Z \geq x) = 1.0 - P(Z \leq x)$ or $1 - N(x)$. Next, NORM.S.DIST(0.363636,1)=0.64194, so, $1 - 0.6419 = 0.3581$. Therefore, the probability that portfolio return will exceed 20% is about 36% if your normality assumption is accurate.

2. What is the probability that portfolio return will be between 12% and 20%? In other words, what is $P(12\% \leq \text{portfolio return} \leq 20\%)$?

## Solution to 2:

$P(12\% \leq \text{Portfolio return} \leq 20\%) = N(Z \text{ corresponding to } 20\%) - N(Z \text{ corresponding to } 12\%)$. For the first term, $Z = (20\% - 12\%)/22\% = 0.363636$, and $N(0.363636) = 0.6419$ (as in Solution 1). To get the second term immediately, note that 12% is the mean, and for the normal distribution, 50% of the probability lies on either side of the mean. Therefore, $N(Z$ corresponding to 12%) must equal 50%. So $P(12\% \leq \text{Portfolio return} \leq 20\%) = 0.6419 - 0.50 = 0.1419$, or approximately 14%.

3. You can buy a one-year T-bill that yields 5.5%. This yield is effectively a one-year risk-free interest rate. What is the probability that your portfolio's return will be equal to or less than the risk-free rate?

## Solution to 3:

If $X$ is portfolio return, then we want to find $P(\text{Portfolio return} \leq 5.5\%)$. For $X = 5.5\%$, $Z = (5.5\% - 12\%)/22\% = -0.2955$. Using NORM.S.DIST(-0.2955,1)=0.3838, we see an approximately 38% chance the portfolio's return will be equal to or less than the risk-free rate.

Next, we will briefly discuss and illustrate the concept of the central limit theorem, according to which the sum (as well as the mean) of a set of independent, identically distributed random variables with finite variances is normally distributed, whatever distribution the random variables follow.

To illustrate this concept, consider a sample of 30 observations of a random variable that can take a value of just −100, 0, or 100, with equal probability. Clearly, this sample is drawn from a simple discrete uniform distribution, where the possible values of −100, 0, and 100 each have 1/3 probability. We randomly pick 10 elements of this sample and calculate the sum of these elements, and then we repeat this process a total of 100 times. The histogram in Exhibit 11 shows the distribution of these sums: The underlying distribution is a very simple discrete uniform distribution, but the sums converge toward a normal distribution.

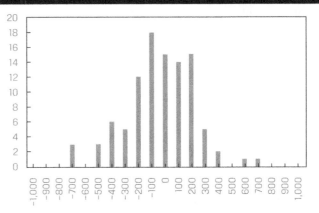

**Exhibit 11: Central Limit Theorem: Sums of Elements from Discrete Uniform Distribution Converge to Normal Distribution**

# 5

## STUDENT'S *T*-, CHI-SQUARE, AND *F*-DISTRIBUTIONS

☐ describe the properties of the Student's *t*-distribution, and calculate and interpret its degrees of freedom

☐ describe the properties of the chi-square distribution and the *F*-distribution, and calculate and interpret their degrees of freedom

### Student's *t*-Distribution

To complete the review of probability distributions commonly used in finance, we discuss Student's *t*-, chi-square, and *F*-distributions. Most of the time, these distributions are used to support statistical analyses, such as sampling, testing the statistical significance of estimated model parameters, or hypothesis testing. In addition, Student's *t*-distribution is also sometimes used to model asset returns in a manner similar to that of the normal distribution. However, since the *t*-distribution has "longer tails," it may provide a more reliable, more conservative downside risk estimate.

# Student's t-, Chi-Square, and F-Distributions

The standard *t*-distribution is a symmetrical probability distribution defined by a single parameter known as **degrees of freedom** (df), the number of independent variables used in defining sample statistics, such as variance, and the probability distributions they measure.

Each value for the number of degrees of freedom defines one distribution in this family of distributions. We will shortly compare *t*-distributions with the standard normal distribution, but first we need to understand the concept of degrees of freedom. We can do so by examining the calculation of the sample variance,

$$s^2 = \frac{\sum_{i=1}^{n}(X_i - \bar{X})^2}{n-1}. \tag{5}$$

Equation 5 gives the unbiased estimator of the sample variance that we use. The term in the denominator, $n - 1$, which is the sample size minus 1, is the number of degrees of freedom in estimating the population variance when using Equation 5. We also use $n - 1$ as the number of degrees of freedom for determining reliability factors based on the *t*-distribution. The term "degrees of freedom" is used because in a random sample, we assume that observations are selected independently of each other. The numerator of the sample variance, however, uses the sample mean. How does the use of the sample mean affect the number of observations collected independently for the sample variance formula? With a sample size of 10 and a mean of 10%, for example, we can freely select only 9 observations. Regardless of the 9 observations selected, we can always find the value for the 10th observation that gives a mean equal to 10%. From the standpoint of the sample variance formula, then, there are nine degrees of freedom. Given that we must first compute the sample mean from the total of $n$ independent observations, only $n - 1$ observations can be chosen independently for the calculation of the sample variance. The concept of degrees of freedom comes up frequently in statistics, and you will see it often later in the CFA Program curriculum.

Suppose we sample from a normal distribution. The ratio $z = (\bar{X} - \mu)/(\sigma/\sqrt{n})$ is distributed normally with a mean of 0 and standard deviation of 1; however, the ratio $t = (\bar{X} - \mu)/(s/\sqrt{n})$ follows the *t*-distribution with a mean of 0 and $n - 1$ degrees of freedom. The ratio represented by $t$ is not normal because $t$ is the ratio of two random variables, the sample mean and the sample standard deviation. The definition of the standard normal random variable involves only one random variable, the sample mean. As degrees of freedom increase (i.e., as sample size increases), however, the *t*-distribution approaches the standard normal distribution. Exhibit 12 shows the probability density functions for the standard normal distribution and two *t*-distributions, one with df = 2 and one with df = 8.

### Exhibit 12: Student's *t*-Distributions vs. Standard Normal Distribution

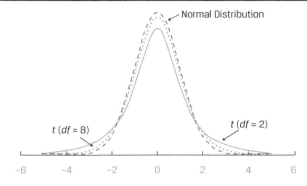

Of the three distributions shown in Exhibit 12, the standard normal distribution has tails that approach zero faster than the tails of the two $t$-distributions. The $t$-distribution is also symmetrically distributed around its mean value of zero, just like the normal distribution. As the degrees of freedom increase, the $t$-distribution approaches the standard normal distribution. The $t$-distribution with df = 8 is closer to the standard normal distribution than the $t$-distribution with df = 2.

Beyond plus and minus four standard deviations from the mean, the area under the standard normal distribution appears to approach 0; both $t$-distributions, however, continue to show some area under each curve beyond four standard deviations. The $t$-distributions have fatter tails, but the tails of the $t$-distribution with df = 8 more closely resemble the normal distribution's tails. As the degrees of freedom increase, the tails of the $t$-distribution become less fat.

Probabilities for the $t$-distribution can be readily computed with spreadsheets, statistical software, and programming languages. As an example of the latter, see the final sidebar at the end of this section for sample code in the R programming language.

## Chi-Square and *F*-Distribution

The chi-square distribution, unlike the normal and $t$-distributions, is asymmetrical. Like the $t$-distribution, the chi-square distribution is a family of distributions. The chi-square distribution with $k$ degrees of freedom is the distribution of the sum of the squares of $k$ independent standard normally distributed random variables; hence, this distribution does not take on negative values. A different distribution exists for each possible value of degrees of freedom, $n - 1$ ($n$ is sample size).

Like the chi-square distribution, the $F$-distribution is a family of asymmetrical distributions bounded from below by 0. Each $F$-distribution is defined by two values of degrees of freedom, called the numerator and denominator degrees of freedom.

The relationship between the chi-square and $F$-distributions is as follows: If $\chi_1^2$ is one chi-square random variable with $m$ degrees of freedom and $\chi_2^2$ is another chi-square random variable with $n$ degrees of freedom, then $F = \left(\chi_1^2/m\right) / \left(\chi_2^2/n\right)$ follows an $F$-distribution with $m$ numerator and $n$ denominator degrees of freedom.

Chi-square and $F$-distributions are asymmetric, and as shown in Exhibit 13, the domains of their pdfs are positive numbers. Like Student's $t$-distribution, as the degrees of freedom of the chi-square distribution increase, the shape of its pdf becomes more similar to a bell curve (see Panel A). For the $F$-distribution, as both the numerator ($df_1$) and the denominator ($df_2$) degrees of freedom increase, the density function will also become more bell curve–like (see Panel B).

## Exhibit 13: PDFs of Chi-Square and F-Distributions

### A. Chi-Square Distributions

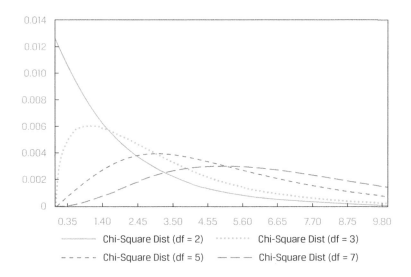

### B. F-Distributions

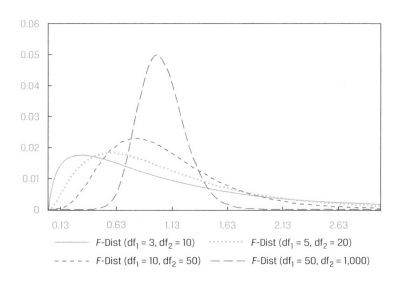

As for typical investment applications, Student's $t$-, chi-square, and $F$-distributions are the basis for test statistics used in performing various types of hypothesis tests on portfolio returns, such as those summarized in Exhibit 14.

### Exhibit 14: Student's *t*-, Chi-Square, and *F*-Distributions: Basis for Hypothesis Tests of Investment Returns

| Distribution | Test Statistic | Hypothesis Tests of Returns |
| --- | --- | --- |
| Student's *t* | *t*-Statistic | Tests of a single population mean, of differences between two population means, of mean difference between paired (dependent) populations |
| Chi-square | Chi-square statistic | Test of variance of a normally distributed population |
| *F* | *F*-statistic | Test of equality of variances of two normally distributed populations from two independent random samples |

### EXAMPLE 7

## Probabilities Using Student's *t*-, Chi-Square, and *F*-Distributions

1. Of the distributions we have covered in this reading, which can take values that are only positive numbers (i.e., no negative values)?

### Solution to 1:

Of the probability distributions covered in this reading, the domains of the pdfs of the lognormal, the chi-square, and the *F*-distribution are only positive numbers.

2. Interpret the degrees of freedom for a chi-square distribution, and describe how a larger value of df affects the shape of the chi-square pdf.

### Solution to 2:

A chi-square distribution with *k* degrees of freedom is the distribution of the sum of the squares of *k* independent standard normally distributed random variables. The greater the degrees of freedom, the more symmetrical and bell curve–like the pdf becomes.

3. Generate cdf tables in Excel for values 1, 2, and 3 for the following distributions: standard normal, Student's *t*- (df = 5), chi-square (df = 5), and *F*-distribution ($df_1$ = 5, $df_2$ = 1). Then, calculate the distance from the mean for probability (*p*) = 90%, 95%, and 99% for each distribution.

### Solution to 3:

In Excel, we can calculate cdfs using the NORM.S.DIST(value,1), T.DIST(value,DF,1), CHISQ.DIST(value,DF,1), and F.DIST(value,DF1,DF2,1) functions for the standard normal, Student's *t*-, chi-square, and *F*-distributions, respectively. At the end of this question set, we also show code snippets in the R language for generating cdfs for the requested values. For values 1, 2, and 3, the following are the results using the Excel functions:

# Student's t-, Chi-Square, and F-Distributions

### CDF Values Using Different Probability Distributions

| Value | Normal | Student's t (df = 5) | Chi-Square (df = 5) | F (df$_1$ = 5, df$_2$ = 1) |
|---|---|---|---|---|
| 1 | 84.1% | 81.8% | 3.7% | 36.3% |
| 2 | 97.7% | 94.9% | 15.1% | 51.1% |
| 3 | 99.9% | 98.5% | 30.0% | 58.9% |

To calculate distances from the mean given probability $p$, we must use the inverse of the distribution functions: NORM.S.INV(p), T.INV(p,DF), CHISQ.INV(p,DF), and F.INV(p,DF1,DF2), respectively. At the end of this question set, we also show code snippets in the R language for calculating distances from the mean for the requested probabilities. The results using the inverse functions and the requested probabilities are as follows:

### Distance from the Mean for a Given Probability (p)

| Probability | Normal | Student's t (df = 5) | Chi-Square (df = 5) | F (df$_1$ = 5, df$_2$ = 1) |
|---|---|---|---|---|
| 90% | 1.28 | 1.48 | 9.24 | 57.24 |
| 95% | 1.64 | 2.02 | 11.07 | 230.16 |
| 99% | 2.33 | 3.36 | 15.09 | 5,763.65 |

4. You fit a Student's $t$-distribution to historically observed returns of stock market index ABC. Your best fit comes with five degrees of freedom. Compare this Student's $t$-distribution (df = 5) to a standard normal distribution on the basis of your answer to Question 3.

## Solution to 4:

Student's $t$-distribution with df of 5 has longer tails than the standard normal distribution. For probabilities 90%, 95%, and 99%, such $t$-distributed random variables would fall farther away from their mean (1.48, 2.02, and 3.36 standard deviations, respectively) than a normally distributed random variable (1.28, 1.64, and 2.33 standard deviations, respectively).

### R CODE FOR PROBABILITIES INVOLVING STUDENT'S T-, CHI-SQUARE, AND F-DISTRIBUTIONS

For those of you with a knowledge of (or interest in learning) readily accessible computer code to find probabilities involving Student's $t$-, chi-square, and $F$-distributions, you can try out the following program. Specifically, this program uses code in the R language to solve for the answers to Example 7, which you have just completed. Good luck and have fun!

```
1  ######### CDF FUNCTIONS in R ################
2
3  #Make a vector of 1, 2, and 3
4  z=1:3
5  print("z values:")
6  print(z)
7
8  #Calculate Standard Normal CDF
9  N_CDF=pnorm(z,mean=0,sd=1)
10 print("Standard Normal CDF:")
11 print(N_CDF)
12
13 #Calculate Student-t CDF
14 #Set degrees of freedom:
15 df=5
16 t_CDF=pt(z,df)
17 print("Student t CDF with df=5:")
18 print(t_CDF)
19
20 #Calculate Chi-Square CDF
21 #Set degrees of freedom:
22 df=5
23 chisq_CDF=pchisq(z,df)
24 print("Chi-Square CDF with df=5:")
25 print(chisq_CDF)
26
27 #Calculate F CDF
28 #Set degrees of freedom:
29 df1=5
30 df2=1
31 F_CDF=pf(z,df1,df2)
32 print("F CDF with df1=5 and df2=1:")
33 print(F_CDF)
34
```

```
35
36  ########## INVERSE FUNCTIONS ##################
37  # Make a vector for p=90%, 95% and 99%
38  P<-c(0.9,0.95,0.99)
39  print("P values:")
40  print(P)
41
42  #Calculate Inverse Standard Normal values
43  N_inv=qnorm(P,mean=0,sd=1)
44  print("Standard Normal values")
45  print(N_inv)
46
47  #Calculate Inverse Student-t values
48  #Set degrees of freedom:
49  df=5
50  t_inv=qt(P,df)
51  print("Student t values with df=5:")
52  print(t_inv)
53
54  #Calculate Inverse Chi-Square values
55  #Set degrees of freedom:
56  df=5
57  chisq_inv=qchisq(P,df)
58  print("Chi-Square values with df=5:")
59  print(chisq_inv)
60
61  #Calculate Inverse F values
62  #Set degrees of freedom:
63  df1=5
64  df2=1
65  F_inv=qf(P,df1,df2)
66  print("F values with df1=5 and df2=1:")
67  print(F_inv)
```

# SUMMARY

In this reading, we have presented the most frequently used probability distributions in investment analysis.

- A probability distribution specifies the probabilities of the possible outcomes of a random variable.
- The two basic types of random variables are discrete random variables and continuous random variables. Discrete random variables take on at most a countable number of possible outcomes that we can list as $x_1, x_2, \ldots$. In contrast, we cannot describe the possible outcomes of a continuous random variable $Z$ with a list $z_1, z_2, \ldots$, because the outcome $(z_1 + z_2)/2$, not in the list, would always be possible.
- The probability function specifies the probability that the random variable will take on a specific value. The probability function is denoted $p(x)$ for a discrete random variable and $f(x)$ for a continuous random variable. For any probability function $p(x)$, $0 \leq p(x) \leq 1$, and the sum of $p(x)$ over all values of $x$ equals 1.

- The cumulative distribution function, denoted $F(x)$ for both continuous and discrete random variables, gives the probability that the random variable is less than or equal to $x$.
- The discrete uniform and the continuous uniform distributions are the distributions of equally likely outcomes.
- The binomial random variable is defined as the number of successes in $n$ Bernoulli trials, where the probability of success, $p$, is constant for all trials and the trials are independent. A Bernoulli trial is an experiment with two outcomes, which can represent success or failure, an up move or a down move, or another binary (twofold) outcome.
- A binomial random variable has a mean equal to $np$ and variance equal to $np(1-p)$.
- A binomial tree is the graphical representation of a model of asset price dynamics in which, at each period, the asset moves up with probability $p$ or down with probability $(1-p)$. The binomial tree is a flexible method for modeling asset price movement and is widely used in pricing options.
- The normal distribution is a continuous symmetric probability distribution that is completely described by two parameters: its mean, $\mu$, and its variance, $\sigma^2$.
- A univariate distribution specifies the probabilities for a single random variable. A multivariate distribution specifies the probabilities for a group of related random variables.
- To specify the normal distribution for a portfolio when its component securities are normally distributed, we need the means, the standard deviations, and all the distinct pairwise correlations of the securities. When we have those statistics, we have also specified a multivariate normal distribution for the securities.
- For a normal random variable, approximately 68% of all possible outcomes are within a one standard deviation interval about the mean, approximately 95% are within a two standard deviation interval about the mean, and approximately 99% are within a three standard deviation interval about the mean.
- A normal random variable, $X$, is standardized using the expression $Z = (X - \mu)/\sigma$, where $\mu$ and $\sigma$ are the mean and standard deviation of $X$. Generally, we use the sample mean, $\overline{X}$, as an estimate of $\mu$ and the sample standard deviation, $s$, as an estimate of $\sigma$ in this expression.
- The standard normal random variable, denoted $Z$, has a mean equal to 0 and variance equal to 1. All questions about any normal random variable can be answered by referring to the cumulative distribution function of a standard normal random variable, denoted $N(x)$ or $N(z)$.
- Student's $t$-, chi-square, and $F$-distributions are used to support statistical analyses, such as sampling, testing the statistical significance of estimated model parameters, or hypothesis testing.
- The standard $t$-distribution is a symmetrical probability distribution defined by degrees of freedom (df) and characterized by fat tails. As df increase, the $t$-distribution approaches the standard normal distribution.
- The chi-square distribution is asymmetrical, defined by degrees of freedom, and with $k$ df is the distribution of the sum of the squares of $k$ independent standard normally distributed random variables, so it does not take on negative values. A different distribution exists for each value of df, $n - 1$.

- The $F$-distribution is a family of asymmetrical distributions bounded from below by 0. Each $F$-distribution is defined by two values of degrees of freedom, the numerator df and the denominator df. If $\chi_1^2$ is one chi-square random variable with $m$ df and $\chi_2^2$ is another chi-square random variable with $n$ df, then $F = \left(\chi_1^2/m\right) / \left(\chi_2^2/n\right)$ follows an $F$-distribution with $m$ numerator df and $n$ denominator df.

# REFERENCES

Campbell, John, Andrew Lo, A. Craig MacKinlay. 1997. The Econometrics of Financial Markets. Princeton, NJ: Princeton University Press.

Cox, Jonathan, Stephen Ross, Mark Rubinstein. 1979. "Options Pricing: A Simplified Approach." Journal of Financial Economics, 7: 229–63. 10.1016/0304-405X(79)90015-1

Fama, Eugene. 1976. Foundations of Finance. New York: Basic Books.

# PRACTICE PROBLEMS

1. A European put option on stock conveys the right to sell the stock at a prespecified price, called the exercise price, at the maturity date of the option. The value of this put at maturity is (exercise price − stock price) or $0, whichever is greater. Suppose the exercise price is $100 and the underlying stock trades in increments of $0.01. At any time before maturity, the terminal value of the put is a random variable.

   A. Describe the distinct possible outcomes for terminal put value. (Think of the put's maximum and minimum values and its minimum price increments.)

   B. Is terminal put value, at a time before maturity, a discrete or continuous random variable?

   C. Letting $Y$ stand for terminal put value, express in standard notation the probability that terminal put value is less than or equal to $24. No calculations or formulas are necessary.

2. Which of the following is a continuous random variable?

   A. The value of a futures contract quoted in increments of $0.05

   B. The total number of heads recorded in 1 million tosses of a coin

   C. The rate of return on a diversified portfolio of stocks over a three-month period

3. $X$ is a discrete random variable with possible outcomes $X = \{1, 2, 3, 4\}$. Three functions—$f(x)$, $g(x)$, and $h(x)$—are proposed to describe the probabilities of the outcomes in $X$.

   |  | Probability Function | | |
   |---|---|---|---|
   | $X = x$ | $f(x) = P(X = x)$ | $g(x) = P(X = x)$ | $h(x) = P(X = x)$ |
   | 1 | −0.25 | 0.20 | 0.20 |
   | 2 | 0.25 | 0.25 | 0.25 |
   | 3 | 0.50 | 0.50 | 0.30 |
   | 4 | 0.25 | 0.05 | 0.35 |

   The conditions for a probability function are satisfied by:

   A. $f(x)$.

   B. $g(x)$.

   C. $h(x)$.

4. The value of the cumulative distribution function $F(x)$, where $x$ is a particular outcome, for a discrete uniform distribution:

   A. sums to 1.

   B. lies between 0 and 1.

   C. decreases as $x$ increases.

5. In a discrete uniform distribution with 20 potential outcomes of integers 1–20, the probability that $X$ is greater than or equal to 3 but less than 6, $P(3 \leq X < 6)$, is:

   A. 0.10.

   B. 0.15.

   C. 0.20.

6. You are forecasting sales for a company in the fourth quarter of its fiscal year. Your low-end estimate of sales is €14 million, and your high-end estimate is €15 million. You decide to treat all outcomes for sales between these two values as equally likely, using a continuous uniform distribution.

   A. What is the expected value of sales for the fourth quarter?

   B. What is the probability that fourth-quarter sales will be less than or equal to €14,125,000?

7. The cumulative distribution function for a discrete random variable is shown in the following table.

   | $X = x$ | Cumulative Distribution Function $F(x) = P(X \leq x)$ |
   | --- | --- |
   | 1 | 0.15 |
   | 2 | 0.25 |
   | 3 | 0.50 |
   | 4 | 0.60 |
   | 5 | 0.95 |
   | 6 | 1.00 |

   The probability that $X$ will take on a value of either 2 or 4 is *closest* to:

   A. 0.20.

   B. 0.35.

   C. 0.85.

8. A random number between zero and one is generated according to a continuous uniform distribution. What is the probability that the first number generated will have a value of exactly 0.30?

   A. 0%

   B. 30%

   C. 70%

9. Define the term "binomial random variable." Describe the types of problems for which the binomial distribution is used.

10. For a binomial random variable with five trials and a probability of success on each trial of 0.50, the distribution will be:

    A. skewed.

    B. uniform.

C. symmetric.

11. Over the last 10 years, a company's annual earnings increased year over year seven times and decreased year over year three times. You decide to model the number of earnings increases for the next decade as a binomial random variable. For Parts B, C, and D of this problem, assume the estimated probability is the actual probability for the next decade.

   A. What is your estimate of the probability of success, defined as an increase in annual earnings?

   B. What is the probability that earnings will increase in exactly 5 of the next 10 years?

   C. Calculate the expected number of yearly earnings increases during the next 10 years.

   D. Calculate the variance and standard deviation of the number of yearly earnings increases during the next 10 years.

   E. The expression for the probability function of a binomial random variable depends on two major assumptions. In the context of this problem, what must you assume about annual earnings increases to apply the binomial distribution in Part B? What reservations might you have about the validity of these assumptions?

12. A portfolio manager annually outperforms her benchmark 60% of the time. Assuming independent annual trials, what is the probability that she will outperform her benchmark four or more times over the next five years?

   A. 0.26

   B. 0.34

   C. 0.48

13. You are examining the record of an investment newsletter writer who claims a 70% success rate in making investment recommendations that are profitable over a one-year time horizon. You have the one-year record of the newsletter's seven most recent recommendations. Four of those recommendations were profitable. If all the recommendations are independent and the newsletter writer's skill is as claimed, what is the probability of observing four or fewer profitable recommendations out of seven in total?

14. If the probability that a portfolio outperforms its benchmark in any quarter is 0.75, the probability that the portfolio outperforms its benchmark in three or fewer quarters over the course of a year is *closest* to:

   A. 0.26.

   B. 0.42.

   C. 0.68.

15. Which of the following events can be represented as a Bernoulli trial?

   A. The flip of a coin

   B. The closing price of a stock

**C.** The picking of a random integer between 1 and 10

16. A stock is priced at $100.00 and follows a one-period binomial process with an up move that equals 1.05 and a down move that equals 0.97. If 1 million Bernoulli trials are conducted and the average terminal stock price is $102.00, the probability of an up move (*p*) is *closest* to:

    **A.** 0.375.

    **B.** 0.500.

    **C.** 0.625.

17. A call option on a stock index is valued using a three-step binomial tree with an up move that equals 1.05 and a down move that equals 0.95. The current level of the index is $190, and the option exercise price is $200. If the option value is positive when the stock price exceeds the exercise price at expiration and $0 otherwise, the number of terminal nodes with a positive payoff is:

    **A.** one.

    **B.** two.

    **C.** three.

18. State the approximate probability that a normal random variable will fall within the following intervals:

    **A.** Mean plus or minus one standard deviation.

    **B.** Mean plus or minus two standard deviations.

    **C.** Mean plus or minus three standard deviations.

19. Which of the following is characteristic of the normal distribution?

    **A.** It is asymmetric.

    **B.** It has definitive limits or boundaries.

    **C.** It is defined by the mean and the standard distribution.

20. Which of the following assets *most likely* requires the use of a multivariate distribution for modeling returns?

    **A.** A call option on a bond

    **B.** A portfolio of technology stocks

    **C.** A stock in a market index

21. A portfolio has an expected mean return of 8% and standard deviation of 14%. The probability that its return falls between 8% and 11% is *closest* to:

    **A.** 8.5%.

    **B.** 14.8%.

    **C.** 58.3%.

22. A portfolio has an expected return of 7%, with a standard deviation of 13%. For

an investor with a minimum annual return target of 4%, the probability that the portfolio return will fail to meet the target is *closest* to:

A. 33%.

B. 41%.

C. 59%.

23. Which parameter equals zero in a normal distribution?

    A. Kurtosis

    B. Skewness

    C. Standard deviation

24. An analyst develops the following capital market projections.

    |  | Stocks | Bonds |
    | --- | --- | --- |
    | Mean Return | 10% | 2% |
    | Standard Deviation | 15% | 5% |

    Assuming the returns of the asset classes are described by normal distributions, which of the following statements is correct?

    A. Bonds have a higher probability of a negative return than stocks.

    B. On average, 99% of stock returns will fall within two standard deviations of the mean.

    C. The probability of a bond return less than or equal to 3% is determined using a Z-score of 0.25.

25. Which one of the following statements about Student's *t*-distribution is *false*?

    A. It is symmetrically distributed around its mean value, like the normal distribution.

    B. It has shorter (i.e., thinner) tails than the normal distribution.

    C. As its degrees of freedom increase, Student's *t*-distribution approaches the normal distribution.

26. Which one of the following statements concerning chi-square and *F*-distributions is *false*?

    A. They are both asymmetric distributions.

    B. As their degrees of freedom increase, the shapes of their pdfs become more bell curve–like.

    C. The domains of their pdfs are positive and negative numbers.

# SOLUTIONS

1.
   **A.** The put's minimum value is $0. The put's value is $0 when the stock price is at or above $100 at the maturity date of the option. The put's maximum value is $100 = $100 (the exercise price) − $0 (the lowest possible stock price). The put's value is $100 when the stock is worthless at the option's maturity date. The put's minimum price increments are $0.01. The possible outcomes of terminal put value are thus $0.00, $0.01, $0.02, . . . , $100.

   **B.** The price of the underlying has minimum price fluctuations of $0.01: These are the minimum price fluctuations for terminal put value. For example, if the stock finishes at $98.20, the payoff on the put is $100 − $98.20 = $1.80. We can specify that the nearest values to $1.80 are $1.79 and $1.81. With a continuous random variable, we cannot specify the nearest values. So, we must characterize terminal put value as a discrete random variable.

   **C.** The probability that terminal put value is less than or equal to $24 is $P(Y \leq 24)$, or $F(24)$ in standard notation, where $F$ is the cumulative distribution function for terminal put value.

2. C is correct. The rate of return is a random variable because the future outcomes are uncertain, and it is continuous because it can take on an unlimited number of outcomes.

3. B is correct. The function $g(x)$ satisfies the conditions of a probability function. All of the values of $g(x)$ are between 0 and 1, and the values of $g(x)$ all sum to 1.

4. B is correct. The value of the cumulative distribution function lies between 0 and 1 for any x: $0 \leq F(x) \leq 1$.

5. B is correct. The probability of any outcome is 0.05, $P(1) = 1/20 = 0.05$. The probability that $X$ is greater than or equal to 3 but less than 6 is expressed as $P(3 \leq X < 6) = P(3) + P(4) + P(5) = 0.05 + 0.05 + 0.05 = 0.15$.

6.
   **A.** The expected value of fourth-quarter sales is €14,500,000, calculated as (€14,000,000 + €15,000,000)/2. With a continuous uniform random variable, the mean or expected value is the midpoint between the smallest and largest values.

   **B.** The probability that fourth-quarter sales will be less than or equal to €14,125,000 is 0.125, or 12.5%, calculated as (€14,125,000 − €14,000,000)/ (€15,000,000 − €14,000,000).

7. A is correct. The probability that $X$ will take on a value of 4 or less is $F(4) = P(X \leq 4) = p(1) + p(2) + p(3) + p(4) = 0.60$. The probability that $X$ will take on a value of 3 or less is $F(3) = P(X \leq 3) = p(1) + p(2) + p(3) = 0.50$. So, the probability that $X$ will take on a value of 4 is $F(4) − F(3) = p(4) = 0.10$. The probability of $X = 2$ can be found using the same logic: $F(2) − F(1) = p(2) = 0.25 − 0.15 = 0.10$. The probability of $X$ taking on a value of 2 or 4 is $p(2) + p(4) = 0.10 + 0.10 = 0.20$.

8. A is correct. The probability of generating a random number equal to any fixed point under a continuous uniform distribution is zero.

## Solutions

9. A binomial random variable is defined as the number of successes in $n$ Bernoulli trials (a trial that produces one of two outcomes). The binomial distribution is used to make probability statements about a record of successes and failures or about anything with binary (twofold) outcomes.

10. C is correct. The binomial distribution is symmetric when the probability of success on a trial is 0.50, but it is asymmetric or skewed otherwise. Here, it is given that $p = 0.50$.

11.

   **A.** The probability of an earnings increase (success) in a year is estimated as $7/10 = 0.70$, or 70%, based on the record of the past 10 years.

   **B.** The probability that earnings will increase in 5 of the next 10 years is about 10.3%. Define a binomial random variable $X$, counting the number of earnings increases over the next 10 years. From Part A, the probability of an earnings increase in a given year is $p = 0.70$ and the number of trials (years) is $n = 10$. Equation 2 gives the probability that a binomial random variable has $x$ successes in $n$ trials, with the probability of success on a trial equal to $p$:

   $$P(X = x) = \binom{n}{x} p^x (1-p)^{n-x} = \frac{n!}{(n-x)!\,x!} p^x (1-p)^{n-x}.$$

   For this example,

   $$\binom{10}{5} 0.7^5 0.3^{10-5} = \frac{10!}{(10-5)!\,5!} 0.7^5 0.3^{10-5}$$
   $$= 252 \times 0.16807 \times 0.00243 = 0.102919.$$

   We conclude that the probability that earnings will increase in exactly 5 of the next 10 years is 0.1029, or approximately 10.3%.

   **C.** The expected number of yearly increases is $E(X) = np = 10 \times 0.70 = 7$.

   **D.** The variance of the number of yearly increases over the next 10 years is $\sigma^2 = np(1-p) = 10 \times 0.70 \times 0.30 = 2.1$. The standard deviation is 1.449 (the positive square root of 2.1).

   **E.** You must assume that (1) the probability of an earnings increase (success) is constant from year to year and (2) earnings increases are independent trials. If current and past earnings help forecast next year's earnings, Assumption 2 is violated. If the company's business is subject to economic or industry cycles, neither assumption is likely to hold.

12. B is correct. To calculate the probability of four years of outperformance, use the formula

    $$p(x) = P(X = x) = \binom{n}{x} p^x (1-p)^{n-x} = \frac{n!}{(n-x)!\,x!} p^x (1-p)^{n-x}.$$

    Using this formula to calculate the probability in four of five years, $n = 5$, $x = 4$, and $p = 0.60$.
    Therefore,

    $$p(4) = \frac{5!}{(5-4)!\,4!} 0.6^4 (1-0.6)^{5-4} = [120/24](0.1296)(0.40) = 0.2592.$$

    $$p(5) = \frac{5!}{(5-5)!\,5!} 0.6^5 (1-0.6)^{5-5} = [120/120](0.0778)(1) = 0.0778.$$

    The probability of outperforming four or more times is $p(4) + p(5) = 0.2592 + 0.0778 = 0.3370$.

13. The observed success rate is 4/7 = 0.571, or 57.1%. The probability of four or fewer successes is $F(4) = p(4) + p(3) + p(2) + p(1) + p(0)$, where $p(4), p(3), p(2), p(1)$, and $p(0)$ are, respectively, the probabilities of 4, 3, 2, 1, and 0 successes, according to the binomial distribution with $n = 7$ and $p = 0.70$. We have the following probabilities:

    $p(4) = (7!/4!3!)(0.70^4)(0.30^3) = 35(0.006483) = 0.226895$.

    $p(3) = (7!/3!4!)(0.70^3)(0.30^4) = 35(0.002778) = 0.097241$.

    $p(2) = (7!/2!5!)(0.70^2)(0.30^5) = 21(0.001191) = 0.025005$.

    $p(1) = (7!/1!6!)(0.70^1)(0.30^6) = 7(0.000510) = 0.003572$.

    $p(0) = (7!/0!7!)(0.70^0)(0.30^7) = 1(0.000219) = 0.000219$.

    Summing all these probabilities, you conclude that $F(4) = 0.226895 + 0.097241 + 0.025005 + 0.003572 + 0.000219 = 0.352931$, or 35.3%.

14. C is correct. The probability that the performance is at or below the expectation is calculated by finding $F(3) = p(3) + p(2) + p(1) + p(0)$ using the formula:

    $$p(x) = P(X = x) = \binom{n}{x} p^x (1-p)^{n-x} = \frac{n!}{(n-x)!x!} p^x (1-p)^{n-x}.$$

    Using this formula,

    $p(3) = \frac{4!}{(4-3)!3!} 0.75^3 (1 - 0.75)^{4-3} = [24/6](0.42)(0.25) = 0.42$.

    $p(2) = \frac{4!}{(4-2)!2!} 0.75^2 (1 - 0.75)^{4-2} = [24/4](0.56)(0.06) = 0.20$.

    $p(1) = \frac{4!}{(4-1)!1!} 0.75^1 (1 - 0.75)^{4-1} = [24/6](0.75)(0.02) = 0.06$.

    $p(0) = \frac{4!}{(4-0)!0!} 0.75^0 (1 - 0.75)^{4-0} = [24/24](1)(0.004) = 0.004$.

    Therefore,

    $F(3) = p(3) + p(2) + p(1) + p(0) = 0.42 + 0.20 + 0.06 + 0.004$
    $= 0.684$, or approximately 68%.

15. A is correct. A trial, such as a coin flip, will produce one of two outcomes. Such a trial is a Bernoulli trial.

16. C is correct. The probability of an up move ($p$) can be found by solving the equation $(p)uS + (1 - p)dS = (p)105 + (1 - p)97 = 102$. Solving for $p$ gives $8p = 5$, so $p = 0.625$.

17. A is correct. Only the top node value of $219.9488 exceeds $200.

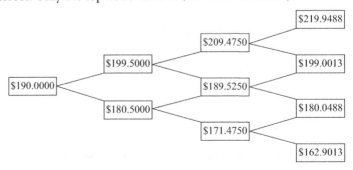

# Solutions

18.

    **A.** Approximately 68% of all outcomes of a normal random variable fall within plus or minus one standard deviation of the mean.

    **B.** Approximately 95% of all outcomes of a normal random variable fall within plus or minus two standard deviations of the mean.

    **C.** Approximately 99% of all outcomes of a normal random variable fall within plus or minus three standard deviations of the mean.

19. C is correct. The normal distribution is symmetric and is completely described by the mean and the standard distribution.

20. B is correct. Multivariate distributions specify the probabilities for a group of related random variables. A portfolio of technology stocks represents a group of related assets. Accordingly, statistical interrelationships must be considered, resulting in the need to use a multivariate normal distribution.

21. A is correct. $P(8\% \leq$ Portfolio return $\leq 11\%) = N(Z$ corresponding to 11%) $- N(Z$ corresponding to 8%). For the first term, NORM.S.DIST((11% − 8%)/14%) = 58.48%. To get the second term immediately, note that 8% is the mean, and for the normal distribution, 50% of the probability lies on either side of the mean. Therefore, $N(Z$ corresponding to 8%) must equal 50%. So, $P(8\% \leq$ Portfolio return $\leq 11\%) = 0.5848 - 0.50 = 0.0848$, or approximately 8.5%.

22. B is correct. By using Excel's NORM.S.DIST() function, we get NORM.S.DIST((4% − 7%)/13%) = 40.87%. The probability that the portfolio will underperform the target is about 41%.

23. B is correct. A normal distribution has a skewness of zero (it is symmetrical around the mean). A non-zero skewness implies asymmetry in a distribution.

24. A is correct. The chance of a negative return falls in the area to the left of 0% under a standard normal curve. By standardizing the returns and standard deviations of the two assets, the likelihood of either asset experiencing a negative return may be determined: Z-score (standardized value) = $(X - \mu)/\sigma$.

    Z-score for a bond return of 0% = $(0 - 2)/5 = -0.40$.

    Z-score for a stock return of 0% = $(0 - 10)/15 = -0.67$.

    For bonds, a 0% return falls 0.40 standard deviations below the mean return of 2%. In contrast, for stocks, a 0% return falls 0.67 standard deviations below the mean return of 10%. A standard deviation of 0.40 is less than a standard deviation of 0.67. Negative returns thus occupy more of the left tail of the bond distribution than the stock distribution. Thus, bonds are more likely than stocks to experience a negative return.

25. A is correct, since it is false. Student's $t$-distribution has longer (fatter) tails than the normal distribution and, therefore, it may provide a more reliable, more conservative downside risk estimate.

26. C is correct, since it is false. Both chi-square and $F$-distributions are bounded from below by zero, so the domains of their pdfs are restricted to positive numbers.

# LEARNING MODULE 5

## Sampling and Estimation

by Richard A. DeFusco, PhD, CFA, Dennis W. McLeavey, DBA, CFA, Jerald E. Pinto, PhD, CFA, and David E. Runkle, PhD, CFA.

*Richard A. DeFusco, PhD, CFA, is at the University of Nebraska-Lincoln (USA). Dennis W. McLeavey, DBA, CFA, is at the University of Rhode Island (USA). Jerald E. Pinto, PhD, CFA, is at CFA Institute (USA). David E. Runkle, PhD, CFA, is at Jacobs Levy Equity Management (USA).*

| LEARNING OUTCOMES | |
|---|---|
| Mastery | The candidate should be able to: |
| ☐ | identify and describe desirable properties of an estimator |
| ☐ | contrast a point estimate and a confidence interval estimate of a population parameter |
| ☐ | calculate and interpret a confidence interval for a population mean, given a normal distribution with 1) a known population variance, 2) an unknown population variance, or 3) an unknown population variance and a large sample size |
| ☐ | describe the issues regarding selection of the appropriate sample size, data snooping bias, sample selection bias, survivorship bias, look-ahead bias, and time-period bias |

## INTRODUCTION

Estimation of a parameter seeks precise answers to the question "What is this parameter's value?" In the financial markets, investment analysts are accustomed to estimating the performance of a particular market by reference to an index. Indexes such as the S&P 500 Index or the Nikkei 225 Stock Average, for example, contain certain samples of stocks. Although the S&P 500 and the Nikkei do not represent the population of US or Japanese stocks, we view them as valid indicators of the whole population's behavior. However, any statistics that we compute with sample information are only estimates of the underlying population parameters.

In this reading, we will discuss what constitutes a good estimator of the population parameter. We will compare a point estimate with a confidence interval estimate. We will also discuss the interpretation of statistical results based on samples of financial data, and the possible pitfalls in this process.

CFA Institute would like to thank Jian Wu, PhD, at State Street (USA), for this major revision of Sampling & Estimation, including new visuals, graphics, Excel functions and related text content throughout the reading.

## 2  POINT ESTIMATES OF THE POPULATION MEAN

☐ identify and describe desirable properties of an estimator

Statistical inference traditionally consists of two branches, hypothesis testing and estimation. Hypothesis testing addresses the question "Is the value of this parameter (say, a population mean) equal to some specific value (0, for example)?" In this process, we have a hypothesis concerning the value of a parameter, and we seek to determine whether the evidence from a sample supports or does not support that hypothesis. The topic of hypothesis testing will be discussed later.

The second branch of statistical inference, and what we focus on now, is estimation. Estimation seeks an answer to the question "What is this parameter's (for example, the population mean's) value?" In estimating, unlike in hypothesis testing, we do not start with a hypothesis about a parameter's value and seek to test it. Rather, we try to make the best use of the information in a sample to form one of several types of estimates of the parameter's value. With estimation, we are interested in arriving at a rule for best calculating a single number to estimate the unknown population parameter (a point estimate). In addition to calculating a point estimate, we may also be interested in calculating a range of values that brackets the unknown population parameter with some specified level of probability (a confidence interval). We first discuss point estimates of parameters and then turn our attention to the formulation of confidence intervals for the population mean.

### Point Estimators

An important concept introduced here is that sample statistics viewed as formulas involving random outcomes are random variables. The formulas that we use to compute the sample mean and all the other sample statistics are examples of estimation formulas or **estimators**. The particular value that we calculate from sample observations using an estimator is called an **estimate**. An estimator has a sampling distribution; an estimate is a fixed number pertaining to a given sample and thus has no sampling distribution. To take the example of the mean, the calculated value of the sample mean in a given sample, used as an estimate of the population mean, is called a **point estimate** of the population mean. As we have seen earlier, the formula for the sample mean can and will yield different results in repeated samples as different samples are drawn from the population.

In many applications, we have a choice among a number of possible estimators for estimating a given parameter. How do we make our choice? We often select estimators because they have one or more desirable statistical properties. Following is a brief description of three desirable properties of estimators: unbiasedness (lack of bias), efficiency, and consistency.

- **Unbiasedness.** An unbiased estimator is one whose expected value (the mean of its sampling distribution) equals the parameter it is intended to estimate.

For example, as shown in Exhibit 1 of the sampling distribution of the sample mean, the expected value of the sample mean, $\overline{X}$, equals $\mu$, the population mean, so we say that the sample mean is an unbiased estimator (of the population mean). The sample variance, $s^2$, calculated using a divisor of $n - 1$, is an unbiased estimator of the population variance, $\sigma^2$. If we were to calculate the sample variance using a divisor of $n$, the estimator would be biased: Its expected value would be smaller than

# Point Estimates of the Population Mean

the population variance. We would say that sample variance calculated with a divisor of *n* is a biased estimator of the population variance. We will discuss the concept of expected value in more detail in the CFA Program curriculum.

### Exhibit 1: Unbiasedness of an Estimator

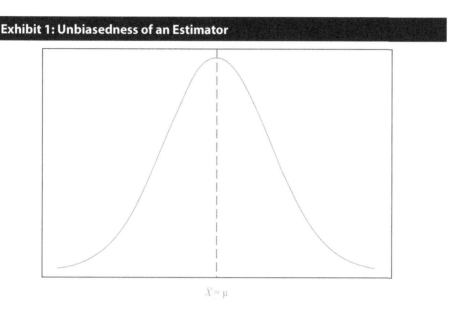

$\bar{X} = \mu$

Whenever one unbiased estimator of a parameter can be found, we can usually find a large number of other unbiased estimators. How do we choose among alternative unbiased estimators? The criterion of efficiency provides a way to select from among unbiased estimators of a parameter.

- **Efficiency.** An unbiased estimator is efficient if no other unbiased estimator of the same parameter has a sampling distribution with smaller variance.

To explain the definition, in repeated samples we expect the estimates from an efficient estimator to be more tightly grouped around the mean than estimates from other unbiased estimators. For example, Exhibit 2 shows the sampling distributions of two different estimators of the population mean. Both estimators A and B are unbiased because their expected values are equal to the population mean ($\bar{X}_A = \bar{X}_B = \mu$), but estimator A is more efficient because it shows smaller variance. Efficiency is an important property of an estimator. Sample mean $\bar{X}$ is an efficient estimator of the population mean; sample variance $s^2$ is an efficient estimator of $\sigma^2$.

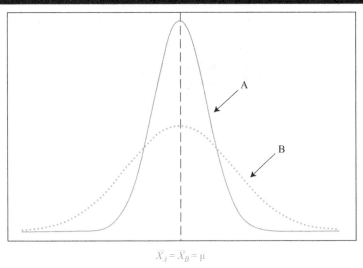

Exhibit 2: Efficiency of an Estimator

$\bar{X}_A = \bar{X}_B = \mu$

Recall that a statistic's sampling distribution is defined for a given sample size. Different sample sizes define different sampling distributions. For example, the variance of sampling distribution of the sample mean is smaller for larger sample sizes. Unbiasedness and efficiency are properties of an estimator's sampling distribution that hold for any size sample. An unbiased estimator is unbiased equally in a sample of size 100 and in a sample of size 1,000. In some problems, however, we cannot find estimators that have such desirable properties as unbiasedness in small samples. In this case, statisticians may justify the choice of an estimator based on the properties of the estimator's sampling distribution in extremely large samples, the estimator's so-called asymptotic properties. Among such properties, the most important is consistency.

- **Consistency.** A consistent estimator is one for which the probability of estimates close to the value of the population parameter increases as sample size increases.

Somewhat more technically, we can define a consistent estimator as an estimator whose sampling distribution becomes concentrated on the value of the parameter it is intended to estimate as the sample size approaches infinity. The sample mean, in addition to being an efficient estimator, is also a consistent estimator of the population mean: As sample size $n$ goes to infinity, its standard error, $\sigma/\sqrt{n}$, goes to 0 and its sampling distribution becomes concentrated right over the value of population mean, $\mu$. Exhibit 3 illustrates the consistency of the sample mean, in which the standard error of the estimator narrows as the sample size increases. To summarize, we can think of a consistent estimator as one that tends to produce more and more accurate estimates of the population parameter as we increase the sample's size. If an estimator is consistent, we may attempt to increase the accuracy of estimates of a population parameter by calculating estimates using a larger sample. For an inconsistent estimator, however, increasing sample size does not help to increase the probability of accurate estimates.

# Point Estimates of the Population Mean

**Exhibit 3: Consistency of an Estimator**

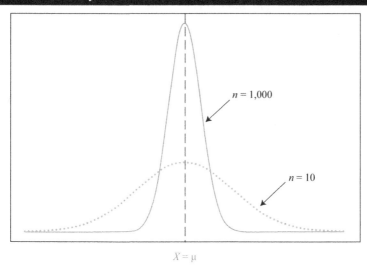

It is worth noting that in a Big Data world, consistency is much more crucial than efficiency, because the accuracy of a population parameter's estimates can be increasingly improved with the availability of more sample data. In addition, given a big dataset, a biased but consistent estimator can offer considerably reduced error. For example, $s^2/n$ is a biased estimator of variance. As $n$ goes to infinity, the distinction between $s^2/n$ and the unbiased estimator $s^2/(n-1)$ diminishes to zero.

## EXAMPLE 1

**Exhibit 4: Sampling Distributions of an Estimator**

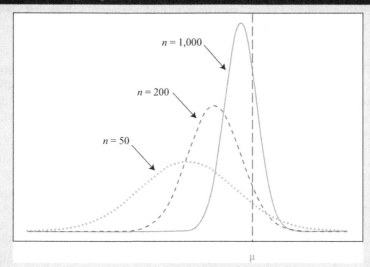

1. Exhibit 4 plots several sampling distributions of an estimator for the population mean, and the vertical dash line represents the true value of population mean.

Which of the following statements *best* describes the estimator's properties?

   **A.** The estimator is unbiased.

**B.** The estimator is biased and inconsistent.

**C.** The estimator is biased but consistent.

### Solution:

C is correct. The chart shows three sampling distributions of the estimator at different sample sizes ($n$ = 50, 200, and 1,000). We can observe that the means of each sampling distribution—that is, the expected value of the estimator—deviate from the population mean, so the estimator is biased. As the sample size increases, however, the mean of the sampling distribution draws closer to the population mean with smaller variance. So, it is a consistent estimator.

## 3. CONFIDENCE INTERVALS FOR THE POPULATION MEAN AND SAMPLE SIZE SELECTION

☐ contrast a point estimate and a confidence interval estimate of a population parameter

☐ calculate and interpret a confidence interval for a population mean, given a normal distribution with 1) a known population variance, 2) an unknown population variance, or 3) an unknown population variance and a large sample size

When we need a single number as an estimate of a population parameter, we make use of a point estimate. However, because of sampling error, the point estimate is not likely to equal the population parameter in any given sample. Often, a more useful approach than finding a point estimate is to find a range of values that we expect to bracket the parameter with a specified level of probability—an interval estimate of the parameter. A confidence interval fulfills this role.

- **Definition of Confidence Interval.** A confidence interval is a range for which one can assert with a given probability $1 - \alpha$, called the **degree of confidence**, that it will contain the parameter it is intended to estimate. This interval is often referred to as the $100(1 - \alpha)\%$ confidence interval for the parameter.

The endpoints of a confidence interval are referred to as the lower and upper confidence limits. In this reading, we are concerned only with two-sided confidence intervals—confidence intervals for which we calculate both lower and upper limits.

Confidence intervals are frequently given either a probabilistic interpretation or a practical interpretation. In the probabilistic interpretation, we interpret a 95% confidence interval for the population mean as follows. In repeated sampling, 95% of such confidence intervals will, in the long run, include or bracket the population mean. For example, suppose we sample from the population 1,000 times, and based on each sample, we construct a 95% confidence interval using the calculated sample mean. Because of random chance, these confidence intervals will vary from each other, but we expect 95%, or 950, of these intervals to include the unknown value of the population mean. In practice, we generally do not carry out such repeated sampling. Therefore, in the practical interpretation, we assert that we are 95% confident that a single 95% confidence interval contains the population mean. We are justified in making this statement because we know that 95% of all possible confidence intervals constructed in the same manner will contain the population mean. The confidence intervals that we discuss in this reading have structures similar to the following basic structure:

- **Construction of Confidence Intervals.** A $100(1 - \alpha)\%$ confidence interval for a parameter has the following structure:

Point estimate ± Reliability factor × Standard error

> where
>
> Point estimate = a point estimate of the parameter (a value of a sample statistic)
>
> Reliability factor = a number based on the assumed distribution of the point estimate and the degree of confidence $(1 - \alpha)$ for the confidence interval
>
> Standard error = the standard error of the sample statistic providing the point estimate
>
> The quantity "Reliability factor × Standard error" is sometimes called the precision of the estimator; larger values of the product imply lower precision in estimating the population parameter.

The most basic confidence interval for the population mean arises when we are sampling from a normal distribution with known variance. The reliability factor in this case is based on the standard normal distribution, which has a mean of 0 and a variance of 1. A standard normal random variable is conventionally denoted by $Z$. The notation $z_\alpha$ denotes the point of the standard normal distribution such that $\alpha$ of the probability remains in the right tail. For example, 0.05 or 5% of the possible values of a standard normal random variable are larger than $z_{0.05} = 1.65$. Similarly, 0.025 or 2.5% of the possible values of a standard normal random variable are larger than $z_{0.025} = 1.96$.

Suppose we want to construct a 95% confidence interval for the population mean and, for this purpose, we have taken a sample of size 100 from a normally distributed population with known variance of $\sigma^2 = 400$ (so, $\sigma = 20$). We calculate a sample mean of $\bar{X} = 25$. Our point estimate of the population mean is, therefore, 25. If we move 1.96 standard deviations above the mean of a normal distribution, 0.025 or 2.5% of the probability remains in the right tail; by symmetry of the normal distribution, if we move 1.96 standard deviations below the mean, 0.025 or 2.5% of the probability remains in the left tail. In total, 0.05 or 5% of the probability is in the two tails and 0.95 or 95% lies in between. So, $z_{0.025} = 1.96$ is the reliability factor for this 95% confidence interval. Note the relationship $100(1 - \alpha)\%$ for the confidence interval and the $z_{\alpha/2}$ for the reliability factor. The standard error of the sample mean, given by Equation 1, is $\sigma_{\bar{X}} = 20/\sqrt{100} = 2$. The confidence interval, therefore, has a lower limit of $\bar{X} - 1.96\,\sigma_{\bar{X}} = 25 - 1.96(2) = 25 - 3.92 = 21.08$. The upper limit of the confidence interval is $\bar{X} + 1.96\,\sigma_{\bar{X}} = 25 + 1.96(2) = 25 + 3.92 = 28.92$. The 95% confidence interval for the population mean spans 21.08 to 28.92.

- **Confidence Intervals for the Population Mean (Normally Distributed Population with Known Variance).** A $100(1 - \alpha)\%$ confidence interval for population mean $\mu$ when we are sampling from a normal distribution with known variance $\sigma^2$ is given by

$$\bar{X} \pm z_{\alpha/2} \frac{\sigma}{\sqrt{n}} \qquad (1)$$

The reliability factors for the most frequently used confidence intervals are as follows.

- **Reliability Factors for Confidence Intervals Based on the Standard Normal Distribution.** We use the following reliability factors when we construct confidence intervals based on the standard normal distribution:

  - 90% confidence intervals: Use $z_{0.05} = 1.65$
  - 95% confidence intervals: Use $z_{0.025} = 1.96$
  - 99% confidence intervals: Use $z_{0.005} = 2.58$

These reliability factors highlight an important fact about all confidence intervals. As we increase the degree of confidence, the confidence interval becomes wider and gives us less precise information about the quantity we want to estimate.

Exhibit 5 demonstrates how a confidence interval works. We again use the daily returns of the fictitious Euro-Asia-Africa Equity Index shown in earlier readings. The dataset consists of 1,258 observations with a population mean of 0.035% and a population standard deviation of 0.834%. We conduct random sampling from the population 1,000 times, drawing a sample of a hundred daily returns ($n = 100$) each time.

We construct a histogram of the sample means, shown in Exhibit 5. The shape appears to be that of a normal distribution, in line with the central limit theorem. We next pick one random sample to construct confidence intervals around its sample mean. The mean of the selected sample is computed to be 0.103% (as plotted with a solid line). Next we construct 99%, 95%, and 50% confidence intervals around that sample mean. We use Equation 4 to compute the upper and lower bounds of each pair of confidence intervals and plot these bounds in dashed lines.

The resulting chart shows that confidence intervals narrow with decreasing confidence level, and vice versa. For example, the narrowest confidence interval in the chart corresponds to the lowest confidence level of 50%—that is, we are only 50% confident that the population mean falls within the 50% confidence interval around the sample mean. Importantly, as shown by Equation 1, given a fixed confidence level, the confidence interval narrows with smaller population deviation and greater sample size, indicating higher estimate accuracy.

### Exhibit 5: Illustration of Confidence Intervals

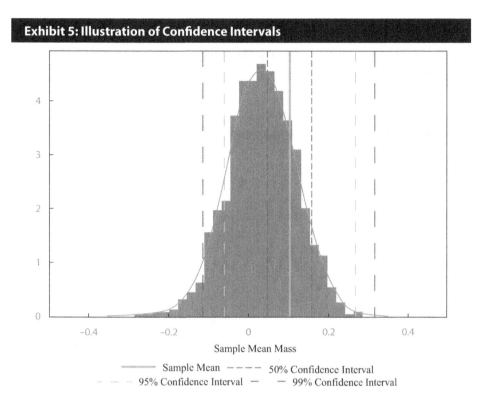

In practice, the assumption that the sampling distribution of the sample mean is at least approximately normal is frequently reasonable, either because the underlying distribution is approximately normal or because we have a large sample and the central limit theorem applies. Rarely do we know the population variance in practice, however. When the population variance is unknown but the sample mean is at least approximately normally distributed, we have two acceptable ways to calculate the confidence interval for the population mean. We will soon discuss the more conservative approach, which is based on Student's $t$-distribution (the $t$-distribution, for short and covered earlier). In investment literature, it is the most frequently used approach in both estimation and hypothesis tests concerning the mean when the population variance is not known, whether sample size is small or large.

A second approach to confidence intervals for the population mean, based on the standard normal distribution, is the $z$-alternative. It can be used only when sample size is large. (In general, a sample size of 30 or larger may be considered large.) In contrast to the confidence interval given in Equation 1, this confidence interval uses the sample standard deviation, $s$, in computing the standard error of the sample mean (Equation 2).

- **Confidence Intervals for the Population Mean—The $z$-Alternative (Large Sample, Population Variance Unknown).** A $100(1 - \alpha)\%$ confidence interval for population mean $\mu$ when sampling from any distribution with unknown variance and when sample size is large is given by

$$\overline{X} \pm z_{\alpha/2} \frac{s}{\sqrt{n}} \tag{2}$$

Because this type of confidence interval appears quite often, we illustrate its calculation in Example 2.

## EXAMPLE 2

### Confidence Interval for the Population Mean of Sharpe Ratios—z-Statistic

1. Suppose an investment analyst takes a random sample of US equity mutual funds and calculates the average Sharpe ratio. The sample size is 100, and the average Sharpe ratio is 0.45. The sample has a standard deviation of 0.30. Calculate and interpret the 90% confidence interval for the population mean of all US equity mutual funds by using a reliability factor based on the standard normal distribution. One of the commonly used portfolio performance evaluation metrics is the Sharpe ratio, which measures the historical risk-adjusted returns. It is defined as the mean excess portfolio return over the risk-free rate divided by the standard deviation of mean returns. The concept of Sharpe ratio will be covered later in the CFA Program curriculum.

   The reliability factor for a 90% confidence interval, as given earlier, is $z_{0.05} = 1.65$. The confidence interval will be

   $$\overline{X} \pm z_{0.05}\frac{s}{\sqrt{n}} = 0.45 \pm 1.65\frac{0.30}{\sqrt{100}} = 0.45 \pm 1.65(0.03) = 0.45 \pm 0.0495$$

   The confidence interval spans 0.4005 to 0.4995, or 0.40 to 0.50, carrying two decimal places. The analyst can say with 90% confidence that the interval includes the population mean.

   In this example, the analyst makes no specific assumption about the probability distribution describing the population. Rather, the analyst relies on the central limit theorem to produce an approximate normal distribution for the sample mean.

As Example 2 shows, even if we are unsure of the underlying population distribution, we can still construct confidence intervals for the population mean as long as the sample size is large because we can apply the central limit theorem.

We now turn to the conservative alternative, using the $t$-distribution, for constructing confidence intervals for the population mean when the population variance is not known. For confidence intervals based on samples from normally distributed populations with unknown variance, the theoretically correct reliability factor is based on the $t$-distribution. Using a reliability factor based on the $t$-distribution is essential for a small sample size. Using a $t$ reliability factor is appropriate when the population variance is unknown, even when we have a large sample and could use the central limit theorem to justify using a $z$ reliability factor. In this large sample case, the $t$-distribution provides more-conservative (wider) confidence intervals.

Suppose we sample from a normal distribution. The ratio $z = (\overline{X} - \mu)/(\sigma/\sqrt{n})$ is distributed normally with a mean of 0 and standard deviation of 1; however, the ratio $t = (\overline{X} - \mu)/(s/\sqrt{n})$ follows the $t$-distribution with a mean of 0 and $n - 1$ degrees of freedom. The ratio represented by $t$ is not normal because $t$ is the ratio of two random variables, the sample mean and the sample standard deviation. The definition of the standard normal random variable involves only one random variable, the sample mean.

Values for the $t$-distribution are available from Excel, using the function T.INV(p,DF). For each degree of freedom, five values are given: $t_{0.10}$, $t_{0.05}$, $t_{0.025}$, $t_{0.01}$, and $t_{0.005}$. The values for $t_{0.10}$, $t_{0.05}$, $t_{0.025}$, $t_{0.01}$, and $t_{0.005}$ are such that, respectively, 0.10, 0.05, 0.025,

# Confidence Intervals for the Population Mean and Sample Size Selection

0.01, and 0.005 of the probability remains in the right tail, for the specified number of degrees of freedom. For example, for df = 30, $t_{0.10} = 1.310$, $t_{0.05} = 1.697$, $t_{0.025} = 2.042$, $t_{0.01} = 2.457$, and $t_{0.005} = 2.750$.

We now give the form of confidence intervals for the population mean using the $t$-distribution.

- **Confidence Intervals for the Population Mean (Population Variance Unknown)—$t$-Distribution.** If we are sampling from a population with unknown variance and either of the conditions below holds:
  - the sample is large, or
  - the sample is small, but the population is normally distributed, or approximately normally distributed,

  then a $100(1 - \alpha)\%$ confidence interval for the population mean $\mu$ is given by

$$\bar{X} \pm t_{\alpha/2} \frac{s}{\sqrt{n}} \tag{3}$$

  where the number of degrees of freedom for $t_{\alpha/2}$ is $n - 1$ and $n$ is the sample size.

Example 3 reprises the data of Example 2 but uses the $t$-statistic rather than the $z$-statistic to calculate a confidence interval for the population mean of Sharpe ratios.

### EXAMPLE 3

### Confidence Interval for the Population Mean of Sharpe Ratios—$t$-Statistic

As in Example 2, an investment analyst seeks to calculate a 90% confidence interval for the population mean Sharpe ratio of US equity mutual funds based on a random sample of 100 US equity mutual funds. The sample mean Sharpe ratio is 0.45, and the sample standard deviation of the Sharpe ratios is 0.30. Now recognizing that the population variance of the distribution of Sharpe ratios is unknown, the analyst decides to calculate the confidence interval using the theoretically correct $t$-statistic.

Because the sample size is 100, df = 99. Using the Excel function T.INV(0.05,99), $t_{0.05} = 1.66$. This reliability factor is slightly larger than the reliability factor $z_{0.05} = 1.65$ that was used in Example 2. The confidence interval will be

$$\bar{X} \pm t_{0.05} \frac{s}{\sqrt{n}} = 0.45 \pm 1.66 \frac{0.30}{\sqrt{100}} = 0.45 \pm 1.66(0.03) = 0.45 \pm 0.0498.$$

The confidence interval spans 0.4002 to 0.4998, or 0.40 to 0.50, carrying two decimal places. To two decimal places, the confidence interval is unchanged from the one computed in Example 2.

Exhibit 6 summarizes the various reliability factors that we have used.

### Exhibit 6: Basis of Computing Reliability Factors

| Sampling from | Statistic for Small Sample Size | Statistic for Large Sample Size |
|---|---|---|
| Normal distribution with known variance | $z$ | $z$ |
| Normal distribution with unknown variance | $t$ | $t^*$ |

| Sampling from | Statistic for Small Sample Size | Statistic for Large Sample Size |
|---|---|---|
| Non-normal distribution with known variance | not available | $z$ |
| Non-normal distribution with unknown variance | not available | $t^*$ |

*Use of z also acceptable.*

Exhibit 7 shows a flowchart that helps determine what statistics should be used to produce confidence intervals under different conditions.

**Exhibit 7: Determining Statistics for Confidence Intervals**

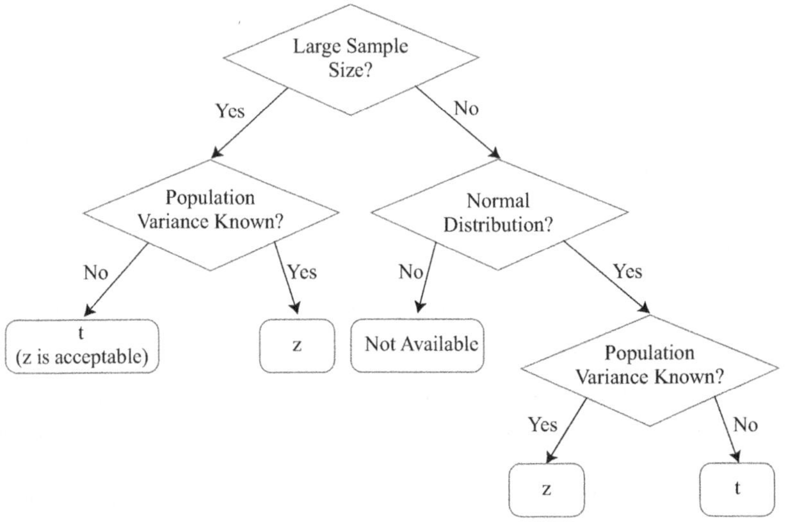

## Selection of Sample Size

What choices affect the width of a confidence interval? To this point we have discussed two factors that affect width: the choice of statistic ($t$ or $z$) and the choice of degree of confidence (affecting which specific value of $t$ or $z$ we use). These two choices determine the reliability factor. (Recall that a confidence interval has the structure Point estimate ± Reliability factor × Standard error.)

The choice of sample size also affects the width of a confidence interval. All else equal, a larger sample size decreases the width of a confidence interval. Recall the expression for the standard error of the sample mean:

$$\text{Standard error of the sample mean} = \frac{\text{Sample standard deviation}}{\sqrt{\text{Sample size}}}$$

We see that the standard error varies inversely with the square root of sample size. As we increase sample size, the standard error decreases and consequently the width of the confidence interval also decreases. The larger the sample size, the greater precision with which we can estimate the population parameter.

# Confidence Intervals for the Population Mean and Sample Size Selection

At a given degree of confidence $(1 - \alpha)$, we can determine the sample size needed to obtain a desired width for a confidence interval. Define $E$ = Reliability factor × Standard error; then $2E$ is the confidence interval's width. The smaller $E$ is, the smaller the width of the confidence interval. Accordingly, the sample size to obtain a desired value of $E$ at a given degree of confidence $(1 - \alpha)$ can be derived as $n = [(t \times s)/E]^2$. It is worth noting that appropriate sample size is also needed for performing a valid power analysis and determining the minimum detectable effect in hypothesis testing, concepts that will be covered at a later stage.

All else equal, larger samples are good, in that sense. In practice, however, two considerations may operate against increasing sample size. First, increasing the size of a sample may result in sampling from more than one population—for example, expanding the sample size may involve pooling together apparently similar samples, when they are actually from different populations (with different population means and variances). A smaller sample size may sometimes be preferred because it represents a more homogeneous distribution than a larger one. Second, increasing sample size may involve additional expenses that outweigh the value of additional precision. Thus three issues that the analyst should weigh in selecting sample size are the need for precision, the risk of sampling from more than one population, and the expenses of different sample sizes.

## EXAMPLE 4

### A Money Manager Estimates Net Client Inflows

A money manager wants to obtain a 95% confidence interval for fund inflows and outflows over the next six months for his existing clients. He begins by calling a random sample of 10 clients and inquiring about their planned additions to and withdrawals from the fund. The manager then computes the change in cash flow for each client sampled as a percentage change in total funds placed with the manager. A positive percentage change indicates a net cash inflow to the client's account, and a negative percentage change indicates a net cash outflow from the client's account. The manager weights each response by the relative size of the account within the sample and then computes a weighted average.

As a result of this process, the money manager computes a weighted average of 5.5%. Thus, a point estimate is that the total amount of funds under management will increase by 5.5% in the next six months. The standard deviation of the observations in the sample is 10%. A histogram of past data looks fairly close to normal, so the manager assumes the population is normal.

1. Calculate a 95% confidence interval for the population mean and interpret your findings.

### Solution to 1:

Because the population variance is unknown and the sample size is small, the manager must use the $t$-statistic in Equation 6 to calculate the confidence interval. Based on the sample size of 10, df = $n - 1$ = 10 − 1 = 9. For a 95% confidence interval, he needs to use the value of $t_{0.025}$ for df = 9. This value is 2.262, using Excel function T.INV(0.025,9). Therefore, a 95% confidence interval for the population mean is

$$\overline{X} \pm t_{0.025}\frac{s}{\sqrt{n}} = 5.5\% \pm 2.262\frac{10\%}{\sqrt{10}}$$
$$= 5.5\% \pm 2.262(3.162)$$
$$= 5.5\% \pm 7.15\%$$

The confidence interval for the population mean spans −1.65% to +12.65%. The manager can be confident at the 95% level that this range includes the population mean.

2. The manager decides to see what the confidence interval would look like if he had used a sample size of 20 or 30 and found the same mean (5.5%) and standard deviation (10%).

Compute the confidence interval for sample sizes of 20 and 30. For the sample size of 30, use Equation 3.

### Solution to 2:

Exhibit 8 gives the calculations for the three sample sizes.

**Exhibit 8: The 95% Confidence Interval for Three Sample Sizes**

| Distribution | 95% Confidence Interval | Lower Bound | Upper Bound | Relative Size |
|---|---|---|---|---|
| $t(n = 10)$ | 5.5% ± 2.262(3.162) | −1.65% | 12.65% | 100.0% |
| $t(n = 20)$ | 5.5% ± 2.093(2.236) | 0.82 | 10.18 | 65.5 |
| $t(n = 30)$ | 5.5% ± 2.045(1.826) | 1.77 | 9.23 | 52.2 |

3. Interpret your results from Parts 1 and 2.

### Solution to 3:

The width of the confidence interval decreases as we increase the sample size. This decrease is a function of the standard error becoming smaller as $n$ increases. The reliability factor also becomes smaller as the number of degrees of freedom increases. The last column of Exhibit 8 shows the relative size of the width of confidence intervals based on $n = 10$ to be 100%. Using a sample size of 20 reduces the confidence interval's width to 65.5% of the interval width for a sample size of 10. Using a sample size of 30 cuts the width of the interval almost in half. Comparing these choices, the money manager would obtain the most precise results using a sample of 30.

## 4  SAMPLING-RELATED BIASES

☐ describe the issues regarding selection of the appropriate sample size, data snooping bias, sample selection bias, survivorship bias, look-ahead bias, and time-period bias

We have already discussed that the selection of sample period length may raise the issue of sampling from more than one population. There are, in fact, a range of challenges to valid sampling that arise in working with financial data. In this section we discuss several such sampling-related issues: data snooping bias, sample selection group of biases (including survivorship bias), look-ahead bias, and time-period bias. All of these issues are important for point and interval estimation and hypothesis testing. As we will see, if the sample is biased in any way, then point and interval estimates and any other conclusions that we draw from the sample will be in error.

## Data Snooping Bias

**Data snooping** relates to overuse of the same or related data in ways that we shall describe shortly. Data snooping bias refers to the errors that arise from such misuse of data. Investment strategies that reflect data snooping biases are often not successful if applied in the future. Nevertheless, both investment practitioners and researchers in general have frequently engaged in data snooping. Analysts thus need to understand and guard against this problem.

Data snooping is the practice of determining a model by extensive searching through a dataset for statistically significant patterns (that is, repeatedly "drilling" in the same data until finding something that appears to work).

If an analyst mines the data thoroughly enough, there are always instances that certain data may appear fitting a pattern, even due to random chance alone.

In essence, we have explored the same data again and again until we found some after-the-fact pattern or patterns in the dataset. This is the sense in which data snooping involves overuse of data. If we were to report only the significant variables without also reporting the total number of variables tested that were unsuccessful as predictors, we would be presenting a very misleading picture of our findings. Datasets in the Big Data space are often blindly used to make statistical inferences without a proper hypothesis testing framework, which may lead to inferring higher-than-justified significance.

How can we investigate the presence of data snooping bias? Typically we can split the data into three separate datasets: the training dataset, the validation dataset, and the test dataset. The training dataset is used to build a model and fit the model parameters. The validation dataset is used to evaluate the model fit while tuning the model parameters. The test dataset is used to provide an **out-of-sample test** to evaluate the final model fit. If a variable or investment strategy is the result of data snooping, it should generally not be significant in out-of-sample tests.

A variable or investment strategy that is statistically and economically significant in out-of-sample tests, and that has a plausible economic basis, may be the basis for a valid investment strategy. Caution is still warranted, however. The most crucial out-of-sample test is future investment success. It should be noted that if the strategy becomes known to other investors, prices may adjust so that the strategy, however well tested, does not work in the future. To summarize, the analyst should be aware that many apparently profitable investment strategies may reflect data snooping bias and thus be cautious about the future applicability of published investment research results.

> **UNTANGLING THE EXTENT OF DATA SNOOPING**
>
> To assess the significance of an investment strategy, we need to know how many unsuccessful strategies were tried not only by the current investigator but also by *previous* investigators using the same or related datasets. Much research, in practice, closely builds on what other investigators have done, and so reflects intergenerational data mining (McQueen and Thorley, 1999) that involves using information developed by previous researchers using a dataset to guide current research using the same or a related dataset. Analysts have accumulated many observations about the peculiarities of many financial datasets, and other analysts may develop models or investment strategies

that will tend to be supported within a dataset based on their familiarity with the prior experience of other analysts. As a consequence, the importance of those new results may be overstated. Research has suggested that the magnitude of this type of data-mining bias may be considerable.

McQueen and Thorley (1999) explored data mining in the context of the popular Motley Fool "Foolish Four" investment strategy, a version of the Dow Dividend Strategy tuned by its developers to exhibit an even higher arithmetic mean return than the original Dow Dividend Strategy. The Foolish Four strategy claimed to show significant investment returns over 20 years starting in 1973, and its proponents claimed that the strategy should have similar returns in the future. McQueen and Thorley highlighted the data-mining issues in that research and presented two signs that can warn analysts about the potential existence of data mining:

- *Too much digging/too little confidence.* The testing of many variables by the researcher is the "too much digging" warning sign of a data-mining problem. Although the number of variables examined may not be reported, we should look closely for verbal hints that the researcher searched over many variables. The use of terms such as "we noticed (or noted) that" or "someone noticed (or noted) that," with respect to a pattern in a dataset, should raise suspicions that the researchers were trying out variables based on their own or others' observations of the data.

- *No story/no future.* The absence of an explicit economic rationale for a variable or trading strategy is the "no story" warning sign of a data-mining problem. Without a plausible economic rationale or story for why a variable should work, the variable is unlikely to have predictive power. What if we do have a plausible economic explanation for a significant variable? McQueen and Thorley caution that a plausible economic rationale is a necessary but not a sufficient condition for a trading strategy to have value. As we mentioned earlier, if the strategy is publicized, market prices may adjust to reflect the new information as traders seek to exploit it; as a result, the strategy may no longer work.

## Sample Selection Bias

When researchers look into questions of interest to analysts or portfolio managers, they may exclude certain stocks, bonds, portfolios, or periods from the analysis for various reasons—perhaps because of data availability. When data availability leads to certain assets being excluded from the analysis, we call the resulting problem **sample selection bias**. For example, you might sample from a database that tracks only companies currently in existence. Many mutual fund databases, for instance, provide historical information about only those funds that currently exist. Databases that report historical balance sheet and income statement information suffer from the same sort of bias as the mutual fund databases: Funds or companies that are no longer in business do not appear there. So, a study that uses these types of databases suffers from a type of sample selection bias known as **survivorship bias**.

The issue of survivorship bias has also been raised in relation to international indexes, particularly those representing less established markets. Some of these markets have suffered complete loss of value as a result of hyperinflation, nationalization or confiscation of industries, or market failure. Measuring the performance of markets or particular investments that survive over time will overstate returns from investing. There is, of course, no way of determining in advance which markets will fail or survive.

# Sampling-Related Biases

Survivorship bias sometimes appears when we use both stock price and accounting data. For example, many studies in finance have used the ratio of a company's market price to book equity per share (i.e., the price-to-book ratio, P/B) and found that P/B is inversely related to a company's returns. P/B is also used to create many popular value and growth indexes. The "value" indexes, for example, would include companies trading on relatively low P/B. If the database that we use to collect accounting data excludes failing companies, however, a survivorship bias might result. It can be argued that failing stocks would be expected to have low returns and low P/Bs. If we exclude failing stocks, then those stocks with low P/Bs that are included in the index will have returns that are higher on average than if all stocks with low P/Bs were included. As shown in Exhibit 9, without failing stocks (shown in the bottom left part), we can fit a line with a negative slope indicating that P/B is inversely related to a company's stock return. With all the companies included, however, the fitted line (horizontal, dotted) shows an insignificant slope coefficient.

This bias would then be responsible for some of the traditional findings of an inverse relationship between average return and P/B. Researchers should be aware of any biases potentially inherent in a sample.

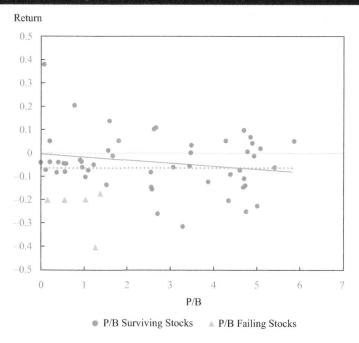

Exhibit 9: Survivorship Bias

## DELISTINGS AND BIAS

A sample can also be biased because of the removal (or delisting) of a company's stock from an exchange. For example, the Center for Research in Security Prices at the University of Chicago is a major provider of return data used in academic research. When a delisting occurs, CRSP attempts to collect returns for the delisted company. Many times, however, it cannot do so because of the difficulty involved; CRSP must simply list delisted company returns as missing. A study in the *Journal of Finance* by Shumway and Warther (1999) documented the bias caused by delisting for CRSP NASDAQ return data. The authors showed that delistings associated with poor company performance (e.g., bankruptcy) are missed more often than delistings associated with good or neutral company performance (e.g., merger or moving to another exchange). In addition, delistings occur more frequently for small companies.

Sample selection bias occurs even in markets where the quality and consistency of the data are quite high. Newer asset classes such as hedge funds may present even greater problems of sample selection bias. Hedge funds are a heterogeneous group of investment vehicles typically organized so as to be free from regulatory oversight. In general, hedge funds are not required to publicly disclose performance (in contrast to, say, mutual funds). Hedge funds themselves decide whether they want to be included in one of the various databases of hedge fund performance. Hedge funds with poor track records clearly may not wish to make their records public, creating a problem of self-selection bias in hedge fund databases. Further, as pointed out by Fung and Hsieh (2002), because only hedge funds with good records will volunteer to enter a database, in general, overall past hedge fund industry performance will tend to appear better than it really is. Furthermore, many hedge fund databases drop funds that go out of business, creating survivorship bias in the database. Even if the database does not drop defunct hedge funds, in the attempt to eliminate survivorship bias, the problem remains of hedge funds that stop reporting performance because of poor results or because successful funds no longer want new cash inflows. In some circumstances, **implicit selection bias** may exist because of a threshold enabling self-selection. For example, compared with smaller exchanges, the NYSE has higher stock listing requirements. Choosing NYSE-listed stocks may introduce an implicit quality bias into the analysis. Although the bias is less obvious, it is important for generalizing findings.

A variation of selection bias is **backfill bias**. For example, when a new hedge fund is added to a given index, the fund's past performance may be backfilled into the index's database, even though the fund was not included in the database in the previous year. Usually a new fund starts contributing data after a period of good performance, so adding the fund's instant history into the index database may inflate the index performance.

## Look-Ahead Bias

A test design is subject to **look-ahead bias** if it uses information that was not available on the test date. For example, tests of trading rules that use stock market returns and accounting balance sheet data must account for look-ahead bias. In such tests, a company's book value per share is commonly used to construct the P/B variable. Although the market price of a stock is available for all market participants at the same point in time, fiscal year-end book equity per share might not become publicly available until sometime in the following quarter. One solution to mitigate the look-ahead bias is to use point-in-time (PIT) data when possible. PIT data is stamped with the date when it was recorded or released. In the previous example, the PIT data of P/B would be accompanied with the company filing date or press release date, rather than the end date of the fiscal quarter the P/B data represents. It is worth noting that the look-ahead bias could also be implicitly introduced. For example, when normalizing input data by deducting the mean and dividing it by standard deviation, we must ensure that the standard deviation of the training data is used as the proxy for standard deviation in validation and test data sets. Using standard deviation of validation or test data to normalize them will implicitly introduce a look-ahead bias as the variance of future data is inappropriately used.

## Time-Period Bias

A test design is subject to **time-period bias** if it is based on a period that may make the results period specific. A short time series is likely to give period-specific results that may not reflect a longer period. A long time series may give a more accurate picture of true investment performance; its disadvantage lies in the potential for a structural change occurring during the time frame that would result in two different return distributions. In this situation, the distribution that would reflect conditions before the change differs from the distribution that would describe conditions after the change. Regime changes, such as low versus high volatility regimes or low versus high interest rate regimes, are highly influential to asset classes. Inferences based on data influenced by one regime, and thus not appropriately distributed, should account for how the regime may bias the inferences.

### EXAMPLE 5

#### Biases in Investment Research

An analyst is reviewing the empirical evidence on historical equity returns in the Eurozone (European countries that use the euro). She finds that value stocks (i.e., those with low P/Bs) outperformed growth stocks (i.e., those with high P/Bs) in recent periods. After reviewing the Eurozone market, the analyst wonders whether value stocks might be attractive in the United Kingdom. She investigates the performance of value and growth stocks in the UK market for a 10-year period. To conduct this research, the analyst does the following:

- obtains the current composition of the Financial Times Stock Exchange (FTSE) All Share Index, a market-capitalization-weighted index;
- eliminates the companies that do not have December fiscal year-ends;
- uses year-end book values and market prices to rank the remaining universe of companies by P/Bs at the end of the year;
- based on these rankings, divides the universe into 10 portfolios, each of which contains an equal number of stocks;
- calculates the equal-weighted return of each portfolio and the return for the FTSE All Share Index for the 12 months following the date each ranking was made; and
- subtracts the FTSE returns from each portfolio's returns to derive excess returns for each portfolio.

She discusses the research process with her supervisor, who makes two comments:

- The proposed process may introduce survivorship bias into her analysis.
- The proposed research should cover a longer period.

1. Which of the following best describes the supervisor's first comment?

    **A.** The comment is false. The proposed method is designed to avoid survivorship bias.

    **B.** The comment is true, because she is planning to use the current list of FTSE stocks rather than the actual list of stocks that existed at the start of each year.

**C.** The comment is true, because the test design uses information unavailable on the test date.

## Solution to 1:

B is correct because the research design is subject to survivorship bias if it fails to account for companies that have gone bankrupt, merged, or otherwise departed the database. Using the current list of FTSE stocks rather than the actual list of stocks that existed at the start of each year means that the computation of returns excluded companies removed from the index. The performance of the portfolios with the lowest P/B is subject to survivorship bias and may be overstated. At some time during the testing period, those companies not currently in existence were eliminated from testing. They would probably have had low prices (and low P/Bs) and poor returns.

A is incorrect because the method is not designed to avoid survivorship bias. C is incorrect because the fact that the test design uses information unavailable on the test date relates to look-ahead bias. A test design is subject to look-ahead bias if it uses information unavailable on the test date. This bias would make a strategy based on the information appear successful, but it assumes perfect forecasting ability.

2. What bias is the supervisor concerned about when making the second comment?

    **A.** Time period bias, because the results may be period specific
    **B.** Look-ahead bias, because the bias could be reduced or eliminated if one uses a longer period
    **C.** Survivorship bias, because the bias would become less relevant over longer periods

## Solution to 2:

A is correct. A test design is subject to time-period bias if it is based on a period that may make the results period specific. Although the research covered a period of 10 years, that period may be too short for testing an anomaly. Ideally, an analyst should test market anomalies over several market cycles to ensure that results are not period specific. This bias can favor a proposed strategy if the period chosen was favorable to the strategy.

# SUMMARY

In this reading, we have presented basic concepts and results in sampling and estimation. We have also emphasized the challenges and biases faced by analysts in appropriately using and interpreting financial data.

- An estimator is a formula for computing a sample statistic used to estimate a population parameter. An estimate is a particular value that we calculate from a sample by using an estimator.
- Because an estimator or statistic is a random variable, it is described by some probability distribution. We refer to the distribution of an estimator as its sampling distribution. The standard deviation of the sampling distribution of the sample mean is called the standard error of the sample mean.

## Sampling-Related Biases

- The desirable properties of an estimator are *unbiasedness* (the expected value of the estimator equals the population parameter), *efficiency* (the estimator has the smallest variance), and *consistency* (the probability of accurate estimates increases as sample size increases).
- The two types of estimates of a parameter are point estimates and interval estimates. A point estimate is a single number that we use to estimate a parameter. An interval estimate is a range of values that brackets the population parameter with some probability.
- A confidence interval is an interval for which we can assert with a given probability $1 - \alpha$, called the degree of confidence, that it will contain the parameter it is intended to estimate. This measure is often referred to as the $100(1 - \alpha)\%$ confidence interval for the parameter.
- A $100(1 - \alpha)\%$ confidence interval for a parameter has the following structure: Point estimate ± Reliability factor × Standard error, where the reliability factor is a number based on the assumed distribution of the point estimate and the degree of confidence $(1 - \alpha)$ for the confidence interval and where standard error is the standard error of the sample statistic providing the point estimate.
- A $100(1 - \alpha)\%$ confidence interval for population mean $\mu$ when sampling from a normal distribution with known variance $\sigma^2$ is given by $\bar{X} \pm z_{\alpha/2} \frac{\sigma}{\sqrt{n}}$, where $z_{\alpha/2}$ is the point of the standard normal distribution such that $\alpha/2$ remains in the right tail.
- A random sample of size $n$ is said to have $n - 1$ degrees of freedom for estimating the population variance, in the sense that there are only $n - 1$ independent deviations from the mean on which to base the estimate.
- A $100(1 - \alpha)\%$ confidence interval for the population mean $\mu$ when sampling from a normal distribution with unknown variance (a *t*-distribution confidence interval) is given by $\bar{X} \pm t_{\alpha/2}(s/\sqrt{n})$, where $t_{\alpha/2}$ is the point of the *t*-distribution such that $\alpha/2$ remains in the right tail and $s$ is the sample standard deviation. This confidence interval can also be used, because of the central limit theorem, when dealing with a large sample from a population with unknown variance that may not be normal.
- We may use the confidence interval $\bar{X} \pm z_{\alpha/2}(s/\sqrt{n})$ as an alternative to the *t*-distribution confidence interval for the population mean when using a large sample from a population with unknown variance. The confidence interval based on the *z*-statistic is less conservative (narrower) than the corresponding confidence interval based on a *t*-distribution.
- Three issues in the selection of sample size are the need for precision, the risk of sampling from more than one population, and the expenses of different sample sizes.
- *Data snooping bias* comes from finding models by repeatedly searching through databases for patterns.
- *Sample selection bias* occurs when data availability leads to certain assets being excluded from the analysis.
- *Survivorship bias* is a subset of sample selection bias and occurs if companies are excluded from the analysis because they have gone out of business or because of reasons related to poor performance.
- *Self-selection* bias reflects the ability of entities to decide whether or not they wish to report their attributes or results and be included in databases or samples. *Implicit selection bias* is one type of selection bias introduced

through the presence of a threshold that filters out some unqualified members. A subset of selection bias is *backfill bias*, in which past data, not reported or used before, is backfilled into an existing database.

- *Look-ahead bias* exists if the model uses data not available to market participants at the time the market participants act in the model.
- *Time-period bias* is present if the period used makes the results period specific or if the period used includes a point of structural change.

# REFERENCES

Fung, William, David Hsieh. 2002. "Hedge-Fund Benchmarks: Information Content and Biases." Financial Analysts Journal, vol. 58, no. 1: 22–34. 10.2469/faj.v58.n1.2507

McQueen, Grant, Steven Thorley. 1999. "Mining Fools Gold." Financial Analysts Journal, vol. 55, no. 2: 61–72. 10.2469/faj.v55.n2.2261

Shumway, Tyler, Vincent A. Warther. 1999. "The Delisting Bias in CRSP's Nasdaq Data and Its Implications for the Size Effect." Journal of Finance, vol. 54, no. 6: 2361–2379. 10.1111/0022-1082.00192

# PRACTICE PROBLEMS

1. An estimator with an expected value equal to the parameter that it is intended to estimate is described as:

   A. efficient.

   B. unbiased.

   C. consistent.

2. If an estimator is consistent, an increase in sample size will increase the:

   A. accuracy of estimates.

   B. efficiency of the estimator.

   C. unbiasedness of the estimator.

3. Petra Munzi wants to know how value managers performed last year. Munzi estimates that the population cross-sectional standard deviation of value manager returns is 4% and assumes that the returns are independent across managers.

   A. Munzi wants to build a 95% confidence interval for the population mean return. How large a random sample does Munzi need if she wants the 95% confidence interval to have a total width of 1%?

   B. Munzi expects a cost of about $10 to collect each observation. If she has a $1,000 budget, will she be able to construct the confidence interval she wants?

4. Find the reliability factors based on the $t$-distribution for the following confidence intervals for the population mean (df = degrees of freedom, $n$ = sample size):

   A. A 99% confidence interval, df = 20

   B. A 90% confidence interval, df = 20

   C. A 95% confidence interval, $n$ = 25

   D. A 95% confidence interval, $n$ = 16

5. Assume that monthly returns are normally distributed with a mean of 1% and a sample standard deviation of 4%. The population standard deviation is unknown. Construct a 95% confidence interval for the sample mean of monthly returns if the sample size is 24.

6. Explain the differences between constructing a confidence interval when sampling from a normal population with a known population variance and sampling from a normal population with an unknown variance.

7. For a two-sided confidence interval, an increase in the degree of confidence will result in:

   A. a wider confidence interval.

   B. a narrower confidence interval.

**Practice Problems**

C. no change in the width of the confidence interval.

8. For a sample size of 17, with a mean of 116.23 and a variance of 245.55, the width of a 90% confidence interval using the appropriate *t*-distribution is *closest to*:

   A. 13.23.

   B. 13.27.

   C. 13.68.

9. For a sample size of 65 with a mean of 31 taken from a normally distributed population with a variance of 529, a 99% confidence interval for the population mean will have a lower limit *closest* to:

   A. 23.64.

   B. 25.41.

   C. 30.09.

10. An increase in sample size is *most likely* to result in a:

    A. wider confidence interval.

    B. decrease in the standard error of the sample mean.

    C. lower likelihood of sampling from more than one population.

11. Suppose we take a random sample of 30 companies in an industry with 200 companies. We calculate the sample mean of the ratio of cash flow to total debt for the prior year. We find that this ratio is 23%. Subsequently, we learn that the population cash flow to total debt ratio (taking account of all 200 companies) is 26%. What is the explanation for the discrepancy between the sample mean of 23% and the population mean of 26%?

    A. Sampling error

    B. Bias

    C. A lack of consistency

12. Alcorn Mutual Funds is placing large advertisements in several financial publications. The advertisements prominently display the returns of 5 of Alcorn's 30 funds for the past 1-, 3-, 5-, and 10-year periods. The results are indeed impressive, with all of the funds beating the major market indexes and a few beating them by a large margin. Is the Alcorn family of funds superior to its competitors?

13. Julius Spence has tested several predictive models in order to identify undervalued stocks. Spence used about 30 company-specific variables and 10 market-related variables to predict returns for about 5,000 North American and European stocks. He found that a final model using eight variables applied to telecommunications and computer stocks yields spectacular results. Spence wants you to use the model to select investments. Should you? What steps would you take to evaluate the model?

14. A report on long-term stock returns focused exclusively on all currently publicly traded firms in an industry is *most likely* susceptible to:

    A. look-ahead bias.

B. survivorship bias.

C. intergenerational data mining.

15. Which sampling bias is *most likely* investigated with an out-of-sample test?
    A. Look-ahead bias
    B. Data-mining bias
    C. Sample selection bias

16. Which of the following characteristics of an investment study *most likely* indicates time-period bias?
    A. The study is based on a short time-series.
    B. Information not available on the test date is used.
    C. A structural change occurred prior to the start of the study's time series.

# SOLUTIONS

1. B is correct. An unbiased estimator is one for which the expected value equals the parameter it is intended to estimate.

2. A is correct. A consistent estimator is one for which the probability of estimates close to the value of the population parameter increases as sample size increases. More specifically, a consistent estimator's sampling distribution becomes concentrated on the value of the parameter it is intended to estimate as the sample size approaches infinity.

3. 

   **A.** Assume the sample size will be large and thus the 95% confidence interval for the population mean of manager returns is $\overline{X} \pm 1.96 s_{\overline{X}}$, where $s_{\overline{X}} = s/\sqrt{n}$. Munzi wants the distance between the upper limit and lower limit in the confidence interval to be 1%, which is

   $$(\overline{X} + 1.96 s_{\overline{X}}) - (\overline{X} - 1.96 s_{\overline{X}}) = 1\%$$

   Simplifying this equation, we get $2(1.96 s_{\overline{X}}) = 1\%$. Finally, we have $3.92 s_{\overline{X}} = 1\%$, which gives us the standard deviation of the sample mean, $s_{\overline{X}} = 0.255\%$. The distribution of sample means is $s_{\overline{X}} = s/\sqrt{n}$. Substituting in the values for $s_{\overline{X}}$ and $s$, we have $0.255\% = 4\%/\sqrt{n}$, or $\sqrt{n} = 15.69$. Squaring this value, we get a random sample of $n = 246$.

   **B.** With her budget, Munzi can pay for a sample of up to 100 observations, which is far short of the 246 observations needed. Munzi can either proceed with her current budget and settle for a wider confidence interval or she can raise her budget (to around $2,460) to get the sample size for a 1% width in her confidence interval.

4. 

   **A.** For a 99% confidence interval, the reliability factor we use is $t_{0.005}$; for df = 20, this factor is 2.845.

   **B.** For a 90% confidence interval, the reliability factor we use is $t_{0.05}$; for df = 20, this factor is 1.725.

   **C.** Degrees of freedom equal $n - 1$, or in this case $25 - 1 = 24$. For a 95% confidence interval, the reliability factor we use is $t_{0.025}$; for df = 24, this factor is 2.064.

   **D.** Degrees of freedom equal $16 - 1 = 15$. For a 95% confidence interval, the reliability factor we use is $t_{0.025}$; for df = 15, this factor is 2.131.

5. Because this is a small sample from a normal population and we have only the sample standard deviation, we use the following model to solve for the confidence interval of the population mean:

   $$\overline{X} \pm t_{\alpha/2} \frac{s}{\sqrt{n}}$$

   where we find $t_{0.025}$ (for a 95% confidence interval) for df = $n - 1 = 24 - 1 = 23$; this value is 2.069. Our solution is $1\% \pm 2.069(4\%)/\sqrt{24} = 1\% \pm 2.069(0.8165) = 1\% \pm 1.69$. The 95% confidence interval spans the range from −0.69% to +2.69%.

6. If the population variance is known, the confidence interval is

$$\bar{X} \pm z_{\alpha/2} \frac{\sigma}{\sqrt{n}}$$

The confidence interval for the population mean is centered at the sample mean, $\bar{X}$. The population standard deviation is $\sigma$, and the sample size is $n$. The population standard deviation divided by the square root of $n$ is the standard error of the estimate of the mean. The value of $z$ depends on the desired degree of confidence. For a 95% confidence interval, $z_{0.025} = 1.96$ and the confidence interval estimate is

$$\bar{X} \pm 1.96 \frac{\sigma}{\sqrt{n}}$$

If the population variance is not known, we make two changes to the technique used when the population variance is known. First, we must use the sample standard deviation instead of the population standard deviation. Second, we use the $t$-distribution instead of the normal distribution. The critical $t$-value will depend on degrees of freedom $n - 1$. If the sample size is large, we have the alternative of using the $z$-distribution with the sample standard deviation.

7. A is correct. As the degree of confidence increases (e.g., from 95% to 99%), a given confidence interval will become wider. A confidence interval is a range for which one can assert with a given probability $1 - \alpha$, called the degree of confidence, that it will contain the parameter it is intended to estimate.

8. B is correct. The confidence interval is calculated using the following equation:

$$\bar{X} \pm t_{\alpha/2} \frac{s}{\sqrt{n}}$$

Sample standard deviation ($s$) = $\sqrt{245.55}$ = 15.670.
For a sample size of 17, degrees of freedom equal 16, so $t_{0.05} = 1.746$.
The confidence interval is calculated as

$$116.23 \pm 1.746 \frac{15.67}{\sqrt{17}} = 116.23 \pm 6.6357$$

Therefore, the interval spans 109.5943 to 122.8656, meaning its width is equal to approximately 13.271. (This interval can be alternatively calculated as 6.6357 × 2.)

9. A is correct. To solve, use the structure of Confidence interval = Point estimate ± Reliability factor × Standard error, which, for a normally distributed population with known variance, is represented by the following formula:

$$\bar{X} \pm z_{\alpha/2} \frac{\sigma}{\sqrt{n}}$$

For a 99% confidence interval, use $z_{0.005} = 2.58$.
Also, $\sigma = \sqrt{529} = 23$.
Therefore, the lower limit = $31 - 2.58 \frac{23}{\sqrt{65}} = 23.6398$.

10. B is correct. All else being equal, as the sample size increases, the standard error of the sample mean decreases and the width of the confidence interval also decreases.

11. A is correct. The discrepancy arises from sampling error. Sampling error exists whenever one fails to observe every element of the population, because a sample statistic can vary from sample to sample. As stated in the reading, the sample mean is an unbiased estimator, a consistent estimator, and an efficient estimator of the population mean. Although the sample mean is an unbiased estimator of the population mean—the expected value of the sample mean equals the population mean—because of sampling error, we do not expect the sample mean to exactly equal the population mean in any one sample we may take.

12. No, we cannot say that Alcorn Mutual Funds as a group is superior to competitors. Alcorn Mutual Funds' advertisement may easily mislead readers because the advertisement does not show the performance of all its funds. In particular, Alcorn Mutual Funds is engaging in sample selection bias by presenting the investment results from its best-performing funds only.

13. Spence may be guilty of data mining. He has used so many possible combinations of variables on so many stocks, it is not surprising that he found some instances in which a model worked. In fact, it would have been more surprising if he had not found any. To decide whether to use his model, you should do two things: First, ask that the model be tested on out-of-sample data—that is, data that were not used in building the model. The model may not be successful with out-of-sample data. Second, examine his model to make sure that the relationships in the model make economic sense, have a story, and have a future.

14. B is correct. A report that uses a current list of stocks does not account for firms that failed, merged, or otherwise disappeared from the public equity market in previous years. As a consequence, the report is biased. This type of bias is known as survivorship bias.

15. B is correct. An out-of-sample test is used to investigate the presence of data-mining bias. Such a test uses a sample that does not overlap the time period of the sample on which a variable, strategy, or model was developed.

16. A is correct. A short time series is likely to give period-specific results that may not reflect a longer time period.

# LEARNING MODULE

# Basics of Hypothesis Testing

by Pamela Peterson Drake, PhD, CFA.

*Pamela Peterson Drake, PhD, CFA, is at James Madison University (USA).*

| LEARNING OUTCOMES | |
|---|---|
| Mastery | The candidate should be able to: |
| ☐ | define a hypothesis, describe the steps of hypothesis testing, and describe and interpret the choice of the null and alternative hypotheses |
| ☐ | compare and contrast one-tailed and two-tailed tests of hypotheses |
| ☐ | explain a test statistic, Type I and Type II errors, a significance level, how significance levels are used in hypothesis testing, and the power of a test |
| ☐ | explain a decision rule and the relation between confidence intervals and hypothesis tests, and determine whether a statistically significant result is also economically meaningful |
| ☐ | explain and interpret the *p*-value as it relates to hypothesis testing |
| ☐ | describe how to interpret the significance of a test in the context of multiple tests |
| ☐ | identify the appropriate test statistic and interpret the results for a hypothesis test concerning the population mean of both large and small samples when the population is normally or approximately normally distributed and the variance is (1) known or (2) unknown |
| ☐ | identify the appropriate test statistic and interpret the results for a hypothesis test concerning the equality of the population means of two at least approximately normally distributed populations based on independent random samples with equal assumed variances |
| ☐ | identify the appropriate test statistic and interpret the results for a hypothesis test concerning the mean difference of two normally distributed populations |
| ☐ | identify the appropriate test statistic and interpret the results for a hypothesis test concerning (1) the variance of a normally distributed population and (2) the equality of the variances of two normally distributed populations based on two independent random samples |

# 1. INTRODUCTION

☐ define a hypothesis, describe the steps of hypothesis testing, and describe and interpret the choice of the null and alternative hypotheses

## Why Hypothesis Testing?

Faced with an overwhelming amount of data, analysts must deal with the task of wrangling those data into something that provides a clearer picture of what is going on. Consider an analyst evaluating the returns on two investments over 33 years, as we show in Exhibit 1.

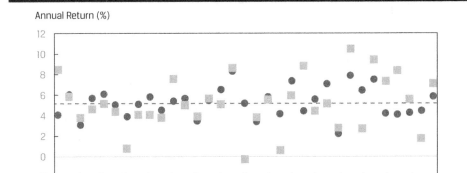

Exhibit 1: Returns for Investments One and Two over 33 Years

Although "a picture is worth a thousand words," what can we actually glean from this plot? Can we tell if each investment's returns are different from an average of 5%? Can we tell whether the returns are different for Investment One and Investment Two? Can we tell whether the standard deviations of the two investments are each different from 2%? Can we tell whether the variability is different for the two investments? For these questions, we need to have more precise tools than simply a plot over time. What we need is a set of tools that aid us in making decisions based on the data.

We use the concepts and tools of **hypothesis testing** to address these questions. Hypothesis testing is part of statistical inference, the process of making judgments about a larger group (a population) based on a smaller group of observations (that is, a sample).

## Implications from a Sampling Distribution

Consider a set of 1,000 asset returns with a mean of 6% and a standard deviation of 2%. If we draw a sample of returns from this population, what is the chance that the mean of this sample will be 6%? What we know about sampling distributions is that

# Introduction

how close any given sample mean will be to the population mean depends on the sample size, the variability within the population, and the quality of our sampling methodology.

For example, suppose we draw a sample of 30 observations and the sample mean is 6.13%. Is this close enough to 6% to alleviate doubt that the sample is drawn from a population with a mean of 6%? Suppose we draw another sample of 30 and find a sample mean of 4.8%. Does this bring into doubt whether the population mean is 6%? If we keep drawing samples of 30 observations from this population, we will get a range of possible sample means, as we show in Exhibit 2 for 100 different samples of size 30 from this population, with a range of values from 5.06 to 7.03%. All these sample means are a result of sampling from the 1,000 asset returns.

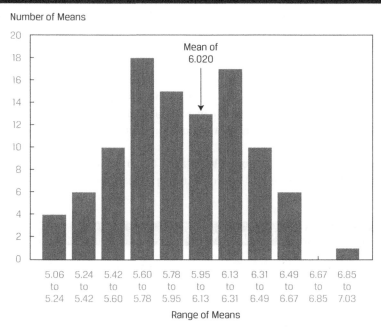

Exhibit 2: Distribution of Sample Means of 100 Samples Drawn from a Population of 1,000 Returns

As you can see in Exhibit 2, a sample mean that is quite different from the population mean can occur; this situation is not as likely as drawing a sample with a mean closer to the population mean, but it can still happen. *In hypothesis testing, we test to see whether a sample statistic is likely to come from a population with the hypothesized value of the population parameter.*

The concepts and tools of hypothesis testing provide an objective means to gauge whether the available evidence supports the hypothesis. After applying a statistical test of a hypothesis, we should have a clearer idea of the probability that a hypothesis is true or not, although our conclusion always stops short of certainty.

The main focus of this reading is on the framework of hypothesis testing of the population mean and variance, parameters that are frequently used in investments.

## 2

# THE PROCESS OF HYPOTHESIS TESTING

☐ compare and contrast one-tailed and two-tailed tests of hypotheses

Hypothesis testing is part of the branch of statistics known as statistical inference. In statistical inference, there is estimation and hypothesis testing. Estimation involves point estimates and interval estimates. Consider a sample mean, which is a point estimate, that we can use to form a confidence interval. In hypothesis testing, the focus is examining how a sample statistic informs us about a population parameter. A **hypothesis** is a statement about one or more populations that we test using sample statistics.

The process of hypothesis testing begins with the formulation of a theory to organize and explain observations. We judge the correctness of the theory by its ability to make accurate predictions—for example, to predict the results of new observations. If the predictions are correct, we continue to maintain the theory as a possibly correct explanation of our observations. Risk plays a role in the outcomes of observations in finance, so we can only try to make unbiased, probability-based judgments about whether the new data support the predictions. Statistical hypothesis testing fills that key role of testing hypotheses when there is uncertainty. When an analyst correctly formulates the question into a testable hypothesis and carries out a test of hypotheses, the use of well-established scientific methods supports the conclusions and decisions made on the basis of this test.

We organize this introduction to hypothesis testing around the six steps in Exhibit 3, which illustrate the standard approach to hypothesis testing.

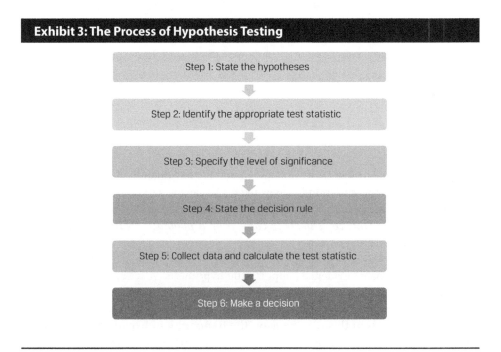

Exhibit 3: The Process of Hypothesis Testing

## Stating the Hypotheses

For each hypothesis test, we always state two hypotheses: the **null hypothesis** (or null), designated $H_0$, and the **alternative hypothesis**, designated $H_a$. For example, our null hypothesis may concern the value of a population mean, $\mu$, in relation to one possible value of the mean, $\mu_0$. As another example, our null hypothesis may concern the population variance, $\sigma^2$, compared with a possible value of this variance, $\sigma_0^2$. The null hypothesis is a statement concerning a population parameter or parameters considered to be true unless the sample we use to conduct the hypothesis test gives convincing evidence that the null hypothesis is false. In fact, the null hypothesis is what we want to reject. If there is sufficient evidence to indicate that the null hypothesis is not true, we reject it in favor of the alternative hypothesis.

Importantly, the null and alternative hypotheses are stated in terms of population parameters, and we use sample statistics to test these hypotheses.

## Two-Sided vs. One-Sided Hypotheses

Suppose we want to test whether the population mean return is equal to 6%. We would state the null hypothesis as

$H_a: \mu \neq 6$.

and the alternative as

$H_0: \mu = 6$

What we just created was a **two-sided hypothesis test**. We are testing whether the mean is equal to 6%; it could be greater than or less than that because we are simply asking whether the mean is different from 6%. If we find that the sample mean is far enough away from the hypothesized value, considering the risk of drawing a sample that is not representative of the population, then we would reject the null in favor of the alternative hypothesis.

What if we wanted to test whether the mean is greater than 6%. This presents us with a **one-sided hypothesis test**, and we specify the hypotheses as follows:

$H_0: \mu \leq 6$.

$H_a: \mu > 6$.

If we find that the sample mean is greater than the hypothesized value of 6 by a sufficient margin, then we would reject the null hypothesis. Why is the null hypothesis stated with a "$\leq$" sign? First, if the sample mean is less than or equal to 6%, this would not support the alternative. Second, the null and alternative hypotheses must be mutually exclusive and collectively exhaustive; in other words, all possible values are contained in either the null or the alternative hypothesis.

Despite the different ways to formulate hypotheses, we always conduct a test of the null hypothesis at the point of equality; for example, $\mu = \mu_0$. Whether the null is $H_0: \mu = \mu_0$, $H_0: \mu \leq \mu_0$, or $H_0: \mu \geq \mu_0$, we actually test $\mu = \mu_0$. The reasoning is straightforward: Suppose the hypothesized value of the mean is 6. Consider $H_0: \mu \leq 6$, with a "greater than" alternative hypothesis, $H_a: \mu > 6$. If we have enough evidence to reject $H_0: \mu = 6$ in favor of $H_a: \mu > 6$, we definitely also have enough evidence to reject the hypothesis that the parameter $\mu$ is some smaller value, such as 4.5 or 5.

Using hypotheses regarding the population mean as an example, the three possible formulations of hypotheses are as follows:

Two-sided alternative: $H_0: \mu = \mu_0$ versus $H_a: \mu \neq \mu_0$

One-sided alternative (right side): $H_0: \mu \leq \mu_0$ versus $H_a: \mu > \mu_0$

One-sided alternative (left side): $H_0: \mu \geq \mu_0$ versus $H_a: \mu < \mu_0$

The reference to the side (right or left) refers to where we reject the null in the probability distribution. For example, if the alternative is $H_a: \mu > 6$, this means that we will reject the null hypothesis if the sample mean is sufficiently higher than (or on the right side of the distribution of) the hypothesized value.

Importantly, the calculation to test the null hypothesis is the same for all three formulations. What is different for the three formulations is how the calculation is evaluated to decide whether to reject the null.

## Selecting the Appropriate Hypotheses

How do we choose the null and alternative hypotheses? The null is what we are hoping to reject. The most common alternative is the "not equal to" hypothesis. However, economic or financial theory may suggest a one-sided alternative hypothesis. For example, if the population parameter is the mean risk premium, financial theory may argue that this risk premium is positive. Following the principle of stating the alternative as the "hoped for" condition and using $\mu_{rp}$ for the population mean risk premium, we formulate the following hypotheses:

$H_0: \mu_{rp} \leq 0$ versus $H_a: \mu_{rp} > 0$

Note that the sign in the alternative hypotheses reflects the belief of the researcher more strongly than a two-sided alternative hypothesis. However, the researcher may sometimes select a two-sided alternative hypothesis to emphasize an attitude of neutrality when a one-sided alternative hypothesis is also reasonable. Typically, the easiest way to formulate the hypotheses is to specify the alternative hypothesis first and then specify the null.

> **EXAMPLE 1**
>
> ### Specifying the Hypotheses
>
> 1. An analyst suspects that in the most recent year excess returns on stocks have fallen below 5%. She wants to study whether the excess returns are less than 5%. Designating the population mean as $\mu$, which hypotheses are most appropriate for her analysis?
>
>    **A.** $H_0: \mu = 5$ versus $H_a: \mu \neq 5$
>    **B.** $H_0: \mu > 5$ versus $H_a: \mu < 5$
>    **C.** $H_0: \mu < 5$ versus $H_a: \mu > 5$
>
> ### Solution
>
> B is correct. The null hypothesis is what she wants to reject in favor of the alternative, which is that population mean excess return is less than 5%. This is a one-sided (left-side) alternative hypothesis.

# IDENTIFY THE APPROPRIATE TEST STATISTIC

☐ explain a test statistic, Type I and Type II errors, a significance level, how significance levels are used in hypothesis testing, and the power of a test

A test statistic is a value calculated on the basis of a sample that, when used in conjunction with a decision rule, is the basis for deciding whether to reject the null hypothesis.

## Test Statistics

The focal point of our statistical decision is the value of the test statistic. The test statistic that we use depends on what we are testing. As an example, let us examine the test of a population mean risk premium. Consider the sample mean, $\overline{X}$, calculated from a sample of returns drawn from the population. If the population standard deviation is known, the standard error of the distribution of sample means, $\sigma_{\overline{X}}$, is the ratio of the population standard deviation to the square root of the sample size:

$$\sigma_{\overline{X}} = \frac{\sigma}{\sqrt{n}}. \tag{1}$$

The test statistic for the test of the mean when the population variance is known is a z-distributed (that is, normally distributed) test statistic:

$$z = \frac{\overline{X}_{rp} - \mu_0}{\sigma/\sqrt{n}}. \tag{2}$$

If the hypothesized value of the mean population risk premium is 6 (that is, $\mu_0 = 6$), we calculate this as $z = \frac{\overline{X}_{rp} - 6}{\sigma/\sqrt{n}}$. If, however, the hypothesized value of the mean risk premium is zero (that is, $\mu_0 = 0$), we can simplify this test statistic as

$$z = \frac{\overline{X}_{rp}}{\sigma/\sqrt{n}}.$$

Notably, the key to hypothesis testing is identifying the appropriate test statistic for the hypotheses and the underlying distribution of the population.

## Identifying the Distribution of the Test Statistic

Following the identification of the appropriate test statistic, we must be concerned with the distribution of the test statistic. We show examples of the test statistics and their corresponding distributions in Exhibit 4.

### Exhibit 4: Test Statistics and Their Distributions

| What We Want to Test | Test Statistic | Probability Distribution of the Statistic | Degrees of Freedom |
|---|---|---|---|
| Test of a single mean | $t = \frac{\overline{X} - \mu_0}{s/\sqrt{n}}$ | t-Distributed | $n - 1$ |
| Test of the difference in means | $t = \frac{(\overline{X}_1 - \overline{X}_2) - (\mu_1 - \mu_2)}{\sqrt{\frac{s_p^2}{n_1} + \frac{s_p^2}{n_2}}}$ | t-Distributed | $n_1 + n_2 - 2$ |
| Test of the mean of differences | $t = \frac{\overline{d} - \mu_{d0}}{s_{\overline{d}}}$ | t-Distributed | $n - 1$ |

| What We Want to Test | Test Statistic | Probability Distribution of the Statistic | Degrees of Freedom |
|---|---|---|---|
| Test of a single variance | $\chi^2 = \dfrac{s^2(n-1)}{\sigma_0^2}$ | Chi-square distributed | $n - 1$ |
| Test of the difference in variances | $F = \dfrac{s_1^2}{s_2^2}$ | $F$-distributed | $n_1 - 1, n_2 - 1$ |

*Note*: $\mu_0$, $\mu_{d0}$, and $\sigma_0^2$ denote hypothesized values of the mean, mean difference, and variance, respectively. The $\bar{x}$, $\bar{d}$, $s^2$, and $s$ denote for a sample the mean, mean of the differences, variance, and standard deviation, respectively, with subscripts indicating the sample, if appropriate. The sample size is indicated as n, and the subscript indicates the sample, if appropriate.

## 4. SPECIFY THE LEVEL OF SIGNIFICANCE

The level of significance reflects how much sample evidence we require to reject the null hypothesis. The required standard of proof can change according to the nature of the hypotheses and the seriousness of the consequences of making a mistake. There are four possible outcomes when we test a null hypothesis, as shown in Exhibit 5. A **Type I error** is a false positive (reject when the null is true), whereas a **Type II error** is a false negative (fail to reject when the null is false).

### Exhibit 5: Correct and Incorrect Decisions in Hypothesis Testing

| Decision | True Situation | |
|---|---|---|
| | $H_0$ True | $H_0$ False |
| Fail to reject $H_0$ | Correct decision: Do not reject a true null hypothesis. | Type II error: Fail to reject a false null hypothesis. False negative |
| Reject $H_0$ | Type I error: Reject a true null hypothesis. False positive | Correct decision: Reject a false null hypothesis. |

When we make a decision in a hypothesis test, we run the risk of making either a Type I or a Type II error. As you can see in Exhibit 5, these errors are mutually exclusive: If we mistakenly reject the true null, we can only be making a Type I error; if we mistakenly fail to reject the false null, we can only be making a Type II error.

Consider a test of a hypothesis of whether the mean return of a population is equal to 6%. How far away from 6% could a sample mean be before we believe it to be different from 6%, the hypothesized population mean? We are going to tolerate sample means that are close to 6%, but we begin doubting that the population mean is equal to 6% when we calculate a sample mean that is much different from 0.06. How do we determine "much different"? We do this by setting a risk tolerance for a Type I error and determining the critical value or values at which we believe that the sample mean is much different from the population mean. These critical values depend on

# Specify the Level of Significance

(1) the alternative hypothesis, whether one sided or two sided, and (2) the probability distribution of the test statistic, which, in turn, depends on the sample size and the level of risk tolerance in making a Type I error.

The probability of a Type I error in testing a hypothesis is denoted by the lowercase Greek letter alpha, $\alpha$. This probability is also known as the **level of significance** of the test, and its complement, $(1 - \alpha)$, is the **confidence level**. For example, a level of significance of 5% for a test means that there is a 5% probability of rejecting a true null hypothesis and corresponds to the 95% confidence level.

Controlling the probabilities of the two types of errors involves a trade-off. All else equal, if we decrease the probability of a Type I error by specifying a smaller significance level (say, 1% rather than 5%), we increase the probability of making a Type II error because we will reject the null less frequently, including when it is false. Both Type I and Type II errors are risks of being wrong. Whether to accept more of one type versus the other depends on the consequences of the errors, such as costs. The only way to reduce the probabilities of both types of errors simultaneously is to increase the sample size, $n$.

Quantifying the trade-off between the two types of errors in practice is challenging because the probability of a Type II error is itself difficult to quantify because there may be many different possible false hypotheses. Because of this, we specify only $\alpha$, the probability of a Type I error, when we conduct a hypothesis test.

Whereas the significance level of a test is the probability of incorrectly rejecting the true null, the **power of a test** is the probability of *correctly* rejecting the null—that is, the probability of rejecting the null when it is false. The power of a test is, in fact, the complement of the Type II error. The probability of a Type II error is often denoted by the lowercase Greek letter beta, $\beta$. We can classify the different probabilities in Exhibit 6 to reflect the notation that is often used.

### Exhibit 6: Probabilities Associated with Hypothesis Testing Decisions

| | True Situation | |
|---|---|---|
| **Decision** | $H_0$ True | $H_0$ False |
| Fail to reject $H_0$ | Confidence level $(1 - \alpha)$ | $\beta$ |
| Reject $H_0$ | Level of significance $\alpha$ | Power of the test $(1 - \beta)$ |

*The standard approach to hypothesis testing involves choosing the test statistic with the most power and then specifying a level of significance.* It is more appropriate to specify this significance level prior to calculating the test statistic because if we specify it after calculating the test statistic, we may be influenced by the result of the calculation. The researcher is free to specify the probability of a Type I error, but the most common are 10%, 5%, and 1%.

### EXAMPLE 2

### Significance Level

1. If a researcher selects a 5% level of significance for a hypothesis test, the confidence level is:

    **A.** 2.5%.

> **B.** 5%.
> **C.** 95%.
>
> ## Solution
>
> C is correct. The 5% level of significance (i.e., probability of a Type I error) corresponds to 1 − 0.05 = 0.95, or a 95% confidence level (i.e., probability of not rejecting a true null hypothesis). The level of significance is the complement to the confidence level; in other words, they sum to 1.00, or 100%.

# 5. STATE THE DECISION RULE

☐ explain a decision rule and the relation between confidence intervals and hypothesis tests, and determine whether a statistically significant result is also economically meaningful

The fourth step in hypothesis testing is stating the decision rule. Before any sample is drawn and before a test statistic is calculated, we need to set up a decision rule: When do we reject the null hypothesis, and when do we not? The action we take is based on comparing the calculated test statistic with a specified value or values, which we refer to as **critical values**. The critical value or values we choose are based on the level of significance and the probability distribution associated with the test statistic. If we find that the calculated value of the test statistic is more extreme than the critical value or values, then we reject the null hypothesis; we say the result is **statistically significant**. Otherwise, we fail to reject the null hypothesis; there is not sufficient evidence to reject the null hypothesis.

## Determining Critical Values

For a two-tailed test, we indicate two critical values, splitting the level of significance, α, equally between the left and right tails of the distribution. Using a $z$-distributed (standard normal) test statistic, for example, we would designate these critical values as $\pm z_{\alpha/2}$. For a one-tailed test, we indicate a single rejection point using the symbol for the test statistic with a subscript indicating the specified probability of a Type I error—for example, $z_\alpha$.

As we noted in our discussion of Exhibit 2, it is possible to draw a sample that has a mean different from the true population mean. In fact, it is likely that a given sample mean is different from the population mean because of sampling error. The issue becomes whether a given sample mean is far enough away from what is hypothesized to be the population mean that there is doubt about whether the hypothesized population mean is true. Therefore, we need to decide how far is too far for a sample mean in comparison to a population mean. That is where the critical values come into the picture.

Suppose we are using a $z$-test and have chosen a 5% level of significance. In Exhibit 7, we illustrate two tests at the 5% significance level using a $z$-statistic: A two-sided alternative hypothesis test in Panel A and a one-sided alternative hypothesis test in Panel B, with the white area under the curve indicating the confidence level and the shaded areas indicating the significance level. In Panel A, if the null hypothesis that $\mu = \mu_0$ is true, the test statistic has a 2.5% chance of falling in the left rejection region and a 2.5% chance of falling in the right rejection region. Any calculated value of the test statistic that falls in either of these two regions causes us to reject the null hypothesis at the 5% significance level.

We determine the cut-off values for the reject and fail-to-reject regions on the basis of the distribution of the test statistic. For a test statistic that is normally distributed, we determine these cut-off points on the basis of the area under the normal curve; with a Type I error (i.e., level of significance, α) of 5% and a two-sided test, there is 2.5% of the area on either side of the distribution. This results in rejection points of −1.960 and +1.960, dividing the distribution between the rejection and fail-to-reject regions. Similarly, if we have a one-sided test involving a normal distribution, we would have 5% area under the curve with a demarcation of 1.645 for a right-side test, as we show in Exhibit 7 (or −1.645 for a left-side test).

### Exhibit 7: Decision Criteria Using a 5% Level of Significance

**A. $H_0: \mu = \mu_0$ versus $H_a: \mu \neq \mu_0$**

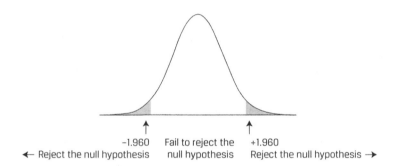

**B. $H_0: \mu \leq \mu_0$ versus $H_a: \mu > \mu_0$**

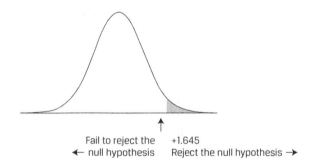

*Determining the cut-off points using programming*

The programs in Microsoft Excel, Python, and R differ slightly, depending on whether the user specifies the area to the right or the left of the cut-off in the code:

| Cut-off for ... | Excel | Python | R |
| --- | --- | --- | --- |
| Right tail, 2.5% | NORM.S.INV(0.975) | norm.ppf(.975) | qnorm(.025,lower.tail=FALSE) |
| Left tail, 2.5% | NORM.S.INV(0.025) | norm.ppf(.025) | qnorm(.025,lower.tail=TRUE) |
| Right tail, 5% | NORM.S.INV(0.95) | norm.ppf(.95) | qnorm(.05,lower.tail=FALSE) |
| Left tail, 5% | NORM.S.INV(0.05) | norm.ppf(.05) | qnorm(.05,lower.tail=TRUE) |

*For Python, install scipy.stats and import:* from scipy.stats import norm.

## Decision Rules and Confidence Intervals

Exhibit 7 provides an opportunity to highlight the relationship between confidence intervals and hypothesis tests. A 95% confidence interval for the population mean, $\mu$, based on sample mean, $\overline{X}$, is given by:

$$\left\{\overline{X} - 1.96\frac{\sigma}{\sqrt{n}}, \overline{X} + 1.96\frac{\sigma}{\sqrt{n}}\right\}, \tag{3}$$

or, more compactly, $\overline{X} \pm 1.96\frac{\sigma}{\sqrt{n}}$.

Now consider the conditions for rejecting the null hypothesis:

$$\frac{\overline{X} - \mu_0}{\sigma/\sqrt{n}} < -1.96 \text{ or } \frac{\overline{X} - \mu_0}{\sigma/\sqrt{n}} > 1.96, \text{ where } z = \frac{\overline{X} - \mu_0}{\sigma/\sqrt{n}}.$$

As you can see by comparing these conditions with the confidence interval, we can address the question of whether $\overline{X}$ is far enough away from $\mu_0$ by either comparing the calculated test statistic with the critical values or comparing the hypothesized population parameter ($\mu = \mu_0$) with the bounds of the confidence interval, as we show in Exhibit 8. Thus, a significance level in a two-sided hypothesis test can be interpreted in the same way as a $(1 - \alpha)$ confidence interval.

### Exhibit 8: Making a Decision Based on Critical Values and Confidence Intervals for a Two-Sided Alternative Hypothesis

| Method | Procedure | Decision |
|---|---|---|
| 1 | Compare the calculated test statistic with the critical values. | If the calculated test statistic is less than the lower critical value or greater than the upper critical value, reject the null hypothesis. |
| 2 | Compare the calculated test statistic with the bounds of the confidence interval. | If the hypothesized value of the population parameter under the null is outside the corresponding confidence interval, the null hypothesis is rejected. |

## Collect the Data and Calculate the Test Statistic

The fifth step in hypothesis testing is collecting the data and calculating the test statistic. The quality of our conclusions depends on not only the appropriateness of the statistical model but also the quality of the data we use in conducting the test. First, we need to ensure that the sampling procedure does not include biases, such as sample selection or time-period bias. Second, we need to cleanse the data, checking inaccuracies and other measurement errors in the data. Once assured that the sample is unbiased and accurate, the sample information is used to calculate the appropriate test statistic.

### EXAMPLE 3

### Using a Confidence Interval in Hypothesis Testing

1. Consider the hypotheses $H_0$: $\mu = 3$ versus $H_a$: $\mu \neq 3$. If the confidence interval based on sample information has a lower bound of 2.75 and an upper bound of 4.25, the *most* appropriate decision is:

    **A.** reject the null hypothesis.

    **B.** accept the null hypothesis.

**c.** fail to reject the null hypothesis.

## Solution

C is correct. Since the hypothesized population mean (μ = 3) is within the bounds of the confidence interval (2.75, 4.25), the correct decision is to fail to reject the null hypothesis. It is only when the hypothesized value is outside these bounds that the null hypothesis is rejected. Note that the null hypothesis is never accepted; either the null is rejected on the basis of the evidence or there is a failure to reject the null hypothesis.

# MAKE A DECISION 6

☐ explain a decision rule and the relation between confidence intervals and hypothesis tests, and determine whether a statistically significant result is also economically meaningful

## Make a Statistical Decision

The sixth step in hypothesis testing is making the decision. Consider a test of the mean risk premium, comparing the population mean with zero. If the calculated $z$-statistic is 2.5 and with a two-sided alternative hypothesis and a 5% level of significance, we reject the null hypothesis because 2.5 is outside the bounds of ±1.96. This is a statistical decision: The evidence indicates that the mean risk premium is not equal to zero.

## Make an Economic Decision

Another part of the decision making is making the economic or investment decision. The economic or investment decision takes into consideration not only the statistical decision but also all pertinent economic issues. If, for example, we reject the null that the risk premium is zero in favor of the alternative hypothesis that the risk premium is greater than zero, we have found evidence that the US risk premium is different from zero. The question then becomes whether this risk premium is economically meaningful. On the basis of these considerations, an investor might decide to commit funds to US equities. A range of non-statistical considerations, such as the investor's tolerance for risk and financial position, might also enter the decision-making process.

## Statistically Significant but Not Economically Significant?

We frequently find that slight differences between a variable and its hypothesized value are statistically significant but not economically meaningful. For example, we may be testing an investment strategy and reject a null hypothesis that the mean return to the strategy is zero based on a large sample. In the case of a test of the mean, the smaller the standard error of the mean, the larger the value of the test statistic and the greater the chance the null will be rejected, all else equal. The standard error decreases as the sample size, $n$, increases, so that for very large samples, we can reject the null for small departures from it. We may find that although a strategy provides a statistically significant positive mean return, the results may not be economically significant when we account for transaction costs, taxes, and risk. Even if we conclude that a strategy's results are economically meaningful, we should explore the logic of why the strategy might work in the future before implementing it. Such considerations cannot be incorporated into a hypothesis test.

> **EXAMPLE 4**
>
> ### Decisions and Significance
>
> 1. An analyst is testing whether there are positive risk-adjusted returns to a trading strategy. He collects a sample and tests the hypotheses of $H_0$: $\mu \leq 0\%$ versus $H_a$: $\mu > 0\%$, where $\mu$ is the population mean risk-adjusted return. The mean risk-adjusted return for the sample is 0.7%. The calculated $t$-statistic is 2.428, and the critical $t$-value is 2.345. He estimates that the transaction costs are 0.3%. The results are *most likely*:
>
>     **A.** statistically and economically significant.
>
>     **B.** statistically significant but not economically significant.
>
>     **C.** economically significant but not statistically significant.
>
> ### Solution
>
> A is correct. The results indicate that the mean risk-adjusted return is greater than 0% because the calculated test statistic of 2.428 is greater than the critical value of 2.345. The results are also economically significant because the risk-adjusted return exceeds the transaction cost associated with this strategy by 0.4% (= 0.7 − 0.3).

## 7. THE ROLE OF *P*-VALUES

☐ explain and interpret the *p*-value as it relates to hypothesis testing

Analysts, researchers, and statistical software often report the *p*-value associated with hypothesis tests. The ***p*-value** is the area in the probability distribution outside the calculated test statistic; for a two-sided test, this is the area outside ± the calculated test statistic, but for a one-sided test, this is the area outside the calculated test statistic on the appropriate side of the probability distribution. We illustrated in Exhibit 7 the rejection region, which corresponds to the probability of a Type I error. However, the *p*-value is the area under the curve (so, the probability) associated with the calculated test statistic. Stated another way, the *p*-value is the smallest level of significance at which the null hypothesis can be rejected.

Consider the calculated *z*-statistic of 2.33 in a two-sided test: The *p*-value is the area in the *z*-distribution that lies outside ±2.33. Calculation of this area requires a bit of calculus, but fortunately statistical programs and other software calculate the *p*-value for us. For the value of the test statistic of 2.33, the *p*-value is approximately 0.02, or 2%. Using Excel, we can get the precise value of 0.019806 [(1-NORM.S.DIST(2.33,TRUE))*2]. We can reject the null hypothesis because we were willing to tolerate up to 5% outside the calculated value. The smaller the *p*-value, the stronger the evidence against the null hypothesis and in favor of the alternative hypothesis; if the *p*-value is less than the level of significance, we reject the null hypothesis.

# The Role of p-Values

We illustrate the comparison of the level of significance and the *p*-value in Exhibit 9. The fail-to-reject region is determined by the critical values of ±1.96, as we saw in Exhibit 7. There is 5% of the area under the distribution in the rejection regions—2.5% on the left side, 2.5% on the right. But now we introduce the area outside the calculated test statistic. For the calculated *z*-statistic of 2.33, there is 0.01, or 1%, of the area under the normal distribution above 2.33 and 1% of the area below −2.33 (or, in other words, 98% of the area between ±2.33). Since we are willing to tolerate a 5% Type I error, we reject the null hypothesis in the case of a calculated test statistic of 2.33 because there is a *p*-value of 2%; there is 2% of the distribution *outside* the calculated test statistic.

**Exhibit 9: Comparison of the Level of Significance and the *p*-Value**

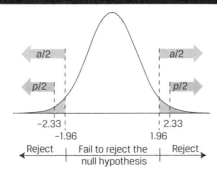

What if we are testing a one-sided alternative hypothesis? We focus solely on the area outside the calculated value on the side indicated by the alternative hypothesis. For example, if we are testing an alternative hypothesis that the population mean risk premium is greater than zero, calculate a *z*-statistic of 2.5, and have a level of significance of 5%, the *p*-value is the area in the probability distribution that is greater than 2.5. This area is 0.00621, or 0.621%. Since this is less than what we tolerate if the α is 5%, we reject the null hypothesis.

Consider a population of 1,000 assets that has a mean return of 6% and a standard deviation of 2%. Suppose we draw a sample of 50 returns and test whether the mean is equal to 6%, calculating the *p*-value for the calculated *z*-statistic. Then, suppose we repeat this process, draw 1,000 different samples, and, therefore, get 1,000 different calculated *z*-statistics and 1,000 different *p*-values. If we use a 5% level of significance, we should expect to reject the true null 5% of the time; if we use a 10% level of significance, we should expect to reject the true null 10% of the time.

Now suppose that with this same population, whose mean return is 6%, we test the hypothesis that the population mean is 7%, with the same standard deviation. As before, we draw 1,000 different samples and calculate 1,000 different *p*-values. If we use a 5% level of significance and a two-sided alternative hypothesis, we should expect to reject this false null hypothesis on the basis of the power of the test.

Putting this together, consider the histograms of *p*-values for the two different tests in Exhibit 10. The first bin is the *p*-values of 5% or less. What we see is that with the true null hypothesis of 6%, we reject the null approximately 5% of the time. For the false null hypothesis, that the mean is equal to 7%, we reject the null approximately 0.973, or 97.3%, of the time.

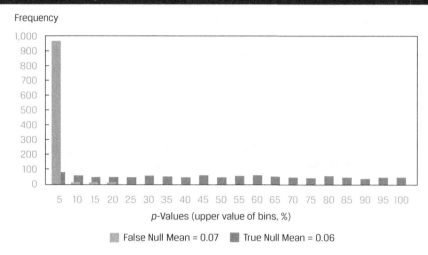

**Exhibit 10: Distribution of p-values for 1,000 Different Samples of Size 50 Drawn from a Population with a Mean of 6%**

The $p$-values for the true null hypothesis are generally uniformly distributed between 0% and 100% because under the null hypothesis, there is a 5% chance of the $p$-values being less than 5%, a 10% chance being less than 10%, and so on. Why is it not completely uniform? Because we took 1,000 samples of 50; taking more samples or larger samples would result in a more uniform distribution of $p$-values. When looking at the $p$-values for the false null hypothesis in Exhibit 10, we see that this is not a uniform distribution; rather, there is a peak around 0% and very little elsewhere. You can see the difference in the $p$-values for two false hypothesized means of 6.5% and 7% in Exhibit 11. It shows that the further the false hypothesis is away from the truth (i.e., mean of 6%), the greater the power of the test and the better the ability to detect the false hypothesis.

Software, such as Excel, Python, and R, is available for calculating $p$-values for most distributions.

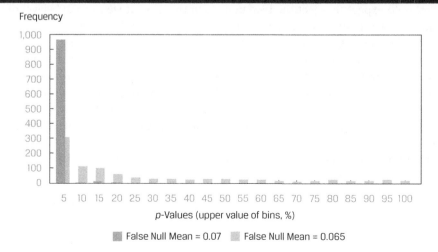

**Exhibit 11: Comparison of the Distribution of p-Values for the False Null Hypotheses $H_0: \mu = 7\%$ and $H_0: \mu = 6.5\%$**

### EXAMPLE 5

#### Making a Decision Using p-Values

1. An analyst is testing the hypotheses $H_0: \sigma^2 = 0.01$ versus $H_a: \sigma^2 \neq 0.01$. Using software, she determines that the *p*-value for the test statistic is 0.03, or 3%. Which of the following statements is correct?

    **A.** Reject the null hypothesis at both the 1% and 5% levels of significance.

    **B.** Reject the null hypothesis at the 5% level but not at the 1% level of significance.

    **C.** Fail to reject the null hypothesis at both the 1% and 5% levels of significance.

#### Solution

B is correct. Rejection of the null hypothesis requires that the *p*-value be less than the level of significance. On the basis of this requirement, the null is rejected at the 5% level of significance but not at the 1% level of significance.

# MULTIPLE TESTS AND SIGNIFICANCE INTERPRETATION

☐ describe how to interpret the significance of a test in the context of multiple tests

A Type I error is the risk of rejection of a true null hypothesis. Another way of phrasing this is that it is a false positive result; that is, the null is rejected (the positive), yet the null is true (hence, a false positive). The expected portion of false positives is the **false discovery rate** (FDR). In the previous example of drawing 1,000 samples of 50 observations each, it is the case that there are samples in which we reject the true null hypothesis of a population mean of 6%. If we draw enough samples with a level of significance of 0.05, approximately 0.05 of the time you will reject the null hypothesis, even if the null is true. In other words, if you run 100 tests and use a 5% level of significance, you get five false positives, on average. This is referred to as the **multiple testing problem**.

The **false discovery approach** to testing requires adjusting the *p*-value when you have a series of tests. The idea of adjusting for the likelihood of significant results being false positives was first introduced by Benjamini and Hochberg (BH) in 1995. What they proposed is that the researcher rank the *p*-values from the various tests, from lowest to highest, and then make the following comparison, starting with the lowest *p*-value (with $k = 1$), $p(1)$:

$$p(1) \leq \alpha \frac{\text{Rank of } i}{\text{Number of tests}}.$$

This comparison is repeated, such that $k$ is determined by the highest ranked $p(k)$ for which this is a true statement. If, say, $k$ is 4, then the first four tests (ranked on the basis of the lowest *p*-values) are said to be significant.

Suppose we test the hypothesis that the population mean is equal to 6% and repeat the sampling process by drawing 20 samples and calculating 20 test statistics; the six test statistics with the lowest *p*-values are shown in Exhibit 12. Using a significance level of 5%, if we simply relied on each test and its $p$-value, then there are five tests in which we would reject the null. However, using the BH criteria, only one test is considered significant, as shown in Exhibit 12.

### Exhibit 12: Applying the Benjamini and Hochberg Criteria

| (1) | (2) | (3) | (4) | (5) | (6) |
|---|---|---|---|---|---|
| $\bar{X}$ | Calculated z-Statistic | $p$-Value | Rank of $p$-Value (lowest to highest) | $\alpha \dfrac{\text{Rank of i}}{\text{Number of tests}}$ | Is value in (3) less than or equal to value in (5)? |
| 0.0664 | 3.1966 | 0.0014 | 1 | 0.0025 | Yes |
| 0.0645 | 2.2463 | 0.0247 | 2 | 0.0050 | No |
| 0.0642 | 2.0993 | 0.0358 | 3 | 0.0075 | No |
| 0.0642 | 2.0756 | 0.0379 | 4 | 0.0100 | No |
| 0.0641 | 2.0723 | 0.0382 | 5 | 0.0125 | No |
| 0.0637 | 1.8627 | 0.0625 | 6 | 0.0150 | No |

*Note:* Level of significance = 5%.

So, what is the conclusion from looking at $p$-values and the multiple testing problem?

- First, if we sample, test, and find a result that is not statistically significant, this result is not wrong; in fact, the null hypothesis may well be true.
- Second, if the power of the test is low or the sample size is small, we should be cautious because there is a good chance of a false positive.
- Third, when we perform a hypothesis test and determine the critical values, these values are based on the assumption that the test is run once. Running multiple tests on data risks data snooping, which may result in spurious results. Determine the dataset and perform the test, but do not keep performing tests repeatedly to search out statistically significant results, because you may, by chance, find them (i.e., false positives).
- Fourth, in very large samples, we will find that nearly every test is significant. The approach to use to address this issue is to draw different samples; if the results are similar, the results are more robust.

### EXAMPLE 6

#### False Discovery and Multiple Tests

A researcher is examining the mean return on assets of publicly traded companies that constitute an index of 2,000 mid-cap stocks and is testing hypotheses concerning whether the mean is equal to 15%: $H_0$: $\mu_{ROA}$ = 15 versus $Ha$: $\mu_{ROA}$ ≠ 15. She uses a 10% level of significance and collects a sample of 50 firms. She wants to examine the robustness of her analysis, so she repeats the collection and test of the return on assets 30 times. The results for the samples with the five lowest $p$-values are given in Exhibit 13.

## Exhibit 13: Five Lowest p-Values of the 30 Samples Tested

| Sample | Calculated z-Statistic | p-Value | Ranked p-Value |
|---|---|---|---|
| 1 | 3.203 | 0.00136 | 1 |
| 5 | 3.115 | 0.00184 | 2 |
| 14 | 2.987 | 0.00282 | 3 |
| 25 | 2.143 | 0.03211 | 4 |
| 29 | 1.903 | 0.05704 | 5 |

1. Of the 30 samples tested, how many should the researcher expect, on average, to have $p$-values less than the level of significance?

## Solution to 1

Of the 30 samples tested, she should expect 30 × 0.10 = 3 to have significant results just by chance. Consider why she ended up with more than three. Three is based on large sample sizes and large numbers of samples. Using a limited sample size (i.e., 50) and number of samples (i.e., 30), there is a risk of a false discovery with repeated samples and tests.

2. What are the corrected $p$-values based on her selected level of significance, and what is the effect on her decision?

## Solution to 2

Applying the BH criteria, the researcher determines the adjusted p-values shown in Exhibit 14.

## Exhibit 14: Adjusted p-Values for Five Lowest p-Values from 30 Samples Tested

| Calculated z-Statistic | p-Value | Rank of p-Value | $\alpha \dfrac{\text{Rank of i}}{\text{Number of tests}}$ | Is p-value less than or equal to adjusted p-value? |
|---|---|---|---|---|
| 3.203 | 0.00136 | 1 | 0.00333 | Yes |
| 3.115 | 0.00184 | 2 | 0.00667 | Yes |
| 2.987 | 0.00282 | 3 | 0.01000 | Yes |
| 2.143 | 0.03211 | 4 | 0.01333 | No |
| 1.903 | 0.05704 | 5 | 0.01667 | No |

On the basis of the results in Exhibit 14, there are three samples with $p$-values less than their adjusted $p$-values. So, the number of significant sample results is the same as would be expected from chance, given the 10% level of significance. The researcher concludes that the results for the samples with Ranks 4 and 5 are false discoveries, and she has not uncovered any evidence from her testing that supports rejecting the null hypothesis.

## 9 TESTS CONCERNING A SINGLE MEAN

> identify the appropriate test statistic and interpret the results for a hypothesis test concerning the population mean of both large and small samples when the population is normally or approximately normally distributed and the variance is (1) known or (2) unknown

Hypothesis tests concerning the mean are among the most common in practice. The sampling distribution of the mean when the population standard deviation is unknown is $t$-distributed, and when the population standard deviation is known, it is normally distributed, or $z$-distributed. Since the population standard deviation is unknown in almost all cases, we will focus on the use of a $t$-distributed test statistic.

The $t$-distribution is a probability distribution defined by a single parameter known as degrees of freedom (df). Like the standard normal distribution, a $t$-distribution is symmetrical with a mean of zero, but it has a standard deviation greater than 1 and generally fatter tails. As the number of degrees of freedom increases with the sample size, the $t$-distribution approaches the standard normal distribution.

For hypothesis tests concerning the population mean of a normally distributed population with unknown variance, the theoretically correct test statistic is the $t$-statistic. What if a normal distribution does not describe the population? The $t$-statistic is robust to moderate departures from normality, except for outliers and strong skewness. When we have large samples, departures of the underlying distribution from the normal case are of increasingly less concern. The sample mean is approximately normally distributed in large samples according to the central limit theorem, whatever the distribution describing the population. A traditional rule of thumb is that the normal distribution is used in cases when the sample size is larger than 30, but the more precise testing uses the $t$-distribution. Moreover, with software that aids us in such testing, we do not need to resort to rules of thumb.

If the population sampled has unknown variance, then the test statistic for hypothesis tests concerning a single population mean, $\mu$, is

$$t_{n-1} = \frac{\bar{X} - \mu_0}{s/\sqrt{n}}, \tag{4}$$

where

$\bar{X}$ = sample mean

$\mu_0$ = hypothesized value of the population mean

$s$ = sample standard deviation

$n$ = sample size

$s_{\bar{X}} = s/\sqrt{n}$ = estimate of the sample mean standard error

This test statistic is $t$-distributed with $n - 1$ degrees of freedom, which we can write as $t_{n-1}$. For simplicity, we often drop the subscript $n - 1$ because each particular test statistic has specified degrees of freedom, as we presented in Exhibit 4.

Consider testing whether Investment One's returns (from Exhibit 1) are different from 6%; that is, we are testing $H_0$: $\mu = 6$ versus $H_a$: $\mu \neq 6$. If the calculated $t$-distributed test statistic is outside the bounds of the critical values based on the level of significance, we will reject the null hypothesis in favor of the alternative. If we have a sample

# Tests Concerning a Single Mean

size of 33, there are $n - 1 = 32$ degrees of freedom. At a 5% significance level (two tailed) and 32 degrees of freedom, the critical $t$-values are ±2.037. We can determine the critical values from software:

- Excel [T.INV(0.025,32) and T.INV(0.975,32)]
- R [qt(c(.025,.975),32)]
- Python [from scipy.stats import t and t.ppf(.025,32) and t.ppf(.975,32)]

Suppose that the sample mean return is 5.2990% and the sample standard deviation is 1.4284%. The calculated test statistic is

$$t = \frac{5.2990 - 6}{1.4284/\sqrt{33}} = -2.8192$$

with 32 degrees of freedom. The calculated value is less than −2.037, so we reject the null that the population mean is 6%, concluding that it is different from 6%.

### EXAMPLE 7

## Risk and Return Characteristics of an Equity Mutual Fund

Suppose you are analyzing Sendar Equity Fund, a midcap growth fund that has been in existence for 24 months. During this period, it has achieved a mean monthly return of 1.50%, with a sample standard deviation of monthly returns of 3.60%. Given its level of market risk and according to a pricing model, this mutual fund was expected to have earned a 1.10% mean monthly return during that time period. Assuming returns are normally distributed, are the actual results consistent with an underlying or population mean monthly return of 1.10%?

1. Test the hypothesis using a 5% level of significance.

## Solution to 1

| Step 1 | State the hypotheses. | $H_0$: μ = 1.1% versus $H_a$: μ ≠ 1.1% |
|---|---|---|
| Step 2 | Identify the appropriate test statistic. | $t = \frac{\overline{X} - \mu_0}{s/\sqrt{n}}$ |
| | | with 24 − 1 = 23 degrees of freedom. |
| Step 3 | Specify the level of significance. | α = 5% (two tailed). |
| Step 4 | State the decision rule. | Critical $t$-values = ±2.069. |
| | | Reject the null if the calculated $t$-statistic is less than −2.069, and reject the null if the calculated $t$-statistic is greater than +2.069. |

**Excel**
   *Lower:* T.INV(0.025,23)
   *Upper:* T.INV(0.975,23)
**R** qt(c(.025,.975),23)
**Python** from scipy.stats import t
   *Lower:* t.ppf(.025,23)
   *Upper:* t.ppf(.975,23)

| Step 5 | Calculate the test statistic. | $t = \frac{1.5 - 1.1}{3.6/\sqrt{24}} = 0.54433$ |
|---|---|---|
| Step 6 | Make a decision. | Fail to reject the null hypothesis because the calculated $t$-statistic falls between the two critical values. There is not sufficient evidence to indicate that the population mean monthly return is different from 1.10%. |

2. Test the hypothesis using the 95% confidence interval.

## Solution to 2

The 95% confidence interval is $\overline{X} \pm$ Critical value $\left(\frac{s}{\sqrt{n}}\right)$, so

$\{1.5 - 2.069\,(3.6/\sqrt{24}),\ 1.5 + 2.069\,(3.6/\sqrt{24})\}$
$\{1.5 - 1.5204,\ 1.5 + 1.5204\}$
$\{-0.0204,\ 3.0204\}$

The hypothesized value of 1.1% is within the bounds of the 95% confidence interval, so we fail to reject the null hypothesis.

---

We stated previously that when population variance is not known, we use a $t$-test for tests concerning a single population mean. Given at least approximate normality, the $t$-distributed test statistic is always called for when we deal with small samples and do not know the population variance. For large samples, the central limit theorem states that the sample mean is approximately normally distributed, whatever the distribution of the population. The $t$-statistic is still appropriate, but an alternative test may be more useful when sample size is large.

For large samples, practitioners sometimes use a $z$-test in place of a $t$-test for tests concerning a mean. The justification for using the $z$-test in this context is twofold. First, in large samples, the sample mean should follow the normal distribution at least approximately, as we have already stated, fulfilling the normality assumption of the $z$-test. Second, the difference between the rejection points for the $t$-test and $z$-test becomes quite small when the sample size is large. Since the $t$-test is readily available as statistical program output and theoretically correct for unknown population variance, we present it as the test of choice.

In a very limited number of cases, we may know the population variance; in such cases, the $z$-statistic is theoretically correct. In this case, the appropriate test statistic is what we used earlier (Equation 2):

$$z = \frac{\overline{X} - \mu_0}{\sigma/\sqrt{n}}.$$

In cases of large samples, a researcher may use the $z$-statistic, substituting the sample standard deviation ($s$) for the population standard deviation ($\sigma$) in the formula. When we use a $z$-test, we usually refer to a rejection point in Exhibit 15.

### Exhibit 15: Critical Values for Common Significance Levels for the Standard Normal Distribution

| Level of Significance | Alternative | Reject the Null if... below the Critical Value | Reject the Null if... above the Critical Value |
|---|---|---|---|
| 0.01 | Two sided: $H_0: \mu = \mu_0,\ H_a: \mu \neq \mu_0$ | −2.576 | 2.576 |
|  | One sided: $H_0: \mu \leq \mu_0,\ H_a: \mu > \mu_0$ |  | 2.326 |
|  | One sided: $H_0: \mu \geq \mu_0,\ H_a: \mu < \mu_0$ | −2.326 |  |
| 0.05 | Two sided: $H_0: \mu = \mu_0,\ H_a: \mu \neq \mu_0$ | −1.960 | 1.960 |
|  | One sided: $H_0: \mu \leq \mu_0,\ H_a: \mu > \mu_0$ |  | 1.645 |
|  | One sided: $H_0: \mu \geq \mu_0,\ H_a: \mu < \mu_0$ | −1.645 |  |

**Tests Concerning a Single Mean**

> **EXAMPLE 8**
>
> ### Testing the Returns on the ACE High Yield Index
>
> 1. Suppose we want to test whether the daily return in the ACE High Yield Total Return Index is different from zero. Collecting a sample of 1,304 daily returns, we find a mean daily return of 0.0157%, with a standard deviation of 0.3157%.
>
>    1. Test whether the mean daily return is different from zero at the 5% level of significance.
>
>    2. Using the $z$-distributed test statistic as an approximation, test whether the mean daily return is different from zero at the 5% level of significance.

### Solution to 1

| | | |
|---|---|---|
| **Step 1** | State the hypotheses. | $H_0$: µ = 0% versus $H_a$: µ ≠ 0% |
| **Step 2** | Identify the appropriate test statistic. | $t = \frac{\bar{X} - \mu_0}{s/\sqrt{n}}$ with 1,304 − 1 = 1,303 degrees of freedom. |
| **Step 3** | Specify the level of significance. | α = 5%. |
| **Step 4** | State the decision rule. | Critical $t$-values = ±1.962. Reject the null if the calculated $t$-statistic is less than −1.962, and reject the null if the calculated $t$-statistic is greater than +1.962. |

> **Excel**
>     *Lower*: T.INV(0.025,1303)
>     *Upper*: T.INV(0.975,1303)
> **R** qt(c(.025,.975),1303)
> **Python** from scipy.stats import t
>     *Lower*: t.ppf(.025,1303)
>     *Upper*: t.ppf(.975,1303)

| | | |
|---|---|---|
| **Step 5** | Calculate the test statistic. | $t = \frac{0.0157 - 0}{0.3157/\sqrt{1,304}} = 1.79582$ |
| **Step 6** | Make a decision. | Fail to reject the null because the calculated $t$-statistic falls between the two critical values. There is not sufficient evidence to indicate that the mean daily return is different from 0%. |

### Solution to 2

| | | |
|---|---|---|
| **Step 1** | State the hypotheses. | $H_0$: µ = 0% versus $H_a$: µ ≠ 0% |
| **Step 2** | Identify the appropriate test statistic. | $z = \frac{\bar{X} - \mu_0}{s/\sqrt{n}}$ with 1,304 − 1 = 1,303 degrees of freedom. |
| **Step 3** | Specify the level of significance. | α = 5%. |
| **Step 4** | State the decision rule. | Critical $t$-values = ±1.960. Reject the null if the calculated $z$-statistic is less than −1.960, and reject the null if the calculated $z$-statistic is greater than +1.960. |

> **Excel**     *Lower*: NORM.S.INV(0.025)
>              *Upper*: NORM.S.INV(0.975)

| | |
|---|---|
| R | qnorm(.025,lower.tail=TRUE) |
| | qnorm(.975,lower.tail=FALSE) |
| **Python** from scipy.stats import norm | |
| *Lower*: norm.ppf(.025,23) | |
| *Upper*: norm.ppf(.975,23) | |

**Step 5** Calculate the test statistic. $z = \frac{0.0157 - 0}{0.3157/\sqrt{1,304}} = 1.79582$

**Step 6** Make a decision. Fail to reject the null because the calculated $z$-statistic falls between the two critical values. There is not sufficient evidence to indicate that the mean daily return is different from 0%.

## 10. TEST CONCERNING DIFFERENCES BETWEEN MEANS WITH INDEPENDENT SAMPLES

☐ identify the appropriate test statistic and interpret the results for a hypothesis test concerning the equality of the population means of two at least approximately normally distributed populations based on independent random samples with equal assumed variances

We often want to know whether a mean value—for example, a mean return—differs for two groups. Is an observed difference due to chance or to different underlying values for the mean? We test this by drawing a sample from each group. When it is reasonable to believe that the samples are from populations at least approximately normally distributed and that the samples are also independent of each other, we use the test of the differences in the means. We may assume that population variances are equal or unequal. However, our focus in discussing the test of the differences of means is using the assumption that the population variances are equal. In the calculation of the test statistic, we combine the observations from both samples to obtain a pooled estimate of the common population variance.

Let $\mu_1$ and $\mu_2$ represent, respectively, the population means of the first and second populations. Most often we want to test whether the population means are equal or whether one is larger than the other. Thus, we formulate the following sets of hypotheses:

Two sided:

$H_0$: $\mu_1 - \mu_2 = 0$ versus $H_a$: $\mu_1 - \mu_2 \neq 0$,

or, equivalently,

$H_0$: $\mu_1 = \mu_2$ versus $H_a$: $\mu_1 \neq \mu_2$

One sided (right side):

$H_0$: $\mu_1 - \mu_2 \leq 0$ versus $H_a$: $\mu_1 - \mu_2 > 0$,

or, equivalently,

$H_0$: $\mu_1 \leq \mu_2$ versus $H_a$: $\mu_1 > \mu_2$

# Test Concerning Differences between Means with Independent Samples

One sided (left side):

$H_0: \mu_1 - \mu_2 \geq 0$ versus $H_a: \mu_1 - \mu_2 < 0$,

or, equivalently,

$H_0: \mu_1 \geq \mu_2$ versus $H_a: \mu_1 < \mu_2$

We can, however, formulate other hypotheses, where the difference is something other than zero, such as $H_0: \mu_1 - \mu_2 = 2$ versus $H_a: \mu_1 - \mu_2 \neq 2$. The procedure is the same.

When we can assume that the two populations are normally distributed and that the unknown population variances are equal, we use a $t$-distributed test statistic based on independent random samples:

$$t = \frac{(\overline{X}_1 - \overline{X}_2) - (\mu_1 - \mu_2)}{\sqrt{\frac{s_p^2}{n_1} + \frac{s_p^2}{n_2}}}, \tag{5}$$

where $s_p^2 = \frac{(n_1-1)s_1^2 + (n_2-1)s_2^2}{n_1 + n_2 - 2}$ is a pooled estimator of the common variance.

As you can see, the pooled estimate is a weighted average of the two samples' variances, with the degrees of freedom for each sample as the weight. The number of degrees of freedom for this $t$-distributed test statistic is $n_1 + n_2 - 2$.

### EXAMPLE 9

### Returns on the ACE High Yield Index Compared for Two Periods

Continuing the example of the returns in the ACE High Yield Total Return Index, suppose we want to test whether these returns, shown in Exhibit 16, are different for two different time periods, Period 1 and Period 2.

**Exhibit 16: Descriptive Statistics for ACE High Yield Total Return Index for Periods 1 and 2**

|  | Period 1 | Period 2 |
|---|---|---|
| Mean | 0.01775% | 0.01134% |
| Standard deviation | 0.31580% | 0.38760% |
| Sample size | 445 days | 859 days |

Note that these periods are of different lengths and the samples are independent; that is, there is no pairing of the days for the two periods.

Test whether there is a difference between the mean daily returns in Period 1 and in Period 2 using a 5% level of significance.

| Step 1 | State the hypotheses. | $H_0: \mu_{Period1} = \mu_{Period2}$ versus $H_a: \mu_{Period1} \neq \mu_{Period2}$ |
|---|---|---|
| Step 2 | Identify the appropriate test statistic. | $t = \dfrac{(\overline{X}_{Period1} - \overline{X}_{Period2}) - (\mu_{Period1} - \mu_{Period2})}{\sqrt{\dfrac{s_p^2}{n_{period1}} + \dfrac{s_p^2}{n_{period2}}}}$, |
| | | where $s_p^2 = \dfrac{(n_{period1}-1)s_{Period1}^2 + (n_{period2}-1)s_{Period2}^2}{n_{period1} + n_{period2} - 2}$ |
| | | with $445 + 859 - 2 = 1{,}302$ degrees of freedom. |
| Step 3 | Specify the level of significance. | $\alpha = 5\%$. |

| Step 4 | State the decision rule. | Critical $t$-values = ±1.962. |
|---|---|---|

Reject the null if the calculated $t$-statistic is less than −1.962, and reject the null if the calculated $t$-statistic is greater than +1.962.

> **Excel**
> *Lower:* T.INV(0.025,1302)
> *Upper:* T.INV(0.975,1302)
>
> **R** qt(c(.025,.975),1302)
>
> **Python** from scipy.stats import t
> *Lower:* t.ppf(.025,1302)
> *Upper:* t.ppf(.975,1302)

| Step 5 | Calculate the test statistic. | $s_p^2 = \dfrac{(445-1)0.09973 + (859-1)0.15023}{445+859-2} = 0.1330$ |
|---|---|---|

$$t = \dfrac{(0.01775 - 0.01134) - 0}{\sqrt{\dfrac{0.1330}{445} + \dfrac{0.1330}{859}}} = \dfrac{0.0064}{0.0213} = 0.3009.$$

| Step 6 | Make a decision. | Fail to reject the null because the calculated $t$-statistic falls within the bounds of the two critical values. We conclude that there is insufficient evidence to indicate that the returns are different for the two time periods. |
|---|---|---|

## 11. TEST CONCERNING DIFFERENCES BETWEEN MEANS WITH DEPENDENT SAMPLES

☐ identify the appropriate test statistic and interpret the results for a hypothesis test concerning the mean difference of two normally distributed populations

When we compare two independent samples, we use a $t$-distributed test statistic that uses the difference in the means and a pooled variance. An assumption for the validity of those tests is that the samples are independent—that is, unrelated to each other. When we want to conduct tests on two means based on samples that we believe are dependent, we use the **test of the mean of the differences**.

The $t$-test in this section is based on data arranged in paired observations, and the test itself is sometimes referred to as the **paired comparisons test**. Paired observations are observations that are dependent because they have something in common. For example, we may be concerned with the dividend policy of companies before and after a change in the tax law affecting the taxation of dividends. We then have pairs of observations for the same companies; these are dependent samples because we have pairs of the sample companies before and after the tax law change. We may test a hypothesis about the mean of the differences that we observe across companies. For example, we may be testing whether the mean returns earned by two investment strategies were equal over a study period. The observations here are dependent in the sense that there is one observation for each strategy in each month, and both observations depend on underlying market risk factors. What is being tested are the differences, and the paired comparisons test assumes that the differences are normally distributed. By calculating a standard error based on differences, we can use a $t$-distributed test statistic to account for correlation between the observations.

### Test Concerning Differences between Means with Dependent Samples

How is this test of paired differences different from the test of the differences in means in independent samples? The test of paired comparisons is more powerful than the test of the differences in the means because by using the common element (such as the same periods or companies), we eliminate the variation between the samples that could be caused by something other than what we are testing.

Suppose we have observations for the random variables $X_A$ and $X_B$ and that the samples are dependent. We arrange the observations in pairs. Let $d_i$ denote the difference between two paired observations. We can use the notation $d_i = x_{Ai} - x_{Bi}$, where $x_{Ai}$ and $x_{Bi}$ are the $i$th pair of observations, $i = 1, 2, \ldots, n$, on the two variables. Let $\mu_d$ stand for the population mean difference. We can formulate the following hypotheses, where $\mu_{d0}$ is a hypothesized value for the population mean difference:

Two sided: $H_0: \mu_d = \mu_{d0}$ versus $H_a: \mu_d \neq \mu_{d0}$

One sided (right side): $H_0: \mu_d \leq \mu_{d0}$ versus $H_a: \mu_d > \mu_{d0}$

One sided (left side) $H_0: \mu_d \geq \mu_{d0}$ versus $H_a: \mu_d < \mu_{d0}$

In practice, the most commonly used value for $\mu_{d0}$ is zero.

We are concerned with the case of normally distributed populations with unknown population variances, and we use a $t$-distributed test statistic. We begin by calculating $\bar{d}$, the sample mean difference, or the mean of the differences, $d_i$:

$$\bar{d} = \frac{1}{n}\sum_{i=1}^{n} d_i, \tag{6}$$

where $n$ is the number of pairs of observations. The sample standard deviation, $s_d$, is the standard deviation of the differences, and the standard error of the mean differences is $s_{\bar{d}} = \frac{s_d}{\sqrt{n}}$.

When we have data consisting of paired observations from samples generated by normally distributed populations with unknown variances, the $t$-distributed test statistic is

$$t = \frac{\bar{d} - \mu_{d0}}{s_{\bar{d}}} \tag{7}$$

with $n - 1$ degrees of freedom, where $n$ is the number of paired observations.

For example, suppose we want to see if there is a difference between the returns for Investments One and Two (from Exhibit 1), for which we have returns in each of 33 years. Using a 1% level of significance, the critical values for a two-sided hypothesis test are ±2.7385. Lining up these returns by the years and calculating the differences, we find a sample mean difference ($\bar{d}$) of 0.10353% and a standard deviation of these differences ($s_d$) of 2.35979%. Therefore, the calculated $t$-statistic for testing whether the mean of the differences is equal to zero is

$$t = \frac{0.10353 - 0}{2.35979/\sqrt{33}} = 0.25203$$

with 32 degrees of freedom. In this case, we fail to reject the null because the $t$-statistic falls within the bounds of the two critical values. We conclude that there is not sufficient evidence to indicate that the returns for Investment One and Investment Two are different.

Importantly, if we think of the differences between the two samples as a single sample, then the test of the mean of differences is identical to the test of a single sample mean.

## EXAMPLE 10

### Testing for the Mean of the Differences

In Exhibit 17, we report the quarterly returns for a three-year period for two actively managed portfolios specializing in precious metals. The two portfolios are similar in risk and had nearly identical expense ratios. A major investment services company rated Portfolio B more highly than Portfolio A. In investigating the portfolios' relative performance, suppose we want to test the hypothesis that the mean quarterly return on Portfolio A is equal to the mean quarterly return on Portfolio B during the three-year period. Since the two portfolios share essentially the same set of risk factors, their returns are not independent, so a paired comparisons test is appropriate. Use a 10% level of significance.

**Exhibit 17: Quarterly Returns for Two Actively Managed Precious Metals Portfolios**

| Year | Quarter | Portfolio A (%) | Portfolio B (%) | Difference (Portfolio A − Portfolio B) |
|---|---|---|---|---|
| 1 | 1 | 4.50 | 0.50 | 4.00 |
| 1 | 2 | −4.10 | −3.10 | −1.00 |
| 1 | 3 | −14.50 | −16.80 | 2.30 |
| 1 | 4 | −5.50 | −6.78 | 1.28 |
| 2 | 1 | 12.00 | −2.00 | 14.00 |
| 2 | 2 | −7.97 | −8.96 | 0.99 |
| 2 | 3 | −14.01 | −10.01 | −4.00 |
| 2 | 4 | 4.11 | −6.31 | 10.42 |
| 3 | 1 | 2.34 | −5.00 | 7.34 |
| 3 | 2 | 26.36 | 12.77 | 13.59 |
| 3 | 3 | 10.72 | 9.23 | 1.49 |
| 3 | 4 | 3.60 | 1.20 | 2.40 |
| Average | | 1.46 | −2.94 | 4.40083 |
| Standard deviation | | 11.68 | 8.17 | 5.71776 |

Using this sample information, we can summarize the test as follows:

| | | |
|---|---|---|
| **Step 1** | State the hypotheses. | $H_0: \mu_{d0} = 0$ versus $H_a: \mu_{d0} \neq 0$ |
| **Step 2** | Identify the appropriate test statistic. | $t = \dfrac{\bar{d} - \mu d0}{s_{\bar{d}}}$ |
| **Step 3** | Specify the level of significance. | 10% |
| **Step 4** | State the decision rule. | With 12 − 1 = 11 degrees of freedom, the critical values are ±1.796. |
| | | We reject the null hypothesis if the calculated test statistic is below −1.796 or above +1.796. |

> **Excel**
>     *Lower:* T.INV(0.05,11)
>     *Upper:* T.INV(0.95,11)
> **R** qt(c(.05,.95),11)
> **Python** from scipy.stats import t
>     *Lower:* t.ppf(.05,11)
>     *Upper:* t.ppf(.95,11)

# Test Concerning Differences between Means with Dependent Samples

| Step 5 | Calculate the test statistic. | $\bar{d} = 4.40083$ |
| --- | --- | --- |
| | | $s_{\bar{d}} = \frac{5.71776}{\sqrt{12}} = 1.65058$ |
| | | $t = \frac{4.40083 - 0}{1.65058} = 2.6624$ |
| Step 6 | Make a decision. | Reject the null hypothesis because the calculated $t$-statistic falls outside the bounds of the two critical values. There is sufficient evidence to indicate that the mean of the differences of returns is not zero. |

The following example illustrates the application of this test to evaluate two competing investment strategies.

### EXAMPLE 11

### A Comparison of the Returns of Two Indexes

1. Suppose we want to compare the returns of the ACE High Yield Index with those of the ACE BBB Index. We collect data over 1,304 days for both indexes and calculate the means and standard deviations as shown in Exhibit 18.

**Exhibit 18: Mean and Standard Deviations for the ACE High Yield Index and the ACE BBB Index**

| | ACE High Yield Index (%) | ACE BBB Index (%) | Difference (%) |
| --- | --- | --- | --- |
| Mean return | 0.0157 | 0.0135 | −0.0021 |
| Standard deviation | 0.3157 | 0.3645 | 0.3622 |

Using a 5% level of significance, determine whether the mean of the differences is different from zero.

### Solution

| Step 1 | State the hypotheses. | $H_0: \mu_{d0} = 0$ versus $H_a: \mu_{d0} \neq 0$ |
| --- | --- | --- |
| Step 2 | Identify the appropriate test statistic. | $t = \frac{\bar{d} - \mu_{d0}}{s_{\bar{d}}}$ |
| Step 3 | Specify the level of significance. | 5% |
| Step 4 | State the decision rule. | With 1,304 − 1 = 1,303 degrees of freedom, the critical values are ±1.962. |
| | | We reject the null hypothesis if the calculated $t$-statistic is less than −1.962 or greater than +1.962. |

> **Excel**
>     *Lower:* T.INV(0.025,1303)
>     *Upper:* T.INV(0.975,1303)
> **R** qt(c(.025,.975),1303
> **Python** from scipy.stats import t
>     *Lower:* t.ppf(.025,1303)
>     *Upper:* t.ppf(.975,1303)

| Step 5 | Calculate the test statistic. | $\bar{d} = -0.0021\%$ |
|---|---|---|
| | | $s_{\bar{d}} = \frac{s_d}{\sqrt{n}} = \frac{0.3622}{\sqrt{1,304}} = 0.01003\%$ |
| | | $t = \frac{-0.00210 - 0}{0.01003} = -0.20937$ |
| Step 6 | Make a decision. | Fail to reject the null hypothesis because the calculated $t$-statistic falls within the bounds of the two critical values. There is insufficient evidence to indicate that the mean of the differences of returns is different from zero. |

## 12. TESTING CONCERNING TESTS OF VARIANCES

☐ identify the appropriate test statistic and interpret the results for a hypothesis test concerning (1) the variance of a normally distributed population and (2) the equality of the variances of two normally distributed populations based on two independent random samples

Often, we are interested in the volatility of returns or prices, and one approach to examining volatility is to evaluate variances. We examine two types of tests involving variance: tests concerning the value of a single population variance and tests concerning the difference between two population variances.

### Tests of a Single Variance

Suppose there is a goal to keep the variance of a fund's returns below a specified target. In this case, we would want to compare the observed sample variance of the fund with the target. Performing a test of a population variance requires specifying the hypothesized value of the variance, $\sigma_0^2$. We can formulate hypotheses concerning whether the variance is equal to a specific value or whether it is greater than or less than a hypothesized value:

Two-sided alternative: $H_0: \sigma^2 = \sigma_0^2$ versus $H_a: \sigma^2 \neq \sigma_0^2$

One-sided alternative (right tail): $H_0: \sigma^2 \leq \sigma_0^2$ versus $H_a: \sigma^2 > \sigma_0^2$

One-sided alternative (left tail): $H_0: \sigma^2 \geq \sigma_0^2$ versus $H_a: \sigma^2 < \sigma_0^2$

In tests concerning the variance of a single normally distributed population, we make use of a chi-square test statistic, denoted $\chi^2$. The chi-square distribution, unlike the normal distribution and $t$-distribution, is asymmetrical. Like the $t$-distribution, the chi-square distribution is a family of distributions, with a different distribution for each possible value of degrees of freedom, $n - 1$ ($n$ is sample size). Unlike the $t$-distribution, the chi-square distribution is bounded below by zero; $\chi^2$ does not take on negative values.

If we have $n$ independent observations from a normally distributed population, the appropriate test statistic is

$$\chi^2 = \frac{(n-1)s^2}{\sigma_0^2} \qquad (8)$$

with $n - 1$ degrees of freedom. The sample variance ($s^2$) is in the numerator, and the hypothesized variance ($\sigma_0^2$) is in the denominator.

# Testing Concerning Tests of Variances

In contrast to the *t*-test, for example, the chi-square test is sensitive to violations of its assumptions. If the sample is not random or if it does not come from a normally distributed population, inferences based on a chi-square test are likely to be faulty.

Since the chi-square distribution is asymmetric and bounded below by zero, we no longer have the convenient ± for critical values as we have with the *z*- and the *t*-distributions, so we must either use a table of chi-square values or use software to generate the critical values. Consider a sample of 25 observations, so we have 24 degrees of freedom. We illustrate the rejection regions for the two- and one-sided tests at the 5% significance level in Exhibit 19.

## Exhibit 19: Rejection Regions (Shaded) for the Chi-Square Distribution (df = 24) at 5% Significance

**A.** $H_0: \sigma^2 = \sigma_0^2$ **versus** $H_a: \sigma^2 \neq \sigma_0^2$

Critical values are 12.40115 and 39.36408

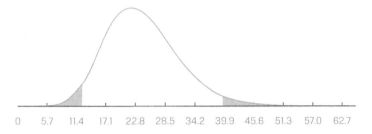

**B.** $H_0: \sigma^2 \leq \sigma_0^2$ **versus** $H_a: \sigma^2 > \sigma_0^2$

Critical value is 36.41503

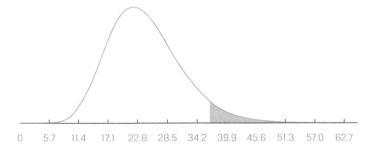

**C.** $H_0: \sigma^2 \geq \sigma_0^2$ **versus** $H_a: \sigma^2 < \sigma_0^2$

Critical value is 13.84843

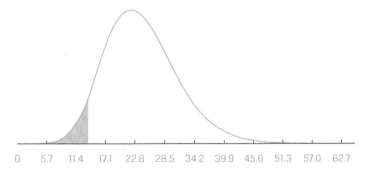

## EXAMPLE 12

### Risk and Return Characteristics of an Equity Mutual Fund

You continue with your analysis of Sendar Equity Fund, a midcap growth fund that has been in existence for only 24 months. During this period, Sendar Equity achieved a mean monthly return of 1.50% and a standard deviation of monthly returns of 3.60%.

1. Using a 5% level of significance, test whether the standard deviation of returns is different from 4%.

### Solution to 1

| | | |
|---|---|---|
| Step 1 | State the hypotheses. | $H_0: \sigma^2 = 16$ versus $H_a: \sigma^2 \neq 16$ |
| Step 2 | Identify the appropriate test statistic. | $\chi^2 = \frac{(n-1)s^2}{\sigma_0^2}$ |
| Step 3 | Specify the level of significance. | 5% |
| Step 4 | State the decision rule. | With 24 − 1 = 23 degrees of freedom, the critical values are 11.68855 and 38.07563. |
| | | We reject the null hypothesis if the calculated $\chi^2$ statistic is less than 11.68855 or greater than 38.07563. |

> **Excel**
>   *Lower:* CHISQ.INV(0.025,23)
>   *Upper:* CHISQ.INV(0.975,23)
> **R** qchisq(c(.025,.975),23)
> **Python** from scipy.stats import chi2
>   *Lower:* chi2.ppf(.025,23)
>   *Upper:* chi2.ppf(.975,23)

| | | |
|---|---|---|
| Step 5 | Calculate the test statistic. | $\chi^2 = \frac{(24-1)12.96}{16} = 18.63000$ |
| Step 6 | Make a decision. | Fail to reject the null hypothesis because the calculated $\chi^2$ statistic falls within the bounds of the two critical values. There is insufficient evidence to indicate that the variance is different from 16% (or, equivalently, that the standard deviation is different from 4%). |

2. Using a 5% level of significance, test whether the standard deviation of returns is less than 4%.

### Solution to 2

| | | |
|---|---|---|
| Step 1 | State the hypotheses. | $H_0: \sigma^2 \geq 16$ versus $H_a: \sigma^2 < 16$ |
| Step 2 | Identify the appropriate test statistic. | $\chi^2 = \frac{(n-1)s^2}{\sigma_0^2}$ |
| Step 3 | Specify the level of significance. | 5% |
| Step 4 | State the decision rule. | With 24 − 1 = 23 degrees of freedom, the critical value is 13.09051. |
| | | We reject the null hypothesis if the calculated $\chi^2$ statistic is less than 13.09051. |

# Testing Concerning Tests of Variances

| | | |
|---|---|---|
| | | **Excel** CHISQ.INV(0.05,23) |
| | | **R** qchisq(.05,23) |
| | | **Python** from scipy.stats import chi2 |
| | | chi2.ppf(.05,23) |
| Step 5 | Calculate the test statistic. | $\chi^2 = \frac{(24-1)12.96}{16} = 18.63000$ |
| Step 6 | Make a decision. | Fail to reject the null hypothesis because the calculated $\chi^2$ statistic is greater than the critical value. There is insufficient evidence to indicate that the variance is less than 16% (or, equivalently, that the standard deviation is less than 4%). |

## Test Concerning the Equality of Two Variances (*F*-Test)

There are many instances in which we want to compare the volatility of two samples, in which case we can test for the equality of two variances. Examples include comparisons of baskets of securities against indexes or benchmarks, as well as comparisons of volatility in different periods. Suppose we have a hypothesis about the relative values of the variances of two normally distributed populations with variances of $\sigma_1^2$ and $\sigma_2^2$, distinguishing the two populations as 1 or 2. We can formulate the hypotheses as two sided or one sided:

Two-sided alternative:

$H_0: \sigma_1^2 = \sigma_2^2$ versus $H_a: \sigma_1^2 \neq \sigma_2^2$

or, equivalently,

$H_0: \frac{\sigma_1^2}{\sigma_2^2} = 1$ versus $H_a: \frac{\sigma_1^2}{\sigma_2^2} \neq 1$

One-sided alternative (right side):

$H_0: \sigma_1^2 \leq \sigma_2^2$ versus $H_a: \sigma_1^2 > \sigma_2^2$

or, equivalently,

$H_0: \frac{\sigma_1^2}{\sigma_2^2} \leq 1$ versus $H_a: \frac{\sigma_1^2}{\sigma_2^2} > 1$

One-sided alternative (left side):

$H_0: \sigma_1^2 \geq \sigma_2^2$ versus $H_a: \sigma_1^2 < \sigma_2^2$

or, equivalently,

$H_0: \frac{\sigma_1^2}{\sigma_2^2} \geq 1$ versus $H_a: \frac{\sigma_1^2}{\sigma_2^2} < 1$

Given independent random samples from these populations, tests related to these hypotheses are based on an *F*-test, which is the ratio of sample variances. Tests concerning the difference between the variances of two populations make use of the *F*-distribution. Like the chi-square distribution, the *F*-distribution is a family of asymmetrical distributions bounded from below by zero. Each *F*-distribution is defined by two values of degrees of freedom, which we refer to as the numerator and denominator degrees of freedom. The $F$-test, like the chi-square test, is not robust to violations of its assumptions.

Suppose we have two samples, the first with $n_1$ observations and a sample variance $s_1^2$ and the second with $n_2$ observations and a sample variance $s_2^2$. The samples are random, independent of each other, and generated by normally distributed populations. A test concerning differences between the variances of the two populations is based on the ratio of sample variances, as follows:

$$F = \frac{s_1^2}{s_2^2} \tag{9}$$

with $df_1 = (n_1 - 1)$ numerator degrees of freedom and $df_2 = (n_2 - 1)$ denominator degrees of freedom. Note that $df_1$ and $df_2$ are the divisors used in calculating $s_1^2$ and $s_2^2$, respectively.

When we rely on tables to arrive at critical values, a convention is to use the larger of the two sample variances in the numerator in Equation 9; doing so reduces the number of $F$-tables needed. The key is to be consistent with how the alternative hypothesis is specified and the order of the sample sizes for the degrees of freedom.

Consider two samples, the first with 25 observations and the second with 40 observations. We show the rejection region and critical values in Exhibit 20 for two- and one-sided alternative hypotheses at the 5% significance level.

# Testing Concerning Tests of Variances

**Exhibit 20: Rejection Regions (Shaded) for the F-Distribution Based on Sample Sizes of 25 and 40 at 5% Significance**

**A.** $H_0$: $\sigma_1^2 = \sigma_2^2$ versus $H_a$: $\sigma_1^2 \neq \sigma_2^2$

Critical values are 0.49587 and 2.15095

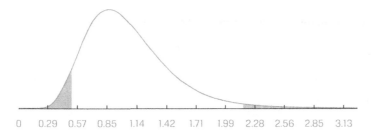

**B.** $H_0$: $\sigma_1^2 \leq \sigma_2^2$ versus $H_a$: $\sigma_1^2 > \sigma_2^2$

Critical value is 1.89566

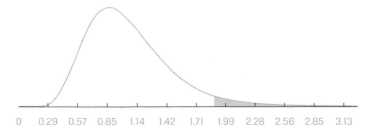

**C.** $H_0$: $\sigma_1^2 \geq \sigma_2^2$ versus $H_a$: $\sigma_1^2 < \sigma_2^2$

Critical value is 0.55551

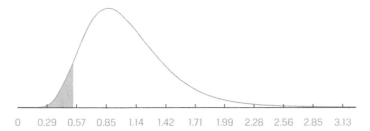

Consider Investments One and Two (from Exhibit 1), with standard deviations of returns of 1.4284 and 2.5914, respectively, calculated over the 33-year period. If we want to know whether the variance of Investment One is different from that of Investment Two, we use the $F$-distributed test statistic. With 32 and 32 degrees of freedom, the critical values are 0.49389 and 2.02475 at the 5% significance level. The calculated $F$-statistic is

$$F = \frac{2.5914^2}{1.4284^2} = 3.29131.$$

Therefore, we reject the null hypothesis that the variances of these two investments are the same because the calculated $F$-statistic is outside of the critical values. We can conclude that one investment is riskier than the other.

# EXAMPLE 13

## Volatility and Regulation

You are investigating whether the population variance of returns on a stock market index changed after a change in market regulation. The first 418 weeks occurred before the regulation change, and the second 418 weeks occurred after the regulation change. You gather the data in Exhibit 21 for 418 weeks of returns both before and after the change in regulation. You have specified a 5% level of significance.

### Exhibit 21: Index Returns and Variances before and after the Market Regulation Change

|  | n | Mean Weekly Return (%) | Variance of Returns |
|---|---|---|---|
| Before regulation change | 418 | 0.250 | 4.644 |
| After regulation change | 418 | 0.110 | 3.919 |

1. Test whether the variance of returns is different before the regulation change versus after the regulation change, using a 5% level of significance.

## Solution to 1

| Step 1 | State the hypotheses. | $H_0: \sigma^2_{Before} = \sigma^2_{After}$ versus $H_a: \sigma^2_{Before} \neq \sigma^2_{After}$ |
|---|---|---|
| Step 2 | Identify the appropriate test statistic. | $F = \dfrac{s^2_{Before}}{s^2_{After}}$ |
| Step 3 | Specify the level of significance. | 5% |
| Step 4 | State the decision rule. | With 418 − 1 = 417 and 418 − 1 = 417 degrees of freedom, the critical values are 0.82512 and 1.21194. |
| | | Reject the null if the calculated $F$-statistic is less than 0.82512 or greater than 1.21194. |
| | | **Excel** |
| | | *Left side:* F.INV(0.025,417,417) |
| | | *Right side:* F.INV(0.975,417,417) |
| | | **R** qf(c(.025,.975),417,417) |
| | | **Python** from scipy.stats import f |
| | | *Left side:* f.ppf(.025,417,417) |
| | | *Right side:* f.ppf(.975,417,417) |
| Step 5 | Calculate the test statistic. | $F = \dfrac{4.644}{3.919} = 1.18500$ |
| Step 6 | Make a decision. | Fail to reject the null hypothesis since the calculated $F$-statistic falls within the bounds of the two critical values. There is not sufficient evidence to indicate that the weekly variances of returns are different in the periods before and after the regulation change. |

# Testing Concerning Tests of Variances

2. Test whether the variance of returns is greater before the regulation change versus after the regulation change, using a 5% level of significance.

## Solution to 2

| Step 1 | State the hypotheses. | $H_0: \sigma^2_{Before} \leq \sigma^2_{After}$ versus $H_a: \sigma^2_{Before} > \sigma^2_{After}$ |
| --- | --- | --- |
| Step 2 | Identify the appropriate test statistic. | $F = \dfrac{s^2_{Before}}{s^2_{After}}$ |
| Step 3 | Specify the level of significance. | 5% |
| Step 4 | State the decision rule. | With 418 − 1 = 417 and 418 − 1 = 417 degrees of freedom, the critical value is 1.17502. |
| | | We reject the null hypothesis if the calculated $F$-statistic is greater than 1.17502. |
| | | **Excel** F.INV(0.95,417,417) |
| | | **R** qf(.95,417,417) |
| | | **Python** from scipy.stats import f |
| | |     f.ppf(.95,417,417) |
| Step 5 | Calculate the test statistic. | $F = \dfrac{4.644}{3.919} = 1.18500$ |
| Step 6 | Make a decision. | Reject the null hypothesis since the calculated $F$-statistic is greater than 1.17502. There is sufficient evidence to indicate that the weekly variances of returns before the regulation change are greater than the variances after the regulation change. |

## EXAMPLE 14

### The Volatility of Derivatives Expiration Days

1. You are interested in investigating whether quadruple witching days—that is, the occurrence of stock option, index option, index futures, and single stock futures expirations on the same day—exhibit greater volatility than normal trading days. Exhibit 22 presents the daily standard deviation of returns for normal trading days and quadruple witching days during a four-year period.

   **Exhibit 22: Standard Deviation of Returns: Normal Trading Days and Derivatives Expiration Days**

   | Period | Type of Day | n | Standard Deviation (%) |
   | --- | --- | --- | --- |
   | 1 | Normal trading days | 138 | 0.821 |
   | 2 | Quadruple witching days | 16 | 1.217 |

   Test to determine whether the variance of returns for quadruple witching days is greater than the variance for non-expiration, normal trading days. Use a 5% level of significance.

## Solution

| | | |
|---|---|---|
| Step 1 | State the hypotheses. | $H_0: \sigma^2_{Period2} \leq \sigma^2_{Period1}$ versus $H_a: \sigma^2_{Period2} > \sigma^2_{Period1}$ |
| Step 2 | Identify the appropriate test statistic. | $F = \dfrac{s^2_{Period2}}{s^2_{Period1}}$ |
| Step 3 | Specify the level of significance. | 5% |
| Step 4 | State the decision rule. | With 16 − 1 = 15 and 138 − 1 = 137 degrees of freedom, the critical value is 1.73997. <br><br> We reject the null hypothesis if the calculated $F$-statistic is greater than 1.73997. <br><br> **Excel** F.INV(0.95,15,137) <br> **R** qf(.95,15,137) <br> **Python** from scipy.stats import f <br>    f.ppf(.95,15,137) |
| Step 5 | Calculate the test statistic. | $F = \dfrac{1.48109}{0.67404} = 2.19733$ |
| Step 6 | Make a decision. | Reject the null hypothesis since the calculated $F$-statistic is greater than 1.73997. There is sufficient evidence to indicate that the variance of returns for quadruple witching days is greater than the variance for normal trading days. |

# SUMMARY

In this reading, we have presented the concepts and methods of statistical inference and hypothesis testing.

- A hypothesis is a statement about one or more populations.
- The steps in testing a hypothesis are as follows:

  1. State the hypotheses.
  2. Identify the appropriate test statistic and its probability distribution.
  3. Specify the significance level.
  4. State the decision rule.
  5. Collect the data and calculate the test statistic.
  6. Make a decision.

- We state two hypotheses: The null hypothesis is the hypothesis to be tested; the alternative hypothesis is the hypothesis accepted if the null hypothesis is rejected.
- There are three ways to formulate hypotheses. Let θ indicate the population parameters:

  1. Two-sided alternative: $H_0: \theta = \theta_0$ versus $H_a: \theta \neq \theta_0$
  2. One-sided alternative (right side): $H_0: \theta \leq \theta_0$ versus $H_a: \theta > \theta_0$
  3. One-sided alternative (left side): $H_0: \theta \geq \theta_0$ versus $H_a: \theta < \theta_0$

  where $\theta_0$ is a hypothesized value of the population parameter and θ is the true value of the population parameter.

- When we have a "suspected" or "hoped for" condition for which we want to find supportive evidence, we frequently set up that condition as the alternative hypothesis and use a one-sided test. However, the researcher may select a "not equal to" alternative hypothesis and conduct a two-sided test to emphasize a neutral attitude.
- A test statistic is a quantity, calculated using a sample, whose value is the basis for deciding whether to reject or not reject the null hypothesis. We compare the computed value of the test statistic to a critical value for the same test statistic to decide whether to reject or not reject the null hypothesis.
- In reaching a statistical decision, we can make two possible errors: We may reject a true null hypothesis (a Type I error, or false positive), or we may fail to reject a false null hypothesis (a Type II error, or false negative).
- The level of significance of a test is the probability of a Type I error that we accept in conducting a hypothesis test. The standard approach to hypothesis testing involves specifying only a level of significance (that is, the probability of a Type I error). The complement of the level of significance is the confidence level.
- The power of a test is the probability of correctly rejecting the null (rejecting the null when it is false). The complement of the power of the test is the probability of a Type II error.
- A decision rule consists of determining the critical values with which to compare the test statistic to decide whether to reject or not reject the null hypothesis. When we reject the null hypothesis, the result is said to be statistically significant.
- The $(1 - \alpha)$ confidence interval represents the range of values of the test statistic for which the null hypothesis cannot be rejected.
- The statistical decision consists of rejecting or not rejecting the null hypothesis. The economic decision takes into consideration all economic issues pertinent to the decision.
- The $p$-value is the smallest level of significance at which the null hypothesis can be rejected. The smaller the $p$-value, the stronger the evidence against the null hypothesis and in favor of the alternative hypothesis. The $p$-value approach to hypothesis testing involves computing a $p$-value for the test statistic and allowing the user of the research to interpret the implications for the null hypothesis.
- For hypothesis tests concerning the population mean of a normally distributed population with unknown variance, the theoretically correct test statistic is the $t$-statistic.
- When we want to test whether the observed difference between two means is statistically significant, we must first decide whether the samples are independent or dependent (related). If the samples are independent, we conduct a test concerning differences between means. If the samples are dependent, we conduct a test of mean differences (paired comparisons test).
- When we conduct a test of the difference between two population means from normally distributed populations with unknown but equal variances, we use a $t$-test based on pooling the observations of the two samples to estimate the common but unknown variance. This test is based on an assumption of independent samples.

- In tests concerning two means based on two samples that are not independent, we often can arrange the data in paired observations and conduct a test of mean differences (a paired comparisons test). When the samples are from normally distributed populations with unknown variances, the appropriate test statistic is $t$-distributed.
- In tests concerning the variance of a single normally distributed population, the test statistic is chi-square with $n - 1$ degrees of freedom, where $n$ is sample size.
- For tests concerning differences between the variances of two normally distributed populations based on two random, independent samples, the appropriate test statistic is based on an $F$-test (the ratio of the sample variances). The degrees of freedom for this $F$-test are $n_1 - 1$ and $n_2 - 1$, where $n_1$ corresponds to the number of observations in the calculation of the numerator and $n_2$ is the number of observations in the calculation of the denominator of the $F$-statistic.

# REFERENCES

Benjamini, Y., Y. Hochberg. 1995. "Controlling the False Discovery Rate: A Practical and Powerful Approach to Multiple Testing." Journal of the Royal Statistical Society. Series B. Methodological, 57: 289–300.

# PRACTICE PROBLEMS

1. Which of the following statements about hypothesis testing is correct?
    A. The null hypothesis is the condition a researcher hopes to support.
    B. The alternative hypothesis is the proposition considered true without conclusive evidence to the contrary.
    C. The alternative hypothesis exhausts all potential parameter values not accounted for by the null hypothesis.

2. Willco is a manufacturer in a mature cyclical industry. During the most recent industry cycle, its net income averaged $30 million per year with a standard deviation of $10 million ($n = 6$ observations). Management claims that Willco's performance during the most recent cycle results from new approaches and that Willco's profitability will exceed the $24 million per year observed in prior cycles.
    A. With $\mu$ as the population value of mean annual net income, formulate null and alternative hypotheses consistent with testing Willco management's claim.
    B. Assuming that Willco's net income is at least approximately normally distributed, identify the appropriate test statistic and calculate the degrees of freedom.
    C. Based on critical value of 2.015, determine whether to reject the null hypothesis.

3. Which of the following statements is correct with respect to the null hypothesis?
    A. It can be stated as "not equal to" provided the alternative hypothesis is stated as "equal to."
    B. Along with the alternative hypothesis, it considers all possible values of the population parameter.
    C. In a two-tailed test, it is rejected when evidence supports equality between the hypothesized value and the population parameter.

4. Which of the following statements regarding a one-tailed hypothesis test is correct?
    A. The rejection region increases in size as the level of significance becomes smaller.
    B. A one-tailed test more strongly reflects the beliefs of the researcher than a two-tailed test.
    C. The absolute value of the rejection point is larger than that of a two-tailed test at the same level of significance.

5. A hypothesis test for a normally distributed population at a 0.05 significance level implies a:
    A. 95% probability of rejecting a true null hypothesis.
    B. 95% probability of a Type I error for a two-tailed test.

**Practice Problems**

   C. 5% critical value rejection region in a tail of the distribution for a one-tailed test.

6. The value of a test statistic is *best* described as the basis for deciding whether to:
   A. reject the null hypothesis.
   B. accept the null hypothesis.
   C. reject the alternative hypothesis.

7. Which of the following is a Type I error?
   A. Rejecting a true null hypothesis
   B. Rejecting a false null hypothesis
   C. Failing to reject a false null hypothesis

8. A Type II error is *best* described as:
   A. rejecting a true null hypothesis.
   B. failing to reject a false null hypothesis.
   C. failing to reject a false alternative hypothesis.

9. The level of significance of a hypothesis test is *best* used to:
   A. calculate the test statistic.
   B. define the test's rejection points.
   C. specify the probability of a Type II error.

10. All else equal, is specifying a smaller significance level in a hypothesis test likely to increase the probability of a:

    |    | Type I error? | Type II error? |
    |----|---------------|----------------|
    | A. | No            | No             |
    | B. | No            | Yes            |
    | C. | Yes           | No             |

11. The probability of correctly rejecting the null hypothesis is the:
    A. $p$-value.
    B. power of a test.
    C. level of significance.

12. The power of a hypothesis test is:
    A. equivalent to the level of significance.
    B. the probability of not making a Type II error.
    C. unchanged by increasing a small sample size.

13. For each of the following hypothesis tests concerning the population mean, $\mu$,

state the conclusion regarding the test of the hypotheses.

A. $H_0: \mu = 10$ versus $H_a: \mu \neq 10$, with a calculated $t$-statistic of 2.05 and critical $t$-values of ±1.984.

B. $H_0: \mu \leq 10$ versus $H_a: \mu > 10$, with a calculated $t$-statistic of 2.35 and a critical $t$-value of +1.679.

C. $H_0: \mu = 10$ versus $H_a: \mu \neq 10$, with a calculated $t$-statistic of 2.05, a $p$-value of 4.6352%, and a level of significance of 5%.

D. $H_0: \mu \leq 10$ versus $H_a: \sigma2 > 10$, with a 2% level of significance and a calculated test statistic with a $p$-value of 3%.

14. In the step "stating a decision rule" in testing a hypothesis, which of the following elements must be specified?

    A. Critical value

    B. Power of a test

    C. Value of a test statistic

15. When making a decision about investments involving a statistically significant result, the:

    A. economic result should be presumed to be meaningful.

    B. statistical result should take priority over economic considerations.

    C. economic logic for the future relevance of the result should be further explored.

16. An analyst tests the profitability of a trading strategy with the null hypothesis that the average abnormal return before trading costs equals zero. The calculated $t$-statistic is 2.802, with critical values of ±2.756 at significance level $\alpha = 0.01$. After considering trading costs, the strategy's return is near zero. The results are *most likely*:

    A. statistically but not economically significant.

    B. economically but not statistically significant.

    C. neither statistically nor economically significant.

17. Which of the following statements is correct with respect to the $p$-value?

    A. It is a less precise measure of test evidence than rejection points.

    B. It is the largest level of significance at which the null hypothesis is rejected.

    C. It can be compared directly with the level of significance in reaching test conclusions.

18. Which of the following represents a correct statement about the $p$-value?

    A. The $p$-value offers less precise information than does the rejection points approach.

    B. A larger $p$-value provides stronger evidence in support of the alternative hypothesis.

**Practice Problems**

C. A *p*-value less than the specified level of significance leads to rejection of the null hypothesis.

19. Which of the following statements on *p*-value is correct?

    A. The *p*-value indicates the probability of making a Type II error.

    B. The lower the *p*-value, the weaker the evidence for rejecting the $H_0$.

    C. The *p*-value is the smallest level of significance at which $H_0$ can be rejected.

20. The following table shows the significance level (α) and the *p*-value for two hypothesis tests.

    |        | α    | *p*-Value |
    |--------|------|-----------|
    | Test 1 | 0.02 | 0.05      |
    | Test 2 | 0.05 | 0.02      |

    In which test should we reject the null hypothesis?

    A. Test 1 only

    B. Test 2 only

    C. Both Test 1 and Test 2

21. Identify the appropriate test statistic or statistics for conducting the following hypothesis tests. (Clearly identify the test statistic and, if applicable, the number of degrees of freedom. For example, "We conduct the test using an *x*-statistic with *y* degrees of freedom.")

    A. $H_0$: $\mu = 0$ versus $H_a$: $\mu \neq 0$, where $\mu$ is the mean of a normally distributed population with unknown variance. The test is based on a sample of 15 observations.

    B. $H_0$: $\mu = 5$ versus $H_a$: $\mu \neq 5$, where $\mu$ is the mean of a normally distributed population with unknown variance. The test is based on a sample of 40 observations.

    C. $H_0$: $\mu \leq 0$ versus $H_a$: $\mu > 0$, where $\mu$ is the mean of a normally distributed population with known variance $\sigma^2$. The sample size is 45.

    D. $H_0$: $\sigma^2 = 200$ versus $H_a$: $\sigma^2 \neq 200$, where $\sigma^2$ is the variance of a normally distributed population. The sample size is 50.

    E. $H_0$: $\sigma_1^2 = \sigma_2^2$ versus $H_a$: $\sigma_1^2 \neq \sigma_2^2$, where $\sigma_1^2$ is the variance of one normally distributed population and $\sigma_2^2$ is the variance of a second normally distributed population. The test is based on two independent samples, with the first sample of size 30 and the second sample of size 40.

    F. $H_0$: $\mu_1 - \mu_2 = 0$ versus $H_a$: $\mu_1 - \mu_2 \neq 0$, where the samples are drawn from normally distributed populations with unknown but assumed equal variances. The observations in the two samples (of size 25 and 30, respectively) are independent.

22. For each of the following hypothesis tests concerning the population mean, state

the conclusion.

**A.** $H_0$: $\sigma^2 = 0.10$ versus $H_a$: $\sigma^2 \neq 0.10$, with a calculated chi-square test statistic of 45.8 and critical chi-square values of 42.950 and 86.830.

**B.** $H_0$: $\sigma^2 = 0.10$ versus $H_a$: $\sigma^2 \neq 0.10$, with a 5% level of significance and a p-value for this calculated chi-square test statistic of 4.463%.

**C.** $H_0$: $\sigma_1^2 = \sigma_2^2$ versus $H_a$: $\sigma_1^2 \neq \sigma_2^2$, with a calculated F-statistic of 2.3. With 40 and 30 degrees of freedom, the critical F-values are 0.498 and 1.943.

**D.** $H_0$: $\sigma^2 \leq 10$ versus $H_a$: $\mu\sigma^2 > 10$, with a calculated test statistic of 32 and a critical chi-square value of 26.296.

# The following information relates to questions 23-24

**Performance in Forecasting Quarterly Earnings per Share**

|  | Number of Forecasts | Mean Forecast Error (Predicted − Actual) | Standard Deviation of Forecast Errors |
|---|---|---|---|
| Analyst A | 10 | 0.05 | 0.10 |
| Analyst B | 15 | 0.02 | 0.09 |

**Critical t-values:**

| | Area in the Right-Side Rejection Area | |
|---|---|---|
| Degrees of Freedom | p = 0.05 | p = 0.025 |
| 8 | 1.860 | 2.306 |
| 9 | 1.833 | 2.262 |
| 10 | 1.812 | 2.228 |
| 11 | 1.796 | 2.201 |
| 12 | 1.782 | 2.179 |
| 13 | 1.771 | 2.160 |
| 14 | 1.761 | 2.145 |
| 15 | 1.753 | 2.131 |
| 16 | 1.746 | 2.120 |
| 17 | 1.740 | 2.110 |
| 18 | 1.734 | 2.101 |
| 19 | 1.729 | 2.093 |
| 20 | 1.725 | 2.086 |
| 21 | 1.721 | 2.080 |
| 22 | 1.717 | 2.074 |
| 23 | 1.714 | 2.069 |
| 24 | 1.711 | 2.064 |
| 25 | 1.708 | 2.060 |
| 26 | 1.706 | 2.056 |
| 27 | 1.703 | 2.052 |

**Practice Problems**

23. Investment analysts often use earnings per share (EPS) forecasts. One test of forecasting quality is the zero-mean test, which states that optimal forecasts should have a mean forecasting error of zero. The forecasting error is the difference between the predicted value of a variable and the actual value of the variable.

    You have collected data (shown in the previous table) for two analysts who cover two different industries: Analyst A covers the telecom industry; Analyst B covers automotive parts and suppliers.

    **A.** With μ as the population mean forecasting error, formulate null and alternative hypotheses for a zero-mean test of forecasting quality.

    **B.** For Analyst A, determine whether to reject the null at the 0.05 level of significance.

    **C.** For Analyst B, determine whether to reject the null at the 0.05 level of significance.

24. Reviewing the EPS forecasting performance data for Analysts A and B, you want to investigate whether the larger average forecast errors of Analyst A relative to Analyst B are due to chance or to a higher underlying mean value for Analyst A. Assume that the forecast errors of both analysts are normally distributed and that the samples are independent.

    **A.** Formulate null and alternative hypotheses consistent with determining whether the population mean value of Analyst A's forecast errors ($\mu_1$) is larger than Analyst B's ($\mu_2$).

    **B.** Identify the test statistic for conducting a test of the null hypothesis formulated in Part A.

    **C.** Identify the rejection point or points for the hypotheses tested in Part A at the 0.05 level of significance.

    **D.** Determine whether to reject the null hypothesis at the 0.05 level of significance.

---

25. An analyst is examining a large sample with an unknown population variance. Which of the following is the *most* appropriate test to test the hypothesis that the historical average return on an index is less than or equal to 6%?

    **A.** One-sided *t*-test

    **B.** Two-sided *t*-test

    **C.** One-sided chi-square test

26. Which of the following tests of a hypothesis concerning the population mean is *most* appropriate?

    **A.** A *z*-test if the population variance is unknown and the sample is small

    **B.** A *z*-test if the population is normally distributed with a known variance

    **C.** A *t*-test if the population is non-normally distributed with unknown variance and a small sample

27. For a small sample from a normally distributed population with unknown variance, the *most* appropriate test statistic for the mean is the:

   A. $z$-statistic.

   B. $t$-statistic.

   C. $\chi^2$ statistic.

28. An investment consultant conducts two independent random samples of five-year performance data for US and European absolute return hedge funds. Noting a return advantage of 50 bps for US managers, the consultant decides to test whether the two means are different from one another at a 0.05 level of significance. The two populations are assumed to be normally distributed with unknown but equal variances. Results of the hypothesis test are contained in the following tables.

   | | Sample Size | Mean Return (%) | Standard Deviation |
   |---|---|---|---|
   | US managers | 50 | 4.7 | 5.4 |
   | European managers | 50 | 4.2 | 4.8 |

   | | |
   |---|---|
   | Null and alternative hypotheses | $H_0: \mu_{US} - \mu_E = 0; H_a: \mu_{US} - \mu_E \neq 0$ |
   | Calculated test statistic | 0.4893 |
   | Critical value rejection points | ±1.984 |

   *The mean return for US funds is $\mu_{US}$, and $\mu_E$ is the mean return for European funds.*

   The results of the hypothesis test indicate that the:

   A. null hypothesis is not rejected.

   B. alternative hypothesis is statistically confirmed.

   C. difference in mean returns is statistically different from zero.

29. A pooled estimator is used when testing a hypothesis concerning the:

   A. equality of the variances of two normally distributed populations.

   B. difference between the means of two at least approximately normally distributed populations with unknown but assumed equal variances.

   C. difference between the means of two at least approximately normally distributed populations with unknown and assumed unequal variances.

30. The following table gives data on the monthly returns on the S&P 500 Index and small-cap stocks for a 40-year period and provides statistics relating to their mean differences. Further, the entire sample period is split into two subperiods of 20 years each, and the return data for these subperiods is also given in the table.

   | Measure | S&P 500 Return (%) | Small-Cap Stock Return (%) | Differences (S&P 500 – Small-Cap Stock) |
   |---|---|---|---|
   | *Entire sample period, 480 months* | | | |
   | Mean | 1.0542 | 1.3117 | −0.258 |
   | Standard deviation | 4.2185 | 5.9570 | 3.752 |

## Practice Problems

| Measure | S&P 500 Return (%) | Small-Cap Stock Return (%) | Differences (S&P 500 − Small-Cap Stock) |
|---|---|---|---|
| *First subperiod, 240 months* | | | |
| Mean | 0.6345 | 1.2741 | −0.640 |
| Standard deviation | 4.0807 | 6.5829 | 4.096 |
| *Second subperiod, 240 months* | | | |
| Mean | 1.4739 | 1.3492 | 0.125 |
| Standard deviation | 4.3197 | 5.2709 | 3.339 |

Use a significance level of 0.05 and assume that mean differences are approximately normally distributed.

- **A.** Formulate null and alternative hypotheses consistent with testing whether any difference exists between the mean returns on the S&P 500 and small-cap stocks.

- **B.** Determine whether to reject the null hypothesis for the entire sample period if the critical values are ±1.96.

- **C.** Determine whether to reject the null hypothesis for the first subperiod if the critical values are ±1.96.

- **D.** Determine whether to reject the null hypothesis for the second subperiod if the critical values are ±1.96.

31. When evaluating mean differences between two dependent samples, the *most* appropriate test is a:
    - **A.** $z$-test.
    - **B.** chi-square test.
    - **C.** paired comparisons test.

32. A chi-square test is *most* appropriate for tests concerning:
    - **A.** a single variance.
    - **B.** differences between two population means with variances assumed to be equal.
    - **C.** differences between two population means with variances assumed to not be equal.

33. During a 10-year period, the standard deviation of annual returns on a portfolio you are analyzing was 15% a year. You want to see whether this record is sufficient evidence to support the conclusion that the portfolio's underlying variance of return was less than 400, the return variance of the portfolio's benchmark.
    - **A.** Formulate null and alternative hypotheses consistent with your objective.
    - **B.** Identify the test statistic for conducting a test of the hypotheses in Part A, and calculate the degrees of freedom.
    - **C.** Determine whether the null hypothesis is rejected or not rejected at the 0.05 level of significance using a critical value of 3.325.

34. You are investigating whether the population variance of returns on an index changed subsequent to a market disruption. You gather the following data for 120 months of returns before the disruption and for 120 months of returns after the disruption. You have specified a 0.05 level of significance.

| Time Period | n | Mean Monthly Return (%) | Variance of Returns |
|---|---|---|---|
| Before disruption | 120 | 1.416 | 22.367 |
| After disruption | 120 | 1.436 | 15.795 |

   A. Formulate null and alternative hypotheses consistent with the research goal.

   B. Identify the test statistic for conducting a test of the hypotheses in Part A, and calculate the degrees of freedom.

   C. Determine whether to reject the null hypothesis at the 0.05 level of significance if the critical values are 0.6969 and 1.4349.

35. Which of the following should be used to test the difference between the variances of two normally distributed populations?

   A. $t$-test

   B. $F$-test

   C. Paired comparisons test

## SOLUTIONS

1. C is correct. Together, the null and alternative hypotheses account for all possible values of the parameter. Any possible values of the parameter not covered by the null must be covered by the alternative hypothesis (e.g., $H_0$: $\mu \leq 5$ versus $H_a$: $\mu > 5$).

2.
    A. As stated in the text, we often set up the "hoped for" or "suspected" condition as the alternative hypothesis. Here, that condition is that the population value of Willco's mean annual net income exceeds $24 million. Thus, we have $H_0$: $\mu \leq 24$ versus $H_a$: $\mu > 24$.
    B. Given that net income is normally distributed with unknown variance, the appropriate test statistic is $t = \frac{\overline{X} - \mu_0}{s/\sqrt{n}} = 1.469694$ with $n - 1 = 6 - 1 = 5$ degrees of freedom.
    C. We reject the null if the calculated $t$-statistic is greater than 2.015. The calculated $t$-statistic is $t = \frac{30 - 24}{10/\sqrt{6}} = 1.469694$. Because the calculated test statistic does not exceed 2.015, we fail to reject the null hypothesis. There is not sufficient evidence to indicate that the mean net income is greater than $24 million.

3. A is correct. The null hypothesis and the alternative hypothesis are complements of one another and together are exhaustive; that is, the null and alternative hypotheses combined consider all the possible values of the population parameter.

4. B is correct. One-tailed tests in which the alternative is "greater than" or "less than" represent the beliefs of the researcher more firmly than a "not equal to" alternative hypothesis.

5. C is correct. For a one-tailed hypothesis test, there is a 5% rejection region in one tail of the distribution.

6. A is correct. Calculated using a sample, a test statistic is a quantity whose value is the basis for deciding whether to reject the null hypothesis.

7. A is correct. The definition of a Type I error is when a true null hypothesis is rejected.

8. B is correct. A Type II error occurs when a false null hypothesis is not rejected.

9. B is correct. The level of significance is used to establish the rejection points of the hypothesis test.

10. B is correct. Specifying a smaller significance level decreases the probability of a Type I error (rejecting a true null hypothesis) but increases the probability of a Type II error (not rejecting a false null hypothesis). As the level of significance decreases, the null hypothesis is less frequently rejected.

11. B is correct. The power of a test is the probability of rejecting the null hypothesis when it is false.

12. B is correct. The power of a hypothesis test is the probability of correctly rejecting the null when it is false. Failing to reject the null when it is false is a Type II error. Thus, the power of a hypothesis test is the probability of not committing a

Type II error.

13. We make the decision either by comparing the calculated test statistic with the critical values or by comparing the $p$-value for the calculated test statistic with the level of significance.

    **A.** Reject the null hypothesis because the calculated test statistic is outside the bounds of the critical values.

    **B.** The calculated $t$-statistic is in the rejection region that is defined by +1.679, so we reject the null hypothesis.

    **C.** The $p$-value corresponding to the calculated test statistic is less than the level of significance, so we reject the null hypothesis.

    **D.** We fail to reject because the $p$-value for the calculated test statistic is greater than what is tolerated with a 2% level of significance.

14. A is correct. The critical value in a decision rule is the rejection point for the test. It is the point with which the test statistic is compared to determine whether to reject the null hypothesis, which is part of the fourth step in hypothesis testing.

15. C is correct. When a statistically significant result is also economically meaningful, one should further explore the logic of why the result might work in the future.

16. A is correct. The hypothesis is a two-tailed formulation. The $t$-statistic of 2.802 falls outside the critical rejection points of less than –2.756 and greater than 2.756. Therefore, the null hypothesis is rejected; the result is statistically significant. However, despite the statistical results, trying to profit on the strategy is not likely to be economically meaningful because the return is near zero after transaction costs.

17. C is correct. When directly comparing the $p$-value with the level of significance, it can be used as an alternative to using rejection points to reach conclusions on hypothesis tests. If the $p$-value is smaller than the specified level of significance, the null hypothesis is rejected. Otherwise, the null hypothesis is not rejected.

18. C is correct. The $p$-value is the smallest level of significance at which the null hypothesis can be rejected for a given value of the test statistic. The null hypothesis is rejected when the $p$-value is less than the specified significance level.

19. C is correct. The $p$-value is the smallest level of significance ($\alpha$) at which the null hypothesis can be rejected.

20. B is correct. The $p$-value is the smallest level of significance ($\alpha$) at which the null hypothesis can be rejected. If the $p$-value is less than $\alpha$, the null is rejected. In Test 1, the $p$-value exceeds the level of significance, whereas in Test 2, the $p$-value is less than the level of significance.

21. 
    **A.** The appropriate test statistic is a $t$-statistic, $t = \frac{\overline{X} - \mu_0}{\frac{s}{\sqrt{n}}}$, with $n - 1 = 15 - 1 = 14$ degrees of freedom. A $t$-statistic is correct when the sample comes from an approximately normally distributed population with unknown variance.

    **B.** The appropriate test statistic is a $t$-statistic, $t = \frac{\overline{X} - \mu_0}{\frac{s}{\sqrt{n}}}$, with $40 - 1 = 39$ degrees of freedom. A $t$-statistic is theoretically correct when the sample comes from a normally distributed population with unknown variance.

**Solutions**

**C.** The appropriate test statistic is a $z$-statistic, $z = \dfrac{\bar{X} - \mu_0}{\frac{\sigma}{\sqrt{n}}}$, because the sample comes from a normally distributed population with a known variance.

**D.** The appropriate test statistic is chi-square, $x^2 = \dfrac{s^2(n-1)}{\sigma_0^2}$, with $50 - 1 = 49$ degrees of freedom.

**E.** The appropriate test statistic is the $F$-statistic, $F = \sigma_1^2/\sigma_2^2$, with 29 and 39 degrees of freedom.

**F.** The appropriate test statistic is a $t$-statistic using a pooled estimate of the population variance: $t = \dfrac{(\bar{X}_1 - \bar{X}_2) - (\mu_1 - \mu_2)}{\sqrt{\dfrac{s_p^2}{n_1} + \dfrac{s_p^2}{n_2}}}$, where $s_p^2 = \dfrac{(n_1 - 1)s_1^2 + (n_2 - 1)s_2^2}{n_1 + n_2 - 2}$. The $t$-statistic has $25 + 30 - 2 = 53$ degrees of freedom. This statistic is appropriate because the populations are normally distributed with unknown variances; because the variances are assumed to be equal, the observations can be pooled to estimate the common variance. The requirement of independent samples for using this statistic has been met.

22. We make the decision either by comparing the calculated test statistic with the critical values or by comparing the $p$-value for the calculated test statistic with the level of significance.

    **A.** The calculated chi-square falls between the two critical values, so we fail to reject the null hypothesis.

    **B.** The $p$-value for the calculated test statistic is less than the level of significance (the 5%), so we reject the null hypothesis.

    **C.** The calculated $F$-statistic falls outside the bounds of the critical $F$-values, so we reject the null hypothesis.

    **D.** The calculated chi-square exceeds the critical value for this right-side test, so we reject the null hypothesis.

23.

    **A.** $H_0: \mu = 0$ versus $H_a: \mu \neq 0$.

    **B.** The $t$-test is based on $t = \dfrac{\bar{X} - \mu_0}{s/\sqrt{n}}$ with $n - 1 = 10 - 1 = 9$ degrees of freedom. At the 0.05 significance level, we reject the null if the calculated $t$-statistic is outside the bounds of $\pm 2.262$ (from the table for 9 degrees of freedom and 0.025 in the right side of the distribution). For Analyst A, we have a calculated test statistic of $t = \dfrac{0.05 - 0}{0.10/\sqrt{10}} = 1.58114$. We, therefore, fail to reject the null hypothesis at the 0.05 level.

    **C.** For Analyst B, the $t$-test is based on $t$ with $15 - 1 = 14$ degrees of freedom. At the 0.05 significance level, we reject the null if the calculated $t$-statistic is outside the bounds of $\pm 2.145$ (from the table for 14 degrees of freedom). The calculated test statistic is $t = \dfrac{0.02 - 0}{0.09/\sqrt{15}} = 0.86066$. Because 0.86066 is within the range of $\pm 2.145$, we fail to reject the null at the 0.05 level.

24.

    **A.** Stating the suspected condition as the alternative hypothesis, we have

    $H_0: \mu_A - \mu_B \leq 0$ versus $H_a: \mu_A - \mu_B > 0$,

    where

    $\mu_A$ = the population mean value of Analyst A's forecast errors

$\mu_B$ = the population mean value of Analyst B's forecast errors

**B.** We have two normally distributed populations with unknown variances. Based on the samples, it is reasonable to assume that the population variances are equal. The samples are assumed to be independent; this assumption is reasonable because the analysts cover different industries. The appropriate test statistic is $t$ using a pooled estimate of the common variance: $t = \dfrac{(\bar{X}_1 - \bar{X}_2) - (\mu_1 - \mu_2)}{\sqrt{\dfrac{s_p^2}{n_1} + \dfrac{s_p^2}{n_2}}}$, where $s_p^2 = \dfrac{(n_1 - 1)s_1^2 + (n_2 - 1)s_2^2}{n_1 + n_2 - 2}$. The number of degrees of freedom is $n_A + n_B - 2 = 10 + 15 - 2 = 23$.

**C.** For df = 23, according to the table, the rejection point for a one-sided (right side) test at the 0.05 significance level is 1.714.

**D.** We first calculate the pooled estimate of variance:
$s_p^2 = \dfrac{(10 - 1)0.01 + (15 - 1)0.0081}{10 + 15 - 2} = 0.0088435.$

We then calculate the $t$-distributed test statistic:

$$t = \dfrac{(0.05 - 0.02) - 0}{\sqrt{\dfrac{0.0088435}{10} + \dfrac{0.0088435}{15}}} = \dfrac{0.03}{0.0383916} = 0.78142.$$

Because 0.78142 < 1.714, we fail to reject the null hypothesis. There is not sufficient evidence to indicate that the mean for Analyst A exceeds that for Analyst B.

25. A is correct. If the population sampled has unknown variance and the sample is large, a $z$-test may be used. Hypotheses involving "greater than" or "less than" postulations are one sided (one tailed). In this situation, the null and alternative hypotheses are stated as $H_0$: $\mu \leq 6\%$ and $H_a$: $\mu > 6\%$, respectively. A one-tailed $t$-test is also acceptable in this case, and the rejection region is on the right side of the distribution.

26. B is correct. The $z$-test is theoretically the correct test to use in those limited cases when testing the population mean of a normally distributed population with known variance.

27. B is correct. A $t$-statistic is the most appropriate for hypothesis tests of the population mean when the variance is unknown and the sample is small but the population is normally distributed.

28. A is correct. The calculated $t$-statistic value of 0.4893 falls within the bounds of the critical $t$-values of ±1.984. Thus, $H_0$ cannot be rejected; the result is not statistically significant at the 0.05 level.

29. B is correct. The assumption that the variances are equal allows for the combining of both samples to obtain a pooled estimate of the common variance.

30.

**A.** We test $H_0$: $\mu_d = 0$ versus $H_a$: $\mu_d \neq 0$, where $\mu_d$ is the population mean difference.

**B.** This is a paired comparisons $t$-test with $n - 1 = 480 - 1 = 479$ degrees of freedom. At the 0.05 significance level, we reject the null hypothesis if the calculated $t$ is less than −1.96 or greater than 1.96.

$$t = \dfrac{\bar{d} - \mu_{d0}}{s_{\bar{d}}} = \dfrac{-0.258 - 0}{3.752/\sqrt{480}} = \dfrac{-0.258}{0.171255} = -1.506529, \text{ or } -1.51.$$

# Solutions

Because the calculated $t$-statistic is between ±1.96, we do not reject the null hypothesis that the mean difference between the returns on the S&P 500 and small-cap stocks during the entire sample period was zero.

**C.** This $t$-test now has $n - 1 = 240 - 1 = 239$ degrees of freedom. At the 0.05 significance level, we reject the null hypothesis if the calculated $t$ is less than $-1.96$ or greater than 1.96.

$$t = \frac{\bar{d} - \mu_{d0}}{s_{\bar{d}}} = \frac{-0.640 - 0}{4.096/\sqrt{240}} = \frac{-0.640}{0.264396} = -2.420615, \text{ or } -2.42.$$

Because $-2.42 < -1.96$, we reject the null hypothesis at the 0.05 significance level. We conclude that during this subperiod, small-cap stocks significantly outperformed the S&P 500.

**D.** This $t$-test has $n - 1 = 240 - 1 = 239$ degrees of freedom. At the 0.05 significance level, we reject the null hypothesis if the calculated $t$-statistic is less than $-1.96$ or greater than 1.96. The calculated test statistic is

$$t = \frac{\bar{d} - \mu_{d0}}{s_{\bar{d}}} = \frac{0.125 - 0}{3.339/\sqrt{240}} = \frac{0.125}{0.215532} = 0.579962, \text{ or } 0.58.$$

At the 0.05 significance level, because the calculated test statistic of 0.58 is between ±1.96, we fail to reject the null hypothesis for the second subperiod.

31. C is correct. A paired comparisons test is appropriate to test the mean differences of two samples believed to be dependent.

32. A is correct. A chi-square test is used for tests concerning the variance of a single normally distributed population.

33.

**A.** We have a "less than" alternative hypothesis, where $\sigma^2$ is the variance of return on the portfolio. The hypotheses are $H_0: \sigma^2 \geq 400$ versus $H_a: \sigma^2 < 400$, where 400 is the hypothesized value of variance, $\sigma_0^2$. This means that the rejection region is on the left side of the distribution.

**B.** The test statistic is chi-square distributed with $10 - 1 = 9$ degrees of freedom: $\chi^2 = \frac{(n-1)s^2}{\sigma_0^2}$.

**C.** The test statistic is calculated as

$$\chi^2 = \frac{(n-1)s^2}{\sigma_0^2} = \frac{9 \times 15^2}{400} = \frac{2{,}025}{400} = 5.0625, \text{ or } 5.06.$$

Because 5.06 is not less than 3.325, we do not reject the null hypothesis; the calculated test statistic falls to the right of the critical value, where the critical value separates the left-side rejection region from the region where we fail to reject.

We can determine the critical value for this test using software:

**Excel** [CHISQ.INV(0.05,9)]
**R** [qchisq(.05,9)]
**Python** [from scipy.stats import chi2 and chi2.ppf(.05,9)]

We can determine the $p$-value for the calculated test statistic of 17.0953 using software:

**Excel** [CHISQ.DIST(5.06,9,TRUE)]

**R** [pchisq(5.06,9,lower.tail=TRUE)]

**Python** [from scipy.stats import chi2 and chi2.cdf(5.06,9)]

34.

**A.** We have a "not equal to" alternative hypothesis:

$$H_0 : \sigma^2_{Before} = \sigma^2_{After} \text{ versus } H_a : \sigma^2_{Before} \neq \sigma^2_{After}$$

**B.** To test a null hypothesis of the equality of two variances, we use an *F*-test:

$$F = \frac{s_1^2}{s_2^2}.$$

$F = 22.367/15.795 = 1.416$, with $120 - 1 = 119$ numerator and $120 - 1 = 119$ denominator degrees of freedom. Because this is a two-tailed test, we use critical values for the $0.05/2 = 0.025$ level. The calculated test statistic falls within the bounds of the critical values (that is, between 0.6969 and 1.4349), so we fail to reject the null hypothesis; there is not enough evidence to indicate that the variances are different before and after the disruption. Note that we could also have formed the *F*-statistic as $15.796/22.367 = 0.706$ and draw the same conclusion.

We could also use software to calculate the critical values:

**Excel** [F.INV(0.025,119,119) and F.INV(0.975,119,119)]

**R** [qf(c(.025,.975),119,119)]

**Python** from scipy.stats import f and f.ppf

[(.025,119,119) and

f.ppf(.975,119,119)]

Additionally, we could use software to calculate the *p*-value of the calculated test statistic, which is 5.896%, and then compare it with the level of significance:

**Excel** [(1-F.DIST(22.367/15.796,119,119,TRUE))*2 or

F.DIST(15.796/22.367,119,119,TRUE)*2]

**R** [(1-pf(22.367/15.796,119,119))*2 or

pf(15.796/22.367,119,119)*2 ]

**Python** from scipy.stats import f and f.cdf

[(15.796/22.367,119,119)*2 or

(1-f.cdf(22.367/15.796,119,119))*2]

35. B is correct. An *F*-test is used to conduct tests concerning the difference between the variances of two normally distributed populations with random independent samples.

# LEARNING MODULE 7

# Appendices

## APPENDICES

**Appendix A**  Cumulative Probabilities for a Standard Normal Distribution
**Appendix B**  Table of the Student's $t$-Distribution (One-Tailed Probabilities)
**Appendix C**  Values of $X^2$ (Degrees of Freedom, Level of Significance)
**Appendix D**  Table of the $F$-Distribution

## Appendix A
## Cumulative Probabilities for a Standard Normal Distribution
$P(Z \leq x) = N(x)$ for $x \geq 0$ or $P(Z \leq z) = N(z)$ for $z \geq 0$

| x or z | 0 | 0.01 | 0.02 | 0.03 | 0.04 | 0.05 | 0.06 | 0.07 | 0.08 | 0.09 |
|---|---|---|---|---|---|---|---|---|---|---|
| 0.00 | 0.5000 | 0.5040 | 0.5080 | 0.5120 | 0.5160 | 0.5199 | 0.5239 | 0.5279 | 0.5319 | 0.5359 |
| 0.10 | 0.5398 | 0.5438 | 0.5478 | 0.5517 | 0.5557 | 0.5596 | 0.5636 | 0.5675 | 0.5714 | 0.5753 |
| 0.20 | 0.5793 | 0.5832 | 0.5871 | 0.5910 | 0.5948 | 0.5987 | 0.6026 | 0.6064 | 0.6103 | 0.6141 |
| 0.30 | 0.6179 | 0.6217 | 0.6255 | 0.6293 | 0.6331 | 0.6368 | 0.6406 | 0.6443 | 0.6480 | 0.6517 |
| 0.40 | 0.6554 | 0.6591 | 0.6628 | 0.6664 | 0.6700 | 0.6736 | 0.6772 | 0.6808 | 0.6844 | 0.6879 |
| 0.50 | 0.6915 | 0.6950 | 0.6985 | 0.7019 | 0.7054 | 0.7088 | 0.7123 | 0.7157 | 0.7190 | 0.7224 |
| 0.60 | 0.7257 | 0.7291 | 0.7324 | 0.7357 | 0.7389 | 0.7422 | 0.7454 | 0.7486 | 0.7517 | 0.7549 |
| 0.70 | 0.7580 | 0.7611 | 0.7642 | 0.7673 | 0.7704 | 0.7734 | 0.7764 | 0.7794 | 0.7823 | 0.7852 |
| 0.80 | 0.7881 | 0.7910 | 0.7939 | 0.7967 | 0.7995 | 0.8023 | 0.8051 | 0.8078 | 0.8106 | 0.8133 |
| 0.90 | 0.8159 | 0.8186 | 0.8212 | 0.8238 | 0.8264 | 0.8289 | 0.8315 | 0.8340 | 0.8365 | 0.8389 |
| 1.00 | 0.8413 | 0.8438 | 0.8461 | 0.8485 | 0.8508 | 0.8531 | 0.8554 | 0.8577 | 0.8599 | 0.8621 |
| 1.10 | 0.8643 | 0.8665 | 0.8686 | 0.8708 | 0.8729 | 0.8749 | 0.8770 | 0.8790 | 0.8810 | 0.8830 |
| 1.20 | 0.8849 | 0.8869 | 0.8888 | 0.8907 | 0.8925 | 0.8944 | 0.8962 | 0.8980 | 0.8997 | 0.9015 |
| 1.30 | 0.9032 | 0.9049 | 0.9066 | 0.9082 | 0.9099 | 0.9115 | 0.9131 | 0.9147 | 0.9162 | 0.9177 |
| 1.40 | 0.9192 | 0.9207 | 0.9222 | 0.9236 | 0.9251 | 0.9265 | 0.9279 | 0.9292 | 0.9306 | 0.9319 |
| 1.50 | 0.9332 | 0.9345 | 0.9357 | 0.9370 | 0.9382 | 0.9394 | 0.9406 | 0.9418 | 0.9429 | 0.9441 |
| 1.60 | 0.9452 | 0.9463 | 0.9474 | 0.9484 | 0.9495 | 0.9505 | 0.9515 | 0.9525 | 0.9535 | 0.9545 |
| 1.70 | 0.9554 | 0.9564 | 0.9573 | 0.9582 | 0.9591 | 0.9599 | 0.9608 | 0.9616 | 0.9625 | 0.9633 |
| 1.80 | 0.9641 | 0.9649 | 0.9656 | 0.9664 | 0.9671 | 0.9678 | 0.9686 | 0.9693 | 0.9699 | 0.9706 |
| 1.90 | 0.9713 | 0.9719 | 0.9726 | 0.9732 | 0.9738 | 0.9744 | 0.9750 | 0.9756 | 0.9761 | 0.9767 |
| 2.00 | 0.9772 | 0.9778 | 0.9783 | 0.9788 | 0.9793 | 0.9798 | 0.9803 | 0.9808 | 0.9812 | 0.9817 |
| 2.10 | 0.9821 | 0.9826 | 0.9830 | 0.9834 | 0.9838 | 0.9842 | 0.9846 | 0.9850 | 0.9854 | 0.9857 |
| 2.20 | 0.9861 | 0.9864 | 0.9868 | 0.9871 | 0.9875 | 0.9878 | 0.9881 | 0.9884 | 0.9887 | 0.9890 |
| 2.30 | 0.9893 | 0.9896 | 0.9898 | 0.9901 | 0.9904 | 0.9906 | 0.9909 | 0.9911 | 0.9913 | 0.9916 |
| 2.40 | 0.9918 | 0.9920 | 0.9922 | 0.9925 | 0.9927 | 0.9929 | 0.9931 | 0.9932 | 0.9934 | 0.9936 |
| 2.50 | 0.9938 | 0.9940 | 0.9941 | 0.9943 | 0.9945 | 0.9946 | 0.9948 | 0.9949 | 0.9951 | 0.9952 |
| 2.60 | 0.9953 | 0.9955 | 0.9956 | 0.9957 | 0.9959 | 0.9960 | 0.9961 | 0.9962 | 0.9963 | 0.9964 |
| 2.70 | 0.9965 | 0.9966 | 0.9967 | 0.9968 | 0.9969 | 0.9970 | 0.9971 | 0.9972 | 0.9973 | 0.9974 |
| 2.80 | 0.9974 | 0.9975 | 0.9976 | 0.9977 | 0.9977 | 0.9978 | 0.9979 | 0.9979 | 0.9980 | 0.9981 |
| 2.90 | 0.9981 | 0.9982 | 0.9982 | 0.9983 | 0.9984 | 0.9984 | 0.9985 | 0.9985 | 0.9986 | 0.9986 |
| 3.00 | 0.9987 | 0.9987 | 0.9987 | 0.9988 | 0.9988 | 0.9989 | 0.9989 | 0.9989 | 0.9990 | 0.9990 |
| 3.10 | 0.9990 | 0.9991 | 0.9991 | 0.9991 | 0.9992 | 0.9992 | 0.9992 | 0.9992 | 0.9993 | 0.9993 |
| 3.20 | 0.9993 | 0.9993 | 0.9994 | 0.9994 | 0.9994 | 0.9994 | 0.9994 | 0.9995 | 0.9995 | 0.9995 |
| 3.30 | 0.9995 | 0.9995 | 0.9995 | 0.9996 | 0.9996 | 0.9996 | 0.9996 | 0.9996 | 0.9996 | 0.9997 |
| 3.40 | 0.9997 | 0.9997 | 0.9997 | 0.9997 | 0.9997 | 0.9997 | 0.9997 | 0.9997 | 0.9997 | 0.9998 |
| 3.50 | 0.9998 | 0.9998 | 0.9998 | 0.9998 | 0.9998 | 0.9998 | 0.9998 | 0.9998 | 0.9998 | 0.9998 |
| 3.60 | 0.9998 | 0.9998 | 0.9999 | 0.9999 | 0.9999 | 0.9999 | 0.9999 | 0.9999 | 0.9999 | 0.9999 |
| 3.70 | 0.9999 | 0.9999 | 0.9999 | 0.9999 | 0.9999 | 0.9999 | 0.9999 | 0.9999 | 0.9999 | 0.9999 |
| 3.80 | 0.9999 | 0.9999 | 0.9999 | 0.9999 | 0.9999 | 0.9999 | 0.9999 | 0.9999 | 0.9999 | 0.9999 |
| 3.90 | 1.0000 | 1.0000 | 1.0000 | 1.0000 | 1.0000 | 1.0000 | 1.0000 | 1.0000 | 1.0000 | 1.0000 |
| 4.00 | 1.0000 | 1.0000 | 1.0000 | 1.0000 | 1.0000 | 1.0000 | 1.0000 | 1.0000 | 1.0000 | 1.0000 |

For example, to find the z-value leaving 2.5 percent of the area/probability in the upper tail, find the element 0.9750 in the body of the table. Read 1.90 at the left end of the element's row and 0.06 at the top of the element's column, to give 1.90 + 0.06 = 1.96. *Table generated with Excel.*

*Quantitative Methods for Investment Analysis*, Second Edition, by Richard A. DeFusco, CFA, Dennis W. McLeavey, CFA, Jerald E. Pinto, CFA, and David E. Runkle, CFA. Copyright © 2004 by CFA Institute.

## Appendix A (continued)
## Cumulative Probabilities for a Standard Normal Distribution
$P(Z \leq x) = N(x)$ for $x \leq 0$ or $P(Z \leq z) = N(z)$ for $z \leq 0$

| x or z | 0 | 0.01 | 0.02 | 0.03 | 0.04 | 0.05 | 0.06 | 0.07 | 0.08 | 0.09 |
|---|---|---|---|---|---|---|---|---|---|---|
| 0.0 | 0.5000 | 0.4960 | 0.4920 | 0.4880 | 0.4840 | 0.4801 | 0.4761 | 0.4721 | 0.4681 | 0.4641 |
| −0.10 | 0.4602 | 0.4562 | 0.4522 | 0.4483 | 0.4443 | 0.4404 | 0.4364 | 0.4325 | 0.4286 | 0.4247 |
| −0.20 | 0.4207 | 0.4168 | 0.4129 | 0.4090 | 0.4052 | 0.4013 | 0.3974 | 0.3936 | 0.3897 | 0.3859 |
| −0.30 | 0.3821 | 0.3783 | 0.3745 | 0.3707 | 0.3669 | 0.3632 | 0.3594 | 0.3557 | 0.3520 | 0.3483 |
| −0.40 | 0.3446 | 0.3409 | 0.3372 | 0.3336 | 0.3300 | 0.3264 | 0.3228 | 0.3192 | 0.3156 | 0.3121 |
| −0.50 | 0.3085 | 0.3050 | 0.3015 | 0.2981 | 0.2946 | 0.2912 | 0.2877 | 0.2843 | 0.2810 | 0.2776 |
| −0.60 | 0.2743 | 0.2709 | 0.2676 | 0.2643 | 0.2611 | 0.2578 | 0.2546 | 0.2514 | 0.2483 | 0.2451 |
| −0.70 | 0.2420 | 0.2389 | 0.2358 | 0.2327 | 0.2296 | 0.2266 | 0.2236 | 0.2206 | 0.2177 | 0.2148 |
| −0.80 | 0.2119 | 0.2090 | 0.2061 | 0.2033 | 0.2005 | 0.1977 | 0.1949 | 0.1922 | 0.1894 | 0.1867 |
| −0.90 | 0.1841 | 0.1814 | 0.1788 | 0.1762 | 0.1736 | 0.1711 | 0.1685 | 0.1660 | 0.1635 | 0.1611 |
| −1.00 | 0.1587 | 0.1562 | 0.1539 | 0.1515 | 0.1492 | 0.1469 | 0.1446 | 0.1423 | 0.1401 | 0.1379 |
| −1.10 | 0.1357 | 0.1335 | 0.1314 | 0.1292 | 0.1271 | 0.1251 | 0.1230 | 0.1210 | 0.1190 | 0.1170 |
| −1.20 | 0.1151 | 0.1131 | 0.1112 | 0.1093 | 0.1075 | 0.1056 | 0.1038 | 0.1020 | 0.1003 | 0.0985 |
| −1.30 | 0.0968 | 0.0951 | 0.0934 | 0.0918 | 0.0901 | 0.0885 | 0.0869 | 0.0853 | 0.0838 | 0.0823 |
| −1.40 | 0.0808 | 0.0793 | 0.0778 | 0.0764 | 0.0749 | 0.0735 | 0.0721 | 0.0708 | 0.0694 | 0.0681 |
| −1.50 | 0.0668 | 0.0655 | 0.0643 | 0.0630 | 0.0618 | 0.0606 | 0.0594 | 0.0582 | 0.0571 | 0.0559 |
| −1.60 | 0.0548 | 0.0537 | 0.0526 | 0.0516 | 0.0505 | 0.0495 | 0.0485 | 0.0475 | 0.0465 | 0.0455 |
| −1.70 | 0.0446 | 0.0436 | 0.0427 | 0.0418 | 0.0409 | 0.0401 | 0.0392 | 0.0384 | 0.0375 | 0.0367 |
| −1.80 | 0.0359 | 0.0351 | 0.0344 | 0.0336 | 0.0329 | 0.0322 | 0.0314 | 0.0307 | 0.0301 | 0.0294 |
| −1.90 | 0.0287 | 0.0281 | 0.0274 | 0.0268 | 0.0262 | 0.0256 | 0.0250 | 0.0244 | 0.0239 | 0.0233 |
| −2.00 | 0.0228 | 0.0222 | 0.0217 | 0.0212 | 0.0207 | 0.0202 | 0.0197 | 0.0192 | 0.0188 | 0.0183 |
| −2.10 | 0.0179 | 0.0174 | 0.0170 | 0.0166 | 0.0162 | 0.0158 | 0.0154 | 0.0150 | 0.0146 | 0.0143 |
| −2.20 | 0.0139 | 0.0136 | 0.0132 | 0.0129 | 0.0125 | 0.0122 | 0.0119 | 0.0116 | 0.0113 | 0.0110 |
| −2.30 | 0.0107 | 0.0104 | 0.0102 | 0.0099 | 0.0096 | 0.0094 | 0.0091 | 0.0089 | 0.0087 | 0.0084 |
| −2.40 | 0.0082 | 0.0080 | 0.0078 | 0.0075 | 0.0073 | 0.0071 | 0.0069 | 0.0068 | 0.0066 | 0.0064 |
| −2.50 | 0.0062 | 0.0060 | 0.0059 | 0.0057 | 0.0055 | 0.0054 | 0.0052 | 0.0051 | 0.0049 | 0.0048 |
| −2.60 | 0.0047 | 0.0045 | 0.0044 | 0.0043 | 0.0041 | 0.0040 | 0.0039 | 0.0038 | 0.0037 | 0.0036 |
| −2.70 | 0.0035 | 0.0034 | 0.0033 | 0.0032 | 0.0031 | 0.0030 | 0.0029 | 0.0028 | 0.0027 | 0.0026 |
| −2.80 | 0.0026 | 0.0025 | 0.0024 | 0.0023 | 0.0023 | 0.0022 | 0.0021 | 0.0021 | 0.0020 | 0.0019 |
| −2.90 | 0.0019 | 0.0018 | 0.0018 | 0.0017 | 0.0016 | 0.0016 | 0.0015 | 0.0015 | 0.0014 | 0.0014 |
| −3.00 | 0.0013 | 0.0013 | 0.0013 | 0.0012 | 0.0012 | 0.0011 | 0.0011 | 0.0011 | 0.0010 | 0.0010 |
| −3.10 | 0.0010 | 0.0009 | 0.0009 | 0.0009 | 0.0008 | 0.0008 | 0.0008 | 0.0008 | 0.0007 | 0.0007 |
| −3.20 | 0.0007 | 0.0007 | 0.0006 | 0.0006 | 0.0006 | 0.0006 | 0.0006 | 0.0005 | 0.0005 | 0.0005 |
| −3.30 | 0.0005 | 0.0005 | 0.0005 | 0.0004 | 0.0004 | 0.0004 | 0.0004 | 0.0004 | 0.0004 | 0.0003 |
| −3.40 | 0.0003 | 0.0003 | 0.0003 | 0.0003 | 0.0003 | 0.0003 | 0.0003 | 0.0003 | 0.0003 | 0.0002 |
| −3.50 | 0.0002 | 0.0002 | 0.0002 | 0.0002 | 0.0002 | 0.0002 | 0.0002 | 0.0002 | 0.0002 | 0.0002 |
| −3.60 | 0.0002 | 0.0002 | 0.0001 | 0.0001 | 0.0001 | 0.0001 | 0.0001 | 0.0001 | 0.0001 | 0.0001 |
| −3.70 | 0.0001 | 0.0001 | 0.0001 | 0.0001 | 0.0001 | 0.0001 | 0.0001 | 0.0001 | 0.0001 | 0.0001 |
| −3.80 | 0.0001 | 0.0001 | 0.0001 | 0.0001 | 0.0001 | 0.0001 | 0.0001 | 0.0001 | 0.0001 | 0.0001 |
| −3.90 | 0.0000 | 0.0000 | 0.0000 | 0.0000 | 0.0000 | 0.0000 | 0.0000 | 0.0000 | 0.0000 | 0.0000 |
| −4.00 | 0.0000 | 0.0000 | 0.0000 | 0.0000 | 0.0000 | 0.0000 | 0.0000 | 0.0000 | 0.0000 | 0.0000 |

For example, to find the z-value leaving 2.5 percent of the area/probability in the lower tail, find the element 0.0250 in the body of the table. Read −1.90 at the left end of the element's row and 0.06 at the top of the element's column, to give −1.90 − 0.06 = −1.96. *Table generated with Excel.*

## Appendix B
## Table of the Student's *t*-Distribution (One-Tailed Probabilities)

| df | p = 0.10 | p = 0.05 | p = 0.025 | p = 0.01 | p = 0.005 | df | p = 0.10 | p = 0.05 | p = 0.025 | p = 0.01 | p = 0.005 |
|---|---|---|---|---|---|---|---|---|---|---|---|
| 1 | 3.078 | 6.314 | 12.706 | 31.821 | 63.657 | 31 | 1.309 | 1.696 | 2.040 | 2.453 | 2.744 |
| 2 | 1.886 | 2.920 | 4.303 | 6.965 | 9.925 | 32 | 1.309 | 1.694 | 2.037 | 2.449 | 2.738 |
| 3 | 1.638 | 2.353 | 3.182 | 4.541 | 5.841 | 33 | 1.308 | 1.692 | 2.035 | 2.445 | 2.733 |
| 4 | 1.533 | 2.132 | 2.776 | 3.747 | 4.604 | 34 | 1.307 | 1.691 | 2.032 | 2.441 | 2.728 |
| 5 | 1.476 | 2.015 | 2.571 | 3.365 | 4.032 | 35 | 1.306 | 1.690 | 2.030 | 2.438 | 2.724 |
| 6 | 1.440 | 1.943 | 2.447 | 3.143 | 3.707 | 36 | 1.306 | 1.688 | 2.028 | 2.434 | 2.719 |
| 7 | 1.415 | 1.895 | 2.365 | 2.998 | 3.499 | 37 | 1.305 | 1.687 | 2.026 | 2.431 | 2.715 |
| 8 | 1.397 | 1.860 | 2.306 | 2.896 | 3.355 | 38 | 1.304 | 1.686 | 2.024 | 2.429 | 2.712 |
| 9 | 1.383 | 1.833 | 2.262 | 2.821 | 3.250 | 39 | 1.304 | 1.685 | 2.023 | 2.426 | 2.708 |
| 10 | 1.372 | 1.812 | 2.228 | 2.764 | 3.169 | 40 | 1.303 | 1.684 | 2.021 | 2.423 | 2.704 |
| 11 | 1.363 | 1.796 | 2.201 | 2.718 | 3.106 | 41 | 1.303 | 1.683 | 2.020 | 2.421 | 2.701 |
| 12 | 1.356 | 1.782 | 2.179 | 2.681 | 3.055 | 42 | 1.302 | 1.682 | 2.018 | 2.418 | 2.698 |
| 13 | 1.350 | 1.771 | 2.160 | 2.650 | 3.012 | 43 | 1.302 | 1.681 | 2.017 | 2.416 | 2.695 |
| 14 | 1.345 | 1.761 | 2.145 | 2.624 | 2.977 | 44 | 1.301 | 1.680 | 2.015 | 2.414 | 2.692 |
| 15 | 1.341 | 1.753 | 2.131 | 2.602 | 2.947 | 45 | 1.301 | 1.679 | 2.014 | 2.412 | 2.690 |
| 16 | 1.337 | 1.746 | 2.120 | 2.583 | 2.921 | 46 | 1.300 | 1.679 | 2.013 | 2.410 | 2.687 |
| 17 | 1.333 | 1.740 | 2.110 | 2.567 | 2.898 | 47 | 1.300 | 1.678 | 2.012 | 2.408 | 2.685 |
| 18 | 1.330 | 1.734 | 2.101 | 2.552 | 2.878 | 48 | 1.299 | 1.677 | 2.011 | 2.407 | 2.682 |
| 19 | 1.328 | 1.729 | 2.093 | 2.539 | 2.861 | 49 | 1.299 | 1.677 | 2.010 | 2.405 | 2.680 |
| 20 | 1.325 | 1.725 | 2.086 | 2.528 | 2.845 | 50 | 1.299 | 1.676 | 2.009 | 2.403 | 2.678 |
| 21 | 1.323 | 1.721 | 2.080 | 2.518 | 2.831 | 60 | 1.296 | 1.671 | 2.000 | 2.390 | 2.660 |
| 22 | 1.321 | 1.717 | 2.074 | 2.508 | 2.819 | 70 | 1.294 | 1.667 | 1.994 | 2.381 | 2.648 |
| 23 | 1.319 | 1.714 | 2.069 | 2.500 | 2.807 | 80 | 1.292 | 1.664 | 1.990 | 2.374 | 2.639 |
| 24 | 1.318 | 1.711 | 2.064 | 2.492 | 2.797 | 90 | 1.291 | 1.662 | 1.987 | 2.368 | 2.632 |
| 25 | 1.316 | 1.708 | 2.060 | 2.485 | 2.787 | 100 | 1.290 | 1.660 | 1.984 | 2.364 | 2.626 |
| 26 | 1.315 | 1.706 | 2.056 | 2.479 | 2.779 | 110 | 1.289 | 1.659 | 1.982 | 2.361 | 2.621 |
| 27 | 1.314 | 1.703 | 2.052 | 2.473 | 2.771 | 120 | 1.289 | 1.658 | 1.980 | 2.358 | 2.617 |
| 28 | 1.313 | 1.701 | 2.048 | 2.467 | 2.763 | 200 | 1.286 | 1.653 | 1.972 | 2.345 | 2.601 |
| 29 | 1.311 | 1.699 | 2.045 | 2.462 | 2.756 | ∞ | 1.282 | 1.645 | 1.960 | 2.326 | 2.576 |
| 30 | 1.310 | 1.697 | 2.042 | 2.457 | 2.750 | | | | | | |

To find a critical *t*-value, enter the table with df and a specified value for $\alpha$, the significance level. For example, with 5 df, $\alpha = 0.05$ and a one-tailed test, the desired probability in the tail would be $p = 0.05$ and the critical *t*-value would be $t(5, 0.05) = 2.015$. With $\alpha = 0.05$ and a two-tailed test, the desired probability in each tail would be $p = 0.025 = \alpha/2$, giving $t(0.025) = 2.571$. Table generated using Excel.

*Quantitative Methods for Investment Analysis*, Second Edition, by Richard A. DeFusco, CFA, Dennis W. McLeavey, CFA, Jerald E. Pinto, CFA, and David E. Runkle, CFA. Copyright © 2004 by CFA Institute.

## Appendix C
## Values of $\chi^2$ (Degrees of Freedom, Level of Significance)

| Degrees of Freedom | Probability in Right Tail | | | | | | | | |
|---|---|---|---|---|---|---|---|---|---|
| | 0.99 | 0.975 | 0.95 | 0.9 | 0.1 | 0.05 | 0.025 | 0.01 | 0.005 |
| 1 | 0.000157 | 0.000982 | 0.003932 | 0.0158 | 2.706 | 3.841 | 5.024 | 6.635 | 7.879 |
| 2 | 0.020100 | 0.050636 | 0.102586 | 0.2107 | 4.605 | 5.991 | 7.378 | 9.210 | 10.597 |
| 3 | 0.1148 | 0.2158 | 0.3518 | 0.5844 | 6.251 | 7.815 | 9.348 | 11.345 | 12.838 |
| 4 | 0.297 | 0.484 | 0.711 | 1.064 | 7.779 | 9.488 | 11.143 | 13.277 | 14.860 |
| 5 | 0.554 | 0.831 | 1.145 | 1.610 | 9.236 | 11.070 | 12.832 | 15.086 | 16.750 |
| 6 | 0.872 | 1.237 | 1.635 | 2.204 | 10.645 | 12.592 | 14.449 | 16.812 | 18.548 |
| 7 | 1.239 | 1.690 | 2.167 | 2.833 | 12.017 | 14.067 | 16.013 | 18.475 | 20.278 |
| 8 | 1.647 | 2.180 | 2.733 | 3.490 | 13.362 | 15.507 | 17.535 | 20.090 | 21.955 |
| 9 | 2.088 | 2.700 | 3.325 | 4.168 | 14.684 | 16.919 | 19.023 | 21.666 | 23.589 |
| 10 | 2.558 | 3.247 | 3.940 | 4.865 | 15.987 | 18.307 | 20.483 | 23.209 | 25.188 |
| 11 | 3.053 | 3.816 | 4.575 | 5.578 | 17.275 | 19.675 | 21.920 | 24.725 | 26.757 |
| 12 | 3.571 | 4.404 | 5.226 | 6.304 | 18.549 | 21.026 | 23.337 | 26.217 | 28.300 |
| 13 | 4.107 | 5.009 | 5.892 | 7.041 | 19.812 | 22.362 | 24.736 | 27.688 | 29.819 |
| 14 | 4.660 | 5.629 | 6.571 | 7.790 | 21.064 | 23.685 | 26.119 | 29.141 | 31.319 |
| 15 | 5.229 | 6.262 | 7.261 | 8.547 | 22.307 | 24.996 | 27.488 | 30.578 | 32.801 |
| 16 | 5.812 | 6.908 | 7.962 | 9.312 | 23.542 | 26.296 | 28.845 | 32.000 | 34.267 |
| 17 | 6.408 | 7.564 | 8.672 | 10.085 | 24.769 | 27.587 | 30.191 | 33.409 | 35.718 |
| 18 | 7.015 | 8.231 | 9.390 | 10.865 | 25.989 | 28.869 | 31.526 | 34.805 | 37.156 |
| 19 | 7.633 | 8.907 | 10.117 | 11.651 | 27.204 | 30.144 | 32.852 | 36.191 | 38.582 |
| 20 | 8.260 | 9.591 | 10.851 | 12.443 | 28.412 | 31.410 | 34.170 | 37.566 | 39.997 |
| 21 | 8.897 | 10.283 | 11.591 | 13.240 | 29.615 | 32.671 | 35.479 | 38.932 | 41.401 |
| 22 | 9.542 | 10.982 | 12.338 | 14.041 | 30.813 | 33.924 | 36.781 | 40.289 | 42.796 |
| 23 | 10.196 | 11.689 | 13.091 | 14.848 | 32.007 | 35.172 | 38.076 | 41.638 | 44.181 |
| 24 | 10.856 | 12.401 | 13.848 | 15.659 | 33.196 | 36.415 | 39.364 | 42.980 | 45.558 |
| 25 | 11.524 | 13.120 | 14.611 | 16.473 | 34.382 | 37.652 | 40.646 | 44.314 | 46.928 |
| 26 | 12.198 | 13.844 | 15.379 | 17.292 | 35.563 | 38.885 | 41.923 | 45.642 | 48.290 |
| 27 | 12.878 | 14.573 | 16.151 | 18.114 | 36.741 | 40.113 | 43.195 | 46.963 | 49.645 |
| 28 | 13.565 | 15.308 | 16.928 | 18.939 | 37.916 | 41.337 | 44.461 | 48.278 | 50.994 |
| 29 | 14.256 | 16.047 | 17.708 | 19.768 | 39.087 | 42.557 | 45.722 | 49.588 | 52.335 |
| 30 | 14.953 | 16.791 | 18.493 | 20.599 | 40.256 | 43.773 | 46.979 | 50.892 | 53.672 |
| 50 | 29.707 | 32.357 | 34.764 | 37.689 | 63.167 | 67.505 | 71.420 | 76.154 | 79.490 |
| 60 | 37.485 | 40.482 | 43.188 | 46.459 | 74.397 | 79.082 | 83.298 | 88.379 | 91.952 |
| 80 | 53.540 | 57.153 | 60.391 | 64.278 | 96.578 | 101.879 | 106.629 | 112.329 | 116.321 |
| 100 | 70.065 | 74.222 | 77.929 | 82.358 | 118.498 | 124.342 | 129.561 | 135.807 | 140.170 |

To have a probability of 0.05 in the right tail when df = 5, the tabled value is $\chi^2(5, 0.05) = 11.070$.

*Quantitative Methods for Investment Analysis*, Second Edition, by Richard A. DeFusco, CFA, Dennis W. McLeavey, CFA, Jerald E. Pinto, CFA, and David E. Runkle, CFA. Copyright © 2004 by CFA Institute.

## Appendix D
## Table of the F-Distribution

**Panel A. Critical values for right-hand tail area equal to 0.05**

| df2:\df1: | 1 | 2 | 3 | 4 | 5 | 6 | 7 | 8 | 9 | 10 | 11 | 12 | 15 | 20 | 21 | 22 | 23 | 24 | 25 | 30 | 40 | 60 | 120 | ∞ |
|---|---|---|---|---|---|---|---|---|---|---|---|---|---|---|---|---|---|---|---|---|---|---|---|---|
| 1 | 161 | 200 | 216 | 225 | 230 | 234 | 237 | 239 | 241 | 242 | 243 | 244 | 246 | 248 | 248 | 249 | 249 | 249 | 249 | 250 | 251 | 252 | 253 | 254 |
| 2 | 18.5 | 19.0 | 19.2 | 19.2 | 19.3 | 19.3 | 19.4 | 19.4 | 19.4 | 19.4 | 19.4 | 19.4 | 19.4 | 19.4 | 19.4 | 19.5 | 19.5 | 19.5 | 19.5 | 19.5 | 19.5 | 19.5 | 19.5 | 19.5 |
| 3 | 10.1 | 9.55 | 9.28 | 9.12 | 9.01 | 8.94 | 8.89 | 8.85 | 8.81 | 8.79 | 8.76 | 8.74 | 8.70 | 8.66 | 8.65 | 8.65 | 8.64 | 8.64 | 8.63 | 8.62 | 8.59 | 8.57 | 8.55 | 8.53 |
| 4 | 7.71 | 6.94 | 6.59 | 6.39 | 6.26 | 6.16 | 6.09 | 6.04 | 6.00 | 5.96 | 5.94 | 5.91 | 5.86 | 5.80 | 5.79 | 5.79 | 5.78 | 5.77 | 5.77 | 5.75 | 5.72 | 5.69 | 5.66 | 5.63 |
| 5 | 6.61 | 5.79 | 5.41 | 5.19 | 5.05 | 4.95 | 4.88 | 4.82 | 4.77 | 4.74 | 4.70 | 4.68 | 4.62 | 4.56 | 4.55 | 4.54 | 4.53 | 4.53 | 4.52 | 4.50 | 4.46 | 4.43 | 4.40 | 4.37 |
| 6 | 5.99 | 5.14 | 4.76 | 4.53 | 4.39 | 4.28 | 4.21 | 4.15 | 4.10 | 4.06 | 4.03 | 4.00 | 3.94 | 3.87 | 3.86 | 3.86 | 3.85 | 3.84 | 3.83 | 3.81 | 3.77 | 3.74 | 3.70 | 3.67 |
| 7 | 5.59 | 4.74 | 4.35 | 4.12 | 3.97 | 3.87 | 3.79 | 3.73 | 3.68 | 3.64 | 3.60 | 3.57 | 3.51 | 3.44 | 3.43 | 3.43 | 3.42 | 3.41 | 3.40 | 3.38 | 3.34 | 3.30 | 3.27 | 3.23 |
| 8 | 5.32 | 4.46 | 4.07 | 3.84 | 3.69 | 3.58 | 3.50 | 3.44 | 3.39 | 3.35 | 3.31 | 3.28 | 3.22 | 3.15 | 3.14 | 3.13 | 3.12 | 3.12 | 3.11 | 3.08 | 3.04 | 3.01 | 2.97 | 2.93 |
| 9 | 5.12 | 4.26 | 3.86 | 3.63 | 3.48 | 3.37 | 3.29 | 3.23 | 3.18 | 3.14 | 3.10 | 3.07 | 3.01 | 2.94 | 2.93 | 2.92 | 2.91 | 2.90 | 2.89 | 2.86 | 2.83 | 2.79 | 2.75 | 2.71 |
| 10 | 4.96 | 4.10 | 3.71 | 3.48 | 3.33 | 3.22 | 3.14 | 3.07 | 3.02 | 2.98 | 2.94 | 2.91 | 2.85 | 2.77 | 2.76 | 2.75 | 2.75 | 2.74 | 2.73 | 2.70 | 2.66 | 2.62 | 2.58 | 2.54 |
| 11 | 4.84 | 3.98 | 3.59 | 3.36 | 3.20 | 3.09 | 3.01 | 2.95 | 2.90 | 2.85 | 2.82 | 2.79 | 2.72 | 2.65 | 2.64 | 2.63 | 2.62 | 2.61 | 2.60 | 2.57 | 2.53 | 2.49 | 2.45 | 2.40 |
| 12 | 4.75 | 3.89 | 3.49 | 3.26 | 3.11 | 3.00 | 2.91 | 2.85 | 2.80 | 2.75 | 2.72 | 2.69 | 2.62 | 2.54 | 2.53 | 2.52 | 2.51 | 2.51 | 2.50 | 2.47 | 2.43 | 2.38 | 2.34 | 2.30 |
| 13 | 4.67 | 3.81 | 3.41 | 3.18 | 3.03 | 2.92 | 2.83 | 2.77 | 2.71 | 2.67 | 2.63 | 2.60 | 2.53 | 2.46 | 2.45 | 2.44 | 2.43 | 2.42 | 2.41 | 2.38 | 2.34 | 2.30 | 2.25 | 2.21 |
| 14 | 4.60 | 3.74 | 3.34 | 3.11 | 2.96 | 2.85 | 2.76 | 2.70 | 2.65 | 2.60 | 2.57 | 2.53 | 2.46 | 2.39 | 2.38 | 2.37 | 2.36 | 2.35 | 2.34 | 2.31 | 2.27 | 2.22 | 2.18 | 2.13 |
| 15 | 4.54 | 3.68 | 3.29 | 3.06 | 2.90 | 2.79 | 2.71 | 2.64 | 2.59 | 2.54 | 2.51 | 2.48 | 2.40 | 2.33 | 2.32 | 2.31 | 2.30 | 2.29 | 2.28 | 2.25 | 2.20 | 2.16 | 2.11 | 2.07 |
| 16 | 4.49 | 3.63 | 3.24 | 3.01 | 2.85 | 2.74 | 2.66 | 2.59 | 2.54 | 2.49 | 2.46 | 2.42 | 2.35 | 2.28 | 2.26 | 2.25 | 2.24 | 2.24 | 2.23 | 2.19 | 2.15 | 2.11 | 2.06 | 2.01 |
| 17 | 4.45 | 3.59 | 3.20 | 2.96 | 2.81 | 2.70 | 2.61 | 2.55 | 2.49 | 2.45 | 2.41 | 2.38 | 2.31 | 2.23 | 2.22 | 2.21 | 2.20 | 2.19 | 2.18 | 2.15 | 2.10 | 2.06 | 2.01 | 1.96 |
| 18 | 4.41 | 3.55 | 3.16 | 2.93 | 2.77 | 2.66 | 2.58 | 2.51 | 2.46 | 2.41 | 2.37 | 2.34 | 2.27 | 2.19 | 2.18 | 2.17 | 2.16 | 2.15 | 2.14 | 2.11 | 2.06 | 2.02 | 1.97 | 1.92 |
| 19 | 4.38 | 3.52 | 3.13 | 2.90 | 2.74 | 2.63 | 2.54 | 2.48 | 2.42 | 2.38 | 2.34 | 2.31 | 2.23 | 2.16 | 2.14 | 2.13 | 2.12 | 2.11 | 2.11 | 2.07 | 2.03 | 1.98 | 1.93 | 1.88 |
| 20 | 4.35 | 3.49 | 3.10 | 2.87 | 2.71 | 2.60 | 2.51 | 2.45 | 2.39 | 2.35 | 2.31 | 2.28 | 2.20 | 2.12 | 2.11 | 2.10 | 2.09 | 2.08 | 2.07 | 2.04 | 1.99 | 1.95 | 1.90 | 1.84 |
| 21 | 4.32 | 3.47 | 3.07 | 2.84 | 2.68 | 2.57 | 2.49 | 2.42 | 2.37 | 2.32 | 2.28 | 2.25 | 2.18 | 2.10 | 2.08 | 2.07 | 2.06 | 2.05 | 2.05 | 2.01 | 1.96 | 1.92 | 1.87 | 1.81 |
| 22 | 4.30 | 3.44 | 3.05 | 2.82 | 2.66 | 2.55 | 2.46 | 2.40 | 2.34 | 2.30 | 2.26 | 2.23 | 2.15 | 2.07 | 2.06 | 2.05 | 2.04 | 2.03 | 2.02 | 1.98 | 1.94 | 1.89 | 1.84 | 1.78 |
| 23 | 4.28 | 3.42 | 3.03 | 2.80 | 2.64 | 2.53 | 2.44 | 2.37 | 2.32 | 2.27 | 2.24 | 2.20 | 2.13 | 2.05 | 2.04 | 2.02 | 2.01 | 2.01 | 2.00 | 1.96 | 1.91 | 1.86 | 1.81 | 1.76 |
| 24 | 4.26 | 3.40 | 3.01 | 2.78 | 2.62 | 2.51 | 2.42 | 2.36 | 2.30 | 2.25 | 2.22 | 2.18 | 2.11 | 2.03 | 2.01 | 2.00 | 1.99 | 1.98 | 1.97 | 1.94 | 1.89 | 1.84 | 1.79 | 1.73 |
| 25 | 4.24 | 3.39 | 2.99 | 2.76 | 2.60 | 2.49 | 2.40 | 2.34 | 2.28 | 2.24 | 2.20 | 2.16 | 2.09 | 2.01 | 2.00 | 1.98 | 1.97 | 1.96 | 1.96 | 1.92 | 1.87 | 1.82 | 1.77 | 1.71 |
| 30 | 4.17 | 3.32 | 2.92 | 2.69 | 2.53 | 2.42 | 2.33 | 2.27 | 2.21 | 2.16 | 2.13 | 2.09 | 2.01 | 1.93 | 1.92 | 1.91 | 1.90 | 1.89 | 1.88 | 1.84 | 1.79 | 1.74 | 1.68 | 1.62 |
| 40 | 4.08 | 3.23 | 2.84 | 2.61 | 2.45 | 2.34 | 2.25 | 2.18 | 2.12 | 2.08 | 2.04 | 2.00 | 1.92 | 1.84 | 1.83 | 1.81 | 1.80 | 1.79 | 1.78 | 1.74 | 1.69 | 1.64 | 1.58 | 1.51 |
| 60 | 4.00 | 3.15 | 2.76 | 2.53 | 2.37 | 2.25 | 2.17 | 2.10 | 2.04 | 1.99 | 1.95 | 1.92 | 1.84 | 1.75 | 1.73 | 1.72 | 1.71 | 1.70 | 1.69 | 1.65 | 1.59 | 1.53 | 1.47 | 1.39 |
| 120 | 3.92 | 3.07 | 2.68 | 2.45 | 2.29 | 2.18 | 2.09 | 2.02 | 1.96 | 1.91 | 1.87 | 1.83 | 1.75 | 1.66 | 1.64 | 1.63 | 1.62 | 1.61 | 1.60 | 1.55 | 1.50 | 1.43 | 1.35 | 1.25 |
| Infinity | 3.84 | 3.00 | 2.60 | 2.37 | 2.21 | 2.10 | 2.01 | 1.94 | 1.88 | 1.83 | 1.79 | 1.75 | 1.67 | 1.57 | 1.56 | 1.54 | 1.53 | 1.52 | 1.51 | 1.46 | 1.39 | 1.32 | 1.22 | 1.00 |

Numerator: $df_1$ and Denominator: $df_2$

## Appendix D (continued)
## Table of the F-Distribution

**Panel B. Critical values for right-hand tail area equal to 0.025**

Numerator: $df_1$ and Denominator: $df_2$

| df1:<br>df2: | 1 | 2 | 3 | 4 | 5 | 6 | 7 | 8 | 9 | 10 | 11 | 12 | 15 | 20 | 21 | 22 | 23 | 24 | 25 | 30 | 40 | 60 | 120 | ∞ |
|---|---|---|---|---|---|---|---|---|---|---|---|---|---|---|---|---|---|---|---|---|---|---|---|---|
| 1 | 648 | 799 | 864 | 900 | 922 | 937 | 948 | 957 | 963 | 969 | 973 | 977 | 985 | 993 | 994 | 995 | 996 | 997 | 998 | 1001 | 1006 | 1010 | 1014 | 1018 |
| 2 | 38.51 | 39.00 | 39.17 | 39.25 | 39.30 | 39.33 | 39.36 | 39.37 | 39.39 | 39.40 | 39.41 | 39.41 | 39.43 | 39.45 | 39.45 | 39.45 | 39.45 | 39.46 | 39.46 | 39.46 | 39.47 | 39.48 | 39.49 | 39.50 |
| 3 | 17.44 | 16.04 | 15.44 | 15.10 | 14.88 | 14.73 | 14.62 | 14.54 | 14.47 | 14.42 | 14.37 | 14.34 | 14.25 | 14.17 | 14.16 | 14.14 | 14.13 | 14.12 | 14.12 | 14.08 | 14.04 | 13.99 | 13.95 | 13.90 |
| 4 | 12.22 | 10.65 | 9.98 | 9.60 | 9.36 | 9.20 | 9.07 | 8.98 | 8.90 | 8.84 | 8.79 | 8.75 | 8.66 | 8.56 | 8.55 | 8.53 | 8.52 | 8.51 | 8.50 | 8.46 | 8.41 | 8.36 | 8.31 | 8.26 |
| 5 | 10.01 | 8.43 | 7.76 | 7.39 | 7.15 | 6.98 | 6.85 | 6.76 | 6.68 | 6.62 | 6.57 | 6.52 | 6.43 | 6.33 | 6.31 | 6.30 | 6.29 | 6.28 | 6.27 | 6.23 | 6.18 | 6.12 | 6.07 | 6.02 |
| 6 | 8.81 | 7.26 | 6.60 | 6.23 | 5.99 | 5.82 | 5.70 | 5.60 | 5.52 | 5.46 | 5.41 | 5.37 | 5.27 | 5.17 | 5.15 | 5.14 | 5.13 | 5.12 | 5.11 | 5.07 | 5.01 | 4.96 | 4.90 | 4.85 |
| 7 | 8.07 | 6.54 | 5.89 | 5.52 | 5.29 | 5.12 | 4.99 | 4.90 | 4.82 | 4.76 | 4.71 | 4.67 | 4.57 | 4.47 | 4.45 | 4.44 | 4.43 | 4.41 | 4.40 | 4.36 | 4.31 | 4.25 | 4.20 | 4.14 |
| 8 | 7.57 | 6.06 | 5.42 | 5.05 | 4.82 | 4.65 | 4.53 | 4.43 | 4.36 | 4.30 | 4.24 | 4.20 | 4.10 | 4.00 | 3.98 | 3.97 | 3.96 | 3.95 | 3.94 | 3.89 | 3.84 | 3.78 | 3.73 | 3.67 |
| 9 | 7.21 | 5.71 | 5.08 | 4.72 | 4.48 | 4.32 | 4.20 | 4.10 | 4.03 | 3.96 | 3.91 | 3.87 | 3.77 | 3.67 | 3.65 | 3.64 | 3.63 | 3.61 | 3.60 | 3.56 | 3.51 | 3.45 | 3.39 | 3.33 |
| 10 | 6.94 | 5.46 | 4.83 | 4.47 | 4.24 | 4.07 | 3.95 | 3.85 | 3.78 | 3.72 | 3.66 | 3.62 | 3.52 | 3.42 | 3.40 | 3.39 | 3.38 | 3.37 | 3.35 | 3.31 | 3.26 | 3.20 | 3.14 | 3.08 |
| 11 | 6.72 | 5.26 | 4.63 | 4.28 | 4.04 | 3.88 | 3.76 | 3.66 | 3.59 | 3.53 | 3.47 | 3.43 | 3.33 | 3.23 | 3.21 | 3.20 | 3.18 | 3.17 | 3.16 | 3.12 | 3.06 | 3.00 | 2.94 | 2.88 |
| 12 | 6.55 | 5.10 | 4.47 | 4.12 | 3.89 | 3.73 | 3.61 | 3.51 | 3.44 | 3.37 | 3.32 | 3.28 | 3.18 | 3.07 | 3.06 | 3.04 | 3.03 | 3.02 | 3.01 | 2.96 | 2.91 | 2.85 | 2.79 | 2.72 |
| 13 | 6.41 | 4.97 | 4.35 | 4.00 | 3.77 | 3.60 | 3.48 | 3.39 | 3.31 | 3.25 | 3.20 | 3.15 | 3.05 | 2.95 | 2.93 | 2.92 | 2.91 | 2.89 | 2.88 | 2.84 | 2.78 | 2.72 | 2.66 | 2.60 |
| 14 | 6.30 | 4.86 | 4.24 | 3.89 | 3.66 | 3.50 | 3.38 | 3.29 | 3.21 | 3.15 | 3.09 | 3.05 | 2.95 | 2.84 | 2.83 | 2.81 | 2.80 | 2.79 | 2.78 | 2.73 | 2.67 | 2.61 | 2.55 | 2.49 |
| 15 | 6.20 | 4.77 | 4.15 | 3.80 | 3.58 | 3.41 | 3.29 | 3.20 | 3.12 | 3.06 | 3.01 | 2.96 | 2.86 | 2.76 | 2.74 | 2.73 | 2.71 | 2.70 | 2.69 | 2.64 | 2.59 | 2.52 | 2.46 | 2.40 |
| 16 | 6.12 | 4.69 | 4.08 | 3.73 | 3.50 | 3.34 | 3.22 | 3.12 | 3.05 | 2.99 | 2.93 | 2.89 | 2.79 | 2.68 | 2.67 | 2.65 | 2.64 | 2.63 | 2.61 | 2.57 | 2.51 | 2.45 | 2.38 | 2.32 |
| 17 | 6.04 | 4.62 | 4.01 | 3.66 | 3.44 | 3.28 | 3.16 | 3.06 | 2.98 | 2.92 | 2.87 | 2.82 | 2.72 | 2.62 | 2.60 | 2.59 | 2.57 | 2.56 | 2.55 | 2.50 | 2.44 | 2.38 | 2.32 | 2.25 |
| 18 | 5.98 | 4.56 | 3.95 | 3.61 | 3.38 | 3.22 | 3.10 | 3.01 | 2.93 | 2.87 | 2.81 | 2.77 | 2.67 | 2.56 | 2.54 | 2.53 | 2.52 | 2.50 | 2.49 | 2.44 | 2.38 | 2.32 | 2.26 | 2.19 |
| 19 | 5.92 | 4.51 | 3.90 | 3.56 | 3.33 | 3.17 | 3.05 | 2.96 | 2.88 | 2.82 | 2.76 | 2.72 | 2.62 | 2.51 | 2.49 | 2.48 | 2.46 | 2.45 | 2.44 | 2.39 | 2.33 | 2.27 | 2.20 | 2.13 |
| 20 | 5.87 | 4.46 | 3.86 | 3.51 | 3.29 | 3.13 | 3.01 | 2.91 | 2.84 | 2.77 | 2.72 | 2.68 | 2.57 | 2.46 | 2.45 | 2.43 | 2.42 | 2.41 | 2.40 | 2.35 | 2.29 | 2.22 | 2.16 | 2.09 |
| 21 | 5.83 | 4.42 | 3.82 | 3.48 | 3.25 | 3.09 | 2.97 | 2.87 | 2.80 | 2.73 | 2.68 | 2.64 | 2.53 | 2.42 | 2.41 | 2.39 | 2.38 | 2.37 | 2.36 | 2.31 | 2.25 | 2.18 | 2.11 | 2.04 |
| 22 | 5.79 | 4.38 | 3.78 | 3.44 | 3.22 | 3.05 | 2.93 | 2.84 | 2.76 | 2.70 | 2.65 | 2.60 | 2.50 | 2.39 | 2.37 | 2.36 | 2.34 | 2.33 | 2.32 | 2.27 | 2.21 | 2.14 | 2.08 | 2.00 |
| 23 | 5.75 | 4.35 | 3.75 | 3.41 | 3.18 | 3.02 | 2.90 | 2.81 | 2.73 | 2.67 | 2.62 | 2.57 | 2.47 | 2.36 | 2.34 | 2.33 | 2.31 | 2.30 | 2.29 | 2.24 | 2.18 | 2.11 | 2.04 | 1.97 |
| 24 | 5.72 | 4.32 | 3.72 | 3.38 | 3.15 | 2.99 | 2.87 | 2.78 | 2.70 | 2.64 | 2.59 | 2.54 | 2.44 | 2.33 | 2.31 | 2.30 | 2.28 | 2.27 | 2.26 | 2.21 | 2.15 | 2.08 | 2.01 | 1.94 |
| 25 | 5.69 | 4.29 | 3.69 | 3.35 | 3.13 | 2.97 | 2.85 | 2.75 | 2.68 | 2.61 | 2.56 | 2.51 | 2.41 | 2.30 | 2.28 | 2.27 | 2.26 | 2.24 | 2.23 | 2.18 | 2.12 | 2.05 | 1.98 | 1.91 |
| 30 | 5.57 | 4.18 | 3.59 | 3.25 | 3.03 | 2.87 | 2.75 | 2.65 | 2.57 | 2.51 | 2.46 | 2.41 | 2.31 | 2.20 | 2.18 | 2.16 | 2.15 | 2.14 | 2.12 | 2.07 | 2.01 | 1.94 | 1.87 | 1.79 |
| 40 | 5.42 | 4.05 | 3.46 | 3.13 | 2.90 | 2.74 | 2.62 | 2.53 | 2.45 | 2.39 | 2.33 | 2.29 | 2.18 | 2.07 | 2.05 | 2.03 | 2.02 | 2.01 | 1.99 | 1.94 | 1.88 | 1.80 | 1.72 | 1.64 |
| 60 | 5.29 | 3.93 | 3.34 | 3.01 | 2.79 | 2.63 | 2.51 | 2.41 | 2.33 | 2.27 | 2.22 | 2.17 | 2.06 | 1.94 | 1.93 | 1.91 | 1.90 | 1.88 | 1.87 | 1.82 | 1.74 | 1.67 | 1.58 | 1.48 |
| 120 | 5.15 | 3.80 | 3.23 | 2.89 | 2.67 | 2.52 | 2.39 | 2.30 | 2.22 | 2.16 | 2.10 | 2.05 | 1.94 | 1.82 | 1.81 | 1.79 | 1.77 | 1.76 | 1.75 | 1.69 | 1.61 | 1.53 | 1.43 | 1.31 |
| Infinity | 5.02 | 3.69 | 3.12 | 2.79 | 2.57 | 2.41 | 2.29 | 2.19 | 2.11 | 2.05 | 1.99 | 1.94 | 1.83 | 1.71 | 1.69 | 1.67 | 1.66 | 1.64 | 1.63 | 1.57 | 1.48 | 1.39 | 1.27 | 1.00 |

## Appendix D (continued)
## Table of the F-Distribution

**Panel C. Critical values for right-hand tail area equal to 0.01**

Numerator: $df_1$ and Denominator: $df_2$

| $df_2$ / $df_1$ | 1 | 2 | 3 | 4 | 5 | 6 | 7 | 8 | 9 | 10 | 11 | 12 | 15 | 20 | 21 | 22 | 23 | 24 | 25 | 30 | 40 | 60 | 120 | ∞ |
|---|---|---|---|---|---|---|---|---|---|---|---|---|---|---|---|---|---|---|---|---|---|---|---|---|
| 1 | 4052 | 5000 | 5403 | 5625 | 5764 | 5859 | 5928 | 5982 | 6023 | 6056 | 6083 | 6106 | 6157 | 6209 | 6216 | 6223 | 6229 | 6235 | 6240 | 6261 | 6287 | 6313 | 6339 | 6366 |
| 2 | 98.5 | 99.0 | 99.2 | 99.2 | 99.3 | 99.3 | 99.4 | 99.4 | 99.4 | 99.4 | 99.4 | 99.4 | 99.4 | 99.4 | 99.5 | 99.5 | 99.5 | 99.5 | 99.5 | 99.5 | 99.5 | 99.5 | 99.5 | 99.5 |
| 3 | 34.1 | 30.8 | 29.5 | 28.7 | 28.2 | 27.9 | 27.7 | 27.5 | 27.3 | 27.2 | 27.1 | 27.1 | 26.9 | 26.7 | 26.7 | 26.6 | 26.6 | 26.6 | 26.6 | 26.5 | 26.4 | 26.3 | 26.2 | 26.1 |
| 4 | 21.2 | 18.0 | 16.7 | 16.0 | 15.5 | 15.2 | 15.0 | 14.8 | 14.7 | 14.5 | 14.5 | 14.4 | 14.2 | 14.0 | 14.0 | 14.0 | 13.9 | 13.9 | 13.9 | 13.8 | 13.7 | 13.7 | 13.6 | 13.5 |
| 5 | 16.3 | 13.3 | 12.1 | 11.4 | 11.0 | 10.7 | 10.5 | 10.3 | 10.2 | 10.1 | 10.0 | 9.89 | 9.72 | 9.55 | 9.53 | 9.51 | 9.49 | 9.47 | 9.45 | 9.38 | 9.29 | 9.20 | 9.11 | 9.02 |
| 6 | 13.7 | 10.9 | 9.78 | 9.15 | 8.75 | 8.47 | 8.26 | 8.10 | 7.98 | 7.87 | 7.79 | 7.72 | 7.56 | 7.40 | 7.37 | 7.35 | 7.33 | 7.31 | 7.30 | 7.23 | 7.14 | 7.06 | 6.97 | 6.88 |
| 7 | 12.2 | 9.55 | 8.45 | 7.85 | 7.46 | 7.19 | 6.99 | 6.84 | 6.72 | 6.62 | 6.54 | 6.47 | 6.31 | 6.16 | 6.13 | 6.11 | 6.09 | 6.07 | 6.06 | 5.99 | 5.91 | 5.82 | 5.74 | 5.65 |
| 8 | 11.3 | 8.65 | 7.59 | 7.01 | 6.63 | 6.37 | 6.18 | 6.03 | 5.91 | 5.81 | 5.73 | 5.67 | 5.52 | 5.36 | 5.34 | 5.32 | 5.30 | 5.28 | 5.26 | 5.20 | 5.12 | 5.03 | 4.95 | 4.86 |
| 9 | 10.6 | 8.02 | 6.99 | 6.42 | 6.06 | 5.80 | 5.61 | 5.47 | 5.35 | 5.26 | 5.18 | 5.11 | 4.96 | 4.81 | 4.79 | 4.77 | 4.75 | 4.73 | 4.71 | 4.65 | 4.57 | 4.48 | 4.40 | 4.31 |
| 10 | 10.0 | 7.56 | 6.55 | 5.99 | 5.64 | 5.39 | 5.20 | 5.06 | 4.94 | 4.85 | 4.77 | 4.71 | 4.56 | 4.41 | 4.38 | 4.36 | 4.34 | 4.33 | 4.31 | 4.25 | 4.17 | 4.08 | 4.00 | 3.91 |
| 11 | 9.65 | 7.21 | 6.22 | 5.67 | 5.32 | 5.07 | 4.89 | 4.74 | 4.63 | 4.54 | 4.46 | 4.40 | 4.25 | 4.10 | 4.08 | 4.06 | 4.04 | 4.02 | 4.01 | 3.94 | 3.86 | 3.78 | 3.69 | 3.60 |
| 12 | 9.33 | 6.93 | 5.95 | 5.41 | 5.06 | 4.82 | 4.64 | 4.50 | 4.39 | 4.30 | 4.22 | 4.16 | 4.01 | 3.86 | 3.84 | 3.82 | 3.80 | 3.78 | 3.76 | 3.70 | 3.62 | 3.54 | 3.45 | 3.36 |
| 13 | 9.07 | 6.70 | 5.74 | 5.21 | 4.86 | 4.62 | 4.44 | 4.30 | 4.19 | 4.10 | 4.02 | 3.96 | 3.82 | 3.66 | 3.64 | 3.62 | 3.60 | 3.59 | 3.57 | 3.51 | 3.43 | 3.34 | 3.25 | 3.17 |
| 14 | 8.86 | 6.51 | 5.56 | 5.04 | 4.70 | 4.46 | 4.28 | 4.14 | 4.03 | 3.94 | 3.86 | 3.80 | 3.66 | 3.51 | 3.48 | 3.46 | 3.44 | 3.43 | 3.41 | 3.35 | 3.27 | 3.18 | 3.09 | 3.00 |
| 15 | 8.68 | 6.36 | 5.42 | 4.89 | 4.56 | 4.32 | 4.14 | 4.00 | 3.89 | 3.80 | 3.73 | 3.67 | 3.52 | 3.37 | 3.35 | 3.33 | 3.31 | 3.29 | 3.28 | 3.21 | 3.13 | 3.05 | 2.96 | 2.87 |
| 16 | 8.53 | 6.23 | 5.29 | 4.77 | 4.44 | 4.20 | 4.03 | 3.89 | 3.78 | 3.69 | 3.62 | 3.55 | 3.41 | 3.26 | 3.24 | 3.22 | 3.20 | 3.18 | 3.16 | 3.10 | 3.02 | 2.93 | 2.84 | 2.75 |
| 17 | 8.40 | 6.11 | 5.19 | 4.67 | 4.34 | 4.10 | 3.93 | 3.79 | 3.68 | 3.59 | 3.52 | 3.46 | 3.31 | 3.16 | 3.14 | 3.12 | 3.10 | 3.08 | 3.07 | 3.00 | 2.92 | 2.83 | 2.75 | 2.65 |
| 18 | 8.29 | 6.01 | 5.09 | 4.58 | 4.25 | 4.01 | 3.84 | 3.71 | 3.60 | 3.51 | 3.43 | 3.37 | 3.23 | 3.08 | 3.05 | 3.03 | 3.02 | 3.00 | 2.98 | 2.92 | 2.84 | 2.75 | 2.66 | 2.57 |
| 19 | 8.19 | 5.93 | 5.01 | 4.50 | 4.17 | 3.94 | 3.77 | 3.63 | 3.52 | 3.43 | 3.36 | 3.30 | 3.15 | 3.00 | 2.98 | 2.96 | 2.94 | 2.92 | 2.91 | 2.84 | 2.76 | 2.67 | 2.58 | 2.49 |
| 20 | 8.10 | 5.85 | 4.94 | 4.43 | 4.10 | 3.87 | 3.70 | 3.56 | 3.46 | 3.37 | 3.29 | 3.23 | 3.09 | 2.94 | 2.92 | 2.90 | 2.88 | 2.86 | 2.84 | 2.78 | 2.69 | 2.61 | 2.52 | 2.42 |
| 21 | 8.02 | 5.78 | 4.87 | 4.37 | 4.04 | 3.81 | 3.64 | 3.51 | 3.40 | 3.31 | 3.24 | 3.17 | 3.03 | 2.88 | 2.86 | 2.84 | 2.82 | 2.80 | 2.79 | 2.72 | 2.64 | 2.55 | 2.46 | 2.36 |
| 22 | 7.95 | 5.72 | 4.82 | 4.31 | 3.99 | 3.76 | 3.59 | 3.45 | 3.35 | 3.26 | 3.18 | 3.12 | 2.98 | 2.83 | 2.81 | 2.78 | 2.77 | 2.75 | 2.73 | 2.67 | 2.58 | 2.50 | 2.40 | 2.31 |
| 23 | 7.88 | 5.66 | 4.76 | 4.26 | 3.94 | 3.71 | 3.54 | 3.41 | 3.30 | 3.21 | 3.14 | 3.07 | 2.93 | 2.78 | 2.76 | 2.74 | 2.72 | 2.70 | 2.69 | 2.62 | 2.54 | 2.45 | 2.35 | 2.26 |
| 24 | 7.82 | 5.61 | 4.72 | 4.22 | 3.90 | 3.67 | 3.50 | 3.36 | 3.26 | 3.17 | 3.09 | 3.03 | 2.89 | 2.74 | 2.72 | 2.70 | 2.68 | 2.66 | 2.64 | 2.58 | 2.49 | 2.40 | 2.31 | 2.21 |
| 25 | 7.77 | 5.57 | 4.68 | 4.18 | 3.86 | 3.63 | 3.46 | 3.32 | 3.22 | 3.13 | 3.06 | 2.99 | 2.85 | 2.70 | 2.68 | 2.66 | 2.64 | 2.62 | 2.60 | 2.53 | 2.45 | 2.36 | 2.27 | 2.17 |
| 30 | 7.56 | 5.39 | 4.51 | 4.02 | 3.70 | 3.47 | 3.30 | 3.17 | 3.07 | 2.98 | 2.91 | 2.84 | 2.70 | 2.55 | 2.53 | 2.51 | 2.49 | 2.47 | 2.45 | 2.39 | 2.30 | 2.21 | 2.11 | 2.01 |
| 40 | 7.31 | 5.18 | 4.31 | 3.83 | 3.51 | 3.29 | 3.12 | 2.99 | 2.89 | 2.80 | 2.73 | 2.66 | 2.52 | 2.37 | 2.35 | 2.33 | 2.31 | 2.29 | 2.27 | 2.20 | 2.11 | 2.02 | 1.92 | 1.80 |
| 60 | 7.08 | 4.98 | 4.13 | 3.65 | 3.34 | 3.12 | 2.95 | 2.82 | 2.72 | 2.63 | 2.56 | 2.50 | 2.35 | 2.20 | 2.17 | 2.15 | 2.13 | 2.12 | 2.10 | 2.03 | 1.94 | 1.84 | 1.73 | 1.60 |
| 120 | 6.85 | 4.79 | 3.95 | 3.48 | 3.17 | 2.96 | 2.79 | 2.66 | 2.56 | 2.47 | 2.40 | 2.34 | 2.19 | 2.03 | 2.01 | 1.99 | 1.97 | 1.95 | 1.93 | 1.86 | 1.76 | 1.66 | 1.53 | 1.38 |
| Infinity | 6.63 | 4.61 | 3.78 | 3.32 | 3.02 | 2.80 | 2.64 | 2.51 | 2.41 | 2.32 | 2.25 | 2.18 | 2.04 | 1.88 | 1.85 | 1.83 | 1.81 | 1.79 | 1.77 | 1.70 | 1.59 | 1.47 | 1.32 | 1.00 |

## Appendix D (continued)
## Table of the F-Distribution

**Panel D. Critical values for right-hand tail area equal to 0.005**

| df1: | 1 | 2 | 3 | 4 | 5 | 6 | 7 | 8 | 9 | 10 | 11 | 12 | 15 | 20 | 21 | 22 | 23 | 24 | 25 | 30 | 40 | 60 | 120 | ∞ |
|---|---|---|---|---|---|---|---|---|---|---|---|---|---|---|---|---|---|---|---|---|---|---|---|---|
| df2: 1 | 16211 | 20000 | 21615 | 22500 | 23056 | 23437 | 23715 | 23925 | 24091 | 24222 | 24334 | 24426 | 24630 | 24836 | 24863 | 24892 | 24915 | 24940 | 24959 | 25044 | 25146 | 25253 | 25359 | 25464 |
| 2 | 198.5 | 199.0 | 199.2 | 199.2 | 199.3 | 199.3 | 199.4 | 199.4 | 199.4 | 199.4 | 199.4 | 199.4 | 199.4 | 199.4 | 199.4 | 199.4 | 199.4 | 199.4 | 199.4 | 199.5 | 199.5 | 199.5 | 199.5 | 200 |
| 3 | 55.55 | 49.80 | 47.47 | 46.20 | 45.39 | 44.84 | 44.43 | 44.13 | 43.88 | 43.68 | 43.52 | 43.39 | 43.08 | 42.78 | 42.73 | 42.69 | 42.66 | 42.62 | 42.59 | 42.47 | 42.31 | 42.15 | 41.99 | 41.83 |
| 4 | 31.33 | 26.28 | 24.26 | 23.15 | 22.46 | 21.98 | 21.62 | 21.35 | 21.14 | 20.97 | 20.82 | 20.70 | 20.44 | 20.17 | 20.13 | 20.09 | 20.06 | 20.03 | 20.00 | 19.89 | 19.75 | 19.61 | 19.47 | 19.32 |
| 5 | 22.78 | 18.31 | 16.53 | 15.56 | 14.94 | 14.51 | 14.20 | 13.96 | 13.77 | 13.62 | 13.49 | 13.38 | 13.15 | 12.90 | 12.87 | 12.84 | 12.81 | 12.78 | 12.76 | 12.66 | 12.53 | 12.40 | 12.27 | 12.14 |
| 6 | 18.63 | 14.54 | 12.92 | 12.03 | 11.46 | 11.07 | 10.79 | 10.57 | 10.39 | 10.25 | 10.13 | 10.03 | 9.81 | 9.59 | 9.56 | 9.53 | 9.50 | 9.47 | 9.45 | 9.36 | 9.24 | 9.12 | 9.00 | 8.88 |
| 7 | 16.24 | 12.40 | 10.88 | 10.05 | 9.52 | 9.16 | 8.89 | 8.68 | 8.51 | 8.38 | 8.27 | 8.18 | 7.97 | 7.75 | 7.72 | 7.69 | 7.67 | 7.64 | 7.62 | 7.53 | 7.42 | 7.31 | 7.19 | 7.08 |
| 8 | 14.69 | 11.04 | 9.60 | 8.81 | 8.30 | 7.95 | 7.69 | 7.50 | 7.34 | 7.21 | 7.10 | 7.01 | 6.81 | 6.61 | 6.58 | 6.55 | 6.53 | 6.50 | 6.48 | 6.40 | 6.29 | 6.18 | 6.06 | 5.95 |
| 9 | 13.61 | 10.11 | 8.72 | 7.96 | 7.47 | 7.13 | 6.88 | 6.69 | 6.54 | 6.42 | 6.31 | 6.23 | 6.03 | 5.83 | 5.80 | 5.78 | 5.75 | 5.73 | 5.71 | 5.62 | 5.52 | 5.41 | 5.30 | 5.19 |
| 10 | 12.83 | 9.43 | 8.08 | 7.34 | 6.87 | 6.54 | 6.30 | 6.12 | 5.97 | 5.85 | 5.75 | 5.66 | 5.47 | 5.27 | 5.25 | 5.22 | 5.20 | 5.17 | 5.15 | 5.07 | 4.97 | 4.86 | 4.75 | 4.64 |
| 11 | 12.23 | 8.91 | 7.60 | 6.88 | 6.42 | 6.10 | 5.86 | 5.68 | 5.54 | 5.42 | 5.32 | 5.24 | 5.05 | 4.86 | 4.83 | 4.80 | 4.78 | 4.76 | 4.74 | 4.65 | 4.55 | 4.45 | 4.34 | 4.23 |
| 12 | 11.75 | 8.51 | 7.23 | 6.52 | 6.07 | 5.76 | 5.52 | 5.35 | 5.20 | 5.09 | 4.99 | 4.91 | 4.72 | 4.53 | 4.50 | 4.48 | 4.45 | 4.43 | 4.41 | 4.33 | 4.23 | 4.12 | 4.01 | 3.90 |
| 13 | 11.37 | 8.19 | 6.93 | 6.23 | 5.79 | 5.48 | 5.25 | 5.08 | 4.94 | 4.82 | 4.72 | 4.64 | 4.46 | 4.27 | 4.24 | 4.22 | 4.19 | 4.17 | 4.15 | 4.07 | 3.97 | 3.87 | 3.76 | 3.65 |
| 14 | 11.06 | 7.92 | 6.68 | 6.00 | 5.56 | 5.26 | 5.03 | 4.86 | 4.72 | 4.60 | 4.51 | 4.43 | 4.25 | 4.06 | 4.03 | 4.01 | 3.98 | 3.96 | 3.94 | 3.86 | 3.76 | 3.66 | 3.55 | 3.44 |
| 15 | 10.80 | 7.70 | 6.48 | 5.80 | 5.37 | 5.07 | 4.85 | 4.67 | 4.54 | 4.42 | 4.33 | 4.25 | 4.07 | 3.88 | 3.86 | 3.83 | 3.81 | 3.79 | 3.77 | 3.69 | 3.59 | 3.48 | 3.37 | 3.26 |
| 16 | 10.58 | 7.51 | 6.30 | 5.64 | 5.21 | 4.91 | 4.69 | 4.52 | 4.38 | 4.27 | 4.18 | 4.10 | 3.92 | 3.73 | 3.71 | 3.68 | 3.66 | 3.64 | 3.62 | 3.54 | 3.44 | 3.33 | 3.22 | 3.11 |
| 17 | 10.38 | 7.35 | 6.16 | 5.50 | 5.07 | 4.78 | 4.56 | 4.39 | 4.25 | 4.14 | 4.05 | 3.97 | 3.79 | 3.61 | 3.58 | 3.56 | 3.53 | 3.51 | 3.49 | 3.41 | 3.31 | 3.21 | 3.10 | 2.98 |
| 18 | 10.22 | 7.21 | 6.03 | 5.37 | 4.96 | 4.66 | 4.44 | 4.28 | 4.14 | 4.03 | 3.94 | 3.86 | 3.68 | 3.50 | 3.47 | 3.45 | 3.42 | 3.40 | 3.38 | 3.30 | 3.20 | 3.10 | 2.99 | 2.87 |
| 19 | 10.07 | 7.09 | 5.92 | 5.27 | 4.85 | 4.56 | 4.34 | 4.18 | 4.04 | 3.93 | 3.84 | 3.76 | 3.59 | 3.40 | 3.37 | 3.35 | 3.33 | 3.31 | 3.29 | 3.21 | 3.11 | 3.00 | 2.89 | 2.78 |
| 20 | 9.94 | 6.99 | 5.82 | 5.17 | 4.76 | 4.47 | 4.26 | 4.09 | 3.96 | 3.85 | 3.76 | 3.68 | 3.50 | 3.32 | 3.29 | 3.27 | 3.24 | 3.22 | 3.20 | 3.12 | 3.02 | 2.92 | 2.81 | 2.69 |
| 21 | 9.83 | 6.89 | 5.73 | 5.09 | 4.68 | 4.39 | 4.18 | 4.01 | 3.88 | 3.77 | 3.68 | 3.60 | 3.43 | 3.24 | 3.22 | 3.19 | 3.17 | 3.15 | 3.13 | 3.05 | 2.95 | 2.84 | 2.73 | 2.61 |
| 22 | 9.73 | 6.81 | 5.65 | 5.02 | 4.61 | 4.32 | 4.11 | 3.94 | 3.81 | 3.70 | 3.61 | 3.54 | 3.36 | 3.18 | 3.15 | 3.12 | 3.10 | 3.08 | 3.06 | 2.98 | 2.88 | 2.77 | 2.66 | 2.55 |
| 23 | 9.63 | 6.73 | 5.58 | 4.95 | 4.54 | 4.26 | 4.05 | 3.88 | 3.75 | 3.64 | 3.55 | 3.47 | 3.30 | 3.12 | 3.09 | 3.06 | 3.04 | 3.02 | 3.00 | 2.92 | 2.82 | 2.71 | 2.60 | 2.48 |
| 24 | 9.55 | 6.66 | 5.52 | 4.89 | 4.49 | 4.20 | 3.99 | 3.83 | 3.69 | 3.59 | 3.50 | 3.42 | 3.25 | 3.06 | 3.04 | 3.01 | 2.99 | 2.97 | 2.95 | 2.87 | 2.77 | 2.66 | 2.55 | 2.43 |
| 25 | 9.48 | 6.60 | 5.46 | 4.84 | 4.43 | 4.15 | 3.94 | 3.78 | 3.64 | 3.54 | 3.45 | 3.37 | 3.20 | 3.01 | 2.99 | 2.96 | 2.94 | 2.92 | 2.90 | 2.82 | 2.72 | 2.61 | 2.50 | 2.38 |
| 30 | 9.18 | 6.35 | 5.24 | 4.62 | 4.23 | 3.95 | 3.74 | 3.58 | 3.45 | 3.34 | 3.25 | 3.18 | 3.01 | 2.82 | 2.80 | 2.77 | 2.75 | 2.73 | 2.71 | 2.63 | 2.52 | 2.42 | 2.30 | 2.18 |
| 40 | 8.83 | 6.07 | 4.98 | 4.37 | 3.99 | 3.71 | 3.51 | 3.35 | 3.22 | 3.12 | 3.03 | 2.95 | 2.78 | 2.60 | 2.57 | 2.55 | 2.52 | 2.50 | 2.48 | 2.40 | 2.30 | 2.18 | 2.06 | 1.93 |
| 60 | 8.49 | 5.79 | 4.73 | 4.14 | 3.76 | 3.49 | 3.29 | 3.13 | 3.01 | 2.90 | 2.82 | 2.74 | 2.57 | 2.39 | 2.36 | 2.33 | 2.31 | 2.29 | 2.27 | 2.19 | 2.08 | 1.96 | 1.83 | 1.69 |
| 120 | 8.18 | 5.54 | 4.50 | 3.92 | 3.55 | 3.28 | 3.09 | 2.93 | 2.81 | 2.71 | 2.62 | 2.54 | 2.37 | 2.19 | 2.16 | 2.13 | 2.11 | 2.09 | 2.07 | 1.98 | 1.87 | 1.75 | 1.61 | 1.43 |
| Infinity | 7.88 | 5.30 | 4.28 | 3.72 | 3.35 | 3.09 | 2.90 | 2.74 | 2.62 | 2.52 | 2.43 | 2.36 | 2.19 | 2.00 | 1.97 | 1.95 | 1.92 | 1.90 | 1.88 | 1.79 | 1.67 | 1.53 | 1.36 | 1.00 |

With 1 degree of freedom (df) in the numerator and 3 df in the denominator, the critical F-value is 10.1 for a right-hand tail area equal to 0.05.

*Quantitative Methods for Investment Analysis*, Second Edition, by Richard A. DeFusco, CFA, Dennis W. McLeavey, CFA, Jerald E. Pinto, CFA, and David E. Runkle, CFA. Copyright © 2004 by CFA Institute.

# Glossary

**A priori probability** A probability based on logical analysis rather than on observation or personal judgment.

**Absolute advantage** A country's ability to produce a good or service at a lower absolute cost than its trading partner.

**Absolute dispersion** The amount of variability present without comparison to any reference point or benchmark.

**Absolute frequency** The actual number of observations counted for each unique value of the variable (also called raw frequency).

**Accelerated methods** Depreciation methods that allocate a relatively large proportion of the cost of an asset to the early years of the asset's useful life.

**Accounts payable** Amounts that a business owes to its vendors for goods and services that were purchased from them but which have not yet been paid.

**Accrued expenses** Liabilities related to expenses that have been incurred but not yet paid as of the end of an accounting period—an example of an accrued expense is rent that has been incurred but not yet paid, resulting in a liability "rent payable." Also called *accrued liabilities*.

**Addition rule for probabilities** A principle stating that the probability that A or B occurs (both occur) equals the probability that A occurs, plus the probability that B occurs, minus the probability that both A and B occur.

**Aggregate demand** The quantity of goods and services that households, businesses, government, and non-domestic customers want to buy at any given level of prices.

**Aggregate demand curve** Inverse relationship between the price level and real output.

**Aggregate income** The value of all the payments earned by the suppliers of factors used in the production of goods and services.

**Aggregate output** The value of all the goods and services produced during a specified period.

**Aggregate supply** The quantity of goods and services producers are willing to supply at any given level of price.

**Aggregate supply curve** The level of domestic output that companies will produce at each price level.

**Alternative hypothesis** The hypothesis that is accepted if the null hypothesis is rejected.

**Amortisation** The process of allocating the cost of intangible long-term assets having a finite useful life to accounting periods; the allocation of the amount of a bond premium or discount to the periods remaining until bond maturity.

**Amortised cost** The historical cost (initially recognised cost) of an asset, adjusted for amortisation and impairment.

**Annual percentage rate** The cost of borrowing expressed as a yearly rate.

**Annuity** A finite set of level sequential cash flows.

**Annuity due** An annuity having a first cash flow that is paid immediately.

**Arithmetic mean** The sum of the observations divided by the number of observations.

**Assets** Resources controlled by an enterprise as a result of past events and from which future economic benefits to the enterprise are expected to flow.

**Autarkic price** The price of a good or service in an autarkic economy.

**Autarky** Countries seeking political self-sufficiency with little or no external trade or finance. State-owned enterprises control strategic domestic industries.

**Available-for-sale** Under US GAAP, debt securities not classified as either held-to-maturity or held-for-trading securities. The investor is willing to sell but not actively planning to sell. In general, available-for-sale debt securities are reported at fair value on the balance sheet, with unrealized gains included as a component of other comprehensive income.

**Average fixed cost** Total fixed cost divided by quantity produced.

**Average product** Measures the productivity of inputs on average and is calculated by dividing total product by the total number of units for a given input that is used to generate that output.

**Average total cost** Total cost divided by quantity produced.

**Average variable cost** Total variable cost divided by quantity produced.

**Back-testing** The process that approximates the real-life investment process, using historical data, to assess whether an investment strategy would have produced desirable results.

**Backfill Bias** A problem whereby certain surviving hedge funds may be added to databases and various hedge fund indexes only after they are initially successful and start to report their returns. Also see *survivorship bias*.

**Balance of payments** A double-entry bookkeeping system that summarizes a country's economic transactions with the rest of the world for a particular period of time, typically a calendar quarter or year.

**Balance of trade deficit** When the domestic economy is spending more on non-domestic goods and services than non-domestic economies are spending on domestic goods and services.

**Balance sheet** The financial statement that presents an entity's current financial position by disclosing resources the entity controls (its assets) and the claims on those resources (its liabilities and equity claims), as of a particular point in time (the date of the balance sheet). Also called *statement of financial position* or *statement of financial condition*.

**Bar chart** A chart for plotting the frequency distribution of categorical data, where each bar represents a distinct category and each bar's height is proportional to the frequency of the corresponding category. In technical analysis, a bar chart that plots four bits of data for each time interval—the high, low, opening, and closing prices. A vertical line connects the high and low prices. A cross-hatch left indicates the opening price and a cross-hatch right indicates the closing price.

**Barter economy** An economy where economic agents as house-holds, corporations, and governments "pay" for goods and services with another good or service.

**Bernoulli random variable** A random variable having the outcomes 0 and 1.

**Bernoulli trial** An experiment that can produce one of two outcomes.

**Bimodal** A distribution that has two most frequently occurring values.

**Binomial random variable** The number of successes in $n$ Bernoulli trials for which the probability of success is constant for all trials and the trials are independent.

**Binomial tree** The graphical representation of a model of asset price dynamics in which, at each period, the asset moves up with probability $p$ or down with probability $(1 − p)$.

**Bottom-up analysis** An investment selection approach that focuses on company-specific circumstances rather than emphasizing economic cycles or industry analysis.

**Box and whisker plot** A graphic for visualizing the dispersion of data across quartiles. It consists of a "box" with "whiskers" connected to the box.

**Broad money** Encompasses narrow money plus the entire range of liquid assets that can be used to make purchases.

**Bubble line chart** A line chart that uses varying-sized bubbles to represent a third dimension of the data. The bubbles are sometimes color-coded to present additional information.

**Capital account** A component of the balance of payments account that measures transfers of capital.

**Capital consumption allowance** A measure of the wear and tear (depreciation) of the capital stock that occurs in the production of goods and services.

**Capital deepening investment** Increases the stock of capital relative to labor.

**Capital stock** The accumulated amount of buildings, machinery, and equipment used to produce goods and services.

**Cash flow additivity principle** The principle that dollar amounts indexed at the same point in time are additive.

**Cash flow from operating activities** The net amount of cash provided from operating activities.

**Cash flow from operations** a cash profit measure over a period for an issuer's primary business activities. It includes cash from customers as well as interest and dividends received from financial investments, less cash paid to employees and suppliers as well as taxes paid to governments and interest paid to lenders.

**Categorical data** Values that describe a quality or characteristic of a group of observations and therefore can be used as labels to divide a dataset into groups to summarize and visualize (also called **qualitative data**).

**Central banks** The dominant bank in a country, usually with official or semi-official governmental status.

**Central limit theorem** The theorem that states the sum (and the mean) of a set of independent, identically distributed random variables with finite variances is normally distributed, whatever distribution the random variables follow.

**Classified balance sheet** A balance sheet organized so as to group together the various assets and liabilities into subcategories (e.g., current and noncurrent).

**Closed economy** An economy that does not trade with other countries; an *autarkic economy*.

**Clustered bar chart** See *grouped bar chart*.

**Coefficient of variation** The ratio of a set of observations' standard deviation to the observations' mean value.

**Combination** A listing in which the order of the listed items does not matter.

**Combination Formula (Binomial Formula)** The number of ways that we can choose $r$ objects from a total of $n$ objects, when the order in which the $r$ objects are listed does not matter, is $_nC_r = \binom{n}{r} = \frac{n!}{(n-r)!\,r!}$.

**Comparative advantage** A country's ability to produce a good or service at a lower relative cost, or opportunity cost, than its trading partner.

**Complement** The event not-S, written $S^C$, given the event S. Note that $P(S) + P(S^C) = 1$.

**Complements** Goods that tend to be used together; technically, two goods whose cross-price elasticity of demand is negative.

**Compounding** The process of accumulating interest on interest.

**Comprehensive income** All changes in equity other than contributions by, and distributions to, owners; income under clean surplus accounting; includes all changes in equity during a period except those resulting from investments by owners and distributions to owners. Comprehensive income equals net income plus other comprehensive income.

**Conditional probability** The probability of an event given (conditioned on) another event.

**Confidence level** The complement of the level of significance.

**Confusion matrix** A grid used for error analysis in classification problems, it presents values for four evaluation metrics including true positive (TP), false positive (FP), true negative (TN), and false negative (FN).

**Consumer surplus** The difference between the value that a consumer places on units purchased and the amount of money that was required to pay for them.

**Contingency table** A table of the frequency distribution of observations classified on the basis of two discrete variables.

**Continuous data** Data that can be measured and can take on any numerical value in a specified range of values.

**Continuous random variable** A random variable for which the range of possible outcomes is the real line (all real numbers between $-\infty$ and $+\infty$) or some subset of the real line.

**Contra account** An account that offsets another account.

**Convergence** The tendency for differences in output per capita across countries to diminish over time. In technical analysis, the term describes the case when an indicator moves in the same manner as the security being analyzed.

**Core inflation** Refers to the inflation rate calculated based on a price index of goods and services except food and energy.

**cost averaging** The periodic investment of a fixed amount of money.

**Coupon rate** The interest rate promised in a contract; this is the rate used to calculate the periodic interest payments.

**Credit analysis** The evaluation of credit risk; the evaluation of the creditworthiness of a borrower or counterparty.

**credit risk** the expected economic loss under a potential borrower default over the life of the contract

**Critical values** Values of the test statistic at which the decision changes from fail to reject the null hypothesis to reject the null hypothesis.

**Cross-price elasticity of demand** The percentage change in quantity demanded for a given percentage change in the price of another good; the responsiveness of the demand for Product A that is associated with the change in price of Product B.

**Cross-sectional data** A list of the observations of a specific variable from multiple observational units at a given point in time. The observational units can be individuals, groups, companies, trading markets, regions, etc.

**Cumulative absolute frequency** Cumulates (i.e., adds up) in a frequency distribution the absolute frequencies as one moves from the first bin to the last bin.

**Cumulative distribution function** A function giving the probability that a random variable is less than or equal to a specified value.

**Cumulative frequency distribution chart** A chart that plots either the cumulative absolute frequency or the cumulative relative frequency on the $y$-axis against the upper limit of the interval and allows one to see the number or the percentage of the observations that lie below a certain value.

**Cumulative relative frequency** A sequence of partial sums of the relative frequencies in a frequency distribution.

**Current account** A component of the balance of payments account that measures the flow of goods and services.

**Current assets** Assets that are expected to be consumed or converted into cash in the near future, typically one year or less. *Also called liquid assets.*

**Current cost** With reference to assets, the amount of cash or cash equivalents that would have to be paid to buy the same or an equivalent asset today; with reference to liabilities, the undiscounted amount of cash or cash equivalents that would be required to settle the obligation today.

**Current liabilities** Short-term obligations, such as accounts payable, wages payable, or accrued liabilities, that are expected to be settled in the near future, typically one year or less.

**Cyclical companies** Companies with sales and profits that regularly expand and contract with the business cycle or state of economy.

**Data** A collection of numbers, characters, words, and text—as well as images, audio, and video—in a raw or organized format to represent facts or information.

**Data snooping** The practice of determining a model by extensive searching through a dataset for statistically significant patterns.

**Data table** see **two-dimensional rectangular array**.

**Days of inventory on hand** An activity ratio equal to the number of days in the period divided by inventory turnover over the period.

**Dealing securities** Securities held by banks or other financial intermediaries for trading purposes.

**Deciles** Quantiles that divide a distribution into 10 equal parts.

**default risk premium** n extra return that compensates investors for the possibility that the borrower will fail to make a promised payment at the contracted time and in the contracted amount.

**Defensive companies** Companies with sales and profits that have little sensitivity to the business cycle or state of the economy.

**Deferred income** A liability account for money that has been collected for goods or services that have not yet been delivered; payment received in advance of providing a good or service.

**Deferred revenue** A liability account for money that has been collected for goods or services that have not yet been delivered; payment received in advance of providing a good or service.

**Deferred tax assets** A balance sheet asset that arises when an excess amount is paid for income taxes relative to accounting profit. The taxable income is higher than accounting profit and income tax payable exceeds tax expense. The company expects to recover the difference during the course of future operations when tax expense exceeds income tax payable.

**Degree of confidence** The probability that a confidence interval includes the unknown population parameter.

**Degrees of freedom** The number of independent variables used in defining sample statistics, such as variance, and the probability distributions they measure.

**Demand curve** Graph of the inverse demand function. A graph showing the demand relation, either the highest quantity willingly purchased at each price or the highest price willingly paid for each quantity.

**Demand function** A relationship that expresses the quantity demanded of a good or service as a function of own-price and possibly other variables.

**Dependent** With reference to events, the property that the probability of one event occurring depends on (is related to) the occurrence of another event.

**Depreciation** The process of systematically allocating the cost of long-lived (tangible) assets to the periods during which the assets are expected to provide economic benefits.

**Descriptive statistics** The study of how data can be summarized effectively.

**Diluted shares** The number of shares that would be outstanding if all potentially dilutive claims on common shares (e.g., convertible debt, convertible preferred stock, and employee stock options) were exercised.

**Diminishing balance method** An accelerated depreciation method, i.e., one that allocates a relatively large proportion of the cost of an asset to the early years of the asset's useful life.

**Diminishing marginal productivity** When each additional unit of an input, keeping the other inputs unchanged, increases output by a smaller increment.

**Direct format** With reference to the cash flow statement, a format for the presentation of the statement in which cash flow from operating activities is shown as operating cash receipts less operating cash disbursements. Also called *direct method*.

**Direct method** See *direct format*.

**Direct write-off method** An approach to recognizing credit losses on customer receivables in which the company waits until such time as a customer has defaulted and only then recognizes the loss.

**Discount** To reduce the value of a future payment in allowance for how far away it is in time; to calculate the present value of some future amount. Also, the amount by which an instrument is priced below its face value.

**Discouraged worker** A person who has stopped looking for a job or has given up seeking employment.

**Discrete data** Numerical values that result from a counting process; therefore, practically speaking, the data are limited to a finite number of values.

**Discrete random variable** A random variable that can take on at most a countable number of possible values.

**Dispersion** The variability of a population or sample of observations around the central tendency.

**Double declining balance depreciation** An accelerated depreciation method that involves depreciating the asset at double the straight-line rate. This rate is multiplied by the book value of the asset at the beginning of the period (a declining balance) to calculate depreciation expense.

**Down transition probability** The probability that an asset's value moves down in a model of asset price dynamics.

**Downside risk**  Risk of incurring returns below a specified value.

**Dutch Book Theorem**  A result in probability theory stating that inconsistent probabilities create profit opportunities.

**Economic costs**  All the remuneration needed to keep a productive resource in its current employment or to acquire the resource for productive use; the sum of total accounting costs and implicit opportunity costs.

**Economic profit**  Equal to accounting profit less the implicit opportunity costs not included in total accounting costs; the difference between total revenue (TR) and total cost (TC). Also called *abnormal profit* or *supernormal profit*.

**Effective annual rate**  An interest rate with a periodicity of one.

**Effective interest rate**  The borrowing rate or market rate that a company incurs at the time of issuance of a bond.

**Elastic**  Said of a good or service when the magnitude of elasticity is greater than one.

**Elasticity**  The percentage change in one variable for a percentage change in another variable; a general measure of how sensitive one variable is to a change in the value of another variable.

**Elasticity of demand**  A measure of the sensitivity of quantity demanded to a change in a product's own price: $\%\Delta Q^D/\%\Delta P$.

**Elasticity of supply**  A measure of the sensitivity of quantity supplied to a change in price: $\%\Delta Q^S/\%\Delta P$.

**Empirical probability**  The probability of an event estimated as a relative frequency of occurrence.

**Employed**  The number of people with a job.

**Equity**  Ownership interest in an entity. A residual claim on the assets of an entity after more senior claims, such as debt, have been satisfied. Also known as *net assets*.

**Estimate**  The particular value calculated from sample observations using an estimator.

**Estimator**  An estimation formula; the formula used to compute the sample mean and other sample statistics are examples of estimators.

**Event**  Any outcome or specified set of outcomes of a random variable.

**Exhaustive**  An index construction strategy that selects every constituent of a universe.

**Expected inflation**  The level of inflation that economic agents expect in the future.

**Expenses**  Outflows of economic resources or increases in liabilities that result in decreases in equity (other than decreases because of distributions to owners); reductions in net assets associated with the creation of revenues.

**Exports**  Goods and services that an economy sells to other countries.

**Externalities**  This term refers to situations where the production or consumption of goods and services creates costs or benefits for others that are not reflected in the prices charged for them. In other words, externalities include the consumption, production, and investment decisions of firms (and individuals) that affect people not directly involved in the transactions. Externalities can be either negative or positive.

**Face value**  The amount of principal on a bond, also known as par value.

**Fair value**  A market-based measure of an investment based on observable or derived assumptions to determine a price that market participants would use to exchange an asset or liability in an orderly transaction at a specific time.

**False discovery approach**  An adjustment in the *p*-values for tests performed multiple times.

**False discovery rate**  The rate of Type I errors in testing a null hypothesis multiple times for a given level of significance.

**Finance lease**  A type of lease which is more akin to the purchase or sale of the underlying asset.

**Financial account**  A component of the balance of payments account that records investment flows.

**Financial flexibility**  The ability to react and adapt to financial adversity and opportunities.

**Financing activities**  Activities related to obtaining or repaying capital to be used in the business (e.g., equity and long-term debt).

**First-degree price discrimination**  Where a monopolist is able to charge each customer the highest price the customer is willing to pay.

**Fiscal policy**  The use of taxes and government spending to affect the level of aggregate expenditures.

**Fisher effect**  The thesis that the real rate of interest in an economy is stable over time so that changes in nominal interest rates are the result of changes in expected inflation.

**Foreign direct investment**  Direct investment by a firm in one country (the source country) in productive assets in a foreign country (the host country).

**Foreign portfolio investment**  Shorter-term investment by individuals, firms, and institutional investors (e.g., pension funds) in foreign financial instruments such as foreign stocks and foreign government bonds.

**Fractile**  A value at or below which a stated fraction of the data lies. Also called quantile.

**Fractional reserve banking**  Banking in which reserves constitute a fraction of deposits.

**Free trade**  When there are no government restrictions on a country's ability to trade.

**Frequency distribution**  A tabular display of data constructed either by counting the observations of a variable by distinct values or groups or by tallying the values of a numerical variable into a set of numerically ordered bins (also called a one-way table).

**Frequency polygon**  A graph of a frequency distribution obtained by drawing straight lines joining successive points representing the class frequencies.

**Future value (FV)**  The amount to which a payment or series of payments will grow by a stated future date.

**FX swap**  The combination of a spot and a forward FX transaction.

**Gains**  Asset inflows not directly related to the ordinary activities of the business.

**GDP deflator**  A gauge of prices and inflation that measures the aggregate changes in prices across the overall economy.

**Geometric mean**  A measure of central tendency computed by taking the *n*th root of the product of *n* non-negative values.

**Goodwill**  An intangible asset that represents the excess of the purchase price of an acquired company over the value of the net assets acquired.

**Gross domestic product**  The market value of all final goods and services produced within the economy during a given period (output definition) or, equivalently, the aggregate income earned by all households, all companies, and the government within the economy during a given period (income definition).

**Gross margin**  Sales minus the cost of sales (i.e., the cost of goods sold for a manufacturing company).

**Gross profit**  Sales minus the cost of sales (i.e., the cost of goods sold for a manufacturing company).

**Gross profit margin**  The ratio of gross profit to revenues.

**Grouped bar chart**  A bar chart for showing joint frequencies for two categorical variables (also known as a **clustered bar chart**).

**Grouping by function**  With reference to the presentation of expenses in an income statement, the grouping together of expenses serving the same function, e.g. all items that are costs of goods sold.

**Grouping by nature**  With reference to the presentation of expenses in an income statement, the grouping together of expenses by similar nature, e.g., all depreciation expenses.

**Growth investors**  With reference to equity investors, investors who seek to invest in high-earnings-growth companies.

**harmonic mean**  A type of weighted mean computed as the reciprocal of the arithmetic average of the reciprocals.

**Headline inflation**  Refers to the inflation rate calculated based on the price index that includes all goods and services in an economy.

**Heat map**  A type of graphic that organizes and summarizes data in a tabular format and represents it using a color spectrum.

**Histogram**  A chart that presents the distribution of numerical data by using the height of a bar or column to represent the absolute frequency of each bin or interval in the distribution.

**Historical cost**  In reference to assets, the amount paid to purchase an asset, including any costs of acquisition and/or preparation; with reference to liabilities, the amount of proceeds received in exchange in issuing the liability.

**Hypothesis**  A proposed explanation or theory that can be tested.

**Hypothesis testing**  The process of testing of hypotheses about one or more populations using statistical inference.

**Implicit price deflator for GDP**  A gauge of prices and inflation that measures the aggregate changes in prices across the overall economy.

**Implicit selection bias**  One type of selection bias introduced through the presence of a threshold that filters out some unqualified members.

**Imports**  Goods and services that a domestic economy (i.e., house-holds, firms, and government) purchases from other countries.

**Income**  Increases in economic benefits in the form of inflows or enhancements of assets, or decreases of liabilities that result in an increase in equity (other than increases resulting from contributions by owners).

**Income elasticity of demand**  A measure of the responsiveness of demand to changes in income, defined as the percentage change in quantity demanded divided by the percentage change in income.

**Income tax payable**  The income tax owed by the company on the basis of taxable income.

**Increasing marginal returns**  When the marginal product of a resource increases as additional units of that input are employed.

**Independent**  With reference to events, the property that the occurrence of one event does not affect the probability of another event occurring. With reference to two random variables $X$ and $Y$, they are independent if and only if $P(X,Y) = P(X)P(Y)$.

**Indirect format**  With reference to cash flow statements, a format for the presentation of the statement which, in the operating cash flow section, begins with net income then shows additions and subtractions to arrive at operating cash flow. Also called *indirect method*.

**Indirect method**  See *indirect format*.

**Inelastic**  Said of a good or service when the magnitude of elasticity is less than one. Insensitive to price changes.

**Inferior goods**  A good whose consumption decreases as income increases.

**Inflation**  The percentage increase in the general price level from one period to the next; a sustained rise in the overall level of prices in an economy.

**inflation premium**  An extra return that compensates investors for expected inflation.

**Inflation uncertainty**  The degree to which economic agents view future rates of inflation as difficult to forecast.

**Input productivity**  The amount of output produced by workers in a given period of time—for example, output per hour worked; measures the efficiency of labor.

**Intangible assets**  Assets without a physical form, such as patents and trademarks.

**Interest**  Payment for lending funds.

**Interest rate**  A rate of return that reflects the relationship between differently dated cash flows; a discount rate.

**Interest rate effect**  The effect through which price level changes, through demand for money, impact interest rate, which in turn impacts investment and consumption.

**Interquartile range**  The difference between the third and first quartiles of a dataset.

**Interval**  With reference to grouped data, a set of values within which an observation falls.

**Inventory investment**  Net change in business inventory.

**Inventory turnover**  An activity ratio calculated as cost of goods sold divided by average inventory.

**Inverse demand function**  A restatement of the demand function in which price is stated as a function of quantity.

**Investing activities**  Activities associated with the acquisition and disposal of property, plant, and equipment; intangible assets; other long-term assets; and both long-term and short-term investments in the equity and debt (bonds and loans) issued by other companies.

**Investment property**  Property used to earn rental income or capital appreciation (or both).

**Joint frequencies**  The entry in the cells of the contingency table that represent the joining of one variable from a row and the other variable from a column to count observations.

**Joint probability**  The probability of the joint occurrence of stated events.

**Labor force**  Everyone of working age (ages 16 to 64) who either is employed or is available for work but not working.

**Labor productivity**  The quantity of goods and services (real GDP) that a worker can produce in one hour of work.

**Law of demand**  The principle that as the price of a good rises, buyers will choose to buy less of it, and as its price falls, they will buy more.

**Law of diminishing marginal returns**  The observation that a variable factor's marginal product must eventually fall as more of it is added to a fixed amount of the other factors.

**Law of diminishing returns**  The smallest output that a firm can produce such that its long run average costs are minimized.

**Level of significance**  The probability of a Type I error in testing a hypothesis.

**Liabilities** Present obligations of an enterprise arising from past events, the settlement of which is expected to result in an outflow of resources embodying economic benefits; creditors' claims on the resources of a company.

**LIFO reserve** The difference between the reported LIFO inventory carrying amount and the inventory amount that would have been reported if the FIFO method had been used (in other words, the FIFO inventory value less the LIFO inventory value).

**Line chart** A type of graph used to visualize ordered observations. In technical analysis, a plot of price data, typically closing prices, with a line connecting the points.

**Linear interpolation** The estimation of an unknown value on the basis of two known values that bracket it, using a straight line between the two known values.

**Liquidity** a characteristic of an asset or a liability that reflects its nearness to cash or settlement.

**liquidity premium** An extra return that compensates investors for the risk of loss relative to an investment's fair value if the investment needs to be converted to cash quickly.

**Long-lived assets** Assets that are expected to provide economic benefits over a future period of time, typically greater than one year. Also called *long-term assets*.

**Look-ahead bias** A bias caused by using information that was unavailable on the test date.

**Losses** Asset outflows not directly related to the ordinary activities of the business.

**Macroeconomics** The branch of economics that deals with aggregate economic quantities, such as national output and national income.

**Marginal cost** The cost of producing an additional unit of a good.

**Marginal frequencies** The sums determined by adding joint frequencies across rows or across columns in a contingency table.

**Marginal product** Measures the productivity of each unit of input and is calculated by taking the difference in total product from adding another unit of input (assuming other resource quantities are held constant).

**Marginal propensity to consume** The proportion of an additional unit of disposable income that is consumed or spent; the change in consumption for a small change in income.

**Marginal propensity to save** The proportion of an additional unit of disposable income that is saved (not spent).

**Marginal revenue** The change in total revenue divided by the change in quantity sold; simply, the additional revenue from selling one more unit.

**Marginal value curve** A curve describing the highest price consumers are willing to pay for each additional unit of a good.

**Market rate of interest** The rate demanded by purchasers of bonds, given the risks associated with future cash payment obligations of the particular bond issue.

**Market-oriented investors** With reference to equity investors, investors whose investment disciplines cannot be clearly categorized as value or growth.

**maturity premium** An extra return that compensates investors for the increased sensitivity of the market value of debt to a change in market interest rates as maturity is extended.

**Mean absolute deviation** With reference to a sample, the mean of the absolute values of deviations from the sample mean.

**Measure of central tendency** A quantitative measure that specifies where data are centered.

**Measure of value** A standard for measuring value; a function of money.

**Measures of location** Quantitative measures that describe the location or distribution of data. They include not only measures of central tendency but also other measures, such as percentiles.

**Median** The value of the middle item of a set of items that has been sorted into ascending or descending order (i.e., the 50th percentile).

**Medium of exchange** Any asset that can be used to purchase goods and services or to repay debts; a function of money.

**Microeconomics** The branch of economics that deals with markets and decision making of individual economic units, including consumers and businesses.

**Modal interval** With reference to grouped data, the interval containing the greatest number of observations (i.e., highest frequency).

**Mode** The most frequently occurring value in a distribution.

**Monetarists** Economists who believe that the rate of growth of the money supply is the primary determinant of the rate of inflation.

**Monetary policy** Actions taken by a nation's central bank to affect aggregate output and prices through changes in bank reserves, reserve requirements, or its target interest rate.

**Money** A generally accepted medium of exchange and unit of account.

**Money creation** The process by which changes in bank reserves translate into changes in the money supply.

**Money multiplier** Describes how a change in reserves is expected to affect the money supply; in its simplest form, 1 divided by the reserve requirement.

**Money neutrality** The thesis that an increase in the money supply leads in the long-run to an increase in the price level, while leaving real variables like output and employment unaffected.

**Multi-step format** With respect to the format of the income statement, a format that presents a subtotal for gross profit (revenue minus cost of goods sold).

**Multinational corporation** A company operating in more than one country or having subsidiary firms in more than one country.

**Multinomial formula (general formula for labeling problems)** The number of ways that $n$ objects can be labeled with $k$ different labels, with $n_1$ of the first type, $n_2$ of the second type, and so on, with $n_1 + n_2 + ... + n_k = n$, is given by $\frac{n!}{n_1! n_2! ... n_k!}$.

**Multiple testing problem** The risk of getting statistically significant test results when performing a test multiple times.

**Multiplication rule for counting** If one task can be done in $n_1$ ways, and a second task, given the first, can be done in $n_2$ ways, and a third task, given the first two tasks, can be done in $n_3$ ways, and so on for $k$ tasks, then the number of ways the $k$ tasks can be done is $(n_1)(n_2)(n_3) ... (n_k)$.

**Multiplication rule for independent events** The rule that when two events are independent, the joint probability of $A$ and $B$ equals the product of the individual probabilities of $A$ and $B$.

**Multiplication rule for probability** The rule that the joint probability of events $A$ and $B$ equals the probability of $A$ given $B$ times the probability of $B$.

**Multivariate distribution** A probability distribution that specifies the probabilities for a group of related random variables.

**Multivariate normal distribution** A probability distribution for a group of random variables that is completely defined by the means and variances of the variables plus all the correlations between pairs of the variables.

**Mutually exclusive** Indicates that only one event can occur at a time.

**n Factorial** For a positive integer $n$, the product of the first $n$ positive integers; 0 factorial equals 1 by definition. $n$ factorial is written as $n!$.

**Narrow money** The notes and coins in circulation in an economy, plus other very highly liquid deposits.

**Natural rate of unemployment** Effective unemployment rate, below which pressure emerges in labor markets.

**Net book value** The remaining (undepreciated) balance of an asset's purchase cost. For liabilities, the face value of a bond minus any unamortized discount, or plus any unamortized premium.

**Net exports** The difference between the value of a country's exports and the value of its imports (i.e., value of exports minus imports).

**Net realisable value** Estimated selling price in the ordinary course of business less the estimated costs necessary to make the sale.

**Net revenue** Revenue after adjustments (e.g., for estimated returns or for amounts unlikely to be collected).

**Node** Each value on a binomial tree from which successive moves or outcomes branch.

**Nominal data** Categorical values that are not amenable to being organized in a logical order. An example of nominal data is the classification of publicly listed stocks into sectors.

**Nominal GDP** The value of goods and services measured at current prices.

**Nominal risk-free interest rate** The sum of the real risk-free interest rate and the inflation premium.

**Non-accelerating inflation rate of unemployment** Effective unemployment rate below which pressure emerges in labor markets.

**Non-current assets** Assets that are expected to benefit the company over an extended period of time (usually more than one year).

**Non-current liabilities** Obligations that broadly represent a probable sacrifice of economic benefits in periods generally greater than one year in the future.

**Non-renewable resources** Finite resources that are depleted once they are consumed; oil and coal are examples.

**Normal goods** Goods that are consumed in greater quantities as income increases.

**Normal profit** The level of accounting profit needed to just cover the implicit opportunity costs ignored in accounting costs.

**Null hypothesis** The hypothesis that is tested.

**Numerical data** Values that represent measured or counted quantities as a number. Also called **quantitative data**.

**Objective probabilities** Probabilities that generally do not vary from person to person; includes a priori and empirical probabilities.

**Observation** The value of a specific variable collected at a point in time or over a specified period of time.

**Odds against E** The reciprocal of odds for $E$.

**Odds for E** The probability of $E$ divided by 1 minus the probability of $E$.

**One-dimensional array** The simplest format for representing a collection of data of the same data type.

**One-sided hypothesis test** A test in which the null hypothesis is rejected only if the evidence indicates that the population parameter is greater than or less than the hypothesized parameter; occurs when the alternative hypothesis is stated either as greater than or less than the hypothesized population parameter.

**Open economy** An economy that trades with other countries.

**Operating activities** Activities that are part of the day-to-day business functioning of an entity, such as selling inventory and providing services.

**Operating cash flow** The net amount of cash provided from operating activities.

**Operating profit** A company's profits on its usual business activities before deducting taxes. Also called *operating income*.

**Opportunity cost** The value that investors forgo by choosing a particular course of action; the value of something in its best alternative use.

**Ordinal data** Categorical values that can be logically ordered or ranked.

**Ordinary annuity** An annuity with a first cash flow that is paid one period from the present.

**Other comprehensive income** Items of comprehensive income that are not reported on the income statement; comprehensive income minus net income.

**Out-of-sample test** A test of a strategy or model using a sample outside the period on which the strategy or model was developed.

**Outcome** A possible value of a random variable.

**Own price** The price of a good or service itself (as opposed to the price of something else).

**Own-price elasticity of demand** The percentage change in quantity demanded for a percentage change in good's own price, holding all other things constant.

**Owners' equity** The excess of assets over liabilities; the residual interest of shareholders in the assets of an entity after deducting the entity's liabilities. Also called *shareholders' equity* or *shareholders' funds*.

**p-Value** The smallest level of significance at which the null is rejected.

**Paired comparisons test** See *test of the mean of the differences*.

**Panel data** A mix of time-series and cross-sectional data that contains observations through time on characteristics of across multiple observational units.

**Per capita real GDP** Real GDP divided by the size of the population, often used as a measure of a country's average standard of living.

**Percentiles** Quantiles that divide a distribution into 100 equal parts that sum to 100.

**Perfectly elastic** When the quantity demanded or supplied of a given good is infinitely sensitive to a change in the value of a specified variable (e.g., price).

**Perfectly inelastic** When the quantity demanded or supplied of a given good is completely insensitive to a change in the value of a specified variable (e.g., price).

**Permutation** An ordered listing.

**Permutation formula** The number of ways that we can choose $r$ objects from a total of $n$ objects, when the order in which the $r$ objects are listed does matter, is $_nP_r = \frac{n!}{(n-r)!}$.

**Perpetuity** A perpetual annuity, or a set of never-ending level sequential cash flows, with the first cash flow occurring one period from now. A bond that does not mature.

**Point estimate** A single numerical estimate of an unknown quantity, such as a population parameter.

**Population** All members of a specified group.

**Potential GDP** The maximum amount of output an economy can sustainably produce without inducing an increase in the inflation rate. The output level that corresponds to full employment with consistent wage and price expectations.

**Power of a test** The probability of correctly rejecting the null—that is, rejecting the null hypothesis when it is false.

**Precautionary money balances** Money held to provide a buffer against unforeseen events that might require money.

**Prepaid expense** A normal operating expense that has been paid in advance of when it is due.

**Present value (PV)** The present discounted value of future cash flows: For assets, the present discounted value of the future net cash inflows that the asset is expected to generate; for liabilities, the present discounted value of the future net cash outflows that are expected to be required to settle the liabilities.

**Principal** The amount that an issuer agrees to repay the debtholders on the maturity date.

**Probability** A number between 0 and 1 describing the chance that a stated event will occur.

**Probability density function** A function with non-negative values such that probability can be described by areas under the curve graphing the function.

**Probability distribution** A distribution that specifies the probabilities of a random variable's possible outcomes.

**Probability function** A function that specifies the probability that the random variable takes on a specific value.

**Production function** Provides the quantitative link between the levels of output that the economy can produce and the inputs used in the production process.

**Productivity** The amount of output produced by workers during a given period—for example, output per hour worked measures the efficiency of labor.

**Profit** The return that owners of a company receive for the use of their capital and the assumption of financial risk when making their investments.

**Profit and loss (P&L) statement** A financial statement that provides information about a company's profitability over a stated period of time. Also called the *income statement*.

**Promissory note** A written promise to pay a certain amount of money on demand.

**Property, plant, and equipment** Tangible assets that are expected to be used for more than one period in either the production or supply of goods or services, or for administrative purposes.

**Qualitative data** see **categorical data**.

**Quantile** A value at or below which a stated fraction of the data lies. Also referred to as a fractile.

**Quantitative data** see **numerical data**.

**Quantity equation of exchange** An expression that over a given period, the amount of money used to purchase all goods and services in an economy, $M \times V$, is equal to monetary value of this output, $P \times Y$.

**Quantity theory of money** Asserts that total spending (in money terms) is proportional to the quantity of money.

**Quartiles** Quantiles that divide a distribution into four equal parts.

**Quintiles** Quantiles that divide a distribution into five equal parts.

**Quoted interest rate** A quoted interest rate that does not account for compounding within the year. Also called *stated annual interest rate*.

**Random variable** A quantity whose future outcomes are uncertain.

**Range** The difference between the maximum and minimum values in a dataset.

**Raw data** Data available in their original form as collected.

**Real exchange rate effect** The effect through which changing price level impacts real exchange rate which in turn impacts net exports and aggregate demand.

**Real GDP** The value of goods and services produced, measured at base year prices.

**Real income** Income adjusted for the effect of inflation on the purchasing power of money. Also known as the *purchasing power of income*. If income remains constant and a good's price falls, real income is said to rise, even though the number of monetary units (e.g., dollars) remains unchanged.

**Real interest rate** Nominal interest rate minus the expected rate of inflation.

**real risk-free interest rate** The single-period interest rate for a completely risk-free security if no inflation were expected.

**Realizable (settlement) value** With reference to assets, the amount of cash or cash equivalents that could currently be obtained by selling the asset in an orderly disposal; with reference to liabilities, the undiscounted amount of cash or cash equivalents expected to be paid to satisfy the liabilities in the normal course of business.

**Recession** A period during which real GDP decreases (i.e., negative growth) for at least two successive quarters, or a period of significant decline in total output, income, employment, and sales usually lasting from six months to a year.

**Relative dispersion** The amount of dispersion relative to a reference value or benchmark.

**Relative frequency** The absolute frequency of each unique value of the variable divided by the total number of observations of the variable.

**Renewable resources** Resources that can be replenished, such as a forest.

**Rent** Payment for the use of property.

**Reserve requirement** The requirement for banks to hold reserves in proportion to the size of deposits.

**Revaluation model** Under IFRS, the process of valuing long-lived assets at fair value, rather than at cost less accumulated depreciation. Any resulting profit or loss is either reported on the income statement and/or through equity under revaluation surplus.

**Revenue** The amount charged for the delivery of goods or services in the ordinary activities of a business over a stated period; the inflows of economic resources to a company over a stated period.

**Rule of 72** The principle that the approximate number of years necessary for an investment to double is 72 divided by the stated interest rate.

**Sales** Generally, a synonym for revenue; "sales" is generally understood to refer to the sale of goods, whereas "revenue" is understood to include the sale of goods or services.

**Sample** A subset of a population.

**Sample mean** The sum of the sample observations divided by the sample size.

**Sample selection bias** Bias introduced by systematically excluding some members of the population according to a particular attribute—for example, the bias introduced when data availability leads to certain observations being excluded from the analysis.

**Sample standard deviation**   The positive square root of the sample variance.

**Sample statistic**   A quantity computed from or used to describe a sample.

**Sample variance**   The sum of squared deviations around the mean divided by the degrees of freedom.

**Scatter plot**   A two-dimensional graphical plot of paired observations of values for the independent and dependent variables in a simple linear regression.

**Scatter plot matrix**   A tool for organizing scatter plots between pairs of variables, making it easy to inspect all pairwise relationships in one combined visual.

**Screening**   The application of a set of criteria to reduce a set of potential investments to a smaller set having certain desired characteristics.

**Second-degree price discrimination**   When the monopolist charges different per-unit prices using the quantity purchased as an indicator of how highly the customer values the product.

**Shareholders' equity**   Total assets minus total liabilities.

**Simple interest**   The interest earned each period on the original investment; interest calculated on the principal only.

**Single-step format**   With respect to the format of the income statement, a format that does not subtotal for gross profit (revenue minus cost of goods sold).

**Speculative demand for money**   The demand to hold speculative money balances based on the potential opportunities or risks that are inherent in other financial instruments. Also called *portfolio demand for money*.

**Speculative money balances**   Monies held in anticipation that other assets will decline in value.

**Stacked bar chart**   An alternative form for presenting the frequency distribution of two categorical variables, where bars representing the sub-groups are placed on top of each other to form a single bar. Each sub-section is shown in a different color to represent the contribution of each sub-group, and the overall height of the stacked bar represents the marginal frequency for the category.

**Stagflation**   The combination of a high inflation rate with a high level of unemployment and a slowdown of the economy.

**Standard deviation**   The positive square root of the variance; a measure of dispersion in the same units as the original data.

**Standard normal distribution**   The normal density with mean ($\mu$) equal to 0 and standard deviation ($\sigma$) equal to 1.

**Standardizing**   A transformation that involves subtracting the mean and dividing the result by the standard deviation.

**Stated annual interest rate**   A quoted interest rate that does not account for compounding within the year. Also called *quoted interest rate*.

**Statement of changes in equity**   (statement of owners' equity) A financial statement that reconciles the beginning-of-period and end-of-period balance sheet values of shareholders' equity; provides information about all factors affecting shareholders' equity. Also called *statement of owners' equity*.

**Statement of financial condition**   The financial statement that presents an entity's current financial position by disclosing resources the entity controls (its assets) and the claims on those resources (its liabilities and equity claims), as of a particular point in time (the date of the balance sheet).

**Statement of financial position**   The financial statement that presents an entity's current financial position by disclosing resources the entity controls (its assets) and the claims on those resources (its liabilities and equity claims), as of a particular point in time (the date of the balance sheet).

**Statement of operations**   A financial statement that provides information about a company's profitability over a stated period of time.

**Statistic**   A summary measure of a sample of observations.

**Statistically significant**   A result indicating that the null hypothesis can be rejected; with reference to an estimated regression coefficient, frequently understood to mean a result indicating that the corresponding population regression coefficient is different from zero.

**Store of wealth**   Goods that depend on the fact that they do not perish physically over time, and on the belief that others would always value the good.

**Straight-line method**   A depreciation method that allocates evenly the cost of a long-lived asset less its estimated residual value over the estimated useful life of the asset.

**Structured data**   Data that are highly organized in a pre-defined manner, usually with repeating patterns.

**Subjective probability**   A probability drawing on personal or subjective judgment.

**Substitutes**   Said of two goods or services such that if the price of one increases the demand for the other tends to increase, holding all other things equal (e.g., butter and margarine).

**Survivorship bias**   Relates to the inclusion of only current investment funds in a database. As such, the returns of funds that are no longer available in the marketplace (have been liquidated) are excluded from the database. Also see *backfill bias*.

**Sustainable rate of economic growth**   The rate of increase in the economy's productive capacity or potential GDP.

**Tag cloud**   see *word cloud*.

**Target semideviation**   A measure of downside risk, calculated as the square root of the average of the squared deviations of observations below the target (also called target downside deviation).

**Technology**   The process a company uses to transform inputs into outputs.

**Terms of trade**   The ratio of the price of exports to the price of imports, representing those prices by export and import price indexes, respectively.

**Test of the mean of the differences**   A statistical test for differences based on paired observations drawn from samples that are dependent on each other.

**Third-degree price discrimination**   When the monopolist segregates customers into groups based on demographic or other characteristics and offers different pricing to each group.

**Time value of money**   The principles governing equivalence relationships between cash flows with different dates.

**Time-period bias**   The possibility that when we use a time-series sample, our statistical conclusion may be sensitive to the starting and ending dates of the sample.

**Time-series data**   A sequence of observations for a single observational unit of a specific variable collected over time and at discrete and typically equally spaced intervals of time (such as daily, weekly, monthly, annually, or quarterly).

**Top-down analysis**   An investment selection approach that begins with consideration of macroeconomic conditions and then evaluates markets and industries based upon such conditions.

**Total comprehensive income**   The change in equity during a period resulting from transaction and other events, other than those changes resulting from transactions with owners in their capacity as owners.

**Total cost**  The summation of all costs, for which costs are classified as fixed or variable.

**Total factor productivity**  A scale factor that reflects the portion of growth unaccounted for by explicit factor inputs (e.g., capital and labor).

**Total fixed cost**  The summation of all expenses that do not change as the level of production varies.

**Total invested capital**  The sum of market value of common equity, book value of preferred equity, and face value of debt.

**Total probability rule**  A rule explaining the unconditional probability of an event in terms of probabilities of the event conditional on mutually exclusive and exhaustive scenarios.

**Total variable cost**  The summation of all variable expenses.

**Trade payables**  Amounts that a business owes to its vendors for goods and services that were purchased from them but which have not yet been paid.

**Trade protection**  Government policies that impose restrictions on trade, such as tariffs and quotas.

**Trade surplus (deficit)**  When the value of exports is greater (less) than the value of imports.

**Trading securities**  Under US GAAP, a category of debt securities held by a company with the intent to trade them. Also called *held-for-trading securities*.

**Transactions money balances**  Money balances that are held to finance transactions.

**Tree-Map**  Another graphical tool for displaying categorical data. It consists of a set of colored rectangles to represent distinct groups, and the area of each rectangle is proportional to the value of the corresponding group.

**Trimmed mean**  A mean computed after excluding a stated small percentage of the lowest and highest observations.

**Trimodal**  A distribution that has the three most frequently occurring values.

**Two-dimensional rectangular array**  A popular form for organizing data for processing by computers or for presenting data visually. It is comprised of columns and rows to hold multiple variables and multiple observations, respectively (also called a **data table**).

**Two-sided hypothesis test**  A test in which the null hypothesis is rejected in favor of the alternative hypothesis if the evidence indicates that the population parameter is either smaller or larger than a hypothesized value; occurs when the alternative hypothesis is stated as not equal to the hypothesized population parameters.

**Type I error**  The error of rejecting a true null hypothesis; a false positive.

**Type II error**  The error of not rejecting a false null hypothesis; false negative.

**Underemployed**  A person who has a job but has the qualifications to work a significantly higher-paying job.

**Unearned revenue**  A liability account for money that has been collected for goods or services that have not yet been delivered; payment received in advance of providing a good or service. Also called *deferred revenue* or *deferred income*.

**Unemployed**  People who are actively seeking employment but are currently without a job.

**Unemployment rate**  The ratio of unemployed to the labor force.

**Unexpected inflation**  The component of inflation that is a surprise.

**Unimodal**  A distribution with a single value that is most frequently occurring.

**Unit elastic**  An elasticity with a magnitude of negative one. Also called *unitary elastic*.

**Unit labor cost**  The average labor cost to produce one unit of output.

**Unit normal distribution**  The normal density with mean ($\mu$) equal to 0 and standard deviation ($\sigma$) equal to 1.

**Units-of-production method**  A depreciation method that allocates the cost of a long-lived asset based on actual usage during the period.

**Univariate distribution**  A distribution that specifies the probabilities for a single random variable.

**Unstructured data**  Data that do not follow any conventionally organized forms.

**Up transition probability**  The probability that an asset's value moves up.

**Value investors**  With reference to equity investors, investors who are focused on paying a relatively low share price in relation to earnings or assets per share.

**Variable**  A characteristic or quantity that can be measured, counted, or categorized and that is subject to change (also called a field, an attribute, or a feature).

**Variable costs**  Costs that fluctuate with the level of production and sales.

**Variance**  The expected value (the probability-weighted average) of squared deviations from a random variable's expected value.

**Visualization**  The presentation of data in a pictorial or graphical format for the purpose of increasing understanding and for gaining insights into the data.

**Voluntarily unemployed**  A person voluntarily outside the labor force, such as a jobless worker refusing an available vacancy.

**Wealth effect**  An increase (decrease) in household wealth increases (decreases) consumer spending out of a given level of current income.

**Weighted mean**  An average in which each observation is weighted by an index of its relative importance.

**Winsorized mean**  A mean computed after assigning a stated percentage of the lowest values equal to one specified low value and a stated percentage of the highest values equal to one specified high value.

**Word cloud**  A visual device for representing textual data, which consists of words extracted from a source of textual data. The size of each distinct word is proportional to the frequency with which it appears in the given text (also known as **tag cloud**).

**Working capital**  The difference between current assets and current liabilities.

**World price**  The price prevailing in the world market.

| | | |
|---|---|---|
| 18 | Jesús Nunca Desperdició Tiempo Para Responder A Los Críticos | 73 |
| 19 | Jesús Sabía Que Había Un Tiempo Oportuno Y Un Tiempo Inoportuno Para Acercarse A La Gente | 77 |
| 20 | Jesús Instruyó A Quienes Discipulaba | 81 |
| 21 | Jesús Rechazó Desalentarse Cuando Otros Juzgaron Mal Sus Motivaciones | 85 |
| 22 | Jesús Rechazó Llenarse De Amargura Cuando Otros Fueron Desleales O Lo Traicionaron | 87 |
| 23 | Jesús Se Relacionó Con Personas De Todos Los Trasfondos Sociales | 91 |
| 24 | Jesús Resistió La Tentación | 93 |
| 25 | Jesús Tomó Decisiones Que Crearon El Futuro Deseado En Vez De Un Presente Deseado | 95 |
| 26 | Jesús Nunca Juzgó A La Gente Por Su Apariencia Externa | 97 |
| 27 | Jesús Reconoció La Ley De La Repetición | 99 |
| 28 | Jesús Era Un Pensador Del Mañana | 101 |
| 29 | Jesús Sabía Que El Dinero Por Sí Solo No Puede Traer Contentamiento | 103 |
| 30 | Jesús Conocía El Poder De Las Palabras Y El Poder Del Silencio | 105 |
| 31 | Jesús Sabía Que Cuando Quieres Algo Que Nunca Has Tenido, Debes Hacer Algo Que No Has Hecho Nunca | 107 |
| 32 | Jesús Permitió Que Las Personas Corrigieran Sus Errores | 109 |

Made in the USA
Las Vegas, NV
06 November 2024

11122828R00195